CAMDEN MISCELLANY
XXXI

CAMDEN MISCELLANY XXXI

CAMDEN FOURTH SERIES
Volume 44

LONDON
OFFICES OF THE ROYAL HISTORICAL SOCIETY
UNIVERSITY COLLEGE LONDON, GOWER STREET, WC1E 6BT
1992

© Royal Historical Society

British Library Cataloguing in Publication Data

Camden Miscellany XXXI—(Camden fourth
  series; v. 44).
  1. History—Periodicals
  I. Royal Historical Society   II. Series
ISBN 0–86193–132–7

Printed and bound in Great Britain by
Butler & Tanner Ltd, Frome and London

CONTENTS

I
Letters of the Cliffords, lords Clifford and earls of Cumberland, $c.1500$–$c.1565$

Edited by
R. W. Hoyle

CONTENTS

ACKNOWLEDGEMENTS

Quite properly in the acknowledgements to an edition, the manuscripts' custodians must be thanked first. I remain (several years after the event) most grateful to the hospitality and courtesy shown to me at Chatsworth by Peter Day and Michael Pearman. At the British Library Dr Frances Harris first made the manuscripts available and took the trouble to discuss them on subsequent occasions. Permission to publish the texts was given, in the case of the Clifford Letter Book at Chatsworth, by the Trustees of the Chatsworth Settlement and for the Althorp letters by the British Library.

My work on the Chatsworth manuscript began when I was funded as a postgraduate by the DES, latterly the British Academy, and my work on the whole was brought to a conclusion during my tenure of a British Academy post-doctoral research fellowship.

In the first stages of preparing the text I was much aided by Dr Joan Thirsk, Dr Gerald Aylmer and Professor Eric Ives. Dr R. T. Spence told me of the Althorp letters many years before they became accessible to the public. In many matters I have been guided by Professor A. G. Dickens's previous edition of letters addressed to members of the Clifford family. A few weeks after his eightieth birthday, it is a pleasure to salute one of the few historians to have brought genuine distinction to the study of Northern History. But in the eight or so years in which this text has been prepared in odd moments as a refuge from more pressing matters, I have had cause to be grateful to the many friends who have joined in correspondence and conversation about the letters. Dr George Bernard may not recall that in a jocular aside he offered the clue which identified the castle of Loyalty and I am additionally grateful to him for looking over the completed text. Bill Sheils gave me his copy of Dickens's Clifford Letters. Amongst others, I recall with gratitude the aid of Margaret Condon, Steven Ellis, Steve Gunn, Richard Hall, David Palliser, Tony Pollard and Jenny Wormald.

September 1990

The delay whilst the letters awaited their turn for publication has allowed me to incorporate some additional material. In particular I have been able to take advantage of the calendar of the Ancient Indictments of King's Bench in the Public Record Office for the northern counties, 1509–58, which is being prepared by Dr Henry

Summerson under the direction of Professor Anthony Tuck and myself. This is the first occasion on which Professor Tuck and I can acknowledge the generosity of the Leverhulme Trust in funding this project and our debt to Dr Summerson for his exemplary work on the records. I am also grateful to Professor Michael Jones for his thorough reading of the typescript and overseeing its progress through the press.

May 1992

ABBREVIATIONS

BL	British Library, Department of Manuscripts
Bodl.	Bodleian Library, Oxford
Chatsw.	Mss of His Grace the Duke of Devonshire at Chatsworth House, Derbyshire
Chatsw., BA	Bolton Abbey Mss at Chatsworth
Clay, 'Clifford Family'	J. W. Clay, 'The Clifford Family', *YAJ* xviii (1905), 354-411
CPR	*Calendar of Patent Rolls*
CW²	*Transactions of the Cumberland and Westmorland Antiquarian and Archaeological Society*, second ser. (1900-)
Dickens, *Clifford Letters*	A. G. Dickens (ed.), *Clifford Letters of the Sixteenth Century*, (Surtees Soc. clxxii, 1962 for 1957)
DNB	*Dictionary of National Biography*
Dodds, *Pilgrimage*	M. H. and R. Dodds, *The Pilgrimage of Grace and the Exeter Conspiracy* (2 vols., 1917)
Hall, *Chronicle*	Edward Hall, *The union of the two noble and illustre famelies of Lancastre and Yorke*, H. Ellis (ed.) (1809).
Harrison, *Pilgrimage of Grace*	S. M. Harrison, *The Pilgrimage of Grace in the Lake Counties, 1536 7* (1981)
HMC	Historical Manuscripts Commission reports
HP 1509-1558	S. T. Bindoff (ed.), *The History of Parliament, 1509-1558. The House of Commons* (3 vols., 1982)
HP 1558-1603	P. W. Hasler (ed.), *The History of Parliament, 1558-1603. The House of Commons* (3 vols., 1981)
Hoyle, 'The fall of the house of Percy'	R. W. Hoyle, 'Henry sixth earl of Northumberland and the fall of the house of Percy, 1527-1537', in G. W. Bernard (ed.), *The English Nobility in the Sixteenth Century* (1992), 180-211
Hoyle, 'First Earl'	R. W. Hoyle, 'The first earl of Cumberland, a reputation reassessed', *NH* xxii (1986), 63-94
Hoyle, 'Land and Landed Relations'	R. W. Hoyle, 'Land and Landed Relations in Craven, Yorkshire, c.1520-1600', (Unpublished D.Phil thesis, University of Oxford, 1987)
James, 'First Earl'	M. E. James, 'The first earl of Cumberland and the decline of Northern Feudalism', *NH* i (1965), reprinted in James, *Society, Politics and Culture. Studies in early modern England* (1986), 148-75
LP	*Letters and Papers Foreign and Domestic of the reign of Henry VIII* (21 vols and addenda, 1862-1932)

Ms Dodsw.	Manuscript collections by Roger Dodsworth in the Bodleian Library, Oxford
NH	*Northern History* (1965–)
Nicolson and Burn	J. Nicolson and R. Burn, *History and Antiquities of the Counties of Westmorland and Cumberland* (2 vols., 1777, repr. 1976)
PRO	Public Record Office
Rae, *Scottish Frontier*	T. I. Rae, *The administration of the Scottish Frontier, 1513–1603* (1966)
Scots Peerage	Sir John Balfour Paul (ed.), *The Scots Peerage* (9 vols., 1904–1914)
Smith, *Land and Politics*	R. B. Smith, *Land and Politics in the Reign of Henry VIII. The West Riding* (1970)
Test. Ebor.	*Testamenta Eboracensia* v (Surtees Soc. lxxix, 1884); vi (*ibid.* cvi, 1902)
Whitaker, *Craven*	T. D. Whitaker, *The history and antiquities of the Deanery of Craven* (1805, third edn. by A. W. Morant, 1878, repr. in 2 vols., 1973, is used here)
YAJ	*Yorkshire Archaeological Journal* (1869–)
YASRS	Yorkshire Archaeological Society Record Series

EDITORIAL PROCEDURES

My guiding principle in the preparation of the edition which follows has been to produce as simple and readily comprehensible a text as possible, uncluttered by excessive footnoting of English usage, the identification of the individuals mentioned or the merely curious. To this end editorial comment is gathered into notes following each letter which it is hoped will satisfy most queries about the date and content.

Punctuation and a division into paragraphs has been introduced into most letters. In the case of the original letters, the address written on the dorse of the latter is placed after the text, but I have followed the practice of the transcribers of the letter book by placing it before the letter in the items drawn from that source.

In the text, 'y' standing for the modern 'th' has been transliterated, so ye, the, yt, that, but 'ye' as a form of address has been retained. Yogh, which appears from time to time (especially in Wharton's letters) and the letters u/v appear as in modern practice. Abbreviations have been expanded silently in the majority of cases; in a few instances they are marked within square brackets. Gaps in the text appear as empty square brackets, so [   ]; illegible sections as [.....]. Cancellations are placed within angle brackets < >; illegible cancellations are marked by points within the brackets, so <......>. Roman numerals are reproduced as they appear, but it might be noticed that the second of the two transcribers of the Clifford Letter Book converted roman numerals into arabic characters as he proceeded.

INTRODUCTION

Private letters are amongst the most valuable, but also least well preserved sources for the historian. Dealing with events of the moment rather than of legal consequence, there was little reason to safeguard documents whose very ephemerality was shown by the medium on which they were written (paper) and their language (English). The survival of some notable collections of fifteenth-century letters, Paston, Plumpton, Cely, Stonor, and from the 1530s, the Lisle letters, should not disguise the fact that sixteenth-century letters between individuals (as opposed to letters between central government and its local lieuten-ants, and *vice versa*) are found relatively infrequently.

Little material of this sort survives for the northern baronial houses. There is practically nothing for the Stanley family, earls of Derby or the Percy family, earls of Northumberland. A single letter book for 1522–4 is extant from the office of the third lord Dacre.[1] There are, it is true, large collections of correspondence for the north Midland houses of Rutland and Shrewsbury, but this is preponderantly of late sixteenth-century date.[2] It was therefore a happy good fortune when a group of 43 letters, mostly addressed to the tenth lord Clifford (d. 1523) or his son the first earl of Cumberland (d. 1542) were acquired through a saleroom by the British Museum in 1955. In 1962 Professor A. G. Dickens published the texts of these letters (with one more) in an edition for the Surtees Society.[3] This group of letters then formed the largest available in print for a northern noble house of the early sixteenth century.

The present edition is a supplement to Dickens's volume. In 1982 the present writer was fortunate to find in the Clifford archive at Chatsworth a volume of transcripts of some 60 letters addressed to the tenth lord Clifford and the first earl dating from $c.1494$–$c.1544$.[4] An

---

[1] BL Add. Ms. 24,965. A series of Dacre letter books of slightly later date survived until the eighteenth century; Nicolson and Burn, i, p. lx.

[2] *The manuscripts of His Grace the duke of Rutland preserved at Belvoir Castle,* i, HMC, Twelfth Report App. iv (1888); *A Calendar of Shrewsbury and Talbot Papers in Lambeth Palace Library and the College of Arms,* i, ed. C. Jamison, rev. E. G. W. Bill; ii, ed. G. R. Batho (Derbyshire Archaeological Society Record Ser., i, iv, 1966, 1971). (The College of Arms collection is now also at Lambeth.)

[3] A. G. Dickens (ed.), *Clifford Letters of the Sixteenth Century* (Surtees Soc. clxxii, 1962 for 1957), hereafter Dickens, *Clifford Letters.*

[4] Chatsw., BA, unnumbered volume.

edition of this material was proposed and accepted for the Camden Series. In 1985, with the purchase of the Spencer manuscripts from Althorp by the British Library, it became possible to double the size of the original undertaking. In its final shape, this edition contains 122 letters, all of which (bar a small minority) have been previously unknown to historians.

By some chance the two collections show a heavy concentration on the 1510s, 1520s and 1530s, the latter decade in particular being strongly represented by substantial groups of letters covering the period of the Anglo-Scottish war of 1532–4 and the Pilgrimage of Grace. It is curious that each archival group contains a distinctive range of correspondents. All the royal letters are in the Clifford letter book, the clerics in Dickens's collection, the nobles in the Chatsworth transcript, the letters of Sir Thomas Clifford and Sir Thomas Wharton in the Althorp letters. Very few writers appear in two of the collections and none in all three. Without pressing the matter too far, it would almost appear that before their division the letters were sorted by the character of their author. The result is that the collections complement each other in a most satisfactory fashion and illustrate the wide range of letters which the family received in the early sixteenth century. For this edition the two collections have been merged into a continuous series, the royal letters placed first, then the major groups of correspondence. At the end (**79–122**)[5] will be found the letters of correspondents who contribute only one or two letters to the collection, arranged alphabetically by name of author.

The manuscript at Chatsworth, which for convenience I have chosen to call the Clifford Letter Book, was presumably brought from the duke of Devonshire's house at Bolton Abbey with the remainder of the Bolton Abbey manuscripts in 1937.[6] The transcript was written by two hands, one of whom wrote in an early seventeenth-century secretary hand similar to that of Christopher Towneley. The manuscript is untitled and gives no clues as to who the transcribers were, where or when they worked or where the original manuscripts were then to be found. Other than a few which survive in the State Papers as drafts of outgoing letters, all are unknown.

It needs to be emphasised that the transcribers produced a work of demonstration quality on large paper pages.[7] The letter book is certainly

---

[5] Numbers in bold refer to a letter printed in this edition.

[6] The volume does not appear in the list of Bolton Abbey Books brought to Chatsworth from the Estate Office.

[7] The book is rectangular with pages $8\frac{1}{2}$" wide and $12\frac{1}{2}$" long. Each page has a ruled margin of approximately 1" along all edges. It is not clear whether the manuscript was bound before the present inter-war binding of white leather-covered boards was added. Internally the book is very clean suggesting that it has been little used.

not the crabbed personal record of an antiquarian like Nathaniel Johnson. Both copyists wrote quickly and fluently, but also extremely legibly and clearly, and took care to make minor emendations to the text as first written. In a few cases they left gaps where words could not be read. Names, especially personal names or titles, were written in upper case to catch the reader's eye. There are errors of transcription and in a few places the text seems to make less than perfect sense, perhaps because of minor omissions. There are also a few cases in which the recipient of the letter is misidentified, but this may have been true of the copy from which the transcribers worked. A comparison of the text of the letter book with the few duplicate or draft copies of individual letters which survive elsewhere shows that the compilers of the letter book were individuals of the highest competence, fully familiar with the sort of materials with which they were working. They arranged the letters by correspondent, starting with royal letters, then the single letter from the Pilgrims' council at York, the Privy Council, the fifth and sixth earls of Northumberland, the first duke of Suffolk, dukes of Norfolk and so on. Within this arrangement the transcribers made no attempt to date letters or place them in chronological order, nor did they identify their authors or offer an overall contents list or general title page. Two later letters in the letter book have been omitted from this edition.[8]

A further collection of letters at Chatsworth, mostly drafts in the hand of John Holmes of Hampole near Doncaster, the second earl's secretary, and dating from the late 1550s and early 1560s, has been partly published in abstract by the Historical Manuscripts Commission and is excluded from the present edition.[9]

The Spencer letters from Althorp are original letters and have been allotted by the British Library the provisional call-number of Althorp B1. (They will in time be assigned an Additional Manuscript number.) When received by the library, they were contained in a single modern slip case with a number of late sixteenth- or early seventeenth-century letters (now mostly transferred to Althorp B2). Each letter had been flattened, a few had been lightly repaired and each was contained within a (twentieth-century) paper sheet which bore a brief (and often inaccurate) note of the correspondents' identities. Previously the letters were in a bundle, the wrapper of which survives with the letters and bears the title 'Under this cover four bundles of letters wrote by several

---

[8] On fo. 16r is a copy of a letter of Elizabeth I to the third earl of Cumberland, from Bishop's Waltham, 19 September 1591. At fo. 37r is found a copy of a 'letter from the Great Magull to King James [I]'.

[9] HMC, *Third Report* (1872), 37. (These letters now form Chatsw., Londesborough D.)

persons unto the two first earls of Cumberl[an]d'. The present edition reproduces all the items in Althorp B1 which can certainly be dated before 1579 and one or two more where the date cannot be certainly ascertained but which might be of slightly later date.[10]

It would appear that the letters and the later Clifford and Burlington papers now in the British Library left the possession of the dukes of Devonshire in the late eighteenth century. They were bequeathed to Georgiana, countess Spencer and after her Lavinia, countess Spencer by Rachel Lloyd in 1803. She probably had them from Georgiana, wife of the fifth duke of Devonshire. The papers remained at Althorp until their sale to the British Library.[11]

Virtually all the letters collected here are in-letters; there is very little from the hands of the Cliffords themselves (with the major exceptions of Sir Thomas Clifford's letters, **29–40** and two from the future second earl to his father, **41–2**). It is to the careers of the three generations of the family to whom the letters are addressed that we must briefly turn.[12]

The Cliffords were amongst the outstanding northern landowners of their age. The tenth lord (b. *c*.1454, d. 1523) was the owner of estates in the West Riding (in Craven around their castle at Skipton and house at Barden), at Londesborough in the East Riding and in the Eden valley in Westmorland. His son and grandson progressively enlarged their Yorkshire holdings. The first earl bought the manor of Carleton in Craven before his inheritance in 1514, lands formerly of Marton priory at Threapland, Cracoe and Appletreewick in 1541 and he secured the estates of Bolton Priory for the family shortly before his death in 1542. The second earl continued to purchase land in Craven. He inherited the Percy estate and jurisdiction in north Craven in 1537 on the death of his uncle, the sixth earl of Northumberland (although these lands were subject to the payment of a rent charge to Northumberland's heirs, initially the Crown). In 1554 he purchased the manor of Litton and had the assignment of a lease of tithes belonging to Christ Church, Oxford. He also made various minor purchases in Craven, but his executors failed to put into effect the earl's injunction

---

[10] There remain in B1 five letters, of which four are addressed to the third earl, the accounts of Thomas Clifford, receiver of the coheirs of the duke of Suffolk for lands in Lincolnshire etc, 4 Elizabeth (fos. 95–104), a seventeenth-century tract on free trade (fos. 107r-113v), a printed oath of the East India Company and the wrapper mentioned previously.

[11] These details of the descent of the manuscripts are taken from the draft catalogue of the Althorp papers available in the manuscript reading room of the British Library.

[12] The basic sources for the history of the family are contained in Clay, 'Clifford Family'. In this section I have also drawn upon the introduction to Dickens's *Clifford Letters*. Lady Anne Clifford's account remains useful especially for family tradition; it is printed by Dickens, 127–150.

that they should buy lands on his son's behalf.[13] None of the family troubled to buy land in Westmorland. The extensive monastic estates around Kirkby Stephen were secured by Thomas lord Wharton and neither earl purchased lands belonging to Shap Abbey despite the family's traditional association with the house. The second earl did take a lease of the Crown's holdings in the barony of Kendal in 1554, but this was the only enlargement of their Westmorland interests.[14] This should not be taken to mean that the family withdrew from Westmorland, since the second earl in particular resided for long periods at his castle at Brougham near Penrith.

The tenth lord was restored to the family estates in 1485 upon the reversal of the attainder of his father. Clifford married somewhat late in life Anne St John of the family of Bletsoe, Bedfordshire, and the elder of his surviving sons, Henry, later first earl of Cumberland, was born in 1493. Clifford married secondly Florence, the widow of Thomas Talbot of Bashall in Craven. There is every sign of a large disparity in age between the two – she certainly survived beyond 1550 – but the marriage broke down before his death and his widow went on to marry a third time, remaining, with her new husband, a charge on the estates.[15]

Clifford had some military pretensions. He attempted to suppress the Yorkshire rebellion of 1487 and took part in the Scottish campaigns of 1497 and 1513 (he was too ill to serve in 1522, **115**).[16] For most of his life he remained detached from political affairs, preferring, if Lady Anne Clifford (who wrote much later) may be believed, to reside at his house at Barden and dabble in alchemy and astrology. He also, as Dickens was the first to point out, deserves mention as a major benefactor of the Carthusians at Mountgrace.[17] The only addition to our knowledge of relations between the family and the house in this collection is a letter of Clifford's son in which he tries to borrow money to cover the costs of unexpected royal service (**86**).

Clifford was, in essence, a second rank peer without (so far as can be told) the stomach for politics. His son, however, was made of a different metal. Henry Clifford, created first earl of Cumberland in 1525, d. 1542, has attracted much recent scholarly attention and there is no real agreement on the interpretation which should be placed on his life. The facts, though, are clear enough. Clifford went to court

[13] For an account of the enlargement of the estates in Craven, Hoyle, 'Land and Landed Relations', 33–6.

[14] *Calendar of Patent Rolls, Mary*, i, 116–7.

[15] See the notes to letters **63** and **101** below.

[16] For Clifford's undistinguished performance in 1487, A. Goodman, *The Wars of the Roses* (1981), 103–4.

[17] Dickens, *Clifford Letters*, 28–9, 62–74.

aged about 10.[18] By the mid-1510s he was estranged from his father who accused him of both malice and inordinate pride and criticised him for dressing himself (and his horse) 'more lyk a duke than a poor baron's son as hee ys'. If the father is to be believed, the younger Clifford was leading a wild life, beating his father's servants, stealing his goods and extorting tithes from various (unnamed) monastic houses. Clifford was driven to complain of his son's behaviour to Henry VIII who instructed the father to pay him £40.[19]

Evidence for this period of the earl's life is hard to find and the present letters add none. It is known that both Clifford and Sir George Darcy (elder son of lord Darcy, another child born late in life to a peer) were imprisoned in the Fleet for a while in the late summer of 1517 although their specific offence is unrecorded.[20] When the evidence for Cumberland's life becomes fuller after 1523, he had clearly settled down and the only trait he retained from his hell-raising years was the noble taste for bullying monastic houses into making leases.[21]

The first earl married twice. His first marriage, made as a child to a daughter of the fourth earl of Shrewsbury, was ended by his spouse's premature death. For his second wife he married Margaret, daughter of the fifth earl of Northumberland and whilst the date of their marriage is unknown, their eldest son Henry was christened in January 1516. A second son, Ingram, and several daughters, followed later. Margaret Clifford died in November 1540 and the first earl survived her by only eighteen months, dying in May 1542 aged about 49.

During this short life Cumberland lacked nothing in the way of honours. He was created earl in 1525 at the same moment as the king's bastard son, Henry Fitzroy, was raised to be duke of Richmond. Elsewhere I have suggested that this must be seen as part and parcel of the refurbishment of provincial government of that year.[22] Cumberland became deputy warden in the West Marches under Richmond during the summer of 1525 and served until late in 1527 when he was either dismissed or allowed to resign. In 1534 he was again appointed warden, serving until the aftermath of the Pilgrimage of Grace when he was effectively replaced by Sir Thomas Wharton (although Cumberland remained titular warden until his death). In 1537, as a reward for his staunch loyalty in the Pilgrimage, he was raised to the Order of the Garter (58). Further royal favour can be seen in the appointment of his brother, Sir Thomas, to the Captainship of Berwick in 1529 and in

---

[18] Batho (ed.), *Shrewsbury and Talbot Papers*, 325.

[19] On this period of the earl's life, see Dickens, *Clifford Letters*, 21–2. The letter is printed in Whitaker, *Craven*, 327.

[20] Dickens, *Clifford Letters*, 22.

[21] Cf. Dickens, *Clifford Letters*, no. 1 and below, **93.**

[22] Hoyle, 'First Earl', 91.

the king's agreement to the marriage of Cumberland's heir, Sir Henry, to a daughter of the duke of Suffolk (who through her mother was a royal niece) in 1535.

Yet the earl's career has been seen as one of failure. In a paper published some years ago (and recently reprinted), Dr M. E. James argued that the earl, through a combination of ambition and incompetence, successfully undermined his own position and incited the Pilgrimage against him. Three specific charges can be separated out; that his ambition in the West Marches drew him into competition with the Dacres, that his extortion of the estates of the earls of Northumberland from his brother-in-law led the sixth earl to work against him, and that his oppressive estate policies cost him the support of his natural gentry circle.[23] Elsewhere I have suggested that these claims are not sustainable.[24] There is no evidence that Cumberland wanted to hold the wardenship in the West Marches. On the contrary, the evidence of letters in this volume suggests quite the opposite (**58–9**), and it seems much more likely that instead of being driven by his own ambition, the first earl served in the borders as a stopgap when the Dacres were, for political reasons, unacceptable as wardens. This is not to say that the earl was ineffective as warden, but the practical difficulties of exercising the office without local estates should not be understated. Conflict with the Dacres was inevitable if only because the warden needed to exercise a control (which they were bound to resent) over their lands and take from them offices which had traditionally been theirs. This was compounded by the independent conflict between Sir William Musgrave, captain of Bewcastle, and the Dacres which spilled over into accusations that the Dacres had used their contacts in Scotland to divert attacks onto Musgrave during the Anglo-Scottish war of 1532–3 and Dacre's trial (and acquittal) on these charges in 1534.[25] Cumberland's seizure of Dacre's goods at his arrest started a further dispute between them. Cumberland's alleged purloining of Dacre's possessions was the subject of a settlement arranged by Cromwell in late 1534 but there are indications that the dispute dragged on beyond the first earl's death. (As late as 1554 Lord Dacre still held it as a grievance against Wharton that restitution had not been made for 300 sheep taken by Cumberland in 1534.) The Clifford-Dacre feud was

---

[23] James, 'First Earl'.

[24] Hoyle, 'First Earl'.

[25] My understanding of this derives mostly from an unpublished paper lent me by Dr Steven Ellis. See also **111** below. At one level this was a straightforward dispute over the possession of property in Bewcastledale (Cumberland), but Dr Ellis has suggested to me in correspondence that it also relates to the defection of Musgrave from the Dacre circle to Cumberland.

only healed by the marriage of the second earl with Anne Dacre in 1552–3.[26]

Of course, Cumberland's second term on the borders ended in tears. His decision to report Richard Dacre's assault on Sir William Musgrave in Carlisle on 9 December and the disturbances which followed (21) revealed to the king the degree of factional infighting in the northwest. Henry forcibly reconciled the parties and delivered Cumberland a most fulsome rebuke (22) but whether he recognised the degree to which the conflict between Cumberland and Dacre was of his own making may be doubted. It was an admission of the failure of royal policy rather than the collapse of Cumberland's ambitions which led to the appointment of Sir Thomas Wharton and a feed council of gentry in the West Marches in 1537. It is worthy of comment that Cumberland's position was protected by the appointment of his servant - Wharton - and his own maintenance as titular warden. Whether Cumberland was active is another matter. A letter of 1541 (25) suggests that he was, but this dates from the period of high alertness with the expected visit of James V and may not necessarily be taken at face value.

The analogy which should be drawn with Cumberland's wardenship is surely with the periods in the late 1520s and early 1530s when the earl of Ormond served as lord deputy in Ireland in place of Kildare. Like the Cliffords, the Butlers were faced with the problem of their geographical distance from the theatre of action and the practical problem of disentangling the private administration of their predecessors from the public offices which they were charged with exercising. Neither Butler nor Clifford appear to have served willingly in their respective offices, but acted at moments when the normal royal servants were for whatever reason unacceptable to Henry.[27]

As to the claim that the earl of Northumberland acted to undermine the first earl, I have attempted to show (using in part 49–52) that relations between Cumberland and his brother in law were exceptionally good, at least in the early 1530s.[28] Nor was the first earl an oppressive landlord.[29] The need to assume that he was, and in the same way the

---

[26] The purloining of Dacre's goods is described by Harrison, *Pilgrimage of Grace*, 36–7, the notes to **88** below and Dickens, *Clifford Letters*, no. 28 (which I would date rather later than Dickens). The triangular factional feuding between the second earl of Cumberland, lord Dacre and lord Wharton in mid-century forms the subject of a paper in preparation. For the moment see PRO STAC 10/15 fos. 114–15 endorsed '15 Dec. 1554, the lord Dacre's articles against the l[ord] Wharton'. I owe this reference to the kindness of Alan Fellows.

[27] S. G. Ellis, 'Nationalist historiography and the English and Gaelic Worlds in the late Middle Ages', *Irish Historical Studies* xxv (1986), 14.

[28] Hoyle, 'First Earl', 78–83.

[29] *Ibid.* 75–8.

postulation of a Clifford-Percy feud, arises from an attempt to explain the Pilgrimage of Grace in terms which are themselves a major misapprehension of the character of that movement.

It is thus unfortunate that the first earl's career has recently been discussed in terms of what he did not do rather than in terms of what he did. In trying to assess his achievements and personality, we are hindered by the fact that virtually all the material relating to his life, both in this collection and in Dickens's, is written to him and not by him. Although it is difficult to judge an audience by reading a play, an acquaintance with the letters suggests that several observations might usefully be made. First of all, it seems likely that the earl was liked and that he encouraged in those who knew him well a relaxed familiarity. This is particularly apparent in the letters of the earls of Northumberland, but also those of his social inferiors, Wharton (**73–8**), Crackenthorpe (**92**) and Musgrave (**111**). Sir Thomas Clifford comes over as being a more business-like correspondent. Suffolk's letters are marked with a concern about the welfare of his daughter and his suspicion that Cumberland was perhaps being mean towards the young couple (especially **55**, **60** and **61**) although he welcomed the thought that the earl might join him at Hatfield for hunting (**65**). Only the letters of the third duke of Norfolk are marked by an obvious coolness (**67–72**). Elsewhere we have occasional comments on Cumberland's generosity (**98** and perhaps **115**).

Secondly there are enough clues within the letters to suggest that the Cliffords had a relationship with Henry VIII that had special qualities (eg. **98**). It is particularly remarkable that Henry was prepared to go to such lengths on behalf of Sir Thomas Clifford (see the notes to **29–40**). But Henry had his reward in the earl's impeccable loyalty and physical bravery during the Pilgrimage of Grace.[30] The significance of the earl's stand against the Pilgrims arises not from any defeat he inflicted upon them, for in military terms he was impotent, but from his determined and public refusal to compromise with the insurgents. This he demonstrated by remaining within his castle and refusing to travel to York (**79**). In fact the correspondence presented here reveals how the king was slow to appreciate the gravity of the situation and failed in the early days of the movement to mobilise assistance for his supporters in the North.[31]

There is much less to say about the second earl of Cumberland (born *c*.1516, d. 1570) in part because of the paucity of sources. He married Eleanor, daughter of the earl of Suffolk (and a niece of Henry

---

[30] For the earl's troubles during the Pilgrimage, Hoyle, 'First Earl', 83–91.

[31] I hope to show in a forthcoming book on the Pilgrimage that the same is true of Henry's dealings with Darcy.

VIII) in 1536; she predeceased him in 1547. He married secondly in 1552 or 1553 Anne, daughter of the fourth lord Dacre. The only surviving issue of the first marriage was a daughter Margaret; of the second there survived two sons, George (third earl, d. 1605), Francis (fourth earl, d. 1641) and a daughter who married Philip lord Wharton. Cumberland never held office on the borders, nor played any prominent role in the Anglo-Scottish wars of the 1540s. Indeed he withdrew from public life after the death of his first wife and Lady Anne Clifford claims, perhaps rightly, that he went to London only three times in the last twenty years of his life. Like his grandfather he was an alchemist and Lady Anne tells us that he had an extensive library of books although no record survives of its contents.[32]

Two reasons may be offered for this disengagement. It appears that the earl's health broke down in the late 1540s. Lady Anne Clifford reports that he was laid out for dead on one occasion, but after being revived by his servants was sustained by a suckling woman. Nonetheless she also tells us that he was finally restored to being 'a strong able man', so ill-health is only a partial explanation.[33] It may be suggested that in the 1560s his withdrawal was politically motivated. Cumberland was suspected of religious conservatism and found little favour with Elizabeth, who deprived him of his place on the York High Commission.[34] His will is noticeably devoid of protestant sympathies and his widow, with the surviving members of his immediate circle, were accounted as catholics after his death.[35]

But he was perhaps finally politique. In 1553 he had no qualms about marrying his daughter Margaret (a great-granddaughter of Henry VII through her mother) into the Dudley family. On 26 January 1553 the second earl authorised Ralph Rokeby, serjeant at law, Marmaduke Wyvill, Thomas Clifford (his half-brother and London agent) and his counsel William Tankard to negotiate a settlement with the duke of Northumberland. Articles for a marriage between Margaret Clifford and the duke's son Guildford survive at Chatsworth, but the marriage that was finally agreed upon was between her and Northumberland's brother Andrew Dudley.[36] Arrangements for the nuptials were well advanced when Northumberland's régime collapsed. Cumberland broke

---

[32] Dickens, *Clifford Letters*, 149.

[33] *Ibid.* 149. His illness can be dated to the summer of 1549; PRO STAC3/4/46. A letter of the earl's of 12 June 1564 refers to a moment of illness 'worse than any of the previous seven years', Chatsw., Londesborough D.

[34] P. Tyler, 'The Ecclesiastical Commission for the province of York, 1561–1641' (unpublished Oxford D.Phil thesis, 1965), 191.

[35] H. Aveling, 'The Catholic Recusants of the West Riding of Yorkshire, 1558–1790', *Proc. Leeds Phil. and Lit. Soc.*, x (1963), 206, 280, 283.

[36] Chatsw., Londesborough K.

off the engagement and seized Dudley's goods at Skipton (which his nephew and executor, Robert earl of Leicester, was still trying to recover in the 1560s). Margaret was subsequently (with royal sanction) married to Henry lord Strange, later fourth duke of Derby.[37] A further example of his ambition and willingness to flirt with protestants comes from his negotiations in the mid-1560s for a marriage between his elder son George and a daughter of the earl of Bedford. Interestingly his intermediary with the Queen was Leicester.[38] His lack of stomach for the catholic cause is finally revealed in his failure to rise with the other northern earls in 1569. He died in January 1570 leaving as his heir a child, George, who came into his inheritance in 1579. An absentee courtier, the third earl was responsible for the dissolution of much of the estates and undid many of the achievements of his father and grandfather.[39]

[37] C. C. Stopes, *Shakespeare's Environment* (1918), 247–57 (based on Requests pleadings in the PRO which I have been unable to locate). For the disastrous Strange-Clifford marriage, B. Coward, *The Stanleys, lords Stanley and earls of Derby, 1385–1672* (Chetham Soc. third ser., xxx, 1983), 28–32.

[38] Whitaker, *Craven*, 338.

[39] We await the full study of the Clifford estates after 1579 which Dr R. T. Spence has in hand.

APPENDIX:
THE ANGLO-SCOTTISH WAR OF 1532-3

The brief Anglo-Scottish war of 1532–3, which was concluded by the Treaty of London in May 1534, has attracted little notice in the standard accounts of relations between the two nations.[1] Indeed, compared with the campaigns of 1513, 1522–3 and the Rough Wooing, this war was small beer indeed. The lack of importance contemporaries attached to it is reflected in the fact that its day to day conduct was left in the hands of the wardens, especially Northumberland, aided by a council of Sir Thomas Clifford, Sir Richard Tempest, Sir Arthur Darcy and others. Sir George Lawson acted as Treasurer. There was no general invasion and the only territory that either side occupied was the small (and derelict) pele of Cawmills, to the north of Berwick, which was taken by the English. Moreover the war was conducted almost entirely on the East and Middle Marches, with little or no activity in the West. Indeed, the war may be seen as an acceleration of the normal border activities of raiding and burning but with the involvement of much larger numbers of men; certainly no attempt was made to penetrate deeply into Scottish territory. Because no other account of the war is available, a brief sketch may be found useful to assist in understanding the letters in the collection which refer to the progress of the war or the negotiations which followed the cessation of hostilities.

It may be said that the war was unintended and unwelcome not only to the protagonists but also to the French, who, as will appear, attempted to bring about the reconciliation of England and Scotland. Its origins may be traced to the slow and progressive deterioration of relations between the English and Scottish wardens in the West Marches during the autumn and winter of 1531–2 which was prompted by jurisdictional disputes. The most serious of these concerned the status of the priory and grounds of Canonbie (now in Scotland) which, it was argued by the English, formed a part of the Debateable Lands. The Scottish claim was that in the recent past the English had made redress to the

[1] J. D. Mackie, 'Henry VIII and Scotland', *Trans. Royal Hist. Soc* 4th ser. xxix (1947); Rae, *Scottish Frontier*; W. Ferguson, *Scotland's Relations with England to 1707* (1977).

23

inhabitants of Canonbie thereby showing that it formed a part of the possessions of the king of Scots.[2]

In March 1532 the English were looking to the restoration of normal working relations between the wardens and advocating that all disputes over Canonbie should be put in the hands of commissioners. By May they were faced with unacceptable demands over the conduct of future meetings of the wardens which Henry rejected in a letter to Sir Thomas Clifford.[3] The dowager Queen of Scotland was sufficiently alarmed to write to her brother (Henry VIII) and Norfolk in mid-May to warn of the dangers of the situation, the responsibility for which she placed on the shoulders of Henry's border officials. James V was active in the borders in early June and seemed likely to direct raids into the Debateable Lands and Liddesdale but withdrew before they could be launched. He did write to Dacre asking for his co-operation in suppressing thieves in the Debateable Lands who used the markets at Carlisle, but Henry would not permit Dacre to offer any assistance.[4] Throughout 1532 these and other matters were the subject of a great deal of diplomatic activity, the Scots having an ambassador in London as late as December 1532.[5]

By 23 August Northumberland had put the eastern borders on a war footing and was reporting an increased number of border incursions into Northumberland. He wrote more fully of the problems he faced on 3 September.[6] At about this same moment Henry decided to heighten tension by ordering Northumberland to set the men of Tynedale and Redesdale with those of Liddesdale on the Scots.[7] Privy seals were sent out on 24 August for the mustering of 1,000 men at Newcastle on 12 September. The business of preparing his share of the force was still exercising Cumberland's officers in Westmorland some days after this (7, 33 and 73). But Henry's decision to mobilise was also accompanied by the signing of an agreement on 25 August with the exiled Scottish nobleman, the earl of Angus, whereby Angus agreed to aid the English king if Henry chose to wage war on Scotland, to acknowledge him as king of Scotland and to take an oath of allegiance to Henry. In return Henry promised him an annuity of £1,000 sterling

---

[2] For the problem of Canonbie, W. Mackay Mackenzie, 'The Debateable Land', *Scottish Hist. Rev.* xxx (1951); *LP* v nos. 535, 537 (amongst other references there).

[3] *Ibid.* nos. 844, 845, 854, 1047, 1078.

[4] *The Hamilton Papers*, J. Bain (ed.), i, (1890), 2–6; *LP* v no. 1079.

[5] *LP* vi no. 19. The gradually deteriorating relations between two kingdoms makes sense of Hall's report that after Easter 1532 the Commons were told of the need to refurbish the defences of the English border to prevent Scottish incursions and offered a fifteenth towards this end. Hall, *Chronicle*, 785–6.

[6] *LP* v nos. 1246, 1286.

[7] *Ibid.* no. 1286.

until Angus regained his Scottish estates. Henry further undertook not to make peace with Scotland without seeking Angus's advice.[8] The association of Henry with the Douglas interest thus became an additional Scottish grievance.[9] But whatever the merits of each party's grievances against the other, it seems certain that Henry should be blamed for the progressive deterioration of relations. Sir Thomas Clifford told his brother in October that James V was anxious to avoid war (10). In an undated letter from November or early December, Thomas Magnus reported that James and his nobles were set on peace but that the borderers did all they could to provoke war.[10]

During October and November the war took the form of raids into England by the Scots and into Scotland by the English garrison at Berwick assisted by their supporters in Liddesdale. A major raid into England on 20–21 November was answered with a raid carried out on Henry's instructions on or about 11 December and the decision was taken during Henry's return from the Calais meeting with Francis I to add a further 1,500 men to the 1,000 men already stationed at Berwick.[11] There was also a naval aspect to the war. In mid-October Sir Thomas Clifford captured a Scots ship which he put to good use until it was seized by the mayor of Hull.[12]

On 23 December the Berwick garrison invaded Scotland and took the small pele tower of Cawmills. This was placed in the charge of George Douglas, younger brother of the earl of Angus.[13] Retaining it proved problematical. By March 1533 the two alternatives of refurbishing the fortification or razing it to prevent it returning to being a gathering place for thieves were under consideration.[14] This however, was the only occasion on which territory was held by either side. Instead the war continued as a series of raids conducted against the other. The impression gained from the scanty correspondence in *Letters and Papers* and that offered here is that the English were the more active

[8] Bodl, Ms Jesus College 74 fo. 213v; *LP* v no. 1254. For Archibald Douglas, 6th earl of Angus (*c.*1489–1557), exiled from Scotland 1528–1542, see *Scots Peerage*, i, 190–3. He was active during the war, raiding into Scotland, advising the warden and council at Berwick and Warkworth and using his servants to spy in Scotland (*LP* v no. 1635, 1638; vi no. 143). His brother George acted as Northumberland's 'underofficer' in a raid into Scotland (49) and was appointed keeper of the Cawmills. On the evidence of the letters printed subsequently, Angus was on good terms with Cumberland with whom he shared a taste in hawking (35 and 36)

[9] *LP* v no. 1367, vi no. 19.

[10] *Calendar of State Papers relating to Scotland*, i, (1858), 31. The letter is abstracted here, without source (and I have been unable to locate it) and palpably misdated to July 1533.

[11] *LP* v nos. 1460, 1559, 1635, 1638; 9, 35, 49 and 74 below.

[12] 8, *LP* v nos. 1559, 1674.

[13] *Ibid.* no. 1655.

[14] *LP* vi nos. 205, 260.

side, keeping up a constant pressure on the coastal plain of Berwickshire with small mobile raiding parties. But larger raids occurred intermittently, their timing in part being determined by the phase of the moon.[15]

The lands of the earl of Buccleugh were attacked and burnt in early February, but the raid planned for early March was cancelled on the king's instructions, probably to aid the French ambassador's negotiations. A raid later in March was also deferred because James V was reported to be in the borders.[16] The normal round of raids was recommenced in April with the English crossing into Scotland on 9, 20 and 21 April, the last nearly ending in disaster. The Scots retaliated on 26 April with a daytime raid which was pursued back into Scotland.[17]

This may have been the last major engagement of the war. The English raid of 20 April coincided with the passage through Berwick of the French ambassador, M. Beauvais, who expressed surprise that no order had been sent to Northumberland instructing him to cease hostilities.[18] Henry accepted a truce for six months on 4 May and ordered his officers in the North to suspend all hostile actions for its duration whilst remaining alert to Scottish attacks (11). On 27 May Lawson wrote to say that there was little activity on the borders and on 29 May he received orders to discharge the 2,500 men of the Berwick garrison placed in arms the previous autumn.[19] If the English appear (on the evidence of English sources) to have achieved a local dominance in their raids, they lost heavily in other respects, having a number of their transport ships carrying grain to the Berwick garrison taken by the Scots.

The key to the cessation of hostilities was the French. Henry may have asked for Francis's mediation with Scotland at their meeting in November 1532 or Francis, given his hostility to James V, may have offered to intervene to heal an unnecessary diversion.[20] His ambassador, Beauvais, was in Scotland in early 1533 and returned to England towards the end of February. After a few days at the court, he set out for France on 28 February.[21] His immediate return was expected in France in March but he did not reach London until about 8 April and as we have seen, crossed into Scotland on 20 April. His mission was

---

[15] *Ibid.* nos. 51, 124.
[16] *Ibid.* nos. 124–5, 217, 260; **75** below.
[17] *Ibid.* nos. 322, 375–6, 409.
[18] *Ibid.* no. 409.
[19] *Ibid.* nos. 544, 553, 664.
[20] *Ibid.* no. 259.
[21] *Ibid.* nos. 184, 198. In his absence, Henry instructed Rochford (newly appointed ambassador to France) to warn Francis that he was prepared to escalate the war. *Ibid.* no. 230.

to secure the cessation of hostilities for a year to allow an opportunity for a peace to be negotiated.[22] Within Scotland Beauvais was viewed as the harbinger of peace and whilst the relevant correspondence is lost, he must quickly have obtained the offer of a truce for six months from James, Henry's acceptance of which was communicated to the ambassador by a letter printed below (**12**).[23] Nonetheless, both kings continued to blame the other for the initial outbreak of hostilities. It appears that James's position was the weaker for he faced a great deal of internal dissent and conspicuously failed to attract support from France despite his pleas.[24] If the lesson needed learning, the special relationship of the Auld Alliance flowed in one direction only.

On 19 June the Scots appointed commissioners to treat at Newcastle where they arrived with Beauvais on 28 June. The immediate sticking point was the Scots's demand for the return of Cawmills. The English commissioners were not authorised to negotiate on this matter (or the question of the Douglas alliance) and expected to agree to an unconditional truce, not one which restored the territorial *status quo ante*.[25] As appears from a letter of 12 September (**14**), the determination to keep Cawmills was very much Henry's own; his local lieutenants doubted whether it could be held or even if it was worth holding. The possibility of putting a flat roof over the collapsed vaults to permit the mounting of artillery was considered but deemed impossible and the persistent advice of both Northumberland and Lawson was that the pele should be demolished.[26]

The king's instructions that the English commissioners were only to accept an unconditional cessation of hostilities forced the negotiations at Newcastle into a stalemate and throughout the summer an uneasy peace was maintained by extending the truce for short periods. Nonetheless, there was a fear after the Berwick garrison was disbanded that the Scots would attempt to seize back Cawmills and the earl of Northumberland went so far as to circulate a warning of an invasion in August.[27]

By early September the patience of the English commissioners was wearing thin and they attempted to force the Scottish commissioners

---

[22] *Ibid.* nos. 242, 259, 351, 408.

[23] cf. *LP* vi no. 485.

[24] On tensions within Scotland, see Northumberland's comments in **49** below and *LP* v nos. 1286, 1460. James sought assistance from the parlement of Paris on 28 Feb. and had an ambassador in France in late April; *LP* vi nos. 190, 408.

[25] *Ibid.* nos. 722, 745.

[26] *Ibid.* nos. 745, 777, 895, 897. In a neat piece of racialism, Lawson reported that no *Englishman* would be garrisoned there in either peace or war unless it was repaired: the English garrison there under Douglas were doubtless Scots.

[27] *Ibid.* no. 968.

into accepting an unconditional truce. After consideration this was declined and a further prorogation agreed. This followed a period in which Henry's attention appears to have strayed from the negotiations (the commissioners having complained about not having received any instructions from him on 27 July)[28], until he laid down his policy in a long letter written on 12 September (**14**). In this he states his willingness to accept an unconditional truce, but rejects the Scots' conditions over Cawmills and other matters, using the example of Tournai and the seizure of English ships by the Scots earlier in the year as an illustration of conventional practice. Welcoming the commissioners' negotiation of a further truce, he regretted that it was not for a longer period and urged them to seek an extension. But, by announcing a general (but temporary) mobilisation of the borders, Henry also hoped to forestall any attempt by the Scots to recover Cawmills while intimidating them into accepting the unconditional truce he required. Orders to supply men for the reestablishment of the Berwick garrison went out to Cumberland the following day.[29]

The extant correspondence is far from clear as to whether Beauvais was still active in the negotiations, but the impasse alarmed Francis I to the point where he wrote to Henry VIII on 10 September urging him to make concessions over Cawmills rather than prolong the dispute further.[30] In the event, the bluff of ordering a remobilisation served its purpose. An unconditional truce had been agreed by 24 September and bands of men making to assemble at Newcastle were caught at Darlington, Chester-le-Street and Durham and turned back.[31] A truce until Michaelmas 1534 was signed on 1 October, the English remaining in possession of Cawmills.[32]

By early 1534 the English appear to have been eager for a settlement of the dispute and as the question of the succession came into consideration, were willing to offer the possibility of including the Stuarts in the entail as an incentive to a speedy agreement.[33] The bishop of Aberdeen arrived in London during March 1534 to negotiate the peace treaty which was finally signed on 11 May. The following day the English agreed to return Cawmills to Scotland.[34] The treaty was to last for the joint lives of the two kings and a year longer, but was overtaken

---

[28] *Ibid.* no. 908.

[29] If the redating of this letter (**13**) can be accepted. Dickens, *Clifford Letters* no. 33 clearly bears on this mobilisation. Unfortunately it is undated and in the light of this argument Dickens's estimate of *c.*23 Aug. 1533 needs to be revised by perhaps three weeks.

[30] *LP* vi nos. 1113–4.

[31] *Ibid.* nos. 1162, 1187, 1283.

[32] *Ibid.* nos. 1196, 1283.

[33] *LP* vii nos. 114, 393.

[34] *Ibid.* nos. 252, 393, 647–8.

by the outbreak of hostilities in 1542. The larger question of the status of Canonbie had to wait until the definition of the Anglo-Scottish border achieved in 1552.[35]

[35] Mackenzie, 'The Debateable Land'.

Letters of Henry VII and Henry VIII

1 Henry VII to the tenth lord Clifford, 7 August [1494 x 1500]. Chatsw., Clifford Letter Book, fo. 12r.

To our right trusty and welbeloved the lord Clifford.

H[enricus] R[ex]   By the Kinge

Right trusty and welbeloved wee greet yow wele, and have understanden your lettre at length written at Skipton the 30 of July, and have perceyved thereby and otherwise the misbehavings on eyther side betweene the bishopp of Duresme our privy seale and yow: for the which yee may be well assured wee be nothing contented nor pleased with yow nor him. And for a restfullnes to be had in this cause, and in avoyding diverse other inconveniencyes, wee have commaunded our said privy seale for to cease forthwith of any further process or execucion against you upon endytement, citacion or otherwise, but to putt all things in respite unto *crastinum animarum* coming. And in the meane season to keepe our peace and to deliver forthwith upon suerty your servauntes and tenantes out of prison to theire liberty for to appeare before us and our counsaile at the said day to annswere unto all that he shall then lay against them. Wherefore wee will and straightly charge yow that ye for your part neyther doe nor attempt any manner of thinge against the said bishopp, his servantes or tenantes by way of fact, assembling of our people, affraies or any other willfull dealing, but inviolably to keepe our peace for yow and all yours, and to lett all things depending betweene yow and him to rest as they now be unto the said *crastinum animarum* upon the perill that may ensue. And then wee shall provide with the leave of our Lord soe as yee shall have all that right requireth in that behalfe. Yeoven under our signet at the mannor of Farlborn the 7th day of August.

This letter can be dated within the Durham episcopate of Richard Foxe, privy seal to Henry VII from 1487 and bishop 1494–1501. It refers to the dispute between Foxe and the 10th lord Clifford over the manor of Hart and Hartlepool in County Durham.[1] This had been seized by the bishop on the attainder of

[1] For the history of the manor of Hart, D. Austin, 'Fieldwork and Excavation at Hart, co. Durham, 1965–1975', *Archaeoligia Aeliana*, 5th ser. iv (1976), 72–78. Cf C. Kitching in D. Marcombe (ed.), *The Last Principality. Politics, Religion and Society in the bishopric of Durham, 1494–1660* (1987), 64–5.

31

the ninth lord Clifford in 1461 on the premise that the bishop had *jure regalia* within the palatinate of Durham. The manor was not restored when the Yorkist attainder was reversed in 1485 and the bishop was still in possession in the mid-1490s.[2] As early as 1494–5 Foxe was marshalling evidence to support his continued possession. Likewise Clifford bought the exemplification of a number of medieval texts in November 1496 which together served to define and limit the bishops' liberties.[3]

From the present letter it would appear that Clifford was at least partially successful in securing possession of the premises, but that his tenants and servants were subjected to litigation and imprisonment. The date at which Clifford appealed to the king is uncertain: Henry, typically, sought to defuse tension by calling the parties before him. It is perhaps from this moment that there survives both an incomplete roll of proceedings before the council and briefs of the litigants' cases.[4] The extant receiver's account for 13 March – 25 July 1500 shows receipts from the manor being paid to both Clifford and Foxe and suggests that Clifford regained possession at mid-summer that year.[5] The letter may possibly be dated from the previous autumn. Certainly the dispute had a local notoriety: the compiler of the Durham chronicle, William Chambre, although writing much later, thought that it explained Foxe's translation to Winchester.[6] The Cliffords remained in possession until the manor was sold by the third earl in 1580.

2 Henry VIII to the tenth lord Clifford, 3 May [1517].
Chatsw., Clifford Letter Book, fos. 8v-9r.

To our right trustie and welbeloved the lord Clifforde.

Henricus Rex   By the Kinge
Trustie and welbeloved wee greete you well. Soe it is upon the Even of Phillip and Jacob last paste [30 April] a great number of insolent prentices and malicious jorneymen of theire sensuall appetites and rancorous disposition against aliens and strangers, artificers and others inhabited within our citty of London soddenly assembled themselves wethein our said citty in the night time under colour of mayeinge,

---

[2] Durham, Dept of Paleography and Diplomatic, CC 189984–6, *ex inf* (in common with the other Durham references) Dr. M. G. Snape.

[3] Durham, Dept of Paleography and Diplomatic, CC 220197 fo. 88v, *CPR 1494–1509*, 81–3.

[4] Chatsw., Londesborough A unlisted. The roll lacks Clifford's bill, but has Foxe's answer and further pleadings yet adds little to our understanding of the case. J. Raine (ed.), *Historiae Dunelmensis, Scriptores Tres*, (Surtees Soc., ix, 1839), pp. ccccxlix-ccccliv; J. Hutchinson, *History of Durham* (1817 ed), i, 433–5 (which I owe to Dr A. J. Pollard). Miss Margaret Condon kindly searched her itinerary of Henry VII for a year when he was at 'Farlborn' on the appropriate day but without success.

[5] Durham, Dept of Paleography and Diplomatic, CC 189986 m. 2; 189987.

[6] Raine (ed.), *Historiae Dunelmensis*, 150.

breakeinge upp, entringe and robbinge the houses of certaine French
and Dutch men, makeinge also greate comminations to other strangers
to the mervellous inquiete and commotion of our said citty and
disturbance of our peace within the same. And albeit the insolent and
rebellous assemble, by our citty sheriffs and other substantiall and well
disposed cittizens with and by the policies, powers and assistance of
the noblemen and others of our counsell, was not onely furthwith
repressed and pacified, but also a greate number of the malefactors
and offenders taken and accordinge to our lawes and theire demerittes
openly convicted and put to execution so that it is now thorowly
pacified and put in quietnes (our Lord be thanked). Yet wee thought
right expedient t'advertise you thereof aswell for the declaracion of the
truth in puttinge all sinister and seditious brutes to silence if any such
shalbe made by indisposed personns as also that yee by your wisdome
should not onely forsee and have good espiall in the places and country
neere adjoyninge to you to know the disposition of our subjectes if upon
untrue reportes they should be stirred to any semblable commotions by
perverse counsaill either against marchantes, strangers or for any
other grownde or cause, but also by your wisedome and power with
thassistance of other our faithfull servantes and subjectes in those partes
furwith to represse the same by takeing aswell the principall moveres
and stirrers thereof as also the offenders accompaninge them for such
unlawfull ententes and purpose, comittinge them to warde and also
advertiscinge [fo. 9] us thereof with all speedy diligence as our speciall
trust is in you and as yee entend to do unto us acceptable pleasure
and service to bee remembred hereafter accordingly. Yeven under our
sigenett att our mannor of Richmonte the third day of May.

The king's circular letter is clearly designed to bring calm and dispel rumour
in the aftermath of the so-called 'Evil May Day' of 1517, a day of rioting in
London against aliens and the city authorities. The day's events and the
subsequent repression are described at length by Edward Hall, and more
recently, R. B. Manning.[7]

---

[7]Hall, *Chronicle*, 588–592; R. B. Manning, *Village Revolts. Social Protest and Popular
Disturbances in England, 1509–1640* (1988), 196–9.

3 Henry VIII to the tenth lord Clifford, 18 May [1520]. Chatsw., Clifford Letter Book, fo. 10r-v.

To our right trustie and welbeloved the lord Clifforde.

Henricus Rex   By the Kinge

Right trustie and welbeloved wee greete you well. And where as wee at this time have written aswell to the sheriffe of that our shire (as shall appeare unto [you] by the coppie of the same writtinge here inclosed) as also to the justices of our peace [fo. 10v] within our said shire whereof yee bee one (as in likewise shall appeare to you by our lettres to you and them addressed), comaundinge and straitly chargeinge that as well the said sheriffe as the said justices endeavor them for the keepinge of our peace and entertainment of our subjectes in good quiet and restfullnes dureinge the time of our jorney into the partes beyonde the sea to the which wee intend to dispose us aboute the latter end of this present month of May.

And forasmuch also as wee have for your great ease spared you of your attendance uppon us in our said jorney and left you at home to doe us service in the keepinge of our peace and good rule and order amongstes our said subjectes, wee will therfore and comaunde you that dureinge the time of our said absence out of this our realme yee have a speciall oversight, regarde and respecte aswell to the said sheriffe as the said justices how and with what diligence they doe and execute our comaundmentes comprised in our said lettres. And that yee also from time to time as yee shall see neede, quickly and sharply call uppon them in our name for the execution of our said commaundmentes. And if yee shall find any of them remisse or negligent in that behalf, wee will that yee lay it sharply to theire charge, advertiseinge them that in case they amende not theire default, yee will thereof advertise our counsaile attendinge uppon our deerest daughter the Princesse and so wee charge you to doe indeed. And if our said sheriffe or justices or any other sheriffe or justices of any other shire next to you uppon any side adjoyninge shall need and require your assistance for the execution of our said comaundementes, wee will and desire you that with the best power that yee can make of our subjectes in harneis, yee be to them aidinge and assistinge from tyme to time as the case shall require, not faileinge hereof as yee intend to please us and as wee singularly trust you. Yeven under our signett at our mannor of Greenewich the xviijth day of May.

Henry's letter to Clifford takes the form of a circular offering instructions for the government of the country in the king's absence abroad for his meeting with Francis I in 1520 ('The Field of Cloth of Gold'). This occurred on 7 June, having been delayed by Henry's meeting with Charles V at Canterbury in the last week of May.[8]

4 Henry VIII to the first earl of Cumberland, 7 September [1525]. Chatsw., Clifford Letter Book, fo. 10v.

To our right trustie and right welbeloved cousin therle of Cumberland.

Henricus Rex   By the Kinge

Right trustie and right welbeloved cousin wee greete you well. And forasmuch as wee understand that the late lord Clifford, your Father deceassed (whose soule God pardon) by his sufficient writtinge granted and lett to farme to our trustie and welbeloved servant Edward Gouldsbrough the mannor and lordshipp of Gouldsbrough with the appurtenances in our countie of Yorke, to have and to hold the same to our said servant dureinge the nonage of Thomas Goldsbrough, sonne and heire of Richard Goldsbrough deceased, yeildinge and paieinge therfore yearly like rent and ferme as in the said writinge is specified more at large. Wee therefore desire and pray you cousin to permitt and suffer our said servant peaceably and quietly to enjoy and occupy the said mannor dureinge the nonage of the said Thomas Goldsbrough accordinge to the effect and purporte of your said Fathers grante without any interruption to the contrary. And in your so doeinge yee shall administer unto us full good pleasure to be remembred accordingly hereafter. Yeven under our signett att our towene of Stony Stratford the vijth day of September.

The dating of this letter is relatively straightforward. That the receipient was the earl of Cumberland can make it no earlier than September 1525: that it was written during the minority of Thomas Goldesborough places it before May 1528. As Henry VIII was at Stony Stratford (Northants) on the appropriate day in 1525, that year can confidently be adopted. This fits well with what can be discovered of the tangled background to the letter.[9]

Richard Goldesborough of Goldesborough near Knaresborough died in 1504, leaving a son, Richard junior. In 1508 Richard junior, who married in his father's lifetime, established a use of his manors of Creskeld and Pool in Wharfedale in favour of his heirs male, with remainder to the use of his brother Edward (on whose behalf the present letter was written) and his heirs male and for lack to other younger brothers. His other lands, including the manor of Goldesborough, were left unentailed. Richard died later in 1508, leaving an infant son, Thomas, born on 26 May 1507. His widow Anne subsequently

[8]J. J. Scarisbrick, *Henry VIII* (1968), 76.
[9]Much of the material is gathered together in A. Goldesborough, *Memorials of the Family of Goldesborough* (1930), 95–8.

married Robert Warcop of Warcop in Westmorland, a man in the Clifford circle, who had a royal grant of the wardship in 1509 then, after Warcop was killed at Flodden, Thomas Wriothesley, Garter King of Arms.[10] An *inquisition post mortem* of 1513 found that Goldesborough was held of the duchy of Lancaster, but this was traversed in 1515 by Clifford who showed that the manor was held of his manor of Londesborough by knight service. Wriothesley's claim to the wardship was thereby made uncertain and he clearly had to compete with Clifford's grantee, Edward Goldesborough, for possession. As early as 1513–4 Goldesborough had been sued by Warcop for trespass at Goldesborough and the removal of goods worth £40. At this time Wriothesley and his wife did not have custody of the young Thomas. An undated petition, but of the mid-1510s, complains that Anne Wriothesley had voluntarily delivered Thomas to Henry lord Clifford who now refused to give him up him, and there were further disputes between Cumberland and Wriothesley.[11] The outstanding disputes between the Cliffords and Wriothesley over the wardship and the chattels of Robert Warcop were settled by arbitration in July 1525. Wriothesley claimed to have the manor of Goldesborough by virtue of a grant of wardship, doubtless that made to Robert Warcop, and claimed Warcop's goods which (it was alleged) had been seized by the 10th lord Clifford. The arbitrators decided that Wriothesley should have the goods, but Cumberland was awarded the manor of Goldesborough although paying Wriothesley 450 marks in compensation.[12]

This settlement excluded Clifford's lessee, Edward Goldesborough. He may probably be identified with the man of that name who served as the duchy of Lancaster's feodary in Knaresborough after 1512 and became a serjeant at arms in 1528.[13] The reference in this letter to Goldesborough being a servant possibly needs to be read literally and if this is so, the letter may be seen as an illustration of the capacity of household servants to obtain royal letters of commendation favourable to them.[14]

5 Henry VIII to the first earl of Cumberland, 27 November 1528. Chatsw., Clifford Letter Book, fo. 3r.

To our right trusty and right welbeloved cousin therle of Cumberland.

Henricus Rex   By the Kinge

Right trustie and right welbeloved cousin, wee greete you well. And understand that one Dicke of the Woodfoote otherwise called Richard

---

[10]*LP* i (1) no. 132 (73), also (2) no. 2137 (26); ii (1) no. 2541; also PRO STAC2/32/58. For Wriothesley see DNB.

[11]PRO, STAC2/32/58; Goldesborough, *Memorials of the Goldesborough Family*, 96.

[12]BL Harleian Ms 4900, fo. 33, cited Goldesborough, *Memorials of the Goldesborough Family*, 97.

[13]R. Somerville, *History of the Duchy of Lancaster* (2 vols, 1953, 1970), i, 526; *LP* iv (2) no. 4687 (20).

[14]It might be added that in 1566 the second earl of Cumberland claimed and sold the wardship of Anne Goldesborough, granddaughter of Richard. Chatsw., Curry 46/4.

Urwen, Scottishman and a simple person who hath committed felony within this our realme upon our subjectes on our borders of Scottland is taken and in ward with you under your charge with our castle of Carlisle. And that also our trusty subject Gefferey Middelton squire is taken in Scotland by the Urwens and delivered to the Armestronges, outlawes there, as hee was goeinge in his pilgrimage unto Saint Trewnym [sic] and so is kept with the said Armestrongs in duresie and shall not be delivered without restoringe of the said Dicke of the Woodfoote otherwise called Richard Urwen, beinge in ward with you.

Wherefore, wee in consideracion thereof will and commaunde you, that yee forthwith upon the sight hereof, deliver or cause to bee delivered the said Dicke of the Woodfoote otherwise called Richard Urwen unto the said Gefferey Middelton for to bee convaiede into Scotland for redeemeinge and pledgeinge of the same Gefferey out of the handes of the said Armestronges, without faileinge thus to doe as wee trust you, and as yee tender our pleasure. And these our letters shalbee your sufficient warrant and discharge in this behalfe att all times hereafter. Yeven under our signett att our mannor of Bridwell the xxvijth day of November, the xxth yeare of our raigne [1528].

Geoffrey Middleton was of an obscure gentry family settled at Middleton Hall in the parish of Kirkby Lonsdale, Westmorland.[15] *Letters and Papers* contains two additional letters relating to his kidnapping and captivity in Scotland during 1528. On 18 July lord Dacre reported that whilst returning from St Ninian's shrine, Middleton had been captured by John Urwen, brother of Richard Urwen (Dick of the Woodfoot), Cumberland's prisoner at Carlisle, and was being held hostage to compel the release of Richard Urwen. Later in the year the intercession of James V was sought to secure the return of pledges left with William Armstrong when Middleton and his servant were released, but from the present letter it seems that Middleton was still in the hands of William Armstrong in late November.[16]

The other letters make it clear that it was the shrine of St Ninian at Whithorn on the Galloway coast to which Middleton was travelling. Little is known about northern support for this shrine, but amongst the adherents of the cult was Richard III.[17]

---

[15] See Nicolson and Burn, i, 253–4.
[16] *LP* iv (2) nos. 4531, 4829.
[17] R. B. Dobson, 'Richard III and the Church of York', in R. A. Griffiths and J. Sherborne (eds), *Kings and Nobles in the Later Middle Ages*, (1986), 142.

6 Henry VIII to the first earl of Cumberland, 13 June [1530].
Chatsw., Clifford Letter Book, fo. 11v.

To our right trustie and right welbeloved cousin therle of Cumberlande.

Henricus Rex By the Kinge

Right trustie and right welbeloved cousin wee greete you well. And albeit for certaine matters of great importance touchinge us and the wealth of this our realme, wee were minded to send for you to repaire hither unto us. Yet tendringe your labors and eschewinge your charges in the same, wee have thought good to send unto you our trustie servantes William Brererton [sic], one of the Gentlemen of our Privie Chamber and Robert Leighton our Chaplin and Thomas Writhesley one of the clerkes of our Signet, to open and declare our mind and pleasure unto you, desireinge you to give firme credence unto the same. And straightly charge you to keepe secret such matter as they shall shew unto you without disclosinge or communicatinge it to any personne or then those whome ye understand by your said servantes to be made privie thereunto without failing as wee singulerly trust you. Yeven under our signett at our castell of Windesor the xiijth day of June.

The 'matter of great importance' and secrecy which formed the subject of this letter of commendation was, inevitably, the divorce. The privy seal is dated on the day following the assembly of a great council of nobles, bishops and others, called to secure their subscription to a petition to the pope calling on him to bring the divorce to a speedy conclusion. Of the delegation, Brereton was executed in 1536, a victim of the fall of Anne Boleyn and Wriothesley served as lord chancellor and was created earl of Southampton in 1547, d. 1550. Robert Leighton is correctly Edward Leighton of Cardinal College and subsequently Henry VIII College, Oxford.[18]

7 Henry VIII to the sixth earl of Northumberland, 24 August [1532].
Chatsw., Clifford Letter Book, fo. 10r.

A coppie of a lettre from his majestie to my lord of Cumberlande [sic].

Right trustie and right welbeloved cousin wee greete you well. And forasmuch as wee bee enformed the borderers of Scotland have of late

---

[18] Scarisbrick, *Henry VIII*, 259–60; E. W. Ives, *Anne Boleyn* (1986), 164. For Leighton, A. B. Emden, *A Biographical Register of the University of Oxford, 1501–1540* (1974), 349. The present reference to Leighton as king's chaplain predates the earliest known to Emden by three years. For Wriothesley, *HP 1509–1558*, iii, 663–6. The accounts for this journey survive in *LP* iv (3) no. 6489.

made divers roades into our East and Middle Marches to the greate damage and hurt of our subjectes there, due redresse whereof our officers, as they write unto us, cannot attaine of the kinge of Scottes. So as wee accompt our self bound for the safegard and defence of our said subjectes to provide and furnish a convenient garrison to lie uppon the saide borders untill such time as wee may otherwise take order therein, wee therfore will and desire you, and likewise comaundinge you by these presentes authorishe the same, to putt in a readines and retaine of your tenantes and servantes the number of two hundreth able men, well horsed, with bowes and arrowes, in sufficient array so as they faile not to be at our towne of Newcastle the xviijth day of September next comeinge, to serve us in the said garrison under the leadeinge of a captaine to be by you appointed, whome wee require you to make Roger Lassells, a man thought unto us verie meete for the same. Signifieinge unto you that forasmuch as the fewer of thinhabitantes of Northumberland be retained in the said garrison the stronger shall the country bee as yee cann by your wisedome consider, our pleasure is therfore that there bee in no wise above two personages inhabitantes of Northumberland in every hundreth of your said number ne yet of the inhabitantes of your mannor of Cokermouth for disfurnishinge of those partes. And as for conducte money, and money for coates for your said men, wee have appointed payment to be made at our citty of Yorke the xijth day of September next ensueuing [*sic*] by thandes of our trustie and welbeloved servant Sir George Lawson knight where fore sendinge thither therfore ye shall not faile to have the same paid accordingly. And as for instructions how and after what sorte and fashion wee will have the said garrison ordered, wee shall with all diligence send the same unto you. Yeven under our signett att our monastarie of Abbington the xxiiijth day of August.

This letter is the first of a sequence bearing on the Anglo-Scottish War of 1532–3. This brief and unnoticed conflict is considered further in the appendix to the introduction.[19] The present letter is clearly addressed to the earl of Northumberland and not Cumberland. Cumberland had no estates in Northumberland (where the earl of Northumberland was the major landowner) and it was Northumberland and not Cumberland who was lord of Cockermouth. Cumberland had similar instructions to raise men which formed the subject of correspondence during September 1532 (**33** and **73**). In all 1,000 troops were to be mustered for Berwick on this occasion.[20] The garrison was enlarged by a further 1,500 men by privy seals sent out in mid November (**9**).

Roger Lassells of Breckenbrough (Yorkshire North Riding) was the steward of the fifth earl of Northumberland's household. He was reappointed by the

---

[19] Above 23–9.
[20] *LP* v nos. 1286, 1630.

sixth earl on his inheritance but appears to have been eased out of the circle of the sixth earl's intimates.[21]

8 Henry VIII to Sir Thomas Clifford, 3 November [1532].
Chatsw., Clifford Letter Book, fo. 13r.

To our trusty and right welbeloved servant and counsailour Sir Thomas Clifford knight, deputy of our towne of Barwicke.

By the Kinge

Trusty and right welbeloved wee greet yow well. And perceyving by contynew [*sic*] of your lettres to us addressed of the 22th day of October not onely your dexterity and wisedome used in setting forth of the shipp to encounter with the Scot as you writt and in other our affaires, for the which we give unto yow our hartye thancks, but also how sundry attempts have been lately comitted by the Scots on our borders: yee shall understand, that not a little mervayling that our counsaile there have stayd to defyne those actes to be notable entries, wee have at this tyme addressed our lettres generally to our said counsaile, like as ye shall now perceive by the same, willing and desyring yow to follow the contents of the same as much as in you for your part, as our speciall trust and confidence is in yow, whereby yee shall more and more deserve our thanckes to be remembred and your weale here after accordingly. Yeven under our signett at our towne of Calais the 3 day of November.

For Sir Thomas Clifford, brother of the first earl of Cumberland and Captain of Berwick 1529–1538, see the head notes to **29–40** below. The circumstances in which Clifford captured a ship are never described in the surviving letters; neither Clifford's report to the king nor the king's dispatch to the council at Berwick reported in this letter are extant. The ship was later seized by the mayor of Hull and remained at issue in relations between England and Scotland as late as 1538.[22]

[21] Hoyle, 'The fall of the House of Percy', 187, 209.
[22] *LP* v no. 1674; xiii (1) no. 837.

9 Henry VIII to the first earl of Cumberland, 3 November [1531 x 1533].
Chatsw., Clifford Letter Book, fo. 12v.

To our right trusty and right welbeloved cosyn the erle of Cumberland.

Henry R[ex]   By the Kinge

Right trusty and right welbeloved cosyn, wee greet yow well. And whereas our most deerest father of famous memory, whose soule God perdon, by his lettres pattentes, amongst other things, did give and graunt unto our intirely beloved grandmother, Lady Margeret countess of Richmond, Somersett and Derby deceased, many great libertyes, franchesyes and customes to be used with our barrony of Kendalle within our countye of Westmorland as by the same lettres pattentes thereof made more plainely it appeareth. According to the which graunt our said late graundmother peaceably occupied [ex]ercised and enjoyed the same libertyes and customes during her naturall life, all which libertyes and customes wee have of late given and graunted amongst other thinges unto our intyrely beloved cosyn Henry duke of Richmont and Somersett, to have, hold, exercize and use to him and to his heyres males in as large and ample manner as ever they weare exercized and used by our said grandmother.

Nevertheles as wee be informed, yee, being sheriff by inheritaunce of our said county of Westmorland, have of late suffred your officers and ministers of your said sheriffwick to disturb, molest and greive the officers and tenantes of the said duke in the exercising of the said libertyes and customes to the great inquietnes of the tenantes, inhabitantes and officers of the said duke within the said barrony. Wee therefore willing indifferency to be ministred unto all our subjectes, will and comaund you that from henceforth yow charge your officers to permitt and suffer all the officers and tenantes of the said duke to use and occupy the said libertyes, franchesyes and customes and every of them within the said barronry [*sic*] according to our graunt and in like manner and forme as they or any of them weare used by our said grand mother without lett or interrupcion of yow or any of your officers. Faile yee not thus to doe as we especially trust you. Yeoven under our signet at our mannor of Greenwich the third day of November.

This letter can be dated on a number of grounds to the years 1531–4 and is further evidence of a dispute between the first earl of Cumberland and the officers of the duke of Richmond over the sheriff of Westmorland's jurisdiction in the barony of Kendal.[23] The Cliffords were hereditary sheriffs of West-

[23] The letter cannot be dated to 3 November 1532 when Henry VIII was in Calais but could belong to any of the other years. PRO, OBS 1418.

morland, which they occupied through deputies.[24] The barony of Kendal was a complex of manors in southern Westmorland centered on the castle at Kendal. The barony was divided between a number of landowners each of whom held a physically distinct portion. In 1525 a moiety of the whole was granted to Henry's bastard, the duke of Richmond, as a part of his apanage and the crown purchased a further fraction for Richmond in $c.1530$.[25]

S. M. Harrison has already described the dispute between Cumberland and his deputies and Richmond's estate officers in Kendal over the right of the sheriff to hold courts within the barony and draw judicial business from its inhabitants.[26] Unfortunately his chronology is defective, but the construction of a more accurate account is hindered by the fact that none of the letters can be closely dated.

In a letter dated only to 1 April, Sir James Layburn, deputy steward of the barony for Richmond, informed Thomas Cromwell of Cumberland's infringements of Richmond's rights, referring to a previous royal injunction to Cumberland to cease meddling. With the letter was enclosed a bill of complaint against Cumberland. The letter must be dated to either 1532 or 1533 for it is directed to Cromwell as 'Master Thomas Cromwell', an appellation unthinkable later. The complaint which survives cannot directly be connected with this letter, for the letter and complaint are in different hands. It too refers to Cumberland's failure to obey a previous royal injunction.[27]

Where Harrison went astray was in his belief that the disturbances extended beyond 1536. He was persuaded of this by a letter to Layburn from a local officer describing an attempt by Cumberland's deputies to hold a court at Kendal. Layburn's correspondent described how he had reminded Cumberland's men of an oral injunction of the duke of Norfolk against their interference. Harrison takes this to have been an order delivered by Norfolk on his progress through the North in the spring of 1537, but this possibility must be countered by the fact that the letter talks of Richmond as a living person although he had died on 22 July 1536.[28]

From these ill-documented events Harrison reads the lesson that the earl was actively trying to draw the barony into his orbit but that his ambition to do so was frustrated by Layburn's capacity to seek royal aid. Cumberland's failure to capture Kendal was, in Harrison's interpretation, one of a number of failures which made plain the earl's declining influence. The rights and wrongs of the case are too obscure for any such conclusion to be offered with certainty. There was a history of such disputes in Westmorland, witness that with the Abbot of Saint Mary's York in the 1510s.[29] Moreover an unnoticed letter of 1531 shows the duke's officers to have been jealous of their master's rights in the barony.[30] That Cumberland's case might not have been as weak

---

[24] Cf. **91** and **104** below.
[25] For the barony see Nicolson and Burn, i, 30–65. For the purchase of the Lumley fraction for Richmond, below **107**.
[26] Harrison, *Pilgrimage of Grace*, 38–42.
[27] *LP* vi nos. 306, 1620.
[28] *LP* v no. 966.
[29] PRO, REQ2/11/24; Dickens, *Clifford Letters*, 81.
[30] Cumbria RO, Carlisle, D/Ay/1/198.

as Harrison supposes is further indicated by the fact that between 1532 and 1534 Cumberland agreed to take the issues outstanding between himself and Richmond to the arbitration of four judges. Regretably their decision is not known to survive.[31]

The dispute may have occupied only a matter of months within the longer period 1532–4. Richmond's officers complained of 'infringements' of their rights in Kendal by Cumberland. They obtained a letter from the king, which might be the one printed here; there were then further disputes the following spring before the matter was defused by arbitration (and subsequently Richmond's death).[32]

10 Henry VIII to first earl of Cumberland, 19 November 1532. Chatsw., Clifford Letter Book, fo. 3r.

To our right trusty and right welbeloved cousin therle of Cumberland.

Henricus Rex   By the Kinge

Right trustie and right welbeloved cosin wee greete you well. Forasmuch as by advertisementes from our borders of the East and Midle Marches foranempst Scotland, wee understand that it is right expedient and necessarie for the defence of those partes and annoyance of the Scottes (who daily molesteth, harrieth and spoileth our subjectes), to augment and encrease our garrison there, to the number of fifteene hundred men over and above one thousand which is att our charge there already. Wee therefore desire and pray you and by these presentes authorish you so to doe; to levie, retaine and put in aredines of such as be within your rules, auctorities or your owne tennantes the number of two hundred, and the same beinge able personages and furnished in array after the manner of the borders, to send to our towne of Newcastle the fifth day of December, there to be ministred and appointed to such places as they shalbee by order of our right trusty and right welbeloved cosin and counsalour therle of Northumberland and other our counsalours there allotted unto, to whom at theire comeinge thither shalbe allowed and paid money for the conducte thither accordingly, wherfore faile ye not thus to do as wee specially trust you. Yeven under our signet at our citty of Canterbury the xixth daie of November the xxiiijth yeare of our raigne [1532].

---

[31] Bodl., Ms Dodsw. 83 fo. 98. The transcript is dated 8 May [ ] Henry VIII. The careers of the four judges named date the recognisance to one of May 1532, 1533 or 1534.

[32] Chatsw., BA 8 fo. 20r has, under Kendal Ward, £4 4s 7d amerced on the tenants of the duke of Richmond that year (1534) and written off as uncollectable.

11 Henry VIII to sixth earl of Northumberland, Sir Thomas Clifford and other councillors in the East and Middle Marches, 4 May 1533. Chatsw., Clifford Letter Book, fos. 6v-7r.

Copie of the kinges lettre to my lord.

Right trustie and right welbeloved cousin and trustie and welbeloved, wee greete you well. Lettinge you wit wee have lately received lettres from the Monsure Beavois our good brother the French kinges ambassador in Scotland, the effect whereof consisteth cheefly in two pointes. Whereof the first is that where upon mo[ti]ane made unto the said kinge of Scottes by the said Beavois on the behalf of our said good brother to enter with us amitie and peace and to have all manner of matters dependinge betweene us in variance compounded and determined after an amiable and frendly sort, the saide kinge of Scottes and his counsell be resolved to followe our said good brothers advice in that behalf, and remittinge all matters dependinge in controversie betweene us to the decision and determination of our said good brother, to take with us a truce for six monthes, and in that time to endeavour by himself to the establishment of a perfect peace, wee should for conclusion of the said truce send our comissioners to Calstreme furnished with sufficient authoritie for that purpose. The second pointe of the said lettres is to addresse our comaundement to you, our cousin of Northumberland, Sir Thomas Clifford and the rest of you our counsellours there [fo. 7r] to surcease and absteine from any invasion or attemptate to be done or committed on our partie dureinge the time of the said [truce].

To the which two pointes wee have made such answere as yee shall perceive by the copies of our lettres now sent to the said Beavois which ye shall receive herewith. And therfore yee shall understand our pleasure and comaundement is that after the receipt hereof, diligently peruseinge your said lettres and maturely digesting the contentes of the same, puttinge neverthelesse yourself, our garrisons and power there in such a readines furnished with good and assured espiall as ye may not onely be able and ready to defend the violence of any such enterp[r]ise as covertly under the coulor of this desire to peace might by our ennimies be attempted against us, but also by your said espialls have certaine knowledge and advertisement what preparacion is made in Scotland towardes warr or what likelihood yee shall perceive that they doe effectually desire this peace so that ye may therby deciphre theire intentes and purposes. There be in no wise any attemptate done or comitted against them on our partie by any of our garrisons upon the borders, Berwike or by any the inhabitantes of the countrey there aboutes unlesse the said Scottes shall first attempt any exploit against us, in which case our pleasure is ye shall in any wise endeavour yourself to revenge the same so as wee rest at no time with the last buffett. Forseinge there be no attemptate comitted on our partie dureinge the time of the said commition unles it may evidently appeare the same to have proceeded first of theire owne seekeing. Willinge and comaundinge you and every of you not onely to advertise us with diligence from time to time what relation and knowledge yee shall have and attaine from your espialls in Scotland or otherwise of the intentes and purposes of the said Scottes and what your opinions shalbee touchinge the same or any other thinge that may percase occurre there, but also to have such vigilant eye and regard to the premisses as by treason in trust for want of good forsight wee sustaine ne suffer any hourte or damage. Yeven under our signet at our manner of Greenewitche the iiijth day of May [the] xxvth yeare of our raigne [1533].

12 Henry VIII to M. Beauvais, the French Ambassador, [4 May 1533]. Chatsw., Clifford Letter Book, fo. 29r-v.

A true coppy of the kinges lettre in annswere to Monsieur de Beavoir the French kings ambassador in Scotland translated out of French, sent by the said Doctor Fox to the said earle of Cumberland.

Where ye write unto us how that following the tenour of the charge to you given by our deerest brother and perpetually ally the French king, yee have on his behalfe prayed the king of Scottes to make truce with us, to the intent that the differences and contencions between us and him may by way of amiable composicion be compounded and determined, whereto we have found him very difficile. Thereby may yee well perceive that on their behalfe hath begon the varyance and warr, and how high minded and obstinate they be, in so much that, although upon an unjust and unlawfull ground, tytle and pretenced quarrell, they have mooved warr against us, yett notwithstanding they will be prayed (right welbeloved) on our behalfe wee ought to be difficult and have cause to be prayed and so tell them hardely, that if it weare not the instance and intercession of the king our deerest brother and the conjunccion and union of our and his affayres which wee repute for one thinge, and for to shew unto him the amity and union of our hartes to be such that wee would refuse him of nothing whatsoever it be in the world, we would not condiscend or agree to any peace, truces or abstinence of warr, untill such tyme as wee should to our satisfaccion be revenged of all the atrocity and wrongs on their behalfe done against us and our subjects. To the intent the boldnes and temerity which they might conceave to undertake heereafter in like case against us should be repressed, and doubtles after that wee have so long forborne and suffred the tender age and youth of the said Scots kinge, not shewing unto him what displeasure upon a just cause and reason wee might have had done and doe unto him; [fo. 29v] our finall resolucion was to make them to feele how undiscreetly and temerarely they have purchased and procured evill and displeasure to their power unto us his uncle, which have allwayes been readye to doe him pleasure and to shew him continually kindnes and amitye.

And now is the tyme that we had appoynted and determyned to have avenged our injury as right and reason requireth, soe that already we had been about, had not it been at the intercession of our deerest brother the French king, for whose favour wee forbeare and surcease now to goe about and proceed untill now to further extremity and rigour as wee should rightfully use against him.

As to that yee writt how the said king of Scotts after the hearing of your charge, hath annswered unto yow that our said good brother the French king is the prince in the world for the which he should most doe reserving him, by the advice of his counsell to follow all his pleasure, remitting all differences and variances by him to be determined and ordered, also that at the intercession of our said good brother he is contented to make truce with us for six months, during the which space he shall indeavour himselfe to conclude a good peace and union with us.

11–12 Both these letters are the copies of royal correspondence sent to Cumberland by Dr Edward Fox on 4 May 1533 (**98**).[33] The French ambassador, who was charged with bringing the Anglo-Scottish war to an end by his mediation, crossed into Scotland on 20 April and rapidly obtained the consent of James V to a truce for six months. This was accepted by Henry VIII.[34] In the first of the two letters Henry communicates notice of the truce and the cessation of hostilities to Northumberland and the commissioners on the borders, warning them to be on their guard against further Scottish actions. In the second he tells Beauvais of his acceptance, stressing that he did so only out of friendship with Francis I and blaming the Scots for the initial outbreak of war.[35]

---

[33] The heading suggests that it is addressed to Cumberland, but the contents show otherwise. For a similar heading where the letter is clearly to the commissioners in the borders, see **14** below.

[34] Above 27.

[35] **12** reads as though it might be incomplete, Henry stopping short of accepting the truce offered by the Scots.

13 Henry VIII to the first earl of Cumberland, 13 August [*recte* September] 1533.
Chatsw., Clifford Letter Book, fo. 3v.

To our right trustie and right welbeloved cosin therle of Cumberlande.

Henricus Rex By the Kinge

Right trustie and right welbeloved wee greete you well. Lettinge you wite that albeit upon such towardnes of conformytye as appeared unto us to have beene in the kinge of Scotts by such sutes and intercessions as was made unto us by sundry waies and meanes to take att our hand a peace honorable for us and our realme, wee removed and withdrew such our garrisons as wee had upon our borders, yet findinge nowe that our streng[t]h removed and his feare somwhat therby asswaged, hee sayth more coldly and after other sort unto us then was trusted he would, requiringe such condicions of truce as whereunto wee with our honour cannott agree. Wee therfore be now enforced· to renewe our said garrisons and to present him such a visage of our strength and arredines as hee may therupon knowe and understand howe expedient and necessarie it shalbee for him to followe and conclude the truce which hee first desired of us in such sorte as in honour wee may be contented with the same. Wherefore wee will and desire you and by these our lettres authorishe you so to doe to put in arredines for warre upon the borders the number of cc persons furnished with captaines att your choise and with other habilimentes accordingly to be taken of your tennantes and such rules and officies as yee have under us, so as they may repaire to our right trustie and right welbeloved cousin and counsailour therle of Northumberland, warden of those our East and Middle Marches att such time and place as shalbee by his lettres appointed unto you. Yeven under our signet att our parke of [   ] the xiijth day of August the xxvth yeare of our raigne [1533].

14 Henry VIII to Thomas Magnus, Sir Thomas Clifford, Sir Ralph Ellerker the younger and Thomas Wharton, English commissioners negotiating with the Scots at Newcastle, 12 September 1533.
Chatsw., Clifford Letter Book, fos. 9r-10r.

The coppie of a lettre to my lord of Cumberlande.

Trustie and right welbeloved wee greete you well and have received your lettres of the vjth of this month signifieinge unto us how ye, perceiveinge the Scottes to persist in theire demaund of Cawmilles and no likelihode of truce to be agreed upon accordinge to your instructions, have procured the truce to be proroged for other 15 daies and desire us further in your said lettres to knowe more plainly our mind what wee ment by the relation in our former lettres to your instructions, consideringe ye had as ye write none specially sent you heretofore but onely advertisement of our pleasure by lettres not to conclude the truce unlesse the Scottes would agree to a clause written in a schedule, the coppie whereof yee sent unto us at this time.

First as touchinge the truce taken by you for xv daies, like as wee are content with the thinge donne and would wishe as the case standeth that either the time were longer or that wee had beene sooner (if it might have beene) advertised thereof. So if yee had used such manner in the obtaininge of the same, as the Scottes should not have had so great cause of courage in theire obstinacie as they may now gather of your sute for the said truce, wee should have beene much better pleased and content therewith; thinkeinge that the Scottes, perceiveinge you for our partie to bee desirous of truce, doe the more frowardly use themselves and would be more tractable beinge roughly handled then with gentile entreatie. Neverthelesse, consideringe ye had instructions to agree to such a truce and that yee percase had regard to the weaknes of our borders now unfurnished, wee write not the premisses so much to blame and find fault in your doeinges as to shewe you our minde and opinion therein to be regarded and followed hereafter.

As touchinge the second pointe of your lettres and t'advertise you more plainly of our mind concerninge the truce to be taken with the Scottes for a yeare, if they will agree therunto omittinge now all relations of any former instructions whether yee have them or have them not, yee shall understand that in this truce to be taken for a yeare, wee regard principally the conservacion of our honnour, which is touched when the kinge of Scottes to us evermore, hitherto so much inferior, should in conclusion of truce now demaund novelties and like a captaine conqueror prescribe and give lawes unto us, sainge give me this, or doe thus, or I will no truce with you. Whereas the verie nature of a truce is accordinge to the wordes of the schedule, the copie whereof ye sent unto us, now every partie to forbeare and abstaine from warre in the state they be in. And if wee had wonne into our handes the whole countrey unto Edenbrough, although uppon condicions wee would as wee should thinke good percase restore the same uppon comunicacion, yet in the conclusion of a truce no restitution there of can of good congruence be spoken of and he that speaketh of it seemeth himself to stand aloft and his feete to bee where his head shall never come, and to have peace in his hand and to sell if he list, in which case neither the kinge of Scottes is, nor wee can take him so to be.

And to shew you breefly as the Scottish kinge withholdeth our subjectes shipps, which as hee taketh in warre hee calleth nowe his owne, so wee semblable and by the same reason call Cawmills ours. [fo. 9v] And equalitie therefore is that in conclusion of truce neither wee speake of our ships, neither he of his milles, and as wee put no condicion to restraine him in the use of our shipps, no more he to doe to us in thorderinge of Cawmilles. This is reciprocate, this is indifferent. This doe all princes observe and thus did wee keep Turney still in our handes against the French kinge. Now when the kinge of Scottes contrary to all custome, fashion and manner saith 'this I will have' though it be never soe little, yet it is in excesse from equalitie and a pretence of a superior heade which wee cannot abide.

Wherfore if the Scottes will agree upon a truce without demandinge Cawmilles or requireinge of us any speciall condicion to doe thus or doe that, wherby they should be seene to have sold this truce unto us for one yeare, then wee would that yee agree and conclude with them and thinke the wordes contained in the schedule to bee verie good, or els the Scottes speakeinge of restitution of Cawmilles, the removeinge of the Dowglasses or any other speciall matter to be convented by you in the truce be it never so small value or moment, yet beinge dishonorable wee will in noe wise yee agree thereunto. And thus yee be answered to your lettres and sufficiently instructed in that behalf.

And to make you participate to our resolucion how to encounter and meete with purposes of the Scottes who wee feare intend in the expiracion of this truce of xv daies to doe some enterprise uppon Cawmilles for recovery thereof and, perceaveinge us to have discharged our garrison uppon our borders, proceed more slackly with us then they els would, wee are determined (which yee must in any wise keepe secret to yourself) to be at the charge to renewe for one month the garrison of our borders to the number of 2,000 men to appeare to the Scottes ready to withstand theire interprises, wherin consideringe that the last prorogation by you taken for xv daies shall end so shortly as against the last end therof our men cannott be in convenient place assembled, wee thinke therfore more then necessarie that the truce bee proroged for xv daies longer if it could be obtained, so as within those xv daies and against thend there of all our men might be in such preparacion and arreadines uppon the place as they might doe anno-iance and resist and withstand as the case should require; which should give terror to the ennimy and feelinge of his owne damage, stirre and provoke him to [   ] for conclusion of the truce. But in the obtaininge of this truce, wee perceave some difficultie which by your wisedomes must be compassed as attemptinge the matter ye neither comfort the ennimy to understand such suites, ne put him in mistrust for feare of any other entended exploite to agree thereunto, wherefore yee shall understand wee have here handled thambassadors of France in such sorte as they have taken uppon them to entreate us to bee content to prorogue the truce for xx daies longer after these xv daies expired and have taken uppon them by theire lettres to procure the same in Scotland which if they doe then our purpose shalbee served.

Neverthelesse perceiveinge this delay of a longer truce to be verie comodious for us as is before written and yet feareinge that the Scottes perceiveinge any such desire to be in us for the said prorogation should take more courage then were expedient, our pleasure is that notwithstandinge the meanes made by the ambassadours of France, yee knowinge our purpose, doe the best yee cann by indirect meanes and apart that is to say, yee [   ] as of yourself, do procure the said prorogation without makeinge any demonstracion by sendeinge of your lettres commonly to the comissioners of Scotland for that purpose, but takeinge occasion of some other matter do putt forth a word to Adam Otterborne or some other of the part of Scotland wherby the prorogation might be by a compasse induced within which wee might reenforce our borders as afore. Which prorogacion of truce if yee can compasse then shall there be a convenient time for preparacion of the furniture of men for strength of [fo. 10] our borders as afore. And if yee cannott obtaine such prorogation, ne yet espie any likelihode of conformitie in the Scottes otherwise then yee have done, by reason wherof by all likelihode open warre should retorne. Wee have in either of these causes advertised our right trustie etc therle of Northumberland of our minde concerning the garrison of our borders and willinge him to consult with you in the premisses have sent him lettres to such as should make men for that purpose to be sent further as the case shall require.

13–14 Letter 14 to the king's commissioners negotiating with the Scots at Newcastle may be identified as Henry's response to their request of 6 September for instructions, to which he replied on 12 September (the date being provided by their next southwards letter).[36] It shows how in the days before 12 September Henry took the decision to break the stalemate in negotiations with the Scots at Newcastle by ordering a temporary mobilisation of the North. (The basic point at issue appears to have been the Scots' demand for the return of the pele of Cawmills which as the letter shows, Henry would not accept.) The threat of further war proved to be successful: the Scots conceded an unconditional truce which was signed on 1 October. The troops mobilised never reached Newcastle but were turned back *en route*.[37] There appears to be a error in the dating of 13 as it appears in the manuscript; it surely refers to the mobilisation of September 1533 rather than an otherwise unrecorded call to arms of the previous month.

[36] *LP* vi nos. 1080, 1161.
[37] The manoeuvres are described in greater detail at 28 above.

15 Henry VIII to the first earl of Cumberland, 5 October [1536].
Chatsw., Clifford Letter Book, fo. 8r-v; previously printed in abstract,
LP xi no. 544, from the draft, PRO, SP1/106 fo. 257r-v.

To our right trustie and right welbeloved cousin and counsailour therle
of Cumberland.

Henricus Rex   By the Kinge

Right trustie and right welbeloved cousin wee greete you well. And
forasmuch as it is certainly declared unto us how that against such
time as our commissioners in those partes appointed for the dissolucion
of such pettie monasteries as be within the lymitt of the acte passed in
our high courte of parliament for that purpose entended to repaire to
the house of Hexam in the same to execute our most dradd comaundement and comission, the chanons of the same assemblinge unto
them other lewd and light persons did not onely most traitorously
withstand our said comissioners and disobey or rather utterly contemne
our lawes, comissions and comaundmentes made and sent out in that
behalf, but also to put them selves in forceable array to have enterprized
further attemptates if our said comissioners had not wisely withdrawen
themselves in convenient time and season. The enterprise where of
joined with theire resolute answere, which was that accordingly to
theire continuance they made they would indeed lose theire lives all
before wee should execute the order and determinacion of our lawes
against them, is so hainous, traitorouse and detestable that mindinge
to have the advicers thereof punished to the example of all other our
subjectes, wee will and straitly charge and comaund you that imediatly
upon the sight hereof, assemblinge all the force [fo. 8v] yee can make
of your frendes, servantes and tennantes, yee shall addresse yourself
thither. And there with such other of our faithfull subjectes and servantes
as wee have appointed, to doe the semblable either to take and
apprehend by way of theire submission all and every the chanons and
other persons that with them have attempted this traitorous acte, and
the same comitt to sure and stronge prisons in severall places or els in
case they will not yeild, but make resistance, either to take them by
force or in the doeinge thereof to use them like arrant and detestible
traitors to the terror of all other hereafter. And thereupon to put aswell
in possession our said comissioners or such other as they shall limitt
thereunto as to have such vigilant regard to the preservacion of the
quiet of the countrie as our good subjectes theire be not molested with
the misdemeanours of such evill disposed persons hereafter without
faileinge as wee specially trust you. And as yee will answere for your
slacknes herein att your perills. Yeven under our signett att our castle
of Windesor the vth day of October.

The present letter also survives as an undated and unaddressed minute in the state papers.[38] The events at Hexham referred to by the letter took place on 28 September when the commissioners charged with the dissolution of the smaller monasteries arrived to effect the surrender of Hexham priory. They found that the priory had gathered together a sizeable body of armed men who thronged the streets of the town and that the canons had barricaded themselves in the conventual buildings. Having attempted to parley, the commissioners withdrew without any act of violence having taken place. The priory did have a degree of right on its side for the commissioners were shown a confirmation granted by Henry VIII, presumably a licence for the continuation of the house granted earlier in the year.[39] Henry's response was violent and exhibits the intolerance of monastic disobedience which is pronounced throughout the Pilgrimage.

It was known in London by 4 October that the canons had resisted the commissioners.[40] The earl of Northumberland's servant, Sir Raynold Carnaby, rode north with letters, including this, directed to Cumberland and others. Diverted by the Lincolnshire rising, he reached Topcliffe only on the night of 9–10 October.[41] Cumberland's letter of 12 October doubtless reported the impossibility of executing the king's orders, although it was also reported that he set out for Hexham and was forced to turn back.[42] Hexham survived until it surrendered to the duke of Norfolk on 26 February 1537.[43]

16 Henry VIII to the first earl of Cumberland, 14 October [1536]. Chatsw., Clifford Letter Book, fos. 3v-4r.

To our right trustie and right welbeloved cousin and counsailour, therle of Cumberland, wardeigne of our West Marches anempst Scotlande.

Henricus Rex   By the Kinge

Right trustie and right welbeloved cousin, wee greete you well. And forasmuch as by your lettres of the ixth of this present month written to our right trustie and welbeloved counsailour the lord Crowmwell, wee doe not onely perceave the misdeamenours of Gilleslande, but likewise the confederacies made in Dent, Sedbarr and Wensladale by the meane and reporture of such false and untrue matter as was never by us or any of our counsaile purposed or entended, with your good determinacion for the repression of the same, for the which wee doe right hartely thanke you.

[38] *LP* xi no. 544.
[39] Dodds, *Pilgrimage*, i, 193–5; *LP* xi no. 504.
[40] *LP* xi no. 535.
[41] **85** below.
[42] *LP* xi no. 760 (2). The letter of 12 October is lost; for a brief notice of it, R. W. Hoyle, 'Thomas Masters' Narrative of the Pilgrimage of Grace', *NH* xxi (1985), 66.
[43] *LP* xii (1) no. 546.

Consideringe that in this troubelous time when by thoccasion of the traitorous insurrection in Lincolnshire light heades may take courage to attempt thinges displeasant and unlawfull, it shalbee meet for all honest [fo. 4r] true men to have vigilant regard to the repression of all such enterprises with such speedy diligence that they bee in no wise suffered to growe so much that without difficulty they cannott bee subdued. Wee have thought good most instantly to desire and pray you not onely to put all your strength and force in such aredines that you may keepe our borders under your rule in such quiet that for want of redresse or by notable attemptates our leages bee not on our behalf broken, but also that you may endeavour yourself therewith to the repression of all such traitors as would arise and make any unlawfull assembly or insurrection in those partes. Eftsoones desireinge you now to use all your wisedome, manhood and policy that those partes may be brought to quiet and semblably all others aboute you as wee specially trust you. And wee shall not faile soe to recompence you for the same that you shall have cause to bee contented. Yeven under our signett att our castle of Windsor the xiiijth day of October, the xxviijth yeare of our raigne [1536].

Cumberland's letter of 9 October is not extant. The disturbances in Dent, Sedbergh and Wensleydale referred to in the present letter had been brought to his notice by Darcy on 6 October and, as I shall argue elsewhere, were probably a manifestation of a tradition of resistance to taxation in the Yorkshire Dales.[44] The misdemeanours of Gilsland in Cumberland are otherwise unevidenced but doubtless refer to border incursions which concerned Cumberland in his capacity as warden. With this letter came one from Cromwell, **93** below.

17 Henry VIII to the first earl of Cumberland, 19 October [1536]. Chatsw., Clifford Letter Book, fo. 4r-v; previously printed in abstract, *LP* xi no. 712, from the draft, PRO, E36/118 fos. 156r-158r.

To our right trustie and right welbeloved cousin and counsailour, therle of Cumberland, warden of our West Marches foranempst Scotlande.

Henricus Rex   By the Kinge
Right trustie and right welbeloved cousin wee greete you well. And have this day aboute ix of the clocke in the morninge receaved your lettres of the xijth of this month declaringe as well the receipt of ours of the vth of the same addressed unto you for the direction of the matter of Hexam as you purpose for your repaire to the same

---

[44] *LP* xi nos. 564, 604.

which neverthelesse you have not accomplished accordinge to thatt appointment you tooke in that behalf by reason of certaine rebellions in those partes attempted (as you write) which wee marvaile that you would suffer to growe and encrease unto so great force and would not rather studdy to have repressed the same imediatly upon the beginninge thereof without any our lettres or comaundment: then to tarrie parlamentinge and consultinge how to redresse the same. For force is the cheefe remedy in such soddaine enterprises and easie had it beene to have then in the beginninge redressed that which without some paine and difficulty will not now bee staied.

Notwithstandinge you shall understand that [we] beinge also advertised that there is att this time a great rebellion in the county of Yorke and those partes, whereof wee bee assured yee have long [?bef]or this time heard and trust that accordinge to the greate confidence wee have in you, yee have putt all your forces in a redines to represse the same. Wee have for the sure and certaine repressinge thereof addressed with a maine armie unto those partes our cousins of Norffolke, Excestre, Shrewsbury, Rutland and Huntingdon, desireinge and prayinge you therefore not onely in such wise [to] prepare yourself with all your servantes and frendes in those partes if yee have not so done already as wee doubt not but yee have, that you may redouble slacknes if any hath beene already committed and so bend your powers, and shewe you[r] face against the said rebells in such partes as may bee to theire annoyance [fo. 4v] and utter repression, as the same may in every parte perceive theire distructions, unlesse they withdraw againe speedely as other lately have done in Lincolnshire, much lamentinge that upon false and untrewe reportes and surmises sett out amonge them, they did attempt such insurrection as whereby they have most highly offended God and given us theire prince and soveraigne lord just cause extremely to punishe them to the example of all others in time comeinge.

Willinge you further to animate and encourage our true and faithfull subjectes with all the good perswasions you can devise to continue theire [true?] and loiall fidelities towardes us, and to take our parte accordinge to theire bounden duties, and to learne by thexample of those in Lincolnshire what perill it is upon light and false rumors and reportes to rebell against theire naturall lord and kinge against Godes commaundment, and att length to theire owne utter destruction. Declaringe also unto them that it is to our greate marvaile, that any of our subjectes will so prone and ready and therwith so light to attempt such a rebellion without any manner of grownd or cause against us by whom they have beene so many yeares preserved in peace from the annoyance of all owtward ennimes and with such reasons wee desire you to induce and exhort them to persever our true subjectes. Declaringe also unto them theffect of these bookes in the markette place and the most publique and open audience that you shall thinke meet for that purpose.

And for the more extreme punishment of these rebells in case they shall continue in this theire rebellion, our pleasure is that you shall with your forces make excourses uppon such personns as be notable auctors and doers in the same. And for the better encourageinge of your servantes, tennantes and frendes beinge with you, to devide amonge them the spoile of all theire goodes and cattells, not doubtinge but in all these thinges you will proceede so ho[no]rablely as no good subject be for any displeasure damaged nor the great offendors left unpunished. Yeven under our signett at our castle of Windsor the xixth day of October, the xxviijth yeare of our raigne [1536].

The present letter was previously known from an unaddressed and undated draft in the State Papers which, on other evidence, was thought to be addressed to Cumberland.[45] The draft, which is complete, is essentially the same as the first four-fifths of the letter printed here, but omits the final paragraph of the Chatsworth text (beginning 'and for the more extreme punishment ...') in which Cumberland is instructed to make reprisals on the goods of the rebels.

Cumberland's letter of 12 October does not survive. It was seen by the seventeenth-century historian Thomas Masters who noted that it reported the rising of the commons in Richmondshire and Lancashire and the firing of beacons.[46]

18 Henry VIII to the first earl of Cumberland, 1 November 1536. Chatsw., Clifford Letter Book, fos. 4v-5r.

To our right trustie and right welbeloved cousin and counsailour, therle of Cumberland, warden of our Westmarches foranempst Scotlande.

Henricus Rex   By the Kinge

Right trustie and right welbeloved cosin wee greete you well. Lateinge you wite that by your lettres lately addressed unto us and otherwise perceiveinge your most noble harte and loiall courage to be such, as notwithstandinge the great menaces and threatninges of the rebells and the great danger yee were in by the same, yee determined rather to abide the adventure of death and so to make your end if such extremitye had ensued with honor and truth then to put yourself into the handes of those that were traitors and manifest rebells assembled to no purpose but to have destroied us and subverted the state of our whole realme

---

[45] *Ibid.* no. 712 and errata p. 718.
[46] Hoyle, 'Thomas Masters' Narrative', 66.

wherby yee must needes have offended your alleageance, and whatsoever the fyne should have beene, dishonored yourself and your house in the estimacion of honest true men. Like as wee cannott give unto you for the same that praise and those thankes that you have justly merited and deserved, assuringe you neverthelesse wee shall never forgett your most faithfull proceedinges in that behalf but rem[em]ber the same to the singuler [fo. 5r] rejoyce of you and yours hereafter.

So beinge now advertised that the said rebelles be againe disparked and retired to theire houses and dwellinge places, and desireinge verie much aswell your state and condicion, whether yee bee now againe att your libertie, or whether yee keepe your hold and fortresse still; as in what sorte the said rebells thus retired do use themselves now upon theire retirement, whether they remaine in quietnes repentinge the offence of theire insurrection against us, or whether they continue in any parte of that furie and madnes they were in, like men that could be content uppon like purpose to make like adventure and attempt semblable insurrection, wee have thought convenient to desire and pray you not only of all the premisses with all possible diligence to send us perfecte advertisement, but also in case the said rebells beinge retired as is aforsaid doe lament any thinge theire offences in this matter so as with good wordes which wee pray you use unto them, declared [sic] what danger they were in by theire said attemptate unles wee had beene a prince of great mercie, how much they have offended God in the same, howe shamefully they were deceaved and deluded and what inconveniences doe ensue to themselves there of. Yee may thinke yourself assured of the multitude and perswade them by litle and litle not onely to detecte unto you by whose meanes, cou[n]sell and abettment they were first incensed to bee so earnest in that matter, but also to helpe to the apprension of the said auctors of this sedition and to doe what they can from time to time to convay them to your handes.

Then to travell yourself all that you possibly can to get into your custodie such as were notable traitors in this matter, keepeing them in sure gard and custodie, ever putting all the rest in sure conforte that wee wilbe a good and gratious lord unto them. In the conduceinge of which matters to some frame and purpose, wee desire and pray you to use all your accustomed wisedome and dexterity and in no wise to be to hastie in the begininge but to proceed by litle and litle and first to compasse them with policie, and after when yee shalbe stronger and by good meanes more able to accomplish that which shalbe to your wisedome thought convenient, to doe in every condicion towardes them as our further pleasure to be declared unto you and the state of the matter shall require. Yeven under our signet att our castle of Wyndsore the first day of November, the xxviijth yeare of our raigne [1536].

Letters and Papers contains only one letter from Cumberland to the king dated in October and November 1536, a fact which can all too easily lead to the facile conclusion that Cumberland was inactive. Thomas Masters saw two letters, now lost, dated 12 October and 26 October. In the second Cumberland reported that he was safe in his castle at Skipton and had refused the rebels' call to surrender. He had 'none with him but his own family but would live and die the king's true subject'.[47] It seems likely that this letter was written in reply to Cumberland's of 26 October at a time (after the first meeting at Doncaster) when the immediate crisis had passed with the negotiated dispersal of the two rival armies. The interest of the letter lies in Henry's instruction that Cumberland should gather intelligence on the perpetrators of the rebellion and seek to bring about their capture and imprisonment. This action was clearly contrary to the spirit of the truce and reflects the king's assumption that the rebellion had been defused when in fact the North remained ready to rise again. The 'good words' which Cumberland was to use to the rebels may be preserved as the proclamation of 12 November (**87**).

19 Henry VIII to the first earl of Cumberland, 7 November [1536]. Chatsw., Clifford Letter Book, fo. 13v; previously printed in abstract, *LP* xi no. 1002, from a variant text, PRO, SP1/111 fo. 1.

To our right trusty and right welbeloved cousin the earle of Cumberland.

Henry R[ex]

Right trusty and right welbeloved cousyn wee greet you well, and aswell have receyved your lettres written at your castle of Skipton the last day of October declaring your noble and faithfull hart and valient courage in your determinacion to withstand to the uttermost the rebells, with the great damnages and despites yee have susteyned by the same and the good state and service done unto us also at our citty of Carliell by our right trusty and welbeloved the lord Clifforde your sonn, that faithfull and valyant young man. As soone as your other lettres that came to the handes of our cousin of Norff[olk] and by sundry other wayes, [we] perceyved the great loyalty and truth of all your proceedinges. For annswere whereunto yee shall understand that as by these presentes wee give unto you for the same with hart and minde our most intyre and cordiall thancks, so doubt yee not good cousin but wee shall in deedes (God giving us lyfe) so consider and remember, yea and recompence the loss ye have at this tyme for your truth susteyned; that you and yours shall have good cause to be content and satisfyed with the same. And forasmuch as wee trust that the danger

---

[47] *Ibid.* 66, 70.

of that matter is now passed, wee doe most hartily require you not onely to have vigilant regard to the preservacion of your owne person till all thinges shall be reduced againe into perfeccion, but also from tyme to tyme to advertize us of the state of the partyes about yow, conformeable to the tenour of our last lettres sent to the same end. Yeven under our signett at Windesor the 7th of November in the etc.

This and the following letter mark the high point of Cumberland's reputation. His letter of 31 October reported the role of his son, Henry lord Clifford, in stiffening resistance to the rebels in Carlisle and the common's destruction of Cumberland's parks and houses at Carleton and Barden near Skipton.[48] The version of this letter in the State Papers (which is not a draft but an engrossed although unsigned copy prepared for dispatch) contains a concluding section which warned of the king's intention to grant a pardon to all rebels except specified ringleaders. This has been struck through and does not appear in the Chatsworth text.[49] Otherwise the texts are similar apart from minor stylistic revisions.

20 Henry VIII to the first earl of Cumberland, 4 December 1536. Chatsw., Clifford Letter Book, fo. 5r-v.

To our right trusty and right welbeloved cousin therle of Cumberland, warden of our West Marches for anempst Scotlande.

Henricus Rex   By the Kinge

Right trustie and right welbeloved cousin wee greete you well. And have received your lettres of the xxixth day of the last month addressed unto us from your castle of Skipton declaringe aswell the continuance of your noble and faithfull harte towardes us as the malicious attemptates

---

[48] *LP* xi no. 927.

[49] *LP* xi no. 1002. A similar clause has been removed from a letter of the same date to the earl of Westmorland. *Ibid.* no. 1003. The clause Cumberland never saw reads 'And to thintent you may the bettre knowe what we entend to doo in this matier, you shal understand that having pitie of the multitude which have been deceyvid by false and forged tales, lyes and reaportes, we do entend to tak them to mercy and to give them a general free pardon for life, landes and gooddes, a very small nomber of the notable villaines that have begonne this insurrection only excepted. And therfore you maye be bold to put them out of dispair and of your honor to warrant the multitude that we wil not fail to be gracious and merciful towardes them. Advising them thereupon in no wise at any manes wil or comaundment to mak any further assemblie but rather for our satisfaction to take hede that suche escape not from them as were the busiest and the greatest auctors amonges them of this sedicion and thus to put them in hope. For we be resolved with all convenient spede to sende downe our proclamacion for this purpose. Desiring you to handle this matier with suche dexterite as it may work some good effecte in the steyeng of the commons aboute you'. (PRO, SP1/111 fo. 1). But see also the notes to **87** below.

committed against you by the rebelles with that also that the rumor is false that was spredd of the apprehension of your sonne the lord Clifford, which wee know also otherwise by a servant sent hither unto us from him and Sir William Musgrave to be certainly true. Good cousin, wee would you should assure yourself that this [fo. 5v] your loiall demeanor shall never be wiped out of our stomacke, nor that you shall for the same be rewarded onely with wordes, but hereafter with such deedes as you shall have cause to say you serve a good maister.

And like as by the said advertisement from the lord Clifford, wee perceive you have, like a man of wisedome and policie, made such shift for your furniture against the malices of the rebells that the same shall not be able to prevaile against you, so wee desire and hartely pray you before all thinges to use that vigilancie that you may preserve your person out of theire danger which shall not be a little to our contentation. And beinge in that suerty, wee desire you to practise by all the good meanes you cann possibly devise to steere our good subjectes and to recover our rebells to a due obedience. For the better compassinge whereof wee send unto you herewith a proclamacion under our great seale which as wee require you to cause to be proclamed and notified, soe wee promise you for our honor wee shall performe the contentes there of to all men that will submitt themselves unto you and receive such an oath as is contained in a schedule herein enclosed. Desireinge you to travell in this matter with all the dexteritie to you possible. And for the more certaine and assured conduceinge thereof to our desired purpose, to sett aparte all old grudges and displeasures with all men, which wee doe trust att our contemplation you will right gladly doe. And by these lettres wee give you full power and authoritie to receive the said othe and submissions of all men without exception that of the parties conteined in the proclamition shall desire to make the same in such humble sorte as to subjectes doth appertaine. Yeoven under our signet at our mannor of Richmont the fourth day of December, the xxviij yeare of our raigne [1536].

Cumberland's letter of 29 November is also lost but is probably the letter forwarded to the king by Norfolk on 30 November. A servant sent by lord Clifford and Sir William Musgrave was at Lincoln on the same day.[50] The letter casts a light on the multiplicity of policies pursued by the king in early December. Dr Bernard has already shown the way in which the instructions sent to Norfolk and Shrewsbury on 2 December differed in important respects. Both offered the rebels a pardon excluding named ringleaders. If this was refused, then a week's truce was to be offered after which Norfolk was authorised to announce a general pardon, but during this time Shrewsbury was instructed

---

[50] *LP* xi nos. 1207-8.

to try and detach Darcy, Aske and others from the Pilgrims by offering them individual pardons.[51] The present letter outlines a policy of offering a free pardon to anyone who would swear to an oath administered locally. The text of the proclamation and oath remains unpublished.[52] The reference towards the end of the letter to putting aside all old grudges may reflect the king's awareness of Clifford's inability to cooperate with the Dacres, remarked upon by Suffolk on 30 November. The letter probably reached Cumberland with Suffolk's of 11 December (57).[53]

21 Henry VIII to the first earl of Cumberland, 21 December 1536. Chatsw., Clifford Letter Book, fo. 6v.

To our right trustie and right welbeloved cousin and counsellour, therle of Cumberland, warden of our West Marches foranempst Scotland.

Henricus Rex   By the Kinge

Right trustie and right welbeloved cousin wee greet you well. And have recei[ved] your lettres of the xiiijth of this month with the copies therein enclosed, and perceiveinge by the same aswell the lewde and seditious demeanour of Richard Dacer within our towne of Carlisle as the assemble made in Craven uppon the settinge upp of the bills uppon the church doores and that both the same matters be neverthelesse by the wisdome of you, the lord Clifford your sonne and others beinge within, appeased. Like as wee give unto you our most hartie thankes for the same, so for aswell wee have thought convenient to signifie that wee have taken order for the conveiance of the said Dacer hither and for the certificate of the truth of the whole matter to be made unto us. And as concerninge the devisoures of the said bills and procurers of the insurrection made thereupon, wee desire and pray you to endeavor your self to apprehend them and so to keepe them in sure prison till you shall knowe further of our pleasure. And further wee require you not onely to have a vigilant eye to the confirmacion of our peace there and the speedy takeinge of all malefactours and seditious personns that shall from time to time transgresse our lawes in those partes; but also semblably t'advertise us of the state of that country, the conformity of the people and of all other occurrances there, with your opinion touchinge the same. Yeven under our signet att Westminster the xxjth day of December, the xxviijth yeare of our raigne [1536].

Cumberland's letter of 14 December reported the posting of 'bills' on church

[51] G. W. Bernard, *The Power of the early Tudor Nobility* (1985), 44–5.
[52] PRO, PRO30/26/116 fos. 8r-9v, 21r-v; cf *LP* xi no. 1235.
[53] *LP* xi no. 1207.

doors in Craven calling for the destruction of deer. With this letter Cumberland forwarded his son's letter of 9 December which detailed an assault made on Sir William Musgrave in the churchyard in Carlisle.[54] Richard Dacre (whose relationship to lord Dacre is unclear), in the company of a group of Dacre tenants, met Clifford at the door of Carlisle 'church' and insulted him by refusing to raise his cap. Moving through the churchyard Dacre then met Musgrave whom he attacked with a dagger. He was restrained but proceeded to call out the town and Clifford and Musgrave were forced to take refuge in the castle. An ugly scene ensued and before Dacre would evacuate the town the mayor had to rally the townsmen and declare for Clifford by joining him in the castle. On 17 December Dacre again returned to Carlisle looking for trouble.

This outbreak of factional friction followed on a period in which lord Dacre and Clifford had agreed to assist each other should either be threatened by the rebels. But after Dacre went to London in early November, Richard Dacre appears to have turned the movement to factional advantage by calling a muster on 15 November at which he was named 'Grand Captain of all Cumberland'.[55] The animus shown against Musgrave (who had been responsible for the trial of lord Dacre in 1534) is particularly marked.

The result of bringing Richard Dacre's behaviour to Henry's attention was to introduce him to the consequences of his policy of using Cumberland as an alternative to lord Dacre in the government of the West Marches. Rather than learn that lesson, his response was to enforce the reconciliation of the parties in January and the magisterial rebuke he offered Cumberland forms the next letter.

22 Henry VIII to the first earl of Cumberland, 24 January 1537. Chatsw., Clifford Letter Book, fos. 5v-6r.

To our right trustie and right welbeloved cousin and counsailour, therle of Comberland, warden of our West Marches for anempst Scotland.

Henricus Rex   By the Kinge

Right trustie and right welbeloved cosin wee greete you well. And even so do right hartely thanke you for your truth and faithfullnes shewed unto us in the time of the late comotion in those partes. And forasmuch as syethens thappeasing of the same, devising upon the establishment of our subjectes in quiet and how to reduce them to perfect unitie and due obedience, wee perceive and consider that where the head is not whole and perfect to it selfe, but devided into divers contrarie partes and fantazies, the members must needes grow out of due order and so

---

[54] *LP* xi no. 1299. Lord Clifford's letter was misdated by the editors of *Letters and Papers* and may be found at *LP* v no. 573. For Musgrave see **110** below and for these events in general, Dodds, *Pilgrimage*, i, 224–5, 299; ii, 42–3.

[55] *Ibid.* i, 224–5, 299.

put the whole bodie in jeoperdie of destruction unles the head may be againe recovered to that agreement in the self that it may both in all thinges doe his office and direct his members in that order and obedience that every of them may, for his parte, do that office he was made and ordeined for, resemblinge the politique body of a common wealth to the naturall body of a man. And consideringe that as wee be the supreme head of this realme under God, so wee have yet in sundry partes of the same our nobles, officers and ministers which represent our personne and so be heades and governoures of the multitude, every in his quarter and countrie.

And that in those partes of our realme where you doe enhabite and have rule, dominion and auctoritie under us, there hath beene such devision, hatred and emnity betweene you and others being of our [fo. 6r] nobilitie and of worshipp as the lord Dacres, the Parres and the Musgraves that wee cannot otherwise thinke thence that if you would have conformed yourselves to an honest unity and agreement, beinge there in the liew of heades for the direction of that parte of our said politique bodie, the same could not have growen to that trouble and discord it is now in. Wee have thought it our parte and dutie as a personne in that preheminent place that of our office ought looke specally to the quiet of our subjectes and rather to cutt away the corrupt members that will not be healed with wholsom medecine then to suffer them to ranker further and so to offende others that without theire infection would be preserved in health and quiett, aswell to induce and move you to such an honest concord, perfect love, certaine amitie as all old grudges and displeasures dependinge betweene you may be cleane withdrawne out of your stomacke and utterly cast away forever and in stead of the same planted a most entire and assured frendshipp, as to comaund every of either parte to declare the same in such wise to your frendes, servantes, tennantes and all others that be towardes you, that they may perceive your reconsiliacion to be perfect, unfeined and of that plaine sort that may from them amove all rancour and malice and engender in the same a like frendshipp to that which wee have and shall thus establish betweene you.

Whereupon you shall understand that wee have here called before us and our counsell aswell the lord Clifford your sonne and Sir William Musgrave for thone partie and the said lord Dacres, Sir William Aparre knight and William Apparre esquire on thother parte and in the presence of our said counsell have caused every of them to desire [of the] others goodwill and frendshipp, to promise from henceforth to putt all old matters in oblivyon, to nurrish this new agreement betweene them and to cause all theire frendes, tennantes and servantes on either parte to do the semblable to thutter most of theire powers.

Neverthelesse, forasmuch as in this matter of contention betweene you and the said lord Dacres and others, wee do consider you to be a principall partie on thone side and therfore accompte the agreement made betweene your sonne and them as a thinge of small moment unles you shall both approve his doeing therin by our comaundment and for your owne parte also in such wise, conforme yourself to the same that our desire therein may be fully satisfied and accomplished. Albeit we doubt not but besides your dutie, the entire love you beare unto us would enforce you without difficultie to condescende frankely and with good hart therunto, knoweinge how much wee mind the same. Yet for the more certaine conducinge therefore to our purposed effect, wee have thought meete to desire and pray you and neverthelesse straghtly to charge and commaund you, at this our speciall request and contemplacion, to forgett all old displeasures betweene you and the said lord Dacres, Parres and other theire frendes and to use such meanes for the continuance of a sincere amitie and perfect frendshipp betweene you as wee may perceive that for our sake you can be content wholy to frame your minde to our pleasure and so to cause all your frendes, tennantes and servantes to doe the semblable as the said lord Dacres and others before named for theire parte have already promised the inviolable observacion of the same towardes you and yours. Desircinge you further not onely to put this our desire in such experience that our subjectes there by your familiarities and good agreementes may see and perceive an entier desire of perfect love and concord on either parte, but also in writinge to signify your answere hereunto with diligence. Yeven under our signet at our mannor of Gree[n]wiche the xxiiijth of Jannuary, the xxviij yeare of our raigne [1537].

The king's investigation of Richard Dacre's assault on Musgrave exposed the factional conflicts in Cumberland but also came to embrace the intermittant struggle between Cumberland and the Parrs in the barony of Kendal (described in the head note to **9** above).[56]

This letter was probably sent with Sir Anthony Browne (for whose credence see the following letter) who was instructed to command Sir Thomas Clifford to subscribe to the king's injunction for amnity. Cumberland sent the king notice of his acceptance of the reconciliation on 8 February in the same letter which placed his wardenry at the king's disposal.[57]

The analogy of the body and the state is a commonplace in Tudor political thought but can rarely have been worked out so fully or expressed so lucidly as on this occasion.

[56] The two William Parrs must be distinguished. Sir William Parr of Horton, Northants, cr. lord Parr in 1543, d. 1547 was the younger son of Sir William Parr of Kendal. He served as chamberlain in Richmond's household. *HP 1509–1558*, iii, 60–2. William Parr esq. was his nephew, cr. earl of Essex 1543, Marquess of Northampton 1547 and 1553, d. 1571. For a letter from this man, **112** below.

[57] *LP* xii (1) no. 372.

23 Henry VIII to the first earl of Cumberland, 26 January [1537]. Chatsw., Clifford Letter Book, fo. 11v.

To our right trustie and right welbeloved cousin and counsailour, therle of Cumberland, warden of our West Marches fore anempst Scotland.

Henricus Rex   By the Kinge

Right trustie and right welbeloved cousin wee greet you well. And forasmuch as wee have at this time sent into those partes our trustie and right welbeloved servant and counsailour Sir Anthony Browne knight, one of the Gentlemen of our Privie Chamber, whome wee have appointed in certaine thinges to conferre with you, our pleasure is you shall give unto him firme and undoubted credence in all thinges which he shall declare unto you on our behalf and semblably ensue the purporte and effecte of the same as wee specially trust you. Yeven under our signet at our mannor of Greenwich [the] xxvjth day of Jannuary.

Browne was sent north to implement the new design for the government of the Middle and East Marches and was with the earl in early March.[58] He was a relative of the first earl twice over; he was the father-in-law of Sir Thomas Clifford and Cumberland's daughter Mabel married Browne's half-brother, William Fitzwilliam, earl of Southampton.[59]

24 Henry VIII to the first earl of Cumberland, [?January 1541]. Chatsw., Clifford Letter Book, fo. 11r.

To our right trustie and right welbeloved cousin and counsailor, therle of Cumberland.

Henricus Rex   By the Kinge

Right trustie and right welbeloved cousin wee greete you well. And where as wee doe send at this present our right trustie and right entirely welbeloved cousin and counsailour the duke of Norffolke as our lieuetennant into those partes to give order aswell for certaine thinges and fortificacions to be done there for the stay, direction and suerty of those borders. Haveinge a sp[ec]iall confidence in your wisedome and earnest mind to serve us, wee have thought good to desire and pray you not onely to give firme credence unto all such thinges as he shall declare unto you on our behalf, but also to ensue and follow his advise

---

[58] *LP* xii (1) nos. 225, 552–3, 614 and **58–9** below.
[59] For Browne's career see *HP 1509–1558*, i, 518–21.

and order in all such matters as he shall determine and communicate with you accordingly without faileing therof as wee specially trust you.

The lack of a dating clause in the transcript of this letter makes it impossible to decide whether it belongs to the period of Norfolk's tour of inspection in March and April 1539[60] or that of February and March 1541.[61]

25 Henry VIII to the first earl of Cumberland, 12 June 1541.
Chatsw., Clifford Letter Book, fo. 7r-v.

To our right trustie and right welbeloved cousin and counsellor, the erle of Cumberland.

Henricus Rex   By the Kinge

Right trustie and right welbeloved cousin wee greete you well. And whereas wee have purposed, God willinge, to make our progresse this yeare unto our citty of Yorke, and doe perceive and certainly knowe that at our beinge there yee wilbe verie desirous accordinge to your bounden duty to repaire thither to visite and see us like as wee would for our parte be as glad as yourself that your desire therein might be satisfied, so forasmuch as wee doe consider that your absence from our frontiers, which wee mind to have at our beinge in those partes well furnished, were not convenient for sundry good respectes, which wee doubt not but your wisdome doth waigh and ponder, wee have thought meete to will and require you not onely for your owne personne to forbeare your accesse unto us for this time, and rather to take occasion for the same at such other [fo. 7v] season as for yourself shalbe as comodious and to us more agreeable, but also to cause such others as you elected [as you elected *repeated*] at the late beinge there of our right trustie and right entirely beloved cosin and counsellor the duke of Norffolke to doe the semblable. And albeit wee thinke it meete that you should make thus your demore there as is aforesaid in your owne personne, yet wee shalbe contented that the lord Clifford your sonne shall in your liew and stead repaire unto us to attend upon us dureinge our aboade in those partes accordingly. Yeven under our signett at our mannor of Greenwich the xijth of June, the xxxiijth yeare of our raigne [1541].

Henry's decision to visit York, made in April 1541, arose from his plan to meet with his nephew, James V of Scotland. In the event Henry reached York on

---

[60] *LP* xiv (1) nos. 625, 674, 731 and 764; also xii (1) no. 804.
[61] *LP* xvi nos. 496–7, 533, 650. The letter of credence assigned to this tour (*ibid.* no. 497) seems unlikely to refer to this year.

18 September having travelled by way of Lincoln and left on 29 September after James had failed to appear.[62] The letter can be read as a calculated snub to Cumberland. On the other hand, Marillac, the French ambassador who accompanied Henry on his progress, reported that the North was being kept in a state of considerable military preparedness, with no noble or gentleman coming to the court unless summoned or following the court outside his own stewardship.[63] In this light, the letter should probably be read at face value (and compare **6** above).

26 Henry VIII to the second earl of Cumberland, 28 July 1542. Chatsw., Clifford Letter Book, fo. 7v.

To our right trustie and right welbeloved cousin, therle of Cumberland.

Henricus Rex By the Kinge

Right trustie and right welbeloved cousin wee greete you well. Willinge and comaunding you imediatly upon the sight hereof you levie or cause to be levied within the lordshipp of Knasbrough the number of fiftie able personns furnished with horse and harneis for the warre. And the same so levied and putt in order to comitt to the leadeinge of our welbeloved servant Thomas Slingsby whom wee have appointed to be captaine of them. And to see them convaied with all diligence to our borders foranempst Scotland, there to be emploied for the defence and suerty of the same, as shalbe devised and appointed by our right trusty and right welbeloved cousin and counsellour therle of Rutland and in his absence by our trusty and right welbeloved counsellour Sir Robert Bowes knight whom wee have specially dispatched thither for this purpose, without failinge as wee trust you. And these our lettres shalbee your sufficient warrant and discharge in that behalf. Yeoven under our signett att our castle of Windsor the xxviijth day of July the xxxiiijth yeare of our raigne [1542].

27 Henry VIII to the second earl of Cumberland, 25 August 1542. Chatsw., Clifford Letter Book, fo. 7v-8r.

To our right trustie and right welbeloved cousin, therle of Cumberlande.

Henricus Rex By the Kinge

Right trustie and right welbeloved cousin, wee greet you well. Lettinge you wite that sendinge at this present our right trusty and right entirely

---

[62] Scarisbrick, *Henry VIII*, 427–8.
[63] *LP* xvi no. 1130.

beloved cousin and counsalour the duke of Norff[olk] to our borders for anempst Scotland for the suertie and defence of the same, wee have appointed you to give your personall attendance there upon him, willinge and comaundinge you that imediatly upon [fo. 8r] the sight hereof to put yourself with all such able men you can make and furnish for the warre of your servantes, tenantes and others within your romes and offices in such order and a readines as you may sett forth with the same within one hower after yee shalbe comaunded so to doe by our said cousin and counsalour whome wee have made our liuetenant. And therfore you must in all thinges obey him and his comaundmentes even as yee would doe and [sic] if wee were present in person.

And to instructe you how you shall furnish the said number of men which you shalbee able to make and bringe with you. First you shall make as many horsmen as you be able to furnish with such horses as may serve in the feild if need so require, every horsman to have his speere or his javelin and the rest of your number you shall order in manner and forme followinge. The fourth parte thereof our pleasure is shalbee good archers, every one furnished with a good bowe and a good sheffe of arrowes. The residue to be bill-men causinge every man to bringe a good bill on his necke with him. Desireinge and neverthelesse comaundinge you to take paine diligently to serve us herein at this present as wee trust you. And these our lettres shalbee your sufficient warrant and discharge in that behalf. Yeven under our signett att our honnour of Hampton Courte the xxvth of August, the xxxiiijth yeare of our raignc [1542].

26–7 The first earl died on 22 April 1542: this and the following letters are addressed to his son the second earl (d. 1570). Both date from the period of the deterioration in Anglo-Scottish relations in the summer of 1542 which culminated in the débâcle at Solway Moss in November.[64] The first earl was granted the stewardship of Knaresborough (an honour of the duchy of Lancaster) in 1533 to hold in reversion from the death of Thomas lord Darcy. The grant was renewed for the second earl in May 1542. The earls held the stewardship for the remainder of the century, but effective local power remained with the deputy steward, Thomas Slingsby of Scriven.[65] The second letter prompted the earl to write to the city of York reminding them of his claim to have (after the fashion of his ancestors) the captaincy of the city and calling

---

[64] Scarisbrick, *Henry VIII*, 434–5. A version of **27**, with many variants, but of equal date and addressed to Sir John Willoughby, has appeared in print; Historical Manuscripts Commission, *Report on the manuscripts of lord Middleton, preserved at Wollaton Hall, Nottinghamshire* (1911), 510–1.
[65] Somerville, *Duchy of Lancaster*, i, 525.

on the mayor and council to inform him of the number of men with which they could supply him.[66]

28 Henry VIII to the ?second earl of Cumberland and others, subsidy commissioners in the West Riding, 12 August [possibly 1543]. Chatsw., Clifford Letter Book, fo. 11r.

To our right trusty and right welbeloved cousin therle of Cumberland, and to our trustie ande welbeloved Sir Robert Nevell, Sir William Copley, Sir Christopher Danby, Sir Henrie Savell, knightes, Thomas Faierfax, serjeant att lawe and Robert Chalonier esquiers, our comissioners in Westrithinge within our countie of Yorke.

Henricus Rex   By the Kinge

Right trustie and right welbeloved cousin and trustie and welbeloved, wee greet you well. And whereas wee have at this time addressed out our commission for the taxacion and levieing of the first paiment of the subsedie granted unto us at our last Parliament, yee shall understand that for the speciall trust and confidence which wee have in your wisedomes, discretions and fidelities towardes us, wee have named you with others to be our comissioners for that county where yee be inhabited. Wherefore like as wee doubt not but yee will use and emploie all your said wisedomes and dexterities to see the said acte, (sundry coppies where of be also sent thither with the said commission) put in such due and full execution as wee may be loveingly and truly answered accordinge to the purporte of the same. So wee desire and pray you to use such circumspection in the devision of yourselfs and the rest of the commissioners joyned with you into sundry partes for more expedicion as there may be in every parte and quarter at the least one of such discretion, authoritie and creditt as may be able in the due execution of the said acte to do unto us such acceptable service as the case and tender love and zeale which wee beare to our subjectes requireth which they shall the more sacilly [sic] accomplish. In case yee shall discreetly before hand waigh and consider with them the groundes and causes which moved our said good and loveinge subjectes to offer this grant unto us and how thankfull and acceptable it shalbe in respect of theire good willes and towardnes to have them thankfully performe the same. Praieinge you nevertheless not to participate the contentes of theis our lettres to any other personne because wee have onely written to you herein and not generally to the rest of your colleagues in comission with you. Yeven under our signet att our honnour of Hampton Court the xjth day of August.

The dating of the letter is problematical. Of those named, Danby was knighted in 1534: Thomas Fairfax was created serjeant at law in 1521 and died in November 1544. The letter must therefore fall within the decade after 1534. It refers to the first collection of a subsidy (making it of 1534, 1540 or 1543). Of these the most likely is 1543 when the assessment was to be made between 1 September and 16 October. This date however must remain tentative. The dating clause offers no help: the king's itinerary reveals that he was not at Hampton Court on any of the appropriate days although this is hardly conclusive evidence.[67]

Letters to subsidy commissioners offering them instructions for the implementation of the statute must have circulated extremely widely, but are now encountered infrequently and no other examples of a letter of this sort are known to survive. The normal practice was for the subsidy commission to divide itself into subcommissions of two or three members, each responsible for the assessment of a single hundred or wapentake. The existence of a quorum of senior members within the commission charged with the division of the larger body and the rehearsal of justifications for the subsidy was previously unsuspected.

Letters of Sir Thomas Clifford

In recent years there has been some interest amongst historians about the ways and means by which the younger sons of the nobility and gentry made their way in life. The survival of a small group of letters from Sir Thomas Clifford, the younger brother of the first earl of Cumberland, allows us to obtain a glimpse of the relationship between the two men, illustrating, in passing, the means of Sir Thomas's advancement.

Clifford's date of birth is unknown, but the first earl was born in 1493 and so Sir Thomas must have been barely thirty when the first letter was written and in his late forties when he died in 1543. From the summer of 1529 to the autumn of 1538 (when he resigned through ill health) he was captain (technically vice-captain) of Berwick on Tweed. He is known to have married at least once and possibly twice. As will appear, his first wife may have been a daughter of Sir Robert Bellingham of Burneside near Kendal, but at the time of his death he was married to Lucy, daughter of Sir Anthony Browne and widow of

[67] PRO, OBS 1418.

Sir John Cutte of Horham Hall, Essex. His only surviving child was a daughter, Elizabeth, aged 15 at his death.

The letters make it clear that there was a close working relationship between the brothers. Sir Thomas is found acting as his brother's London agent in letters of 1526–8 (**29–31**), trying to arrange loans on the earl's behalf (**39**), supplying him with armour and munitions (**36**), acting in the West Marches during Cumberland's wardenship (**37**) and mediating between Cumberland and petitioners (**34** and **40**). He also served as steward in Craven in the 1520s. But if Clifford was the earl's man, he also had an eye for his own advancement (**30** and **31**). In this he possessed the considerable advantage of a king who was 'good and gracious' to him. Henry went to some lengths to obtain the captaincy of Berwick for him, intervened in the affairs of Sir Roger Bellingham on Clifford's behalf and in 1526–7 granted him stewardships in Lancashire, albeit in reversion.[68]

Sir Roger Bellingham (d. 1533) possessed manors in Westmorland (including the manor of Burneside) and Northumberland (the manor of Bellingham). He was, by the late 1520s, extremely old. In 1531 he was said to be eighty or more, but less modestly called ninety some years before. (For a letter of Sir Roger's, see **80** below.) His son and heir, Sir Robert, had as issue four daughters. Both generations of the family had close Clifford connections, Sir Roger serving as under-sheriff of Westmorland in 1506 or before and Master Forester in Craven, possibly in the 1520s. Sir Robert was a servant in the party that travelled to London for Cumberland's ennoblement in 1525.[69] At some point during the 1520s Sir Robert complained to Chancery that his father, contrary to promises made at the time of Sir Robert's marriage, was trying to disinherit him in favour of Sir Thomas Clifford and a single daughter who Clifford was to marry. By 1531 this dispute had come to the King's notice. In a blatantly partisan move, he gave Clifford permission to obtain recoveries out of Chancery against Sir Robert but ordered that both Clifford and Bellingham should abide the terms of his arbitration over the premises. The king's award, if it was made, appears not to survive, but in Hilary term 1532 Clifford had a fine from Bellingham of his Westmorland lands.[70] Clifford's *inquisition post mortem* shows that he died seized of the manor of Burneside and the indications are that the king's award gave Clifford the Westmorland lands of the Bellingham family and left the Northumberland lands with Sir Robert and his daughters.[71]

[68] Somerville, *Duchy of Lancaster*, i, 501, 508.
[69] PRO, IND 7041 m. 89; Hoyle, 'Land and Landed Relations', 245, 249.
[70] C1/466 no. 32; C54/400 between nos. 39 & 40; W. Farrer, (ed. J. F. Curwen), *Records relating to the Barony of Kendale*, i (Cumberland and Westmorland AAS, record ser., iv, 1923), 269.
[71] Clay, 'The Clifford Family', 373–4 prints the IPM.

It is far from certain that Clifford actually married a daughter of Sir Robert Bellingham. The standard pedigrees show all four daughters marrying local gentry and the marriage was unknown to Lady Anne Clifford in the seventeenth century.[72] Clifford was married by $c.1528$ as his daughter was aged 15 at his death, but Sir John Cutte died only on 1 July 1528.[73] Against this must be weighed Clifford's message to his 'bedfellow' in **30** which may be of 1527. It is possible that Cumberland married a daughter of Sir Robert Bellingham first and Lucy Cutte later and that his claim on the Bellingham estate was that of a widowed son-in-law. It does appear that with royal sanction (and in the face of opposition from Sir Robert), Sir Roger partly disinherited his family by selling Burneside to Clifford in about 1531–2.

In much the same way it must have been apparent to the Dacres in their competition with him over the captaincy of Carlisle (described at **31** below) that he, and not they, held the king's ear. Again advancement came from a king willing to act decisively of behalf of a favoured servant.

29 Sir Thomas Clifford to the first earl of Cumberland, St Luke's day [18 October 1526].
BL, Althorp B1, fo. 1r–v.

Pleaseth it your lordshippe to be advertysed that I accordyng to your commandement have delyvered your letter to my lordes grace wheryn as yet I am not called to shewe his grace further of my credens. Also I have delyvered your letter to Maister Wyatt and have made apparans uppon the prevey seall and hath day yeven yn the next weke to make further answere theryn uppon the kynges pleasure knowen. Also I have delyvered all your oder lettres consernyng your busynesses here sens I come and have entred yn co[muni]cacion for the expedicion of the same. And so shortly as they or eny of them be brought to eny sertente your lordshippe shall have further knolege.

Also my lorde, newes have we here that the Pope shuld be dryven to a holde by the duke Fernando and the Imperours company and there kept yn captyvyte. And as it is seid, Seynt Petre chyrch of Rome spoyled and robbed by soldyours and oder adjonantes. And that the Bisshop of Bathe and Mr Wynter which were goyng towarde the seid

---

[72] Nicolson and Burn, i, 126–7; Joseph Foster, *Pedigrees recorded at the Heralds' visitations of the counties of Cumberland and Westmorland, 1615, 1666* (?1891), 4; Dickens, *Clifford Letters*, 130–1.

[73] G. H. Rogers-Harrison in *Trans. Essex Arch. Soc.* iv (1869), pedigree opp. p. 42.

Pope with grete ryches be taken with the seid Imperours company and armye and there reteyned unto the tyme the kynges plesor be knowen theryn. Also the Grande Turke hath beseged the kyng of Hungry and hath slane hym and have distroyed his contrey and kepeth it yn trybute. And after the seid newes with oder come to London, the Kyng was sent fore and come yn all hast possyble out of the contrey frome Amptyll and contynued at Westmynster with his counsell by v or vj days but wherof they have concludyd it is not yet knowen. Also my lady Clyfforde is sore syk of the ague and dropsey and is not lyke to lyve long as this berer will shewe your good lordshippe with oder thynges more at large. And thus our lorde Jh[es]u have your good lordshippe yn his blyssed kepyng, at London on Seynt Lukys day.

Thomas Clyfford.

Also my lorde I have spoken for the allowance of your fee of the wardenrye wheryn the clerkes of the resceyte sey they must nedys have and see your patent which I wold ye sent up with some sure carier as shortly this terme as ye can convenyently. And then the same clerkes sey ye shall have it allowed without ferther sute to the kynges highnes or to my lorde cardynall which patent I have left at Carleton with my lady Belyngeham.

Clerk's hand. Signed. Addressed [fo. iv] 'To the right honourable and my syngler good lorde the erle of Cumberlonde'.

Sir Thomas Clifford's letter can be dated by the topical foreign news offered in the final paragraph. The king of Hungary, Louis II, was killed at Mohacs on 29 August 1526 and the outbreak of disorder in Rome occurred on 19 September.[74]

Of those mentioned, the Lady Clifford whose death was confidently predicted was probably the widow of the tenth lord Clifford, stepmother of the first earl. She, however, survived this present illness by something like thirty years (the date of her death is unknown); for her life see the commentary to 101 below. Lady Bellingham, resident at Carleton Park, was the wife of Sir Roger Bellingham of Burneside in Westmorland, mentioned previously. It is clear that Clifford was being used as his brother's London agent, carrying letters to Wolsey ('his Grace'), Sir Henry Wyatt (Treasurer of the Chamber) and appearing on privy seals. He had, he reported, delivered other letters and spoken with the Exchequer concerning the payment of Cumberland's wardenry fee. It is tempting to connect this letter with an undated memorandum addressed

[74] For a letter to Cumberland written two days previously which relays much the same news, see Dickens, *Clifford Letters* no. 31.

to Sir Thomas by the first earl which lists a range of matters to be raised with the king and Wolsey.[75] Most of these concern the grant of offices in the West Marches held by the Dacres which Cumberland wished to have to bolster his position as warden. The issue of the earl's fee occurs in both the present letter and the memorandum, but on balance it seems that the memorandum is best dated to the autumn of 1525.

30 Sir Thomas Clifford to the first earl of Cumberland, 15 September [?1527].
BL, Althorp B1, fos 2r-3v.

Jh[es]u

My lord, my duhty remembrd. Plesyd your lordshipe to be advertysid that I have rec' your letter the contentes wher off I have at lenth performed[?]. And accordingly I sente my servand Robert Horsley to the courte to my lord privy sielle to knaw the kynges grace plessour and hys concernyng Wylliam Clyfford and shuyd to hym also your said letter to me direkyd for the saym who died repute your letter and demener in that by halffe substancyall and touk the letter and said he wauld shuyd [it] unto the kynges maygesty. And to the mater he said that he knaw not but the said Wylliam Clyfford was honeste and true and that he myght have and occupye all thynges that ever he had.

And also my lord this day my lord pruwy siell schud me in lyke maner as beffore he shud to my said servaund wherfor ye may wythowt daunger lete hym goo wher he lest <as I thynk> and wher further I presom that ye er not inquiet by meyne of Mr Norton, in that my advice is ye caus sume lernd consell luke substancyally upon your evidens, not doutdinge but ye shall have all that ryght requirs wyth fawfor and the meyne tym my delygens shalbe as the tym wyll serve to the best of my pouer. And over this my lord, I requier your lordshipe to be good to my bydfelow and that shee myay remayne to my comyng unto yow or elles to wryte me more certente for I have beene in comynication wyth the kynges magesty off certen thynges, and as yet we be not threw so that I canne adyvertysse your good lordship the planes, not dow[t]inge wyth the grace of God to be despatchd wyth my resonable dysire and the kynges fawffore and thus owre lord have your good lordshipe in hys blessid keppinge, from London this Sondeday xv day of S[e]ptember.

[fo. 2v] An [my] lord this day I dyned wyth the maire of London wher one merchand of London shud me that he was collector for the kyng wher certen mony is un paid wych is due to be payd by yow and shuld have been payd ij yers past the one payment and thother payment a yer pastd wherfor my lord seeinge as all thynges is, me thynk it good ye se the payment maid wyth delygens.

Thomas Clyfford.

Letter in a very rough clerk's hand. Signed. Addressed [fo. 3v] 'To my lord my brother delyver this'.

Clifford offers few clues which might allow us to date the letter. The reference to the Lord Privy Seal could easily be read as a reference to Cromwell and so after 1536, but the allusion to the trouble that Mr Norton was causing the earl (over Norton's attempt, finally successful, to construct a park at Rilston near Skipton) suggests a date before 1530.[76] Likewise Clifford's hopes for advancement seem to indicate a date before his appointment to Berwick. A date in the late 1520s is therefore plausible and so 1527, the year in which 15 September fell on a Sunday. If this is the case, the payments with which Cumberland was in arrears might perhaps be those for the subsidy granted in 1523. It is far from clear why the earl should have been concerned with the affairs of one William Clifford. The only man of that name to be readily found is William Clifford of Borscombe, Wiltshire, of a cadet branch of the family (but still included in the Clifford entail for want of nearer relatives) who died in 1535.[77] Clifford's servant Horsley may tentatively be associated with the man of that name who was appointed Keeper of the Gates at Warkworth by Northumberland in January 1532, was associated with Clifford at Berwick in 1538 and served as MP for Northumberland in April 1554.[78]

31 Sir Thomas Clifford to the first earl of Cumberland, 18 March [1528].
BL, Althorp B1, fo. 4r-v.

Pleassyth your gud lordship to be advertyssith. And that I have reyceyved your lettre and the coppy of my lord Dacar indentur wherof I am ryght glade notwithstandyng if it hade be doyn afoir the kynges grace it hade beyn the better. And ferther it haith pleassith the kyng to be so gud and gracius unto me that I trust my lord Dacre nor no other shall oppteyn the contrary bot that I may have and in joy the castle of Kyrlylle for terme of my lyff with all ussues, fees and proheyttes therunto ussed and accustomed. Allso Master Tresorer thynkkith that if it myght stond with your plesur it were neccessary and reqesytt for your lordship to se the kynges grace this next terme for ye were never

[76] Hoyle, 'First earl', 73–4.
[77] H. Clifford, *The House of Clifford* (1988), 130.
[78] *HP 1509–1558*, ii, 395.

more hyghely in hys gracios favor then ye be at thys day and no fawytt, <bot> onely your long absence.

And newyelles we have noyn bott this Mounday xvjth day of March at nyght my lord Tressorer and my lord Chamerlayn cam to the kyng and ther was cumanded contenently to returne home in to thair contreys to stay the comonys aswell in Northfolke as in othe placeys for insurrecconys only anenst my lord Cardinall grace and all greitt men of the courtt ar cumanded to returne home and keip thair countres in gud order except my lord marquies of Exetre wich doith remayn styll in the courtt as knawyth Jh[es]u who preserve your noble lordship. Wryttyn at Wyndsour the xviijth day of Marche.

Thomas Clyfford.

Clerk's hand. Signed. Addressed [fo. 4v] 'To the Ryght honorable and my very gud lord therle of Cumberland'.

The letter again reveals Clifford acting on Cumberland's behalf at court, but unlike the previous letter, Clifford shows himself to be equally concerned with his own advancement.

The general political news fixes the letter in March 1528, a period marked by a fear of insurrection arising from the trade depression which followed the decline in diplomatic relations between England and the Low Countries. Hall describes a meeting of Wolsey and the merchantile community on 11 March: on the evidence of this letter a decision was taken the following Monday to send nobles into the counties to keep order. Hall regarded the problem as affecting Essex, Kent, Wiltshire and Suffolk in particular, but this letter suggests that the alarm was more general.[79]

Clifford's machinations over the constableship of Carlisle are obscure and eventually abortive. The titular keeper of the city and castle after 1525 was the duke of Richmond who held the office in his capacity as warden. Nonetheless the captaincy was closely associated with the wardenship (or vice-wardenship during Richmond's lifetime) of the West Marches. Sir Thomas had served as Cumberland's deputy in Carlisle in the period of his (vice-)wardenship in succession to Dacre's appointee, John Leigh. The earl of Cumberland did not surrender control of Carlisle when Dacre was reappointed in late 1527 and this proved to be a source of antagonism between them. The castle garrison refused to aid Dacre in raiding the Debateable Lands in August 1528 and in October of that year Thomas Magnus urged Wolsey to unite the captaincy and the

[79] Hall, *Chronicle*, 745–6. For other accounts of the depression, D. MacCulloch, *Suffolk and the Tudors* (1986), 298 and P. Gwyn, *The King's Cardinal. The rise and fall of Thomas Wolsey* (1990), 459–462. For the work of a nobleman sent to defuse tensions, S. J. Gunn, *Charles Brandon, duke of Suffolk, c.1484–1545* (1988), 80–1.

wardenship in one man's hands.[80] Dacre did not receive Carlisle until the summer of 1529. The reason, as this letter makes clear, was that Sir Thomas was in competition for the office. In the end he failed and his ambitions were satisfied by his appointment to the captaincy of Berwick. This post had been held by Sir Anthony Ughtred since 1515 except for a period during Westmorland's vice-wardenry in 1525–6. He was still in office in May 1528.[81] Ughtred resigned or was removed during the Summer of 1529 to make room for Clifford who paid him 1,000 marks for the 'goodwill' of the office. We may suspect that Henry lay behind the translation. Clifford's appointment to Berwick allowed Dacre's installation at Carlisle.[82] This resolved the struggle for Carlisle, but at the cost of creating the anomaly of a Clifford in the East Marches.

32 Sir Thomas Clifford to the first earl of Cumberland, 27 September [1531].
BL, Althorp B1, fo. 5r-v.

My verray goode lord in moost hartie wies I commende me unto your goode lordeshipe. And wher as I doe perceyve that the mattir in traverce bitwixte Guy Maychell and Richard Maychell is put to thorderinge of your lordeships award to be yevyn furth unto theym in writinge on this syd the feast of Saint Martyn next cummynge, for thobservinge wherof, as I ame likewies informed, the said parties ar enterchangeably bounde by obligacion, I most affectually doe desier your lordeshipe that in the procedinges of the saide award your lordeshipe will, as good right and mattir may and shall appear, tender and consider the manyfold injures susteigned by the said Guy through the commocion and actes of the said Richard, with your lieffull and reasonable favours the rather at the contemplacion of this my letter and desier.

And forsomuch as your lordeshipe all redy haith for the furst part of your award in the premisses ordered that the said Richard should deliver and restore unto the said Guy such cattell as he dyd taike by mean of distres, and the same not fulfilled by the said Richard not withstandinge your lordeshipes letter directed unto hym for the same, it may pleas your lordeship fer the mayntenance of the same furst part of your award that the said Richard may be commaunded eftsons to maike restitucion of the said gooddes and that in the hoolle sequell hirof the right of the said Guy may be stauned for the mayntenance

[80] *LP* iv (1) nos. 705, 1431 (6), 2052; (2) nos. 4828, 2374 (misdated in *LP* but printed in full in R. B. Armstrong, *The History of Liddesdale, Eskdale ... and the Debateable Land*, i (1883), App. xxii).

[81] *LP* ii (1) no. 549; iv (1) no. 1779; (2) nos. 2435, 2729, 4313 (22).

[82] *LP* iv (3) nos. 5748 (22), 5906 (6); 5952. For the purchase, *Calendar of State Papers Domestic, Addenda, 1547–65* (1870), 468.

of his right accordinglie. And thus our lord preserve your good lordeshipe. From Barnardecastell this xxvijth day of September.

Your lordeships at commaundment, Thomas Clyfford.

Clerk's hand. Signed. (Letters **32–4** are probably by the same clerk.) Addressed [fo. 5v] 'To the right honourable and my verray good lord my lord of Cumberland'.

Clifford's letter allows an opening into a longer but obscure dispute between Guy Machell of Crackenthorpe in Westmorland and his cousin Richard Machell of Hesket in Cumberland. The issue appears to have been Guy Machell's levying of a recovery which quashed the entail on his estates, so denying Richard Machell his hope of eventual inheritance. The case was the subject of litigation before the duke of Richmond's council and in Chancery in the 1520s and again in 1532. The letter refers to Richard Machell's seizure of five oxen, a bullock and three cows from Brampton on 19 July 1531, which he drove into Furness, an act which formed the subject of an indictment at Quarter Sessions in August. It would appear that even after the earl wrote to him, Richard Machell continued to withhold the cattle. The latter reveals that Cumberland attempted to arbitrate but if an award was made it has not been discovered. Guy Machell died in or shortly after 1536. In his will he made the earl, Sir Thomas and Henry lord Clifford his supervisors.[83]

33 Sir Thomas Clifford to the first earl of Cumberland, 10 September [1532].
BL, Althorp B1, fo. 6r-v.

My verray good lord, pleasith it the same wher as I doo perceyve ye ar putting in redines one hundreth men to be set forward to me according to the kinges pleasor propoportyd unto your lordeshipe for that purpos by his lettres which as I am enformyd by my servaund John Tempest is by youe limityd to be at the leadinge of my nephew Thomas your sone who shall have in cumpany with him John Skelton. My lord, I doubt not with your favors bot your wisdom woill consaive my said nephew your son is of over tendre yers to have rewll and guyding of such a company and that John Skelton is of such age that he may not take ne susteyn the payn rightly therunto pertenynge. And in as much as the kinges lettre laitly unto [me] addressid, the copie

---

[83] Nicolson and Burn, i, 345–351 for the family and 347 for the dispute; PRO C1/541 no. 96; 656 nos. 16–19, KB9/519 m.14. No arbitration survives amongst the family manuscripts copied by the Rev. Thomas Machell in the seventeenth century, Cumbria RO, Carlisle, Mss of the Dean and Chapter of Carlisle, Machell Mss vol 5. Machell's will is in Nicolson and Burn, i, 348–9.

wherof I sent unto your lordeshipe, manifestid that his hieghnes had appoyntid me to have the leading of one hundreth men and for the same had writtin unto your lordeshipe, wold it pleas youe upon your goodnes so to appoynt and try the same clen men weill horsyd and frech archers as if neide be thei may doo such service as may sounde to your honour and my worshepe and in likewies to caus and suffer my coussing Cristofor Aske to come with the same, which is a man brokin with the world and meat for such buysynes and may by his counceill doo me singler good pleasours or els to send unto me the persones in full noumbre and I shall se theym so orderid as I doubt not bot their service shalbe accepteable, as our lord knawith who ever preserve your good lordeshipe in helth. From Barwik this xth day of Septembre at nyt.

Thomas Clyfford.

Clerk's hand as before. Signed. Addressed [fo. 6v] 'To the right honourable and my verray gud lord my lord of Cumbreland with speed'.

The present letter is a further member of the group describing the mobilisation for war in 1532. By privy seal of 24 August, Northumberland was instructed to raise troops which were to muster at Newcastle on 18 September (7). Wharton wrote from his house at Wharton on 17 September announcing the muster and dispatch of troops from the Clifford estates in Westmorland (73). This appears to be the party of men to which Clifford refers in this letter. Thomas Clifford, the correspondent's nephew, was the first earl's acknowledged bastard who died in 1569. John Skelton was of Armathwaite Castle in Cumberland, sheriff of Cumberland in 1511, d. 1544. He served as Cumberland's steward in Cumberland in 1534.[84] The respective ages of these two makes sense of Clifford's comments about one being too old and the other too young. Clifford's servant John Tempest is possibly the second son of Sir Richard Tempest of Bracewell and Bolling in Bradford, a family associated with the family. Christopher Aske is the brother of the rebel of 1536 and served as the first earl's receiver and steward in Craven.

34 Sir Thomas Clifford to the first earl of Cumberland, 27 October [1532].
BL, Althorp B1, fo. 7r-v.

My verray goode lorde, pleasith it the same for news occurraunt in theis partes sence my lait lettres hir is noon, saving that at this instant

---

[84] Chatsw., BA 8, fo. 11r.

tym ther is with my lord of Northumbrelande a pursevaunte of Scotelande who haith brought lettres from the king of Scottes unto the sam, by the tenour wherof as may be perceyvyd the saide kinge is verray loth and in hiegh fear of warr to succeide, offering and demaunding meatinges to be had verray largely and humblie for the avoding ther of.

My lord, hir haith been with me this berer George Burton with divers his frindes makin instance, that wher your lordship haith the sam George in suyt for sleyng of dere, I should solicyt your lordeshipe in his favors, wherfor wold it pleas the sam at this myn request to seas of the suyt and to tak his humble submyssion with his good hert and service in reacompence of his offence. Considering he beinge so sorowfull and pensif for his trespas and woll offer hym self to abyd such punycion therfor as your lordeshipe woll imput unto hym. I hertly requier your lordeshipe to us and take the maitir in paciens accordinglie rather for the sakes of such his frindes and uther gentilmen as haith movyd me thus to doo as I trust your lordeshipe ye rather wull. And the Holie Trenitie preserve your lordeshipe. From Warkeworth this xxvijth day of Octobre.

Yours, Thomas Clyfford.

Clerk's hand. Signed. The top and lower centre of the page is decayed. The last line of the text partly damaged, and a small piece of paper reading 'Octo' is stuck to the margin and is certainly a part of the dating clause. Addressed [fo. 7v] 'To the right honourable and my verray goode lorde my lord of Cumbreland'.

Although tangential to its main purpose, the news offered at the beginning of the letter probably locates it in October 1532 as the Anglo-Scottish war began in earnest. It can be shown that Northumberland was at Warkworth at that time. Against this dating, it has to be admitted that there is no other explicit notice in the sources of a pursuivant being sent with conciliatory letters from James V although he later complained of the rejection of his overtures made in mid or late October 1532.[85] George Burton can be identified as one of the family who were tenants of the grange at Threapland in Craven (par. Burnsall) which belonged to Marton Priory but lay within the earl's Forest of Skipton.

[85] LP v no. 1558.

35 Sir Thomas Clifford to the first earl of Cumberland, 24 November [1532]
BL, Althorp B1, fo 8r-v.

My verray goode lorde, pleasith it the sam to be advertised of affairs lait occurraunte in theis partes. On Sonday the ix day of this month instante wher as viij^{xx} of the garyson soldiers of this town at nyt issued entendinge to have takin upe a town in Scoteland and by chaunce light upon the lard of Langton, Scotesman, who was accompanyd with cccc men scottes at a place callid Bille Myre and set upon the sam and took therof c prisoners and wan iij^{xx} horses. And on Wednisday last the xx day of this saide month instant, the lard of Sesford, the lard of Farnyhirst his sone and heir, the lard of Buckleugh and Mark Ker with iiij standerdes with theym com and invaydid Englend and cast of ij forrayes, the one of the watter of Brumishe and took upe furth of Ingram, Branton, Reslay and Fawdon many nelt, sheipe and gait[?], and the other of the Watter of Ayll[?] and tuk upe Ryle and Prendewike.

And for your hauke which ye sent for to my lord of Angwysch, he is not providyt therof at this tyme, trustes within one weike of Saint Andrewwes to be stored and to serve your lordeshipe of one than yf your fawconer com over agane. And I trust my self in the meane tym to provid your lordshipe of one other, as knawith the Holie Trenetie who ever preserve your l[ordship]. From Barwek this xxiiijth day of Novembur.

Thomas Clyfford.

Clerk's hand. Signed. Addressed [fo. 8v] 'To the right honourable and my verray good lord my lord of Cumberland'.

Clifford describes clashes between the English and Scots which occurred in November 1532.[86] The earl of Angwysch is the earl of Angus; the promised hawk seems to recur in the next letter.

36 Sir Thomas Clifford to first earl of Cumberland, 3 February [?1533].
BL, Althorp B1, fo. 9r-v.

My verray goode lorde, pleasith it the same, I have resayvede your lordeships lettre daited at youre castell of Skipton the xviijth day of the month of January last. And wher by the same your lordeshipe desierith

---

[86]For other accounts of the same events see a letter of 20 November from Northumberland to Henry VIII, *LP* v no. 1559, and letter **74** below.

me to provide youe of oone yeron jake of the best mayking, thinkinge that oone being maide meat for me woll serve your lordeshipe and to have it maid with joyntes and lithes at such places as may maike it most easye, I shall not fayll, Gode wollinge, to have such one in a redynes for your lordeshipe against your cumyng hithers (if ye so doo). And in caace your lordeshipe shall set forwarde to the west partes, upon knawledge had from your lordeshipe, I shall send it unto youe with all deligencence [*sic*].

And as to provide your lordeshipe of goonepowder, ther is noon in the New Castell, and for that at is heir is of the kinges store which is resayvede by indenture, so that no deliverance therof is maide nor put to no manner of use oneles upon the kinges warraunt. Never theles yf your lordeships repayre shalbe hither I shall maik such shifte as ye may and shall be fornishid therof. And upon knawlege of your pleasour, yf ye thinke goode, I shall writ to London for your fornitor ther of to be sent unto your lordeshipe with all deligence.

And sembleablie accordinge to your pleasor, upon knawlege had by me of my lorde of Northumberlandes writing unto your lordeship and oder nowbill men for your resorting hither with your powers, I shall writ unto my cousinge Lowther wherby he may be in more redines to meat your lordeshipe.

Advertising your lordeshipe I have as yhit kepid your servand and fawconer for bicaus the hawk which I had provyd[y]t for your lordeshipe was not so good at the proyf as she was rakenyd to be, and therfor I have sent heir agane, trustinge to have a better sent which if I have not, I shall doo displeasors therfor the trible value at large. Certefyyng your lordeshipe, my lorde of Angwish sendis youe one by your said servand such one as I undertaike shall right well content your lordshipe, for he had rather have doon youe eny oder pleasor that he could than have parted with heir. And the Holie Trenitie preserve your lordeshipe. From the kinges castell of Barwike this thrid day of February.

Thomas Clyfford.

Clerk's hand. Signed at the bottom of the page. Addressed [fo. 9v] 'To the right honourable and my verray good lord my lord of Cumberland.'

There are few obvious ways of dating this letter. Certainly it must belong to Clifford's period as captain of Berwick from where it is dated and so to 1530–8. The reference to the earl of Northumberland must make it between 1530–6 but as he is said to have put out a call for reinforcements, the period of the Anglo-Scottish war, specifically 1533, seems most plausible. The reference to the hawk promised to Cumberland by Angus may refer back to **35**, and so add further weight to the suggestion of February 1533. A jack is a short sleeveless jacket of leather with either mail or iron plates.

37 Sir Thomas Clifford and Sir John Lowther to the first earl of Cumberland, 18 May [1535].
BL, Althorp B1, fos. 10r-11v.

Pleasith it your lordeshipe to be advertysed that yesterday beinge the xvijth day of May at Arthureth church beinge accompanyt with Jake Musgrave, we dyd meate with Hector Armestronge, Reuyen Armestronge, Habby Armestronge and Antony Armestronge which mayd great suytte for the savegard of Cristofor Armestronge brother to the said Antony whiche remaynith in prison heyr. And so thei have offerd yf your lordeshipe wilbe good lord and save his lyff, that the said Cristofor and Antony with other to theym perteynyng shall draw such draught as thei shall bring the outlawes which dyd clyme Carlill walles to the noumbre of v or vj in such place wher that Maister Capetayn and other your servanttes shall have theym cummynge to their handes within Ynglond ground wher nayn can escaype bot with speid of horsefeet. And in trust that your lordeshipe wilbe content we have graunted Antony forberance upon twoo dayes warnyng. And he, ne noon of his, to doo no harme within Inglond ground in the mean season.

Newes heir my lord is noon bot that the kinge of Scottes hais beyn upon the borders aswell west as myddill marches and hais doon hiegh justice and gyffen many men remission and in especially all the owtlawes of Scoteland dwellinge in the debayteabill ground. And also he hais tayking away with hym the lard of Bucklewgh whiche as the Armestronges shewis ws is attaynted for being with the lord Dacres at the roode of Cavers. And that the said kyng of Scottes hais takyn into his handes all the manerheid and stewartships of all the abbays and bushoppes men within the realme of Scoteland wherby he rakyns hym self much stranger then he was befor.

And also when we rood to the takyn of Cristofor Armestrong we went to John Denton, the mayrs deputie, and desyered of hym to have some company of the town, owther horsemen or footemen lyyk as custom hais ben befor tym, who gave annswer that he wold commaund no man to go, how be it he wold cause his sergiauntes to go through the town and that every man that wold go should have leyf; al beit noon went. Also my lord this town was sore grevyt for lokking of the yaittes at what tym we callyt one hoost down to have sought the owtlawes, which hoost come to soon of the day to the town. And for feer that word should go into the law contrey befor the hoost, we lokked the yayttes [fo. 10v] as custume befor tym have ben. And thus the Holly Trenytye preserve your good lordeshipe. From the castell of Carlill the xviijth day of May.

Your humbill servanttes, Thomas Clyfford, John Lowther.

The body of the text, the commendation and both signatures in a clerk's hand. Addressed [fo. 11v] 'To the Ryght honourabyll my lord of Cumbreland his good lordeshipe'.

Sir Walter Scott, laird of Buccleugh, was attainted at a justice ayre held at Jedburgh in April 1535 for treasonable communications with Dacre and this provides the date for the letter. Anthony Armstrong was sought by Cumberland in the last weeks of 1534 for the march treasons of selling horses into Scotland and leading Scots into England. He avoided arrest with the aid of Dacre's officers and this formed the subject of a complaint to Henry VIII.[87] This letter adds a further stage to the story. Armstrong's brother Christopher fell into Clifford's hands and here we see members of the Armstrong kin negotiating for his release in return for their aid in capturing the outlaws who broke into Carlisle.

38 Sir Thomas Clifford to the first earl of Cumberland, 29 December [?1536].
BL, Althorp B1, fo. 12r-v.

My verray goode lorde, pleasith it the sam. I have resayvede a lettre from Mr Treseror unto your lordeshipe directyd with one oder lettre unto my self wherby he willit me to breke upe[n] your lordiships lettre and to se the contentes therof and to writ unto youe to be towardly myndit for your partin accordinge therunto which by myn oppynnyon shall not onelie be to the hiegh contentacion and plesor of the kinges grace, bot also a great strength, weall and comforth to youe, both your frindes and allyes. And thus after my right hertie recomendacions unto my lady your bedefolloy, I woll commit youe unto the tuicion of the Holie Trinite. From Barweke this xxixth day of Decembre.

Thomas Clyfford.

Clerk's hand, signed. Damaged by damp on left hand side but entirely legible. Addressed [fo. 12v] 'To the right honourable and my verray good lord my lord off Cumberland'.

This letter also offers few clues for dating. It is little more than speculation to suggest that the letter referred to was from Sir William Fitzwilliam, Treasurer of the Household and written in December 1536 when Cumberland's reputation

[87] *LP* vii no. 1558; viii no. 310.

was at its highest. It is known that letters were being sent to Cumberland by way of Berwick during the Pilgrimage (cf **57** below) which might explain the use of this most unusual route. But such a letter is not known to be extant.

39 Sir Thomas Clifford to the first earl of Cumberland, 17 May [1530 x 1538].
BL, Althorp B1, fo. 13r-14v.

My verry good lorde pleasith it the same, I have receyvyd your lettre by your servaunt Richard Graym. And wherr therby ye do requier that I should make shift for your lordship of a certayn some of money, of verrey truyth and of confidence which your lordship may and shall gif unto me, at this tym it is not in me possible to do. Nevertheles I send unto your lordship herinclosed a warrant unto William Bean your lordshipes auditur and William Baylyff of London, fishmonger, upon which they or the one of them shall delyver unto your lordship one hundreth markes. And for full reacompence of suche money as I am indetted unto your lordship the same hundreth markes with xxxli payed upon your lordshipes byll unto William Bayllif and xjli in contentacion of my lord of Carlisle for certan hanginges with certan money payed for my lord your sone allowed, I shall at Mighelmes next cumyng pay unto your lordship the remayndor, not doubting that your lordship woll conceyve or conjector eny thing herin bot to accept this for my reasonable excuse without color, and to tendre not onely my greate charges yerly hertofore susteyned by reason of payment for myn office, bot also that nowe is the tym for me to maike provision for my houshold store, wherby it shall verrey deuly appear unto your lordship accordingly.

And where as further in your lordshipes lettre ye doo move me that in caace I my self can not serve your lordshipes request in the premisses, that I should for your fornytor therof attempt Sir George Lawson therfor as for [fo. 13v] me, of verrey truyth I have doon so albeit as he doith say and alledge that what for provision of corn by the kinges comaundment and in money layd furth for fournyshing of payment of the garryson not yhit comyn to his handes, he haith beside his awn store borrowed a greate some, so that I can in no wies borrowe eny money of hym towardes your lordshipes purpos, for which I am right sory if I could amend it. Trusting your lordship woll rakeyng that I have used my full delygence for the accomplisshing of your request and desyer in the premisses, which to perform, I shall at all tyms do myn utter indevor to my full power, as knowith the Hoolly Trenyte who ever preserve your good lordship. From Alnwik this xvijth day of May.

Your lordeships at comandment, Thomas Clyfford.

Clerk's hand, signed. Addressed [fo. 14v] 'To the right honourable and my verray goode lorde, my lorde of Cumberland'.

This letter is almost completely bereft of clues as to its date. Within broad terms it belongs to Clifford's period as Captain of Berwick, 1529–38, the reference to Clifford's purchase of the captaincy suggesting a date towards the beginning of the period. The reference to the shortage of money to pay the garrison might point to May 1533. Sir George Lawson, merchant of York, served as Treasurer of Berwick from 1517 until his death in 1543.[88]

40 Sir Thomas Clifford to the first earl of Cumberland, 10 June [1530 × 1538].
BL, Althorp B1, fos. 15r-16v.

My verrey goode lord. Aftir my most humble recomendation, wher as I doe undirstonde that ther is certaine proces cum down against my cousinge Sir John Lowther and that in thexecution therof your lordeships commaundement is verrey ernest towart hyme, I beinge of good rememburaunce that at my laite beinge above, my said coussinge and your servantte Thomas Joylye was in communycation and was put in trust by your said servantte, that he wold discharge hyme above for <that> a certain somme <of> then named which my said cousinge dyd promes hyme I beinge afor. <Wherfor> I will besech your goode lordeshipe, consideringe the premysses and also how that upon his goode will he dyd give me monytion of my dangers by reason wherof I have procured his great payn and chargies for his repayr unto the kinges counceill wher likewyse he dyd use hym self right substanncially and frindelye, that he doinge that thinge that sufficiauntely may discharge yor lordeshipe. Ye will so frindelie use hym [...] (the rather at the contemplation of this my lettre) in this bihalve as that he shall thinke his goode will towart me weill bistowed, not doubtinge bot his demerittes towart your lordeshipe shall disserve the same as knawith the Hollie Goost who have your good lordeschipe in eternall tuycion. From the kinges castell of Barwick this <i>xth day of June.

Your lordships at commaundement, Thomas Clyfford.

[88] For his career as a royal officeholder, see *YAJ* xlii (1967–70), 486 and the biography by Palliser in *HP 1509–1558*, ii, 500–2.

Clerk's hand, signed. Addressed [fo. 16v] 'To the right honorabill and my verray good lord my lord of Cumberlande'.

This letter can only be dated within the broad limits of Clifford's captaincy of Berwick. For Sir John Lowther, see the commentary to **104-6** below. Thomas Jolly acted as clerk of courts to the first earl from before 1537 and probably died in office in 1552, serving in 1545 and 1547 as member of parliament for the Cliffords' borough of Appleby. Dickens was mislead into thinking him a vicar of Skipton.[89] The nature of the favour which Lowther had done Clifford is obscure. The letter illustrates the possibilities for misfeasance open to Cumberland as hereditary sheriff of Westmorland and the pressures which might be put on him.

Letters of Henry lord Clifford

41 Henry lord Clifford to the first earl of Cumberland, 14 April [1537]. BL, Althorp B1, fo. 61r-v.

My dewtie remembred. Pleassith your honorable lordsheipe to be advertiseth with humble desyres of your dayly blessyng and that the kynges letter ys delyvered accordyng to your cummandment wherin I corth make no reportt by causse I hade no copy nor credence from your lordshepe of the same and ferther I have maid peticion to hys grace for sum parcelles of the landes of Fournes wherin hys said grace haith answarded me that he wyll have a gareson keiped ther, in so much[?] that I can have no spede therin as yeitt. And also certefeyng you that my lord the duke of Southfolke ys not in the courtt, notwithstandyng I have delyvered your lettres to hys secreyttory wich haith appyved thaym and oppon the syght therof said he wald solucite for the complessement of thaym the best he myght. And thus Jh[es]u have your honorable lordsheipe in his blessed keipeyng. Wrytyng at London the xiiij day of Apprill.

By yowr most lufuyng sun, Henry Clefford.

Clerk's hand as in 42 below. Signed. Addressed [fo. 61v] 'To my ryght honorable and synguler gud lord and father the erlle of Cumbrland ys dilyver'.

Henry lord Clifford – the future second earl – was born in 1517. His adventures during the Pilgrimage of Grace reveal him to have been a resourceful young

---

[89] Hoyle, 'Land and Landed Relations', 251-2; Dickens, *Clifford Letters*, 101; compare *HP 1509-1558*, ii, 450-1.

man, well capable of taking initiatives independently of his father. The young Clifford's request to have a grant of a part of the lands of Furness locates this letter. The surrender of Furness was signed on 9 April 1537 although the monks were still in place some weeks later. The garrison mentioned by Clifford was instituted in the winter of 1537.[90] The earl's letter which Clifford had delivered is probably that of 9 April.[91]

42 Henry lord Clifford to the first earl of Cumberland, 12 January [?late 1530s, no later than 1540].
BL, Althorp B1, fo. 68r-69v.

Pleassith your honorable lordsheipe to be advertisith with harty desyres of your dayly blessyng. And wher ther is a maitter in travers betwyxt one Reme of Clyfton and on Wyber wich haith beyn befor your lordsheipe hertofor and now of lat the said Wyber haith entered hym selfe, hys wyff and hys chylderyn in to the house of the said pour man, oppon whois complayntt I dyd calle the parties befor me and advertisith thaym to abyde my order wich the said Wyber dyd refusse, wheroppon I have cumanded Thomas Sanfurth beyng your lordsheipe stewartt to putt thaym owytt agayn to the matter be forther tryed by the lawe or otherwysse. And also ther was inqere maid at the last sessions at Applebe of a certayn ryott to be comytted and doyn at Overton wich ther wald not be founde and for the ferther examynation therof, I my selfe, the abbott of Shaipe with other gentilmen dyd make ferther inqer as mor playnly doith apper by certayn bylles concernyng the same wich I have sende unto you and of your plesur herin wh[at] ever that ye wyll certefye the counsell or cumand me other wysse concernyng the premysses. I besuch your lordsheipe that I may knawe wich I shall ever be glade to accompleshe with the grace of Jh[es]u who have your honorable lordsheipe in hys blessed keipyng. Wryttyn at Brougham Castle the xijth day of Januarij.

Also my lord they of Perith haith sett a courtt and haith putt dowyn the office of the Skeldrake sheipe for ever by cause ye shall not have your purpos wich me thynk is nott for your honor to be doyn nowe mor in your days then it haith beyn in other menys tyme to for you.

By yowr most lovfuyng sun, Henry Clefford.

Clerk's hand. Signed. Addressed [fo. 69v] 'To my ryght honorable lord and father therlle of Cumberland this dely[vere]d'.

---

[90] For all of this, C. Haigh, *The Last Days of the Lancashire Monasteries and the Pilgrimage of Grace* (Chetham Soc., 3rd ser., xvii, 1969), 104-7.
[91] *LP* xii (1) nos. 882-3.

As **41** shows, by 1537 lord Clifford was acting independently of his father. It seems likely that the present letter dates from around the same time; the reference to the abbot of Shap must place it before the surrender of the abbey in January 1540. The dispute to which Clifford refers is otherwise unknown. 'One Wyber' might be Thomas Wybergh of Clifton, a gentry cornage tenant of the Cliffords' and a distant relative, but this seems an offhand way of referring to a figure of some substance. Thomas Sandford, the earl's steward, was of Askham, Westmorland and is doubtless the man of that name who died in 1564. The Sandford family were cornage tenants of the Cliffords and it appears that Sandford's wardship was sold to Sir Christopher Dacre, Sandford being named as a Dacre household servant in 1525.[92] Cumberland was crown lessee and steward of Penrith, an office associated with the wardenship of the western marches. A survey of 1619 describes the *Skelldrakershipp* as a market toll of a handful of corn or salt from every sack offered for sale.[93]

Letters of the fifth and sixth earls of Northumberland

The following group of letters, written (with one exception) by the fifth earl of Northumberland (d. 1527) and his son, the sixth earl (d. 1537) to the first earl of Cumberland or his wife, when taken with the smaller group of letters between the same parties published by Dickens, sheds a considerable light on the relations between the two families.[94] If there is one predominant tone in the letters, it is friendship coupled with co-operation and a sense of shared concerns and interests. This may surprise those who have been brought up to see the northern nobility as being engaged in a competition for regional pre-eminence.

Henry Clifford, first earl of Cumberland, was married as a youth to Margaret, the daughter of the fourth earl of Shrewsbury. She died young and *sine prole*. Clifford then took for his second wife Margaret, daughter of the fifth earl of Northumberland. Their eldest child, Henry, the future second earl of Cumberland, was born in or before January 1516.[95] Margaret Clifford died in 1540, but a close and cordial relationship between the two families continued after her death.

Little can be discovered about the relationship between the tenth lord Clifford and the fifth earl of Northumberland. It is known that Clifford acted as steward for the Percy estates in Craven which lay

[92] For Wyber, Nicolson and Burn, i, 418; Dickens, *Clifford Letters*, 116. For Sandford *LP* iv (1) no. 1310; for the family, Nicolson and Burn, i, 425–6 and F. W. Ragg in *CW²* xxi (1921), 194–5, also 207–9, 211.

[93] PRO, E164/47 fo. 92r.

[94] Dickens published a letter of 1526–7 from the fifth earl of Northumberland and letters of 1526, 1528, and two of 1533 from the sixth earl, all to Cumberland. *Clifford Letters* nos. 30–34.

[95] *LP* iv (2) no. 3380 (p. 1530).

immediately to the north of the Clifford's own Honour of Skipton.[96] This responsibility was inherited by the first earl of Cumberland, as **43** and **45** make clear. In November 1524 Northumberland also made his son-in-law his 'head commissioner' in Cumberland with the duties of surveying Northumberland's lands, making leases, assessing enclosures and spoils of woods and settling disputes between Northumberland's junior estate officials.[97] The letters printed subsequently, with an additional one published by Dickens, suggest that Clifford and his father-in-law had a close, cordial and co-operative relationship. Against this must be weighed the report of the future sixth earl of Northumberland, who in a letter of late 1526, told how his father had warned Wolsey not to trust his son-in-law because he was 'all with my lord of Norfolk'.[98] The exact meaning of this comment, or the circumstances in which it was made, are obscure.

Of the quality of the relationship between the first earl of Cumberland and his brother-in-law, the sixth earl, there can be little doubt despite an argument offered some years ago by Dr M. E. James. Northumberland, it will be recalled, having dispersed large parts of his patrimony by sale (or, as it is sometimes alleged, gifts) and imprudent leases finally assigned the remainder to Henry VIII and so disinherited his brothers who died the victims of the royal retribution which followed the Pilgrimage. (The earldom was then in abeyance until 1557.) Cumberland was amongst the beneficiaries of Northumberland's distribution of his estates. In 1532 Northumberland granted the reversion of the Percy fee in Craven to his nephew Henry Clifford (later second earl), if Northumberland died without issue. James interpreted this as a *douceur* extorted from the earl for Cumberland's support when Northumberland was in difficulties over his supposed betrothal to Anne Boleyn. Moreover James argued that this act of brigandage poisoned relationships between the two earls, and that Northumberland deliberately set out to undermine Cumberland's position within Craven. I have suggested elsewhere that this argument is not sustained by the available evidence.[99] It must not be forgotten that the grant of the Percy Fee was contingent on the sixth earl's death without issue, but that he also reserved to his heirs the rents of the manors and jurisdictions, making the transfer much less advantageous to Cumberland than James and others have assumed. As the present letters were called

[96] R. W. Hoyle (ed.), *Early Tudor Craven, subsidies and assessments c. 1510–1547* (YASRS cxlv, 1987), 7, 10, 13 etc.

[97] Chatsw., Curry 46/5, signet of 3 November 16 Henry VIII, seen in a very decayed condition.

[98] Dickens, *Clifford Letters*, no. 31.

[99] James, 'First Earl'; Hoyle, 'First Earl'. I have considered the life of the sixth earl of Northumberland further in 'The fall of the House of Percy'.

in evidence in my earlier discussion, it may simply be remarked that the two letters of 1532 and 1533 (**49–50** below) describe a close friendship between the two men. In the first Northumberland invites the earl and countess of Cumberland to spend Christmas with him at Warkworth. In the second Northumberland describes the way in which he wanted Cumberland to subsume identities with him by travelling to the Queen's coronation together and having their servants share a common livery. Wharton's letters from the winter of 1532–3 also testify to the pleasure that Northumberland took in his brother-in-law's company and by implication the concern that Cumberland felt for Northumberland's poor health (**74–5**). Northumberland's simple notes to his sister (**51–2**) reveal a close, almost pathetic, connection.

Unfortunately none of this material bears on the temper of relations in the last few years of Northumberland's life (although it is known that Cumberland visited Topcliffe in September 1535), nor does it assist in elucidating the nature of the earl's declining health or his decision to disinherit his brothers. Nonetheless the relationship between Clifford and Percy did not end with the earl's death and the temporary suppression of the earldom. When the fifth earl's widow (to whom **48** is directed) died in late 1542, she made her grandson, the second earl, the supervisor of her will. The suspicion must be that it was the first or second earl who arranged the marriage of the natural daughter of Sir Ingram Percy with one of the Clifford's retainers, Henry Tempest of Broughton near Skipton, the settlement for which was signed in 1543.[100] And Henry Percy, the future eighth earl of Northumberland, was a member of the Clifford household in the years around 1550[101]

Letters of the fifth earl of Northumberland

43 Fifth earl of Northumberland to the eleventh lord Clifford, 30 September [1523].
Chatsw., Clifford Letter Book, fo. 18r.

To mine owne good lord and soninlawe the lord Clifford.

Myne owne good lord and sonn, in my hartiest manner I thanke your good lordshipp for my good cheire and costes I put you to att my last beinge with you which if it lie in me I shall deserve. My lord I send your bedfellow and your little one and mine hartie Godes blessinge and mine. My lord I have sent the ringe here inclosed which my

---

[100] *Collectanea Topographica et Genealogica*, vi (1840), 374–8.

[101] PRO, STAC3/6/46 in which Percy is named as one of a number of Clifford servants in a hunting party which clashed with the servants of Thomas lord Wharton in September 1549. He received a new years gift in 1551; Chatsw., BA 223 fo. 27r.

servant forgatte to inclose in my last lettre wherein I beseech your good lordshipp to take no displeasure with your servant the bearer of my last lettre for the negligence of my servant.

My lord I have no newes to send you, but there comes fast privey seales to all them which made no lone to the kinge last for them to make payment forthwith and to all them which have not paid the lone that they were sessed att. My lord I perceave that yonge Sir Raufe Elliecar goe over sea for hee is puttinge his men here in a readines and there shall come out an armie into France, who shalbee captaine as yet I knowe not. My servant William Worme is not come home yet, but as soone as hee comes yee shall have such newes as I have.

My lord your clock-smith is comen to me this Mich[aelm]is even which shalbe with you againe as soone as I can possible rid him. My lord I send you by this bearer my booke of all my fines made in Craven at every time and by whome, what is received and what remaines unpaid and what they be that have not fined and are unsessed and my lord, I cann be contented to take cattell as sheepe or neat for that which is behind if they will lett me have it by reasonable prices. And I pray you that I may be advertised herein by this bearer which I sennd unto your good lordshipp att this time. Written att my castell of Wresill the last day of September.

Your kinsman assured, H. Northumberlande.

44 Fifth earl of Northumberland to the eleventh lord Clifford, 6 December [1523].
Chatsw., Clifford Letter Book, fo. 18r-v.

To my lord and soninlawe the lord Clifforde.

Mine owne good lord and soninlawe, in my most hartie manner I recomme[n]d me unto you and sendes my daughter your bedfellowe and your little ones and mine hartie Godes blessinge and mine and giveth [fo. 18v] unto you mine owne good lord my most intire thankes for your loveinge and kind dealinge with me in this my necessitie upon my last writinge unto you and my lord, I am and shalbee assured yours.

And my lord I have yet no word from London but onely that mine attorney is comen home, William Danbye, who Sir William Gascon, Treasurer to my Lord Cardinall spake with att his departure and willed him to shew me that the matters that you and I spake to him on concerninge the lord Conniers should bee spedd and also I should bee spedd in those matters I brake with him in in [*sic*] like forme and that

I should send upp as lait as I canth because he should goe home into his country and that he should shew me that my lord cardinall will cause the kinge to write unto us. And also himself would write in like forme. The kinges lettre is comen unto me which I send you by this bearer to see. If yours bee comen I pray you send it me in like forme. My said attorney grauntes there is a viccar elect at Roym.

My lord, my lord treasurer wrat by post to the abbott of St Marie abbey who send me word on Thursday last, the iiijth day of December, that hee would not faile to be with me uppon Sonday att night next, the vijth day of December, the coppie of my lettre of answere unto the said abbott againe I have sent you here inclosed. My owne good lord and sonn I pray you hast my venison away that I may send it upp for I make the carrier to tarry for it. My lord the soldiers beyond the sea comes a pace against theire captaines wills. The duke of Suffolke shall bide there all this winter. The lord Sannds came over to the kinge by post, the cause why is not yett knowne. The lord Mongey shall goe over with v ml [men] but as yet it restes. My lord, Roger Chamblays matter of the murder is quickly handled by my lord cardinall and by the helpe of Sir Williame Gascon. My lorde there is a new busines in London for a new lone of money in so much as the judges and all other there was stopped att mine attorneys comeinge away for that cause. My lord yet would I know where I shall see you and your bedfellow in the latter end of this Christmas and as I have further newes I shall advertise you. Written att my mannor of Leckingfeld the vjth day of December.

Your kinsman,   H. Northumberland.

45 Fifth earl of Northumberland to the eleventh lord Clifford, [6 x 25 December 1523].
Chatsw., Clifford Letter Book, fos. 18v-19r.

To mine owne good lord the lord Clifforde.

Mine owne good lord, in my full hartie manner I commend me unto you and sendes my daughter your bedfellow and your little ones and mine hartie Godes blessinge and mine. My lord I have no newes to send but I perceave the duke of Suffolke shall over in all hast and that they are mustringe fast and the lord Ferries shall over with him who hath much busines in his country for he is faine to put them in prison [fo. 19r] because they will not in no wise goe over with him and all other as I perceave is in like case for they alleadge for them that they will not lie out in winter. My lord my receavour of Northumberland is with me here and hee sheweth me that my lord treasurer falles well to justice insomuch as he hath hedet [*sic*] of the Fenwiks, Eringtons and other insomuch that there is but hard agreement betwixt him and the lord Dacres. And he sheweth me that the duke of Albany hath broken his day. And as for these Inglish folkes which was said was about the kinge of Scottes, he can tell me of no such thinge, but he sheweth me that the kinge of Scottes hath the lord Hambleton and other about him and is disposed to bee mervelous self willed and uttereth that hee can as evill browke Inglish men as ever did any of his age and doth take as obstinate waies with him for his yeares.

My lord I have worde from London that my marchand goes not abroade and [   ] not to London and other where my lord I perceave that all those that have not lent the kinge already shall have privie seales to pay theire lone or els to come upp this terme and all those that are behind which hath beene sessed and not paid hath mervelous sharpe privie seales and verie rigorous wordes. Your servant can shewe you that my venison (God thanke you) was mervelous well accepted and came well as can bee for the kinge came to [   ] to my lord cardinall as it came thither. What presentes were prepared against the kinges comeinge your servant can shew you. My servantes dragges above for my causes but as yett they can gett none answere to come home.

My lord I have sent my trustie servant Robert Hastinges my baliffe of Nafferton to your good lordshipp with my booke of fynes, what is paid and what is unpaied in that countrey and of every time that the lettes was. My lord, I would bee content to take sheepe or neat or any other cattell for it so that I may have them upon reasonable prices wherein I beseech your good lordshipp of your loveinge kindnes herein and my lord, all other fermholdes of mine which was not lett before, I beseech your good lordshipp to lett them out in like case after the rate as theire farmes comes to a yeare at the least and further as your good lordshippe thinkes best. Also my lord ye shall perceave as I am informed that all the crowners in this country is bound to certifie to the kinges counsaile of all the owtlawries in this country; wherefore it is good your good lordshipp speake with the crowners in your partes for your frendes and servantes for suites, for if the outlawries be delivered it will sure come to a money matter: if they be staid and not delivered and the parties agreed it shall doe no hurt. My lord I shall send you betwixt this and Cristenmas your booke of orders for your house and your booke of otes. I will leave out of it all your prices and the quantites because yee may stint what prices yee will agree to one yeare with another in the *grosse emption* and also what quantites that yee may put in more or lesse as yee thinke good to serve your house.

Your kinsman assured,   H. Northumberlande.

43–5 This sequence of three letters from the fifth earl to his son-in-law can be dated to the autumn of 1523. The subscription to Northumberland's son-in-law *lord* Clifford places them no earlier than the autumn of 1523, the 10th lord having died the previous April. Nor can they be dated later than the autumn of 1524, Clifford being created earl in June 1525. Both the news of the French war and the mention in **43** of the election of a Pope locates them in 1523. (Clement VII, elected on 19 November 1523 and so still news in London in the first week of December.) The reference to the earl of Albany in **45** confirms this identification: Albany was in France from October 1522 until September 1523 and then in Scotland until May 1524. The third of the letters is undated: it is placed last in the sequence on the assumption that the venison called for in **44** is that graciously received in **45**. Against this dating in 1523, the dates offered in **44**, Thursday 4 December and Sunday 7 December fall in 1522 and not 1523 although on other grounds the letter must be of 1523.

The temper of the letters is cordial with substance being given to the earl's salutations to his son-in-law, daughter and grandchildren by his requests that he might see them at Christmas. It is clear that he and Cumberland were cooperating on common concerns. I am unable to identify the matter concerning lord Conyers about which they had made a joint approach to Wolsey. Of those named, the Lord Treasurer is the second earl of Surrey, later third duke of Norfolk (d. 1554), temporarily warden in the East Marches; lord 'Mongey' is William Blount, lord Mountjoy. Roger 'Chambley' may be Roger Cholmley, lawyer and finally Lord Chief Justice 1552–3 (d. 1565), although the nature of his scrape is elusive.

Two further points may be observed. The letters make it clear that the extraction of the Forced Loan of 1522–3 was a more protracted process than is sometimes imagined. Further they suggest real problems in the payment of fines in Yorkshire with Northumberland's reiterated willingness to accept sheep or cattle ('neat') suggesting a shortage of coin. I am not aware of any other instances of fines being paid in kind, although this may mean nothing more than animals were assigned a monetary value in the accounts which form the larger part of our evidence.

46 Fifth earl of Northumberland to the first earl of Cumberland, 29 March [1526 or 1527].
Chatsw., Clifford Letter Book, fo. 19v.

To mine owne good lord and sonne my lord off Cumberlande.

Mine owne good lord and sonne in my hartiest manner I recommende me unto you. And the cause of my writinge unto your good lordshipp att this time is that I receaved your lettre concerninge the chauntrie voide att my castell of Cockermouth for your preist this bearer wherein

I must beseech your good lordshipp to take none unkindnes with it that hee is not spedd, hee hath beene verie importunate. And I perceave it hath beene alwaies accostomed that one of the said preist should keepe a grammer schoole which is a mervelous good and a meritorious deede. Wherefore I would be loath to breake that good president. Wherefore mine owne good lord, I have gotten a maister of grammer to be chauntrie priest there and to be bounden to keepe the said grammer schoole continually. Hee is one that hath beene exercised with teaching and is a sedulous preist and in good yeares. Wherefore my lord I pray your good lordship to be contented with this good deede, by followinge of this good example hereafter. And if such a place in my chauntrie fall in myne hand here after, I will put therin your preist afore any other. Written att my castell of Wresill the xxixth day of Marche.

Your owne assured, H. Northumberlande.

The present letter has to be dated between June 1525 (creation of the earl of Cumberland) and April 1527 (death of the fifth earl). Northumberland has not previously been thought of as a patron of learning but this letter reflects a real commitment to the grammar school at Cockermouth.[102]

Letters of the sixth earl of Northumberland

47 Henry lord Percy to the eleventh lord Clifford, 19 November [1524]. Chatsw., Clifford Letter Book, fos. 19v-20r.

To my owne good lord and brother my lord Clifford.

Mine owne good lord and brother I hartely comend me unto you. And where that nowe by my lordes meanes for my advancement to honnour, the kinge hath appointed me to bee one of them which shall assault the castell of Lowaltie, the circumstances of which castell this bearer shall showe you at length with all the occurrentes here; where by my lord I am likely to be not at a little cost. And my lord my Father will doe nothinge for me but would be gladd to have mee put to lacke. And now my good lord there is no remedy but [   ] my frendes to helpe me or els to make some other shift to save mine honnour. I desier and most hartie pray you to lend me for one yeare the some [fo. 20r] of cli and that I may have it here with me afore St Andrew Day next if it may be possible. And for the repayment thereof againe

---

[102] For references to the medieval school, see J. A. H. Moran, *The Growth of English Schooling, 1340–1548* (1985), 244–5.

assure as yee can devize. Yee shall have mine uncke Alaine Per[c]ie or one or two more substantiall persons bounden. And thus my good lord herein now yee may doe me mervelous pleasure. And I trust in time to come to doe you like pleasure if it may be in my little power. In hast at London the xixth day of November.

Your assured and most faithfull brother,   Henry Percy.

The address of the letter locates it in November 1523 or 1524. The possibility was considered that the letter referred to a stage in the 1523 campaign against Scotland, but no castle with an appropriate name could be located. Instead, it appears that the assault took place not on a real castle but a mock castle called 'Loyalty' erected for the Christmas tournament of 1524 in the tiltyard at Greenwich. Hall provides a full description of the events without naming Percy amongst the 16 knights who undertook the assault. The instruction to build the castle was given on 6 November thus providing time for Percy to be selected and find that he could not raise sufficient money to take part.[103] Whilst the king had appointed Percy to be amongst the knights, it is not clear if the 'lord' who had solicited his inclusion was Wolsey or (less likely) his father.

Percy's pecuniary embarrassment and his acid comments on his father are all of a part with what else we know of the years before his inheritance. It is possible to show that he was borrowing on penal terms in these years and that the obligations he entered into then were satisfied by the sale of parts of the estate after his inheritance.[104]

48 Sixth earl of Northumberland to his mother, the dowager countess, 21 August [1527].
BL, Althorp B1, fo. 25r-v.

My most dere lady and moder, in my hertiest manner I commend me unto your gode ladiship praing therof your daly blissing. And wher as I am informyd that ye ar proposid to go [to] the erle of Cumbreland, surely madam it shall not stand with your honour so to do, pondering that ye have allegid by your writinges that if ye shuld have gone theder when ye were mocioned by my lord cardinall it shuld have put yow in jeoparde of your liff. And now madam for to go theder shuld not onely amonges al wisemen be reputid a gret lightnes in yow, pondering your excuse afor, but also a mervelous inconstancy that ye shuld mak so farr a progres so sone after the deth of my lord and fader whos soull Jh[es]u pardon. Writen at Ohelsan the xxjth day of August.

---

[103] Hall, *Chronicle*, 688–91; also Alan Young, *Tudor and Jacobean Tournaments* (1987), 146 (the castle itself being illustrated on p. 147); *LP* iv (1) no. 965.
[104] Hoyle, 'Fall of the House of Percy', 183–6.

Your humble lovyng son, Henre Northbreland.

No address. Possibly autograph.

The fifth earl of Northumberland died on 27 May 1527: he was buried with both modesty and expedition. By mid-June Cumberland could tell Thomas Hennage that the widowed countess had declined his invitation to remove to Skipton (where he offered to make her 'the chief lady and mistress' of the house), but had decided to stay at Wressle or go to live with lady Pickering. She did, he reported, not wish to go to Craven for her health: she feared the 'coldness of the air there'. The present letter adds a further element to the story. The countess changed her mind within a matter of weeks and attracted this rebuke from her son.[105] As noted previously, connections between the dowager countess and her son-in-law's family remained strong up to her death in 1542.

49 Sixth earl of Northumberland to the first earl of Cumberland, 29 October [1532].
Chatsw., Clifford Letter Book, fos. 20v-21r.

A coppie of a lettre from Henry erle of Northumberland to Henric first erle of Cumberlande his brother in lawe.

My good lord and brother in my hartiest manner I commend me unto you. And accordinge to your desire and my good sisters your bedfellowes as I perceave by my brother Clifforth have admitted Lancelott Martin this bearer to the bowbearershipp and fermehold of my Forest of Langstrothe. And also have send unto your good lordshipp a commission herewith wherein I have denominiated William Gravis as my commissioner and left a space for as many as shall please your good lordshipp to put in to view my game and woodes there.

And for newes here, therle of Murrey is made warden for against me. Neverthelesse he keepeth still Edenbrough for where he should have lien at Coldingham, he was contented that I should bee his steward to make his provision against his comeinge there. And for mine under officer I made George Dowglasse, who two daies afore his comeinge thither did make such a fire to warme him with all that Coldingham with two other townes nye adjoyninge thereunto and all the corne thereunto belonginge to the value of 2,000li sterlinge was burnt and nothinge left standinge but onely the abbey where they toke 80 prisoners and 60 good horse beside 300 head of cattle. And so daily rodes and burninges is betweene us and Scotland by stealth. And

[105] *LP* iv (2) nos. 3134, 3184.

notwithstandinge many outragious actes done by the Scottes to England, oure garrisons here is not determined to feight but all to keepe the peace.

My good lord and brother as him that is most desirous of your good company and my good sisters, if I durst bee so bold to putt you to paine in these rude [fo. 21r] partes I wilbe bold to desire you and my sister to keepe this Christmas with me at me castle of Werkwurth, most hartly beseechinge your good lordshipp for the same, which should be most unto my comforth. And for any army to be raised against the west borders, I will assure you the contrarie, and there is no[ne] likely afore the springe of the yeare any army to be raised against these marches under my rule, pondringe not onely the devision betweene the kinge of Scottes and his nobles but also the longe distance of the partes from which he must bringe his armie. And for lettres enowe there passis betweene the warden of Scotland and me but finally noe redresse nor meetinges. And thus my good lord have you in his keepeinge. Written at my castle of Werkwurthe the xxixth day of October.

Your assured faithfull brother,   H. Northumberlande.

James Stewart, earl of Moray, was appointed warden of the Scottish East March on 12 October 1532 and the burning of Coldingham took place on the evening of Friday, 18 October. George Douglas, who Northumberland describes as his under-officer, was the younger brother of the exiled earl of Angus.[106] Lancelot Martin is correctly Lancelot Marton of Eshton near Skipton, a family closely associated with the Cliffords.[107] Marton came to hold other Craven offices on the Northumberland's estates before his death, but the present letter suggests that he did so as Cumberland's man and not, as has been supposed, Northumberland's.[108] Langstrothdale, of which Marton was made bowbearer, lies at the extreme head of Wharfedale.

50 Sixth earl of Northumberland to the first earl of Cumberland, [May 1533].
Chatsw., Clifford Letter Book, fo. 20r-v.

A coppie of a lettre from Henry erle of Northumberlande to Henrie first erle of Cumberland his brother in lawe.

---

[106] Rae, *Scottish Frontier*, 237; *LP* v no. 1460. For Douglas see 24–5 above.

[107] Marton's father Henry, d. 1533, served as steward of the household, master forester and steward in Craven at different times. Hoyle, 'Land and Landed Relations', 245.

[108] Smith, *Land and Politics*, 202, 207.

My singuler good lord and brother, in my most hartie manner I recomend me unto your lordshipp. And this Tuesday earely in the morninge I receaved your kinde and loveinge lettres with the coppies aswell of the kinges highnes lettres unto your good lordshipp as to my nephew your sonn, whereby I perceave yee goe upp to the queen's corronation, assureinge your good lordshipp I have no knowledge as yet from the kinge whether I shall come upp yet or not. Neverthelesse I have a servant of mine with his grace and all my frendes above to sollicite my comeinge upp seeinge it is a likelihood to be a peace. And concerninge all the doeinge aswell here from the kinge as to the kinge, you shall perceave by the coppies of the lettres there of here inclosed at length and as soone as I have knowledge what I shall doe, I shall not faile to send unto you in post.

My good lord and brother, where of your goodnes it pleaseth you to write what liveries I doe give, ye would give as nigh the same as ye can, for which my lord I most hartelie thanke you, and ye shall perceave that all my gentlemen shall have tawnie with broad gardes of blacke velvet as they use now in the court and my yeomen plaine tawny with redd capps and blacke feathers without any imbrodery as I am yet advised. I am purposed to be seaven score horse and not above and if yee be upp afore me, looke what fashion your coates be made and mine shalbe of the same turne.

Also my lord, where of your goodnes and noble favor toward me, yee bee contented that wee shall meete soe to ride both upp togeather to the kinge or els I to come to you to Skipton, the which my lord, if I goe nott upp in too great post I will not faile. [fo. 20v] And if I doe soe, then I will desire your good lordshipp, my sister may take the paine to meete me at Topcliffe whome of all women I am most desirous to see. And thus my lord I leave of here in this matter because I looke daily for word from the kinge.

My lord I am determined as for yet to lie att my lord Mountjoyes house at Paules Cheave. Also my lord now you must somethinge thinke upon your honnour as well for [your] owne apparell as for my good nephewes uppon which I have made your lordshipp a draught after my foolish opinion. Also my lord I thinke yee shall have henshemen at the coronacion which if yee have, yee shall have three and three of my henshmens coates if yee send unto me.

The coronation of Anne Boleyn took place on Whit Sunday, 1 June 1533. The present latter lacks a dating clause, but may be assigned to the weeks previous when Percy was in Northumberland. It seems unlikely that his invitation ever arrived, but his nephew, the young Henry Clifford, was made a Knight of the Bath in advance of the ceremony.[109] The determination to share livery must

---

[109] It is possible to compile an itinerary of the earl's movements from the dating clauses of his privy seals found (mainly) in Mss of the duke of Northumberland, Alnwick Castle,

be read as the most explicit declaration of close friendship and alliance and adds weight to a comment Northumberland made later that summer, that Cumberland was the man who Northumberland felt himself 'most bounden unto'.[110]

51 Sixth earl of Northumberland to Margaret countess of Cumberland, 10 July [1532].
Chatsw., Clifford Letter Book, fo. 21r.

To my deerest sister the countesse of Cumberlande.

Mine owne good ladie and sister I hartily comende me unto you. And have received your present by your servant Shires for the which I render unto you my right hartie thankes. And yee shalbee assured I shall deserve your kindnes which I have ever found in you as a good naturall sister unto me heretofore which I shall not put in oblivion as Jesus knoweth who keepe you. At Westminster the xth day of July.

Your loveinge brother, H. Northumberlande.

52. Sixth earl of Northumberland to Margaret countess of Cumberland, 18 May [　]．
Chatsw., Clifford Letter Book, fo. 21v.

To my deerest sister my lady of Cumberlande.

Mine owne good lady and sister, after my most hartie recomendacion unto you with cordiall thankes for your paines taken with me at my house wherein you showed yourself so kind and naturall that I must needes count myself most bounden unto you next the kinge above all other, trustinge, God willing, not to faile but affore Trinity Sonday to see you at your owne house which shalbe most my comfort, in hast xviijth day May.

Your faithfull loveinge brother, H. Northumberlande.

51–2 Neither of these two letters is dateable although **51** might possibly be

Northumberland, Letters and Papers no. 2. This shows that Northumberland was at Alnwick in April, has no references for May but has him back at Warkworth on 10 June.
　[110] Dickens, *Clifford Letters*, no. 33.

of 1532 when Northumberland can be shown to have been in London. Northumberland remarks in other letters of the early 1530s on his affection for and desire to see his sister. It would be a reasonable speculation to suppose that he transferred to her some of the affection he might otherwise have given to his wife from whom he separated within a few years of marriage.[111]

Letters of Charles Brandon, first duke of Suffolk

Charles Brandon, duke of Suffolk (1484–1545), the brother-in-law of Henry VIII, needs little introduction having recently been the subject of a full biography.[112] It is far from clear to what degree the friendship of Cumberland and Suffolk pre-dated the marriage in 1535 of Suffolk's daughter Eleanor to Henry lord Clifford, later second earl. The letters which follow reveal a number of aspects of the relationship between the reciprocal father-in-laws: over the arrangement of the marriage and subsequent provisions for the young couple (**53, 60, 61**), over Cumberland's problems in the Pilgrimage of Grace (**54–7**) and the subsequent rearrangement of the administration of the North (**58–9**), and Suffolk's work as a London agent for the earl in his attempt to secure a lease of the lands of Bolton Priory (**62**). The relationship, as seen through Suffolk's eyes, is cordial enough but the letters are also marked by his concern for the welfare of his daughter and suspicion that the young couple might not be adequately served by the arrangements for their household made by Cumberland.

It has been a commonplace of the literature that the first earl strained himself raising the dowry required by Suffolk and in building the eastward extension to Skipton Castle to accommodate his son's new bride.[113] In fact we know little about Cumberland's finances at any point in his life, and whilst it is noteworthy that references to the earl's borrowings and debts occur frequently within these letters, it would be unwarranted to assume that he was abnormally indebted by the standards of the time or that some share of that indebtedness arose from the costs of the Brandon-Clifford marriage.

The Suffolk letters are, with one exception, drawn from the Clifford Letter Book. The main body of letters occupies fos. 22r-24v and is headed by the title 'Lettres from Charles Brandon duke of Suffolke to my lord of Cumbreland'.

---

[111] Cf **50** above and Dickens, *Clifford Letters* no. 34. For the marriage, Bernard, *The power of the early Tudor Nobility*, 153–4.

[112] Gunn, *Brandon*. I am grateful to Dr Gunn for his suggestions as to the dates of a number of the letters.

[113] Cf Lady Anne Clifford printed by Dickens, *Clifford Letters*, 141–2 and Dickens himself, 26, together with Gunn, *Brandon*, 132. It is not clear when the extension to the castle was built.

53 Charles, first duke of Suffolk to the first earl of Cumberland, [?early 1535].
Chatsw., Clifford Letter Book, fo. 22r.

My very good lord in my harty wise I recommend me unto yow. And so it is that I have receyved your lettres, by the which I doe perceive the goodwill and intent of your hart for the accomplishment of the marriage between my lord your sonn and my daughter. And my lord I ansuer yow I have no less good will and minde but that it may take effect (God willing), for my lord I doubt not but you knowe well inough that the delay thereof that hath been never came of me. But my lord I pray you doe herein, as I will not fayle, God willing, at my next coming to the kings grace (which I trust shall be shortly after Easter), and that is or [sic] your departure to knowe the kings pleasure, whether it shall stand with his pleasure the said marriage shall goe forth or not, and upon his graces pleasure knowne, I ensure you there shall be noe delay but you shall knowe myne intent and minde wholly with which I doubt not, but you will be content. And my lord, as concerninge my lord your sonns beinge in the court, I am very glad thereof, for it shall be both to your honour and his weale. And as for changing of his minde, if it shall soe happen I had rather he did now then hereafter, but I mistrust him nought, as knoweth God whoe send you my now good lord as well to doe as I would my selfe. Written at my house at Henham.

By yours assured,   Charles Suffolke.

The wedding of Henry lord Clifford and Eleanor Brandon took place about mid summer 1535 in her father's house at Southwark in the king's presence.[114] It seems reasonable to assume that the present letter dates from the earlier part of 1535. The nature of the delays mentioned are unknown. It reveals the importance of securing royal sanction for the marriage; at much the same time Cumberland used Suffolk as an intermediary with the king to float the idea of a marriage between his daughter Maud and John, third lord Conyers.[115]

[114] Dickens, *Clifford Letters*, 141, 144.
[115] *LP Add.* i no. 1037.

54 Charles, first duke of Suffolk and Sir William Fitzwilliam to the first earl of Cumberland, 22 October [1536].
Chatsw., Clifford Letter Book, fo. 22v.

To our very good lord my lord of Cumberland in hast hast.

Our very good lord in our right harty manner we commend us unto yow. And sorry wee be to heare of the st[i]res that yee be in, nevertheles sithence it is soe laid to your charge that yee must needes defend it eyther in the feild or within your house, my lord, if yee suppose that yee may be able to make your party good with them with your honour in the feild, then in the name of God to advaunce your selfe and sett upon them as yee shall thincke most expedient. And if yee shall thinck your selfe not able to fight with them in the feild, then wee cann say no more to yow but to keepe your house with all the force yee cann devise soe that you keepe you out of theire handes, wherein we pray God to be your ayde, and send you well to overcome these false rebellious and traytors. And thus the Holy Trinity have yow our very good lord in his blessed keepinge. At Lincolne the 22th day of October.

Also my lord as this day my lord of Shroysbury is at Doncaster, and also my lord of Norff[olk] and my lord of Exeter with v thowsand men which, God willinge, shall repulse these false companyes.

Charles Suffolke, W. Fitzwilliames.

The fullest account of Suffolk's role in the Pilgrimage is that recently offered by Gunn.[116] Brandon entered Lincoln on 16 October 1536, and he was to remain there until Christmas or New Year (although in **57** he expresses the hope of going to court soon after 11 December). Cumberland was able to raise a large force of men but lost some or all of them in the face of the Pilgrims, leaving him with the single option of sheltering within the castle at Skipton.[117] Suffolk's co-signatory, Sir William Fitzwilliam, lord admiral, was Cumberland's brother-in-law.

55 Charles, first duke of Suffolk to the first earl of Cumberland, 7 November [1536].
Chatsw., Clifford Letter Book, fo. 24r.

To my very good lord my lord of Cumberland.

My very good lord in my right harty manner I commend me unto

[116] Gunn, *Brandon*, 144–152.
[117] Hoyle, 'First Earl', 87–8.

yow. And forasmuch as I understand my daughter was of late in some daunger by reason of the rebells in your partes: I hartely pray you my lord in eschewing any further danger or perill ye will send her unto me hither if yee thinck yee may so doe by any suertye possible, and here I trust she shall be out of danger, where I intend to have my wyfe shortly by Godes grace whoe have yow my good lord in his keeping. At Lincolne the 7th of 9er.

Yours assured, Charles Suffolke.

Regretably Suffolk offers no clues as to how he had heard of his daughter's adventures. The story of how she, together with her son and sisters-in-law were trapped at Bolton Priory by the insurrection, then rescued by Christopher Aske and brought through the rebels to safety at Skipton, has been told several times.[118]

56 Charles, first duke of Suffolk, Sir Anthony Brown and others to the first earl of Cumberland, 7 November [1536].
Chatsw., Clifford Letter Book, fos. 24r-v; previously printed in abstract, *LP* xi no. 1005, from two copies in the State Papers, PRO, SP1/111 fos. 5r-7v.

A lettre from the duke of Suffolke, Sir Anthony Browne and others unto the earle of Cumberland.

Our very good lord, in our right harty wise we commend us unto yow, acerteyning you we have receaved your lettres dated the 5th of this month by which wee perceive the good and honorable service that yee and my lord your sonne have done unto the kings highnes being no little to all our comfortes and to you and our said lord your sonne great honour, not doubting but considering your quarrell and the high honour that dependeth thereuppon yee will contynue in your good and noble hartes serving the king as yee have done; hartely thancking you of your good advertisement of the state of the people upon the borders and other places named in your said lettres. And albeyt according to your desyre we have debated amongst us how wee might help you with gonns and gonn powder, we consider it is not possible to send them unto you by water neither by land, but it should rather come into thandes of the rebells then unto yow which were to great danger both for us and you; being very sorry we cannot doe you no pleasure therein. And also of the great losses and spoile that yee have susteyned

---

[118] The account of the Dodds, *Pilgrimage*, i, 210, is the most sober.

by the traitors, not doubting but the good and honorable service that ye have done shall be considered to the good satisfaccion for the same. And to acerteyne you how everything proceedeth here, ye shall understand that upon such order and direccion as was taken by my lord of Norffolk and my lord of Shrewsbury with the rebells, they stand and be as yet at a stay trusting all shall be well. Nevertheless as we shall have knowledge [fo. 24v] we shall not faile to advertize you from tyme to tyme with all speed possible; desyring you in likewyse to doe the same unto us from your partes. And in the meane tyme to keepe your selfe in good suerty as yee have done untill ye shall see all thinges in good and perfect assurance. And forasmuch as we perceive that some of your lettres which ye have sent unto the kinges highnes have been taken so that they never came to the kinges graces handes, we shall so see for the sure conveyance of the lettre which ye have sent unto me the duke of Suffolke at this tyme, that it shall shortly come unto the kinges handes to the intent his grace shall perceive the good service ye have done, which we be well assured his grace will not forgett. And thus God have you in his keeping and send you aswell to doe in your affaires and busines as wee would doe ourselves. At Lincolne the 7th day of November.

Neither of the letters referred to in this letter are known to survive, but two copies of the present letter, in which Suffolk declines to supply Cumberland with gunpowder because he and the others at Lincoln found the logistical problems insurmountable, survive in the State Papers.[119] The second of these carries the signatures and messages of Cumberland's correspondents (omitted in the Chatsworth text) as follows; 'by youres assuered, Charles Suffolk; your poore frend, Francis Brian; my lord it ys not a lyttyll comforth to me to here of your doynges, Antonie Browne; J. Russell; W. Par'. There are various minor variants in the wording of the letters but the sense is common to all. Suffolk's role as a staging post for correspondence between Cumberland (and a range of other northern nobles) and the king (and vice versa) is made plainer in the following letter.[120] Aske saw at least one intercepted letter between Suffolk and Cumberland in which Cumberland asked to be supplied with gunpowder (as in the present letter). Aske took this to refer to a need at Skipton when in fact it referred to Carlisle.[121]

[119] *LP* xi no. 1005.
[120] Cf. Gunn's comments, *Brandon*, 149.
[121] *LP* xii (1) no. 698 (3).

57 Charles first duke of Suffolk to the first earl of Cumberland, 11 December [1536].
Chatsw., Clifford Letter Book, fo. 23r.

To my very good lord my lord of Cumberland.

My very good lord in my right harty manner I commend me unto you. Soe it is that 5 or 6 dayes passed I receaved certeyne proclamacions and lettres from the kings highnes, which I should have sent to Barwicke by water unto Sir Thomas Clifford whoe should have sent the same unto you and to my lord your sonne and others as surely as he could devise accordinge to theire direccions, which notwithstanding, because the said lettres and proclamacions were delivered unto me at the tyme appointed for the meetinge, I have kept and stayd the same proclamacions with me untill I might have sure knowledge how all things should come to pass uppon the next meeting. And now forasmuch as (thancked be God) all things be now brought to a good end, I deteyne the said proclamacions in my handes, considering it is not now needfull to putt the same in execution, sending unto you the kings said lettres to the intent yee should perceive how thanckfully the kings highnes doth accept and take your good service done unto his highnes at this tyme, whereof I am more gladd then I cann comitt to penn. And my lord I intend, God willing, shortly to be at the court, and if yee send any servaunt of yours thither I shall advertize yow of such further news as I shall know there by Godes goodnes, whoe have yow my very good lord in his blessed keeping. At Lincolne the 11th day of December.

Yours assured,   Charles Suffolke.

The letter forwarded by Suffolk was the king's of 4 December, above **20**, which was sent to him with other letters and proclamations directed to various northern gentry and the towns of Newcastle and Carlisle. All were to be directed by way of Berwick.[122]

---

[122] *LP* xi no. 1236.

58 First duke of Suffolk and other councillors to the first earl of Cumberland, 31 January [1537].
Chatsw., Clifford Letter Book, fos. 14v 15r.

A lettre from my lord of Suffolke, my lord privy seale, my lord of Sussex, my lord admirall, the bishopps of Hereford and Chichester and Sir William Kingstone unto the earle of Cumberland.

After our right harty commendacions to your good lordshipp, whereas the kings majestie considering the great discord that hath of late chaunced amongst his subjetes of those partes, purposing like a wise and prudent prince with thappeasing of inward trouble to establish such an order for the sure keeping and defence of his marches as may preserve his subjects from all annoyance and danger of outward and forreigne enemyes, hath concluded upon a direccion for his East and Middle Marches. And to putt the same in execucion hath already sent hither Sir Anthony Browne knt, one of the gentlemen of the privy chamber, of whose arrivall and proceeding in that behalfe wee doubt not but you shall have perfitt knowledge before these our lettres shall come to your handes. Albeit his highnes and wee of his counsell doe well see and perceive that a like order to be taken for the West Marches should be both for his graces honour and safety. And doe remember therewith both how loth ye weare to take the office of warden thereof upon you, and how desyrous you have shewed your selfe aswell to me specially the lord privy seale as to others sythence you had the rome thereof to be discharged againe of the same, so it might have ensewed with his majesties favour, whome you have ever showed your selfe ready in all thinges to serve without respect in such place as he hath appointed unto you.

Yet his highnes, considering the faithfull and honorable service you have lately done unto him in the preservacion of your selfe out of the handes of his rebelles, hath determined to stay his proceedinges for the West Marches unles you shall be well contented to leave your offices in the same. Wherein as we doubt not but you will use that conformity that may be to his graces satisfaccion, honour and suerty therein, which also we desyre and advise you to doe; so his majestie hath commaunded us to signify unto yow that in a part of recompence for your loyall [fo. 15r] service lately done unto him, his grace hath resolved to advance yow to the honour of the Gartier [*sic*], and besides further in such wise to consider the same as you shall have cause to thincke it well employed. Wherefore his highnes desireth you not onely to signify your conformity herein unto his grace or to us of his counsell with diligence, but also in the meane season to have such regard to the defence of Carlile and thother partes of those marches as they may be out of all danger of enemyes or rebells that would impugne the same. And thus fare yee most hartely well. From Greenwich the last of January.

59 Charles, first duke of Suffolk, Thomas lord Cromwell (lord privy seal) and Sir William Fitzwilliam (lord admiral) to the first earl of Cumberland, 31 January [1537].
Chatsw., Clifford Letter Book, fo. 15r.

A lettre from the duke of Suffolk, my lord privy seale and my lord admirall unto the erle of Cumberland.

After our right harty commendacions to your good lordshipp, by this bearer you shall receave a generall lettre written unto you from the whole councell by the kinges highnes commaundment touching his graces determinacion for a like order to be established for the West Marches as is devised and putt in execucion upon th'Est and Middle Marches, which (though it shall be much to his highnes honour and suerty), yet the great goodnes and benignity of his grace, considering your good service lately done unto him, will not proceed thereunto unless you shall shew yourself fully conformeable to the same.

Wherefore my lord, albeyt we doubt not but the least knowledge you could atteyne in any thing that may tend to his graces satisfaccion, would easily frame your minde to apply your selfe without desyre unto it. Yet remembring what paine and charge you have in th'occupying of the office of those marches and of Carlile, and how loth you were to receave them, how desyrous you have shewed your selfe to forgoe them, and what quiett shall thereby ensue unto you, wee have thought convenyent in this our privat lettre to advice yow to shew your selfe gladd, as thanckfully for the purpose afforesaid to render them into his graces handes as you did like a good servant and a faithfull minister at the begining receave the same, which as wee doubt not but you will doe right gladly, so wee desyre and pray you by your secrett lettres to advertize us speedily thereof. And in the meane season till this device shall take effect, to have such regard to the sure keepinge and defence thereof as may be for your honour and his grace's suerty. And thus fare you well hartely. From Greenewich the last of January.

58–59 The present letter and its partner, the private letter of Suffolk, Cromwell and Fitzwilliam which accompanied it, are of interest on a number of grounds. They make it clear that in the last week of January 1537 a decision was taken to reorganise the government of all the marches and not just that of the Middle and East Marches, but that the reorganisation of the West Marches was contingent upon Cumberland's willingness to surrender his offices.[123] Sir Anthony Browne was dispatched to implement the new arrangements in the East: Cumberland was warned of Browne's mission by letter of 26 January (**23**).[124] Obviously the option of remaining in office was less than fully open to Cumberland and the advice of his correspondents was that he should place his wardenship at the king's disposal. But most significantly, Cumberland was reminded of his reluctance to accept the wardenship and his correspondents assumed that he would be grateful to abandon his duties. The discrete fashion in which his resignation was sought and the consolation of the Garter suggest that Cumberland's reputation was still high in the king's eyes despite the magisterial rebuke for faction fighting delivered less than a week before (**22**). Cumberland replied to this letter and the king's earlier letter on 8 February placing his office at the king's disposal.[125]

Letter **58** has some additional interest as an early product of the new privy council arrangements. Sadly the text available gives no clues as to whether or not it was signed by all of those named as its authors

60 Charles, first duke of Suffolk to the first earl of Cumberland, 17 September [1537 x 1541].
Chatsw., Clifford Letter Book, fo. 23v.

To my very good lord my lord of Cumberland.

My very good lord, in my right harty wise I commend me unto yow. And understandinge that my daughter Clifforde cann never have her good health at Riche [*sic*] Abby, I desyre you my lord that you would be contented that your sonne my lord Clifford and my said daughter may have your castle at Brome as they have had afore tyme where they may be and contynue for such season as they shall thincke most convenyent for the more confirmacion of both their healths, wherein you shall doe me and them great pleasure. Pray you my lord, of your minde herein yee will advertize me in your writinge by this bearer. And thus the Holy Trinitye have you in his keepinge. At my castell of Tatershall the 17th day of September.

Yours assured,   Charles Suffolke.

Postscript. My lord, if yee have any tame red deere that ye may send me, I pray you send me some of them, and I shall paye for the charges of their conveyaunce.

---

[123] For a discussion of the reorganisation of northern government in the early months of 1537, M. L. Bush, 'The Problem of the Far North: a study of the crisis of 1537 and its consequences', *NH* vi (1971), 40–63.
[124] For Browne's instructions see *LP* xii (1) no. 225.
[125] *LP* xii (1) nos. 372–4.

The present letter can be dated between Suffolk's grant of Tattershall in Lincolnshire in the spring of 1537 and the death of the first earl five years later in 1542. The younger Cliffords were resident at Roche abbey, about five miles east of Rotherham, a house of which the Cliffords were patrons. 'Brome' is Brougham castle in Westmorland (where the second earl was to die in 1570).

61 Charles, first duke of Suffolk to the first earl of Cumberland, 20 December [?1539].
Chatsw., Clifford Letter Book, fo. 22v.

To my very good lord my lord of Cumberland.

My very good lord after my right harty comendacions, yee shall understand that as this day I have receyved your lettres and a hundreth marks towardes the furniture of my lord your sonns and my daughters his wifes charges; which some wilbe very little, and will not serve for that purpose. And therefore I trust yee will disburse a larger some like as yee have promised me you would doe. My part shall not lack as yee shall perceive hereafter. And whereas I perceive by my lord your sonns lettres that he intendeth to resort to London with diligence, and that my daughter his wife shall contynew with you untill the holy dayes shall be passed, and then to be conveyed hither, I am contented therewith as knoweth God whoe have you, my lord, in his keeping. At the kinges castell of Dover the 20th of December.

Yours assured,   Charles Suffolke.

The contents of the letter are straightforward enough. Dr Gunn suggests that it might be dated 1539 given that Suffolk met Anne of Cleves at Dover on her landing there on 29 December.

62 Charles, first duke of Suffolk to the first earl of Cumberland, 4 February [1540].
Chatsw., Clifford Letter Book, fo. 23v.

To my very good lord my lord of Cumberland.

My lord after my harty commendacions theis shall be to advertize you that whereas my lord your sonne and your servaunt have mooved me for the lease of Boulton, with very much difficulty and with the especiall helpe of my frendes I have now a promise thereof, but it must be to your charges for the partyes that had a graunt thereof must be some what compounded and agreed with; assuring you if I had not made great labours therein it would not have been gotten for a great some of mony, as I am sure my lord your sonne cann advertize. And as for the 200 marks which I doe owe yow, I shall disburse that for you out of hand, and ye must send hither with all speed yee cann 200 li more; and therewith I trust to satisfye all partyes in such wise as it shall come to your handes according to your desyre. And thus the Holy Trinity have yow my very good lord in his tuicion. At London the 4th of February.

Yours assured,   Charles Suffolke.

The Cliffords claimed the patronage of Bolton Priory which, with Shap, served as the location of family interments. The stewardship and manrede of the house was a possession of the Cliffords. I have shown elsewhere how during the early months of 1538 the first earl sought to prevent the priory making leases which were disadvantageous to his interest by procuring his own.[126] The house surrendered in January 1539, but Cumberland's crown lease of the whole was not issued until 29 July 1541.[127] Part of the reason for this delay was his insistence on trying the legality of leases made by the prior and convent before the surrender[128] but it is also clear from the present letter that securing the lease was by no means all plain sailing. The inquest into conventual leases made in August 1540 shows that Cumberland had the promise of a lease by then: it seems most likely that the present letter dates to 1540 rather than 1541. The identities of the individuals who secured a lease before Cumberland are unknown. In 1542, shortly before his death, Cumberland secured a grant of the major part of Bolton's estates.

It might be added that Suffolk acted as Cumberland's agent in the purchase of other monastic properties in Craven.[129]

63 Charles, first duke of Suffolk to the first earl of Cumberland, 14 January [1525 x 1542].
Chatsw., Clifford Letter Book, fo. 24v.

To my very good lord my lord of Cumberland.

My very good lord, in my right harty manner I commend me unto you. And so it is that my lord Richard Greye hath shewed me that ye

[126] R. W. Hoyle, 'Monastic Leasing before the Dissolution: the evidence of Bolton Priory and Fountains Abbey', *YAJ* lxi (1989), 111–37.
[127] *LP* xvi no. 1500 at p. 721.
[128] E315/108 nos. 103–4, discussed by Hoyle, 'Monastic Leasing'.
[129] C54/426 nos. 57–8, the originals of which survive in the unlisted Londesborough Mss at Chatsworth.

owe him diverse sommes of mony as in the right of my lady his wife concerning her dower and joincture, whereupon resteth and dependeth a great part of his living. And forasmuch as my said lord is content at my desyre no further to open this matter against you, I pray you my lord to see him payd as speedily as ye conveniently cann so that he have no further cause to complaine against yow. And thus the Holy Trinity have yow, my very good lord, in his keepinge. At the kinges mannor of Greenewich the 14th of January.

Yours assured, Charles Suffolke.

Richard lord Grey, younger brother of the marquess of Dorset (d. 1531) married the widow of the tenth lord Clifford. An impoverished minor noble, he was, as this letter makes clear, reliant upon his wife's dower for much of his income. For a letter from Grey himself asking for the settlement of arrears of his wife's annuity, see **101** below. Dr Gunn points out to me that Grey's nephew, Henry marquess of Dorset, married Suffolk's daughter Francis at some time in the early 1530s. There are no obvious grounds by which this letter can be dated.

64 Charles, first duke of Suffolk to the first earl of Cumberland, 27 January [1536 x 1542].
Chatsw., Clifford Letter Book, fo. 22r.

To my very good lord my lord of Cumberland.

My lord in my right harty manner I commend me unto yow. Soe it is that I have receaved your lettres and as touching such mony as you should have had of Sir Thomas Wentworth, I shall soe provide that you shall be satisfyed and payd thereof shortly. And as for other your affayres in these partes, at my lord your sonns coming home yee shall be advertized of the proceedings of the same, and in everythinge where in my good will and furtherance shall not lacke at all tymes as knoweth God, whoe have you, my very good lord, in his tuicion. At my house besides Charing Cross the 27th day of Januarye.

Yours assured, Charles Suffolke.

Suffolk's letter is clearly addressed to the first earl; the dating from his house at Charing Cross must place it no earlier than 1536. Sir Thomas Wentworth of West Bretton near Wakefield (who must be distinguished from his namesake, ennobled in 1529) was in Suffolk's service in the 1520s.[130] The nature of his debt to Cumberland is unknown.

[130] Gunn, *Brandon*, passim.

65 Charles, first duke of Suffolk to the first earl of Cumberland, 8 July [1537 x 1540].
BL, Althorp B1, fos 72r-73v.

My vere good lord, in my right hertie wise I comend me unto you and also to my lady yor wiff, even so prayng you to remembre your promes concernyng our meting this gresse tyme and to bring my ladye your wiffe withe you to thentent we maye be merie together for I entend, God willing, to be at Hatfeld Thorne the first daye of Septembre as knoythe owr lord who have you in his blessid tuicon. From Tattershalle the viijth daye of Julij.

By yours assurid, Charles Suffolk.

Clerk's hand, signed. Subscribed [fo. 73v] 'To my vere good lord my lord of Cumb[er]lond'.

It is not immediately clear whether Suffolk is writing to his son-in-law or the first earl, but the formal reference to 'my lady your wife' rather than 'my daughter' tips the balance towards the first earl. If so, the letter can be no later than July 1540, for the first earl was widowed a second time in the November of that year. The dating from Tattershall makes it no earlier than 1537, so the letter is probably of 1537–40; but if addressed to the second earl, then 1542–5.[131]

Letters of the second and third dukes of Norfolk

This small group of letters contains one of c.1517 from the second duke of Norfolk (d. 1524) addressed to the tenth lord Clifford (**66**) and five from the third duke (d. 1554) to the first earl of Cumberland, mostly touching events after the Pilgrimage of Grace (**67–70, 72**). A further item is a commission of Norfolk's appointing Cumberland and others his deputies during the invasion scare of 1539 (**71**). All are drawn from the Clifford Letter Book in which the commission is placed before the letters. The letters themselves carry the heading (on fo. 25v) 'letters from the foresaid duke of Norffolke to my lord of Cumberland'.

Little is known of the relations between the two families of Howard and Clifford. The tenth lord Clifford was paying a fee to the second earl of Norfolk in the mid-1510s and the tone of the letter between them seems cordial enough.[132] But in the next generation, members of

---

[131] For the manor of Hatfield and the 'manor house' there, see J. Birch and P. Ryder, 'Hatfield Manor House, South Yorkshire', *YAJ* lx (1988).
[132] Chatsw., BA 3 fo. 41; a further payment of 1515 may be found in an unnumbered accountant's notebook. This last payment was made by Roger Tempest.

the Clifford circle assumed that the Howards would always prefer the Dacres as may be seen by Musgrave's comments in **111** below. Equally Norfolk was not an honest broker in 1537 when he vigorously rooted for Dacre's reappointment to the wardenry of the Western Marches.

66 Second duke of Norfolk to the tenth lord Clifford, 20 July [*c*.1517 x 1520].
Chatsw., Clifford Letter Book, fo. 26v.

To my lord and cousin my lord Clifford.

My lord and cousin in my most herty wise I commend me unto yow. And so it is that your servaunt this bearer hath right well and diligently solicited your causes in these partes, howbeyt there hath been noe small delayes of hearing aswell of your causes as of all others by reason of the ambassadors and other great matters concerninge outward partes. And in that I may doe for the furtherance of your said causes at any tyme, I shall be glad to doe noe less for you there in then I would doe for myne owne. And allwayes as nigh as ye cann you shall have myne advyce to leave pursuytes and busynes, and especially in these parts for they be chargeable and very costly besides longe delayes. And over this my lord, as touchinge your late servaunt Tempeste, noe doubte there is, but he hath done you right good service about your busynes in these partes; for the which it is thought here, that ye ought better to accept and take the same then hitherto ye have done, and to looke unto him therefore as it becometh a man of your honour to doe, and to doe for him what yee may reasonably in recompence of the same; for I knowe right well he hath well deserved largely to have your favour. And of such news as be occurrance [*sic*] in these partes, I have declared my mynde unto your said servaunt and partly he hath seene and heard himselfe to whome aswell therein as in all other your causes I pray you give credence. And thus the Holye Trinitye have you in his safeguard. Written at Lambeth the 20th day of Julye.

Your loving cousin,   T. Norffolke.

At first sight the letter gives few clues as to either date or subject matter. The reference to Clifford's late servant Tempest allows the letter to be assigned with some certainty to the late 1510s, possibly 1517. Tempest can be identified as Roger Tempest, a gentleman of Broughton near Skipton. He was active in the Clifford service in the mid-1510s, serving as steward in 1514 and farmer of the escheatorship in 1516–7, but by 1521 he was a member of Wolsey's household. The present letter must relate to Tempest's defection from the Clifford circle;

he was clearly a man of ability for whom service with Clifford provided an entry into more exalted circles. If this is accepted, then the identity of the correspondents follows and it is possible to proceed further and suggest that the year might be 1517 when the king received ambassadors during the summer.[133]

67 Third duke of Norfolk to the first earl of Cumberland, 18 January [1537].
Chatsw., Clifford Letter Book, fo. 26r.

To my very good lord my lord of Cumberland.

My very good lord in my harty manner I commend me unto you, letting you witte, that whereas the kings majestie hath appointed me with all speed and celerity to repayre into those partes there to reside as his leiuetuante for the due administracion of justice betweene his subjectes, to the intent I may be accompanyed with such part of the nobles and gentlemen of those partes at myne entry into the same as shall be convenyent for his highnes honour, his pleasure was I should desyre yow by these my lettres to meete me at Yorke the third day of February next, which I require and pray you to doe; and in the meane season to use such vigilancye and circumspeccion for the partes about you as at my cominge thither, I may finde the same in such obedyent conformity as to their dutyes apperteyneth. And forasmuch as it is necessary at your being with me at Yorke to have diverse of the most substantiall and hedd yeomen of the partes under your governance afore me to heare the declaracion of the kings pleasure, I pray you bringe with you of every country under your said rule 5 or 6 of the most esteemed yeomen aforesaid. From Greenwich the 18 day of January.

Yours assuredly, T. Norffolk.

Norfolk's appointment as lieutenant in the North and his intention to be at York on 3 February was announced on 16 January 1537. The order to Cumberland to assemble the head yeomen of the area under his control served to reiterate the king's instructions. In the event Norfolk entered York some days later than intended: he was at Pontefract on 4 February but had reached York by 7 February when he was busy swearing gentlemen.[134]

68 Third duke of Norfolk to the first earl of Cumberland, [30 or 31] March [1537]
Chatsw., Clifford Letter Book, fo. 30r.

To my very good lord my lord of Cumberland.

My very good lord, after my very harty commendacions, this shall be to advertize you that the kinges highnes in his lettres addressed unto me which I receaved yesterday, considering that now the king of Scotts is repairing with his wife into Scotland, and is to be doubted what he will attempt, hath commaunded me to require and pray yow at his coming home to have good espiall upon him, to th'intent yow may the better know his proceedinges and to be vigilant in the keeping good rule and order upon your wardenry whereof ye have the charge. And as concerning the Scottishmen that are at Carliell, his pleasure is they shall not be delivered into Scotland though the Regentes should desyre the same, but permitted to remayne still untill ye shall have other advertizement of his highnes or me to the contrary: and therefore I pray you that they using themselves accordingly may have all necessaryes for their mony as to honest men should apperteyne. And thus hartely fare ye well. From Newbrugh the 3 day of March.

Yours assuredly,   T. Norffolke.

My lord, myne advise shall be that in no wise ye depart towardes London unles ye have the kings highnes licence so to doe.

The date of the letter as it appears in the Chatsworth manuscript is impossible. On 5 March Norfolk was at Newcastle having crossed the Pennines from Carlisle by way of Prudhoe, but he was at Newbrugh priory (15 miles north of York) on 31 March, 2 and 4 April.[135] The letter is probably of 30 or 31 March. This suggestion finds support in the reference to the Scots. These were four refugees from Ayr who fled to Carlisle on 21 March after denying the supremacy of the Pope and calling for a vernacular New Testament.[136] The possibility of James V travelling through England was raised in late January or early February. In the event he sailed along the east coast and although expected in late April, landed at Leith on 19 May.[137]

[135] *Ibid.* nos. 775, 777, 809–10, 825, below letter **69**.
[136] *Ibid.* no. 703.
[137] Dodds, *Pilgrimage*, ii, 240–56 summarises the material.

69 Third duke of Norfolk to the first earl of Cumberland, 31 March [1537].
Chatsw., Clifford Letter Book, fo. 30v.

To my very good lord my lord of Cumberland.

My very good lord, after my harty commendacions, this shall be to advise you I have receaved of your servant this bearer the two prisoners ye sent me, and right so acerteyne you that for my part I cann lay nothing to their charges, but onely my lord of Sussex and other the kinges councell in Lancashire. And therefore, as to the preist I have sent him unto the goale at Yorke there to remayne under sure custody untill some matter may be found to be laid against him. And as to the other, I have sent him to yow againe, praying you to take suerty of him of an hundreth poundes to be forthcoming at any time when I send for him; and thereupon to lett him goe at libertye. And as for the fellow ye write to me yee have in prison at Carlile, I knowe nothing to lay to his charge, for consideringe his late departure from me, assured I am he could not be at the assault at Carliel. And thus hartely fare yee well. From Newborough the last day of March.

T. Norffolke.

I have been unable to identify the various prisoners mentioned in the letter.

70 Third duke of Norfolk to the first earl of Cumberland, 10 April [1537].
Chatsw., Clifford Letter Book, fo. 25v.

My very good lord, after my harty comendacions, these shall be to advertize you that the kinges highnes hath commaunded my lord Darcy, Sir Robert Constable and Aske to the Tower for their most heynous and abominable treason which they conspired to attempt sythence the pardon, which I signifye unto your lordshipp forasmuch his highnes hath commaunded me to declare and divulge the same throughout my leiuetenancye that it is for none old matter before the pardon, but onely for new conspiracye sithence the same.

And forasmuch as theis buisines here are somewhat doutfull and not yet fully stablished, I require you not to fayle but to send your servaunt unto me to Sheriff Hutton upon Saturday at night by whome I shall advertize you of more at length. And my minde is no wise (although you have the kings lettres to goe to London) yee shall goe, but to tarry, and in noe wise to departe out of the country untill yee shall heare further from me in that behaulfe, and that alsoe yee shall signify unto the people the cause of their apprehension, and that the same is for none old matter but for new conspiracye sythence the pardon as is aforesaid. And thus hartely farewell. From Duresme the tenth day of Aprill.

Yours assuredly, T. Norffolk.

Darcy and Aske were arrested on 7 April. Norfolk was told of this by a council letter written on the same day which instructed him to stress in his pronouncements that their arrest was for treasons committed since the pardon.[138]

71 Appointment by the third duke of Norfolk of the first earl of Cumberland, Henry lord Clifford and others as his deputies, 5 April 1539.
Chatsw., Clifford Letter Book, fo. 25r-v.

A commission from Thomas duke of Norffolke, lord treasurer and marshall of England to my lord of Cumberland, my lord Clifford etc for to be his deputys in the government of the West Ryding of Yorkshire.

Be it knowne to all men that these presentes shall heare or see, that where it hath pleased the kinges majestie to yeave unto us Thomas, duke of Norffolke, treasurer and marshall of England, his highnes comission under the great seale dated at Westminster the 26 day of March in the 30th yeere of his majestes most prosperous raigne [1539], committinge unto us full power and aucthoritye be the same for defence of all invasions of enemyes by land and sea in the shires of Yorke, Cumberland, Westmerland, Northumberland and Lancashire, the countys of the cittye of Yorke, the towne of Hull, the bishoprick of Duresme and the towne of Barwicke and all other places within the said countyes aswell within libertyes as without, to cause sure watches and beacons to be made in places accostomed for ready monition and warninge to be given to all the kings subjects if any landing of enemyes from the sea or other invasion by land should channce to be made, that they with all diligence might be ready to withstand and expell the said enemyes.

And where also it hath pleased his majestie by the said comission to give unto us, the said duke, full power and aucthority in our absence to name such noble men and others as we shall thincke convenyent to levye the kings subjectes in defensable array for the intent before

[138] *LP* xii (i) nos. 846, 863.

expressed, and that our aucthority by our lettres shall be sufficyent warrant and discharge against his highnes and his lawes for levying his majesties said subjectes in defenseable arraye for the causes afore specifyed; wee therefore considering that yee be most able and meete personns in our absence for that purpose in our opinyon within the West Rydinge of Yorkeshire to have the cheife rule of the kings subjectes, for this intent have appointed you there unto, desyring and hartely praying you and alsoe in the kings name straightly charginge and comaunding you and every of you to have such a vigilant and circumspect eye and regard that your selfes and all others (by vertue here of) committed to your leading be allwayes from henceforth in perfect readynes to withstand the malice, and alsoe to expell the kings majesties enemyes if [fo. 25v] any such invasion or landinge should channce to be.

Commaundinge and straightly charginge uppon the daunger that there of may ensue [that] all the kinges subjetes under the rule committed unto yow by vertue hereof to be in like arreadines when tyme shall require, and to be as obedyent to you as they ought to be to their leader and governor for the tyme. In wittnes whereof wee have signed these presentes with our owne hand and have caused our seale to be putt unto the same the 5th daye of Aprill the 30th yeere of the raigne of our said soveraigne lord Kinge Henry the eighte.

T. Norffolke.

The signature is placed in the left hand margin of fo. 25r doubtless in emulation of the original.

In the early months of 1539 England was convulsed by the expectation of invasion. The King's undated 'device' (assigned by Professor Hale to early February) outlined a blueprint for a range of coastal defences and assigned the defence of sectors of the coast to specified nobles and gentry. In this programme Norfolk was charged with the supervision of the northern counties (although it gave him control of a wider area than that outlined here).[139] The duke's commission is not known to survive. At the time it was issued, he was engaged in inspecting the castles of the Scottish border (cf. 24 above which may be of this date).

[139] *LP* xiv (i) no. 398, discussed by J. R. Hale in H. M. Colvin *et al*, *The History of the King's Works*, iv (ii) (1982), 369–70.

72 Third duke of Norfolk to the first earl of Cumberland, 28 March [   ].
Chatsw., Clifford Letter Book, fo. 26r.

To my very good lord my lord of Cumberland.

My very good lord in my harty manner I commend me unto you. And right soe advize you I have receaved your fawlcon, which I assure you is a very good hawke, for the which most hartely I thancke you. And thus hartely fare yee well. From Sheriff Hotton the 28 day of March.

yours assuredly,   T. Norffolk.

Letters of Sir Thomas Wharton to the first earl of Cumberland

The group of six letters from Sir Thomas Wharton which follow may be regarded as amongst the most interesting of the collection. Wharton's career is well-known to historians not least thanks to an essay by Dr James; but these letters illustrate a period of his life which has previously been obscure.[140]

Wharton was born $c.1495$ into a Westmorland gentry family settled at Wharton in the parish of Kirkby Stephen. He married into the Yorkshire circle of the earls of Northumberland and was one of the major beneficiaries of the sixth earl's dissipation of his estates, receiving the Cumberland estates of the earldom with the Lieutenantship of Cockermouth in fee farm in 1530 (although I have suggested elsewhere that this grant is not all it seems) as well as stewardships and manors in Yorkshire.[141] Wharton was a member of a small group of intimates around the earl but in the early 1530s he was also a rising figure in his own right. James has traced the developing contacts between Henry VIII, Cromwell and Wharton. He became a JP in 1531 and served as one of the four English commissioners in the Anglo-Scottish negotiations of 1533. In 1537 he was appointed deputy (but *de facto*) warden of the West Marches and full warden in 1544. In the early 1530s we have a picture of Wharton as a man detached from his family's traditional loyalty to the Cliffords, progressively moving out of the provincial world of the Percy household into the circle of the Crown.

What has been overlooked in previous accounts is the continuing strength of Wharton's association with the earl of Cumberland. James

---

[140] James, 'Change and Continuity in the Tudor North', *Borthwick Paper*, xxvii (1965), repr. in his *Society, Politics and Culture*, 91–147. For a brief factual account of his life, *HP 1509–1558*, iii, 597–99.

[141] Hoyle, 'The fall of the House of Percy', 189–90, 193.

made little of the fact that Wharton sat in the Reformation Parliament as member for the Clifford borough of Appleby. He was unaware that Wharton acted as Cumberland's steward and Master Forester in Mallerstang (Westmorland). In these letters we see Wharton for the first time as a personality rather than a cipher; as the earl of Northumberland's aide-de-camp, and as a rather wide-eyed observer of the London scene, retailing gossip and news, flattered that Cromwell should share his Irish correspondence with him. But we also see a deferential man, well aware of his obligations to Cumberland for whom he was happy to run errands in London and fulfil his responsibilities as an estate officer in Westmorland, and conscious of the ambiguity of his position as an officer of both Cumberland and Northumberland.

These are sides to Wharton which have remained unexposed. There is no doubt that Wharton was ambitious and in later life ruthless in furthering his ambition. Equally he had qualities which the Crown was all too eager to utilise and it must not be forgotten that he had the considerable good fortune to be in the right place at the right time. Nonetheless his position in the early 1530s can only be understood if we eschew an interpretation of northern history which sees Cumberland and Northumberland as the head of competing power blocs. It has already been suggested that relations between the two families were exceptionally cordial and cooperative. This, more than anything else, allowed Wharton to serve two masters, but in serving them he was also serving a third, the king, in a general but increasingly specific sense. As a member of their circles, Wharton was a member of the royal retinue but one removed, and it was a small step for the Crown to draw upon his services directly.

It is not clear whether the letters which follow are in Wharton's hand or that of a clerk (although the balance of evidence points to the former). Whichever, the letters are amongst the worst written of the collection. (Wharton's comments in **76** about his rude writing may perhaps be read literally.) The process of transcription is also hindered by Wharton's idiosyncratic and phonetic orthography.

73 Sir Thomas Wharton to the first earl of Cumberland, 17 September [1532].
BL, Althorp B1, fos. 37r-38v.

Ryght honourable, hyt maye pleysse your lordshyp to be advertesed that lyke to your lordshyp commandment I have to my lytle poure attendyt every thyng as I am of dewtye most boundon for the settyng forwerdes of your lordshypes tenantes and servantes to serve the kyng. And with in the offyce I have under your lordshyp hayth apoyntyd thre score suche personages and in such redines as assuredly I dow accompte shall be to your lordshyps honore. And so thowght by Sir Johne Lowther, my cosyn Sandfurthe and Thomas Falowfelde thys Sonday last apone Sandfurth moyre mustered. Also my cosyn Sandfurthe of your lordshypes tenantes under hys ruylle makyth xx^{ti} and Thomas Falowfelde of hys awne apoyntment xviij. And thus your lordshyp nowmbre is fully furnessyde. For all the resydew within howre offyces, we have gyffyne in your lordshypes nayme for ther redynes wernyng lyke to your lordshypes commandment.

Hyt may pleyss your lordshyp I dyd my selfe accordyng to my dewtye excercysse sondry days amongst thayme for the preparacion her of and in vewyng the resydew, wiche assuredly is far furthe of frayme, I have noted every man your lordshypes tenantes as hys redynes is. And now after the departure of thes, in my poure opynion thayr wolde by your lordshyp commandment suche a vew be takyn as with the sayme hyt myght appeyr with ther warrantes of your lordshyp, ther fermes with the commodytye, theyr gudes and ther redynes to serve the kyng. Ande thus by a perfyt vewe with thayr personages every thyng myght be orderyt to your lordshypes honore and thayr most surtye. Ande sore I am that I maye not accordyng to my dewtye attend this and other your lordshyps serwes as I am bowndon, most humble besuchyng your lordshyp to consydre now my serwes [fo. 37v] to my lorde frome whome I have beyne long abcent. And yff ther be any serwes ther or elles wher your lordshyp wyll commande me, I shall attende the sayme as k[n]awythe Jh[es]u who ever preserve your lordshyp with increse of honore. At my poure howsse of Wharton, the xvij day of Septembre.

Your lordshypes humble att commandment, Thomas Whartton.

Clerk's hand. Signed at the very bottom of fo. 37v. Addressed [fo. 38v] 'To the ryght honorable my lorde of Cumbrelande hys gude lordshyp'.

The earliest of Wharton's letters details the arrangements for the mustering and dispatch of troops for the Anglo-Scottish borders in 1532 (cf. 7 above) which he undertook as Cumberland's steward and master forester of Mallerstang in southern Westmorland. Of the other officers named, Lowther is discussed further in the notes to 104-6 below; Thomas Sandford, later Sir Thomas, of Askham (Westmorland) was steward of the Clifford estates in Westmorland 'from Appleby downwards' (meaning northwards) in both 1534 and 1541 and Thomas Fallowfield of Great Strickland (Westmorland) was constable of the earl's castle of Brougham.[142] 'My lord', from whom Wharton had been absent,

---

[142] Details of estate offices are taken from Chatsw., BA 8 fo. 23v (1534) and Cumbria RO, Kendal, D/Hoth box 45 (receiver's account for 1541). For Sandford see Nicolson and Burn, i, 425-6; for Fallowfield *ibid.*, 448 and *HP 1509-1558*, ii, 116-7.

is Northumberland. The 'warrants' to which Wharton refers were the indentures by which the tenants held their tenements.

74 Sir Thomas Wharton to the first earl of Cumberland, 25 November [1532].
BL, Althorp B1, fos. 39r-40v.

Plesyth hyt your honorable lordshyp to be advertysyd that the cumyng off Jake was mwche to my lordes plesur and the weneson and wyldfowlle dyd cum in marwelus good tym to my lord his lordshyp. I dyd oftyn before lowke for sum letteres or word from your lordshyp. Off the nowes occurrant in thes partes, your lordshyp may persave the sam by my lordes letteres, assuryng your lordshyp that now the dowynges off the Scotes and that att his and mwst be down agayn to tham inforceth a grete apperance off werre to insow. Thare nowmbre was att thare beyng in apon ye Mydle Merches apon Wedynsday last abowe thre thusand men wyth thre standartes dysplayd as to say Day Kars, the lord of Sesfurth wo his werdayn [warden] by inheretance, allso the lord off Bukclowthes and the lord off Farneerstes. Thankes be to God thare akte was not to the hurt off Yngland a hundreth merk in all and yett thare was run thre sewerall forrays, on before day and two other att towlff off the cloke apon the day leght. The same rode was made by the kyng off Scotes commandment for all his offeycercs was wyth hym streght before and his agayn repared to hym by all espealles. We can not attayn but that thay wyll have a greter rod. The c[...]dty off Scotland his hygh agaynst my lord, allbeyt sum thare his howre frendes. [fo. 39v] Thare purpose was to have sett fyer nere the kassell off Anwyke att this last rode but fere dyd lett tham and we er studeyng to make grete rodes as the tymes may serve us.

My lord his now a lytell mowed agayn wyth his hold deses. His lordshyp allways comfordyly to here from your lordshyp and from tym to tym your lordshypes letteres shallbe plesant to hym and as I may attayn to the knowlege I shall advertyse and serve as your lordshyp shall command me accordyng to my most bowndon dwety. The good myrth mayd by Jake and his takyng in to Scotland your lordshyp may att length persave in wryttyng, wyche was no smalle plesur to my lord as knowyth the Trenety wo preserve your lordshyp in honor. Att Werkwerth the xxv day off Nowembre.

My lord after the makyng of this letter, my lord dyd resave letteres from the kyng and now the contentes off this my letter mwst be put in execucion for my lord shall ryd by the kynges commandment two or thre rodes in the marche and Tewedall. God and Saynt George send his lordshyp good sped wyth honor. His nowbre shallbe xxv^t

hundreth men in gareson bysydes the cuntre whereoff your lordshyp makyth parte and yet hyt mwst not be knowyn to we inter Scotland yff we may kep hyt sekeret.

By your lordshypes ever bowndon att commandment, Thomas Whartton.

Holograph. Subscribed [fo. 40v], 'To the ryght honorable and my were good lord my lord off Cumbreland'. Autograph throughout.

Wharton writes from the household of the earl of Northumberland at Warkworth Castle and describes skirmishes between the English and Scots in the border war of 1532–3.[143] Wharton's opponents can be quickly identified as Andrew Kerr of Cessford, Walter Scott, lord of Buccleuch (tried for treasonable communication with England in 1535, d. 1552) and Andrew Kerr of Fernihurst (d. 1545). Jack is unidentified, but from the little we hear of him in this and the next letter, he may be a fool sent to raise Northumberland's spirits.[144] Northumberland had a history of chronic illness which is never described but referred to as his 'old disease'. For the escalation of the war mentioned in the postscript, see also the signet to Cumberland asking him to supply a further 200 troops, 9 above.

75 Sir Thomas Wharton to the first earl of Cumberland, 2 March [1533]
BL, Althorp B1, fos. 41r-42v.

Plesyth hyt your lordshyp to be advertysed that syth myn humble letteres last sent, thare his no nowes worthe advertysement from thes partes, saveyng the erlle off Mwrray hath beyn in the hede off Redsdayll and dyd cast off a forray and lay hym sellff apon the heght off the fell thre mylle from any inhabetyng. His forray hath burnt abowt twollff howses wherin was few dwelleres and thare was off Scotes takyn seven presoneres and so wyth[o]wt any tareyng he went away. Thay off Rydsdayll by my lordes commandment was in Scotland the second nyght after and thare burnt two twones and two stedes, on town dyd stand wyth in thre mylle off Gedworth where the erlle duth lye. [.....]rsday next I thynke Sir Rauffe Ellerker and I shall [meet with] two knyghtes off the kynges cowncell off Scotland. [Our m]etyng hath beyn the longer delayde bycause as hyt [y]s sayde, thay bryng wyth tham instrukcones from the kyng thare m[aste]r by the holle cowncell thare dewysed.

---

[143] For other accounts of the same events in November 1532, see letter 35 above and LP v no. 1559 (a letter of Northumberland's).

[144] Jack also appears in a letter published by Dickens, Clifford Letters, no. 34.

Allso hyt may plese your lordshyp, my lord duth not comford a lytell in the cumyng off your lordshyp and my lade in to thes partes as his lordshyp hath consaved att the beyng here off Jake and att sondre tymes syth I have by commwnykecion wyth my lord well persaved the sam and, as off dwety I dyd accowmpte my sellff bowndon, hath made sondre perswaciones wyth his lordshyp anempst the sam your cumyng, by wyche hyt may appere a grete loffe and honor that your lordshyp bereth unto hym. Thareby I assure your lordshyp for your comyng and my lades, my lord taketh more comford thar in then I can wrytt and [.....] tymes spekyth to that effekte. My powre adwyse hys [that] your lordshyp wen ye shall cum and [fo. 41v] my lade that ye bryng wyth your lordshyp a good and conwenyent nowmbre lyke to your howshold serwantes fulle and yff hyt wold plese your lordshyp to adresse your lettere as thogh they were sekeret but yett lett tham or sum on bee suche as I may show unto my lord, declareng tharein your lordshypes cumyng lyke a vj or vij dayes before your cumyng and watt your lordshyp wyll command me in the sam anempst any proweseon for your men or horses, I shall accordyngly attend to the best off my smalle powere as off were dwty I am bowndon, as knowyth Jesu wo preserve your lordshyp in honore.

Your lordshyp shall here and see mane strange [.....] att your cumyng. My comford shallbe to see your [lord]shyp here. Att the assyses att Yorke I mwst nedes be for weg[hty?] causes off myn awn. And thus I pray God my powre serwes may be allways to your lordshypes most nobyll contentacion wyche I shall ever attend as [*breaks off*].

After the makyng off this letter this Sonday the second day off Marche, the nowes dyd cum that the sam mornyng by trayn made by the [.....] Rauffe Ellerker, son and heyre to Sir Rauffe, Sir Robert Ellerker, Thomas Ellerker and Thomas Menwell kapetayn to my lord Scrowpp retenow off 1 men was all fowre taken and wyth tham the mowmbre off threscowre and abowe by hastenes and fole abowe West Nowton in makyng a chays wyth[o]ut good order truned [*sic*] to abushement and on off my lord Scropes retenow his slayn and the resedow his all in Scotland.

Your lordshypes awn bowndon att commandment, Thomas Whartton.

Holograph. A few small holes in the letter account for the gaps in the text. Subscribed [fo. 42v] 'To the ryght honorable my lorde of Cumbreland'.

The general context of the letter and the reference to Sunday 2 March place it quite firmly in 1533. The events on the borders which it describes are otherwise ill documented: there appears to be no other reference to the capture of the Ellerkers by the Scots or the earl of Moray's raids into Redesdale.[145] The surviving correspondence makes it clear that Henry was not eager to escalate the war whilst James V was in the Scottish border counties. Raids planned for early March were deferred until James left, which he did about 20–21 March.[146] The letter offers further evidence of the cordial relations which existed between Northumberland and Cumberland.

76 Sir Thomas Wharton to the first earl of Cumberland, 9 December [1533]
BL, Althorp B1, fos. 43r-44v.

My bowndon dwtye humble advertysed un to your honorable lordshype. Plesyth hyt you the sam that syth my powre letteres last sent un to your lordshyp for the nowes occurrant in thes partes, the day off mareage dyd hold betwen the dwke off Rychemond and the lade now his wyffe, the day off wyche mareage was not grete saveyng in danceyng, the quen furst danced wyth the duke and the kyng after wyth the duches his wyffe and after other as thay were dysposed and then the kyng and the quen and after my lord Clyfford and a lade and so passed wyth mwche dansyng and att nyght lykewyse. Thay dyd not lye togyther but thay [.....] off to bed awlowyng [sic]. The kyng was there all that tym. I saw hyt to the duke was gown to his other logeng and hath ever syth tym beyn sumthyng seke and kepyth his cham[b]er by mwche dansyng.

The nowes yett er nothyng plesaunt from the partes beyond the see. We shall have a grete parlayment for hyt his sade that nown shallbe abcent that aught to be here for the surte where off thos that be off the hyyeer[?] howse hath speciall letteres wereoff your lordshyp hath on. Upon Wedynes day next my lade prynces remowyth to Byshop Haytfeld and there settyth upe her howse to the wyche howse shall be broght the lade Mare. The prynces shallbe honorable removed wyth dywers nobylles as the dwke off Northfolke, the lord marques of Exceter and other and the lade Mare shallbe brought thether wyth the erlle off Oxford, the erlle off Sussex, Mr Tresorer and other. The duke [fo. 43v] of Suffalke shuld have fett the lade Mare but he hath wyncheyd his leg att the tenes that he may not ryde. The prynces doweger shall have thre thusand merke a yere and therty persones in her howse. The lord Wylliam his cum hom and the byshope off Wynchester his cumyng and yett we here nothyng but that shypes shallbe wyth artelyre repared and other proweseones [provisions] for the warre. The kyng aukyth att the fesand every day and his mere hyt hys thoght the quen bredyth chyld and she showeth her Grace so. Mr Tresorer shepp wyth tempestes sore betyn his cum hom.

And thus my lord I trobyll your lordshyp from tym to tym wyth my rude wryttyng takyng comford ever in that wyche I thynke may remembre your lordshype to command that wyche allways may lye in my powre serwes the sam as I am bowndon off dwety shallbe rede as knowyth the Trenety wo preserve your lordshype wyth mwche increce off honor. Att Mr Tresoreres the <v> ixth day of Decembre.

Your lordshypes wyth his serwes, Thomas Whartton.

Holograph, very difficult; the spelling notably erratic. A small area of water damage makes for difficulty in reading two line ends on fo. 43v. Subscribed [fo. 44v], 'To the ryght honorable my lord off Cumbreland.'

Wharton's cheerful to letter to Cumberland seems to have no greater purpose than to acquaint him with the latest court news. The king's bastard, Henry duke of Richmond, was married to a daughter of the third duke of Norfolk in early December: the dispensation was dated 28 November 1533. The household of the Princess Mary was moved to Hatfield on 13 December, and although Suffolk may well have lamed himself at tennis, he was still sent to convey Henry's demands to Katherine of Aragon on 17 December.[147] His news of the parliament was correct: the sixth session of the Reformation parliament met on 15 January 1534.

77 Sir Thomas Wharton to the first earl of Cumberland, 12 December [1534].
BL, Althorp B1, fos. 48r-49v.

Plesyth yt your lordshype to be advertysede that for the newys occurrant in thes partes, yt ys comfortable in the courtte to her off the gude redressez downe apon the borders to the gude advancement of the peax betwen bothe the reallmes. Ande for the newys in Irlande, owre men now haythe gude spede ther. Monye Iryche gentyllmen dowythe come in to the lieutenante ther with submyssion frome Garratt. Ande our Inglyshmen hade hyme in on chaysse wher the northorun men dyde verey well ande over threw dyvers of Garrottes power. Ande the chaysse dyde last sex mylles. Yt plesyde master secretore to shew me the newys ande dyde rede Brabsones letter who is treserowr off the werres ther.

When the parlament shall breke or what day, at the makyng her off yt was uncertayne. And wether yt shall desolve or proroge yt is nott certayne but proroge as ytt is sayde. Ther is grauntyde to the kynge ande on acte mayde that hys grace, hys heyrez ande successores shall have of every sperituall person after the dethe, the furst fructes of ther b[e]n[e]fyce what degre in sp[irit]ualtie so ever he be. Ande the tenth part of every sp[irit]uall manes lyeffynge yerlye for ever to be payde. Ande of the temporaltye a subcedye of xijd off the pownde of xxli in valow of gudes or landes and upwerde to be payde in two yeres at two paymentes. And the xvth afor grauntyde to be payde in the thryde yere next after and ther er monye other actes passede as your lordshyp shalbe advertysede in a breffe abstract off the sayme after the conclusion of thys parlament. Ande yff ther be any serwes that your lordshype wyll commande me, I shall her attende the sayme acordyng to my bowndon dewtye. Ande wher yt plesyde your lordeshype to dyrect your honorable letteres to me, declaryng yor plesur in the sayme upon my former suyt mayde to your lordshyp for ande consernynge the offyce I have of stewerdeshype of youre lordshypes landes, I shall eftsons with all convenient spede advertysse your lordshyp off my suyt lyke to your honourable [fo. 48v] letteres sent to me in that sayme.

The kynge kepythe hys Crystynmes at Grenwyche but no hall ther shalbe kepyde as yt is sayde. Ande the saying is that hys grace wyll over see at Apryll wher a metyng shalbe hade betwen the Frenche kynge and hyme. The Inbassetore [sic] is goyne with gret intertaynment ande a grett rewerde. Yt dyde amowntt emongst theyme all xvjth hundrethe pounde besydes horsez, geldynges and other plesures. There was the nyght befor hys departor a gret banckett at the Whyt Hall. Ande thus our lorde preserve your lordshype in honore. At London the xijth day off Decembre by your servant Mr Reydman. I have seyne your lordshypes besynes well attendyt her.

Your lordshyp att commandment to his power, Thomas Whartton.

Possibly holograph; if not a clerk's hand and signed. Subscribed [fo. 49v], 'To the ryght honorable and my verey gude lorde my lorde off Cumbrelande'.

Wharton's letter relates the news current at the court in the closing days of the seventh session of the Reformation Parliament (which was prorogued on 18 December). The statutes which Wharton thought noteworthy of mention are the act for the First Fruits and Tenths (26 Henry VIII c.3) and the subsidy (c.19). He makes no reference to the Royal Supremacy. Of the other news mentioned, the letter shown to Wharton by Master Secretary (Cromwell) came from William Brabazon, under-treasurer in Dublin. (The letter does not survive.) 'Garret's power' is a reference to the forces of Garret Og, 9th earl of Kildare, then a prisoner in the Tower but in whose name rebellion had been raised in

Ireland by his son. The ambassador who had recently left was the Admiral of France, Philip Chabot, sent by Francis I to negotiate a marriage between the Princess Mary and the duc d'Augouleme, Francis's third son. The opulence of his departure was thought worthy of remark by Chapuys.[148]

78 Sir Thomas Wharton to the first earl of Cumberland, 17 January [   ].
BL, Althorp B1, fos. 51r-52v.

Right honorable, pleasithe your lordschipe to be advertessyd that uppon Fryday at nyght the xiijth of this instant, the kyng of Scottes dyd cume to a colege callyd Glencloden a mylle frome Dumfresse and is at this present at Longs Maven cassell. Hys cumyng is werie soden and haithe bot a smalle trayn. Hys abode thei say wyll not be long bot all his procedynges ar so unsertayn that dowtfull it is to wrytte off the same. I dow practysse suche esspyall as I can to atteyn knowlege and as the inportaunce off the same schall occaseon so I schall indevour my selffe to advertesse your lordshipe. Good it is in my powre oppenyon that your lordshype maike your abode at Skeiptton cassell unto the said kynges departur frome hys marches and that the poste horses to lie as your lordshipe dyd appoyntte withe me affore your departor from Brougham and I schall not onlye advertesse your lordshipe bot be moste glade to dow any thyng I may to your honour as almyghttie God knowithe who preserve your lordschipe withe muche encresse off the same. Att the kynges highenes cassell of Carlesle the xvijth of Januar.

Your lordshypes att commandment, Thomas Whartton.

Clerk's hand, signed. Subscribed [fo. 52v], 'To the right honorable and my verey good lord the erle off Cumbreland'.

This letter stands apart from its predecessors. It is noticeably less deferential, the signing clause is less fulsome. This is probably enough to suggest a date after Wharton's appointment as *de facto* warden in 1537. There was however no Friday 13 January between 1537 (which is impossible if only because James V was in France) and 1543 (when James V was recently dead). The previous conjuction of day and date, 1531, is equally unhelpful. Nor do we know of a winter progress into the western Scottish marches by James in this period.[149] The date of the letter must therefore remain unsettled. Of the places named,

[148] R. J. Knecht, *Francis I* (1982), 234–5; *LP* v no. 1507.
[149] Cf Rae, *Scottish Frontier*, app. 6 for dates.

the college in the borders near Dumfries was Lincluden: James was then proceeding to the royal castle at Lochmaben.

Letters arranged alphabetically by correspondent

79 The Council of the Pilgrims of Grace at York to first earl of Cumberland, 22 November [1536].
Chatsw., Clifford Letter Book, fo. 14r.

The coppy of a lettre to my lord of Cumberland from the generall counsell of the commons dated at Yorke the 22th of November Anno etc and signed with their hands as followeth;

MY LORD, this is to advertize yow that the barronage and commonalty of the North is thus contented that the lord Scroope, Sir Richard Tempest, Christofer Metcalfe esq, Robert Chaloner and other[s] shall come to you to Skipton and shall promise upon his [*sic*] honour that your lordshipp shall safely come to them and so to retorne in your castle againe, so that your lordshipp will of your honour make like promise that he and his company may in like manner safely come to you and to retorne from yow in like suerty. And the said lord Scroope shall declare unto your lordshipp the cause of our assembly which is for the mayntenance of the faith of God and the right and liberty of his church militant and the destruction of heretickes and their opinions and other publicke welths in soule and body as by the said lord Scroope shall be to your lordshipp declared and the perill that will ensew to your lordshipp in the contrary done. And that your lordship by your lettre will signify to the barronage if you wilbe thus contented or [not] with hast. Thus in all your honourable affayres God be your governour. From the Counsell at Yorke.

John Scroope, Robert Constable, John Constable, James Strangways, Robert Aske cap[tain], Johannes Latymer and all other knights and squiers.

The first earl's opposition to the Pilgrimage and his success in remaining out of the Pilgrims' hands was justly applauded by contemporaries (although it contributed little of significance to the failure of the movement). This letter from the Pilgrims' council at York reveals their anxiety to secure his support. The delegation never travelled to Skipton but the letter was probably carried there by Robert Bowes whose contact with Cumberland was the subject of a royal complaint in early December.[150]

The members of the delegation named as being ready to travel all had close

[150] *LP* xi no. 1227.

connections with the earl. Scrope was the earl's son-in-law and later one of his executors.[151] Sir Richard Tempest of Bracewell and Bolling, (for whom see **117** below), was a close Clifford neighbour. Christopher Metcalfe (d. 1574), son of Sir James Metcalfe (d. 1539) of Nappa in Wensleydale, later married Elizabeth, daughter of the first earl (although not in the earl's lifetime).[152] Robert Chaloner of Stanley near Wakefield, common lawyer, was a member of the king's Council in the North from 1530 until his death in 1555. He was named as the earl's counsel retained in 1527 and 1529 and acted as an executor of Cumberland's will.[153] The messenger, Bowes, was the earl's brother-in-law through his elder brother Sir Ralph Bowes (d. 1516) who had married a daughter of the tenth lord Clifford.[154]

80 Sir Roger Bellingham to the first earl of Cumberland, Friday before Christmas [1525 x 1533].
BL, Althorp B1, fo. 45r-v.

Jh[es]u
My lord, pleysytt your lordshypp to knaw that I have raysavyd on letter on Fryday last neyxtt be for Crystynmes by Thomas Jonson your servand from mayster Sir Thomas your brother for the wyche he haythe wryttyng un to me for a perffytt and a trew rentalle off the holle extynct off alle my hole landes and to send hym yt with the berrer off hys letter. Sir at thys tym I culd not send hym yt with the berrer off hys letter for I hade no perffytt trew rentale mayd. Wherffor yff yt wylle pleyse your lordshypp to send over Christoffer Aske or som other off your cuncele betwyxt thys and the xijth day on to me, that then they shale have the perffytt and trew rentalle with alle othere thinges att shuld dow hym gud, bot I wylle never agre at he shuld partt my landes for rather or he shuld dow thatt I wald ryde yett up to London my selffe. Theyr for lett hym keypp hys promes for I shall keypp myn. And as for the rentale I shall mayk yt reydey. No mor to your lordshyp at thys tym bot Jh[es]u preserve yow to hys most plesur. At Burnesyd thys layst Fryday neyxt be for Crystynmes.

Yours assurethe servand and beydman, Sir Roger Ballengem, knyghtt.

[151] Clay, 'Clifford Family', 379. Scrope appears to have taken refuge in Skipton earlier in the rising, Hoyle, 'First earl', 83–4.
[152] The marriage probably took place c.1550 and the settlement was still a matter of contention in 1553, W. C. Metcalfe and Gilbert Metcalfe, *Records of the Family of Metcalfe formerly of Nappa in Wensleydale* (1891), 99–101.
[153] Yorkshire Archaeological Society, Leeds, DD121/29/10, 34/1; Clay, 'Clifford Family', 379.
[154] Dickens, *Clifford Letters*, 131; Hoyle, 'First earl', 72.

Holograph. Addressed [fo. 45v], 'To the ryghtt honorable and noble lord Henre heyrle off Cumbrland'.

The letter can only be dated within the broad limits of the first earl's ennoblement in 1525 and Bellingham's death in 1533. His connection with the Cliffords and his attempt to disinherit his son and granddaughters has already been described.[155] Unfortunately the context and sense of this letter is far from clear. Christopher Aske (d. 1538) was the first earl's receiver in Craven.

81 William Beckwith, Mayor of York, to the second earl of Cumberland, 14 December 1555.
BL, Althorp B1, fos. 77r-78v.

Yt may please your honorable lordship to be advertised that of an olde usage of this citie of York, the mayour of the same for the tyme beyng must make his fest of mayoraltie to his bredrne thaldremen and other the worshipfull and honest persones of the same citie on Saynt William day, at whiche fest emonges others they have ben allwayes accustomed to have redde deere wherof I beyng nowe mayour am cleerly unprovyded. And remembryng the speciall good mynd and favour that your lordship and all your noble anncestours have allwayes borne towardes this said citie emboldeneth me thus hom[b]ely to wright unto your honorable lordship besechyng the same of your accustomed goodnesse to helpe me with a pece of redde deere ageynst my sayd fest to be kept the secunde day of Januarie next. And suche poore pleasure or service as I can doo for your lordship or yours, your L[ordship] shall commande me at all tymes as knoweth allmighty God whoo preserve your good lordship in moche honor with good health long to prospare. From York the xiiijth of Decembre 1555.

Your lordships to his power, Wylliam Bekwyth mayor.

Clerk's hand. Signed. The word 'secunde' in the date of the feast added in another hand. Addressed [fo. 78v], 'To the right honorable and 1/4the3/4 my very speciall good lord the earle of Cumbreland yeve theis'. Docquetted, 'L[ett]res from the lorde maior of Yorke for a pycce of flessh ayenst Saynt W[illia]m dye'.

Beckwith may be quickly identified. A York merchant, free of the city in 1540, sheriff 1543-4 and an alderman from 1553, he served as Mayor in 1555 and 1569. He died in 1586.[156]

[155] Above 70-1.
[156] R. H. Skaife, *Catalogue of the Mayors, Bailiffs, Lord Mayors ..... of the City of York* (1895), unpublished Ms *penes* York City Archives, *sub nomine*.

The mayoral feast for which Beckwith required venision was not noticed by Professor Palliser in his survey of the civic year of Tudor York.[157] It was reasonable enough that the mayor, aldermen and other civic figures should feast in commemoration of St William (Archbishop of York, d. 1154, who was the city's patron), but the feast of his translation is normally given as the Sunday after Epiphany (12 January in 1556) and not as this letter would indicate 2 January. It would be useful to ascertain whether the local practice was really at variance with the received wisdom.

Of greater interest is the relationship between York and the Cliffords that this letter touches upon.[158] The application for venison was not, as the letter might suggest, a single request, but a custom of some standing. In 1542, while demanding troops from York, the second earl referred to his grandfather and father having supplied York with venison twice yearly, the feast on St William's day probably being one of those occasions. Significantly, Cumberland's letter on this occasion was carried to York with a gift of deer meat and 20s for wine.

The supply of deer for civic functions was taken by the Cliffords to be indicative of their relationship with the city. The family claimed, mostly without success, to be captains of the city and so entitled to command York's forces in war. In 1513 the tenth lord's claim was rejected, but his grandson's right was accepted by the city in August 1542. However, by the November of that year Cumberland was threatening to complain to the king and council if the city did not cooperate with him and in early 1544 Suffolk was writing to ask the city to honour its 'customary' commitment to Cumberland. York itself was more concerned that Clifford's exclusive claims were amongst several demands made upon it for the supply of troops for the Anglo-Scottish war.[159] It is hard to see that the Cliffords carried much weight within the city; they served as convenient suppliers of venison, which they were doubtless pleased to do to keep alive their claim over the city.

82 Sir William Bulmer to the first earl of Cumberland, [22 April 1526 x 1531].
BL, Althorp B1, fo. 35r-v.

My lord, in my most humble manner I command me unto you. Pleasyth you the same, I have resaved your letter by your servant thys paysse day wich was dyrect unto my lordes grace and other of hys counsell and with all spede that I couth I delyvered yt unto Mr Dyrector and he sentt for Mr Secretory and other of the counsell for to dysspache your sayd servant with all sped that convenyently myght be.

My lorde, your servant asked me wher that my lordes grace dyd

[157] D. M. Palliser, 'Civic Mentality and the Environment in Tudor York', *NH* xviii (1982), 81–5.
[158] For what follows see *York Civic Records*, iv, ed. A. Raine (YASRS cviii, 1945), 79–80, (printing York City Archives, E40 no. 1), 101, 103, 123.
[159] *York Civic Records*, iii, ed. A. Raine (YASRS cvi, 1942), 40–1.

dyne abroode of Saynt Georges day or noo. My lord, ye know that my lordes grace ys knyght of the Garter and ther manner your lordshyp knowys well enoughe. My lord, bothe my lord of Nothumbarland and my lord of Westmoreland hayth sent unto my lordes grace for ther excusys, and so at this tyme we doo looke for no gret men. My lord yf ye warre dysposyd to come, I thynke yt best that ye spayre at this tyme. And your lordshyp may take your eyse well enoughe for we do looke for no sych grett men. My lord your sonne faryth well and commandes hym unto your lordshyp and to my good lady, to whome I beseyche you that I may be recomandyt. From Pomfrett thys Saynt Georges evyn.

By yours at commandment, W. Bulmer.

Clerk's hand. Signed. Addressed [fo. 35v] 'To the ryght honorable and myne especyall good lord my lord of Commerland thys be d[elivere]d'.

Internal evidence suggests strongly that the correspondent is Sir William Bulmer (d. 1531). The reference to the earl of Northumberland makes it no later than April 1537. Bulmer is obviously at the centre of a household based at Pontefract Castle, the unnamed head of which was a Knight of the Garter. This was almost certainly Richmond's household in which Bulmer served as steward. The latter may thus be dated to 1526 or the years immediately following when Richmond was resident in the North.[160]

83 Sir William Butts to the first or second earl of Cumberland, [24 July, before 1545].
BL, Althorp B1, fo. 76r-v.

Ryght honourabyll and my synglar goid lord, my dutye humblye to your goid lordshyppe hadd. Lekythe it the same to take of your lozenges one every mornyng and one an ower a for souper and one at your goyng to bedd and so to contynewe to thei ar don. Of the powder to take by the space of one ower a for dyner or breckfaste the weyght of one grote with aile or beir on to it be don. Wyth the oyntment to a noynte the reynes of your backe from your gyrdylsted downe wardes and the space be twyxte your fundament and coddes every mornyng and evenyng and to bynde a lynyne cloithe up on the place a noynted and thus to do ij or iij days to gether, than to streike of your playster up on a thyne lynyne cloithe after the manner of ys paper and to applye this playster to your backe a long up on it from your gyrdelstede

---

[160] For Bulmer see *HP 1509-1558*, i, 542-3.

downe wardes ther, usyng it iiij or v days. After that, retorne to your oyntement usyng it a gen as ye dyd and than a gen to use your playster renewyd and so to reverte from the one to the other on to thei be don and with dylygent and contynuall use of theise I trust ye shall perceyve helpe. And myche the soner if your lordshyppe wyll for your helthe absteyne from all hoite spyces, salte and sweite meetes and from wynes on lesse it be a drawghte or ij in the myddes of your refectiones. From wych heite of your backe and from all mocyons that[?] may put your backe in ony heite and lyeng on the same in your sleippe, from medycynes for the stone and generally from all swych thynges as sharply provoke the uryne; from late souppyng and from drynckyng or banketyng after souper. Use in your brothes borage, letuce, endyve, vyolett levys and gowldes, prwnes, a few great resynges and sawnders and your brothes shall nat be very thycke. The herbes shall be bownde hole to gether and nat choppyd. Whan ye labur nat greatly ner ryse nat tymely, ij refectiones on the day is sufficient and in ony wyse provyde therbe vij oweres be twyxte dener and souper and ij oweres after your souper or ye go to bedd. Easyly to purge your body shuld be very profytable but I knowe nat your natur suffycyently here. This tyme of the [..]nyonley days is no assuerd tyme to purge and to attempte strong medycynes. Her to for I beseych your lordshyppe to be content with theise thynges for this tyme assertefyeng me who thei do with yow and your lordshyppe shall have my further cownsell with all dylygence as knowithe God who ever have yow in his twiclon to his pleasur. From Cambrydge ys Seint James Evyn.

Yours assuerd, William Butte.

Receyved xxs. Payed for medycynes; lozenges ijs iiijd, a playster xxd, a powder xijd, an oyntement xvjd, summa vjs iiijd and so rest in my handes xiijs viijd.

Holograph. Addressed, 'To my lorde of Comberland'.

Sir William Butts (d. 1545) was perhaps the outstanding court physician of his generation.[161] It is impossible to be certain to which earl of Cumberland the present prescription was addressed. The second earl, despite his poor health later in the 1540s, was only thirty when Butts died and it may be tentatively suggested that a letter concerning a back problem was sought by the older man, the first earl.

[161] For Butts see *DNB*. Recent writers have emphasised his protestantism and association with Anne Boleyn. See M. Dowling, 'Anne Boleyn and Reform', *J. Ecclesiastical History* 35 (1984), 30–46.

84 James Calfhill to the second earl of Cumberland, 28 March 1568. BL, Althorp B1, fos. 80r-81v.

My humble dewtie remembrid to your honour. Wheras I was bold to write unto your l[ordship] as tuching an howse, which yow do hold of the Deane and Chapitre of Powles in Cred Lane, Henry Aykinson your servant sent me in that behalf your l[ordship's] answere, to this effect, that if I did procure a lease unto your l[ordship] for lx yeres from the Deane and Chapitre, and wold be bound upon xiiij daies warning to leve at all tymes the howse unto your l[ordship's] use, and otherwise contynually reserve a lodging for your counsel and servantes when thei cum, then culd your l[ordship] be content to satesfy my desier, for which your curtesy as my part is, I thank your honor with all my hart, and for the ij later conditions I dare and wil assure them to your l[ord], but for a lease longer then your lordships own lif wil not in any wise be grauntid, for so I have recevid the determinat answer from the Deane and Chapitre. In respect wherof if it plese your goodnes to accept my former offer I will not fayle to recompens as I can the good turn recevid. If yor honour be otherwise resolvid, I am right sory for it and wil no further deale in the cawse, but give up again that title that I have to the Deane and Chapitre for so much do I honor your lordships howse that I wil not by law contend with yow. This one thing I must assure your l[ordship], that if I leve it, I shall give place to another which suith for it, which proferith a large fyne for the lease and is well able to recover the possession; which thing I speke not (God is my witnes) for myn own cause furthering but only of good will, that I wold not have your l[ordship] hinderid. If your honor wil let me be tenant to yow, yow shal have a lease for your life tyme, the howse at your commaundment when you will, your counsel and servantes entertayned alwaies and a further benefit if it lye in me. Only I besech your honor to vouch safe to send me your plesure in writing by this berer, for answer I must give to the Deane and Chapitre before the terme begyn. And thus wisshing unto your honor long life and health with increse of honor, I committ yowr l[ordship] to the Almighty. From York the xxviijth of March 1568.

Your l[ordship] to commaund assuredly, Ja[mes] Calfehill.

Holograph. Addressed [fo. 81v] 'To the right honorable and my singuler good lord the erle off Cumberland give these'.

This letter concerns a house in Creed Lane in the city of London, held of the Dean and Chapter of St Paul's by the second earl. The writer, James Calfhill, was a clerical pluralist at St Paul's. Calfhill was appointed to a canonry at

Christ Church, Oxford in 1560 and to the prebend of St Pancras at St Paul's in 1562. He was promoted to the archdeaconry of Colchester in 1565 and it is reported that he was nominated bishop of Worcester shortly before his death in 1570.[162]

Cumberland may have been acquainted with Calfhill through Christ Church. The college was endowed with rectories and tithes in Craven, formerly belonging to Bolton Priory, which the second earl farmed from the college.[163] From the letter it sounds as though Cumberland was trying to extend his lease on the house, using Calfhill as a go-between to secure terms which the Dean and Chapter would not conceed.

85 Sir Reynold Carnaby to the first earl of Cumberland, [10 October 1536].
BL, Althorp B1, fo. 54r-v.

Jh[esu]s

Pleasithe yt your right honorable lordship to be advertisid, my humble dewty unto the same lowly remembryd. On Thursday nyt last beyng the vth of this month, I was commanded by m[aste]r lord privay seal in the kynges highnes name in all hast possible to caws to be sent unto your l[ordship] the kynges most gracys lettres which I send unto the same herewith like as I have to be delyvered to my lord of Westmorland and to dyvers other nobles and gentlemen. The caws why I culd nat make so hasty spede as I thought to have done was for that the comons of Lyncolnshire beyng rebellyd was so sparclyd abode in companyes severally that I did forbere the comon way which hyndered me a days jornay. And tochyng the contentes of your l[ordes] letteres from the kynges highnes at this tyme, I make the hast I can towardes Hexham for the accomplishment of the kynges most dred commandment as far as may ly in my litle powr to do. Where yf I can do your l[ordship] any servyce accordyng to my dewty, I shall nat fale to fulfill the same as far as may ly in me. And I besich almyghty God to preserve your lordship. In great hast rydyng weryly norwardes, frome Toplif this Tewsday at v othe clok in the mornynge.

Therles of Shrosbery, Rutland and Hontyngton was at Nottyngham on Sonday nyt last with a nombe[r] of men reknyd abowt xl m^{le} or above, marchyng forward agaynst the kynges rebells. The commons of Lyncolnshire which was thought to be abowt Newarkk so that men

---

[162] J. and J. A. Venn, *Alumni Cantabrigiensis*, pt i, (4 vols, 1922–7), i, 282 and *DNB* give major references.

[163] The tithes of Long Preston, Bolton in Craven, Broughton, Carleton and Skipton were leased by Christ Church to Sir Thomas Chaloner in October 1547 for 80 years. In 1554 he assigned the remainder of the term to Cumberland for £400. Chatsw., Curry 46/8.

juges theme to mete abowt Thursday next yf the commons withdrawe theme nat som other way.

Yowr l[ordship] humbly with his pore servyce at commandment,
R. Carnaby.

Holograph. Addressed [fo. 54v], 'To the right honorable and my synguler god lord my lord therle of Combeland his good lordship.'

Carnaby's letter has already been considered in the context of the letter he carried from the King to Cumberland instructing the earl to intervene in the affairs of Hexham Priory, (15). Carnaby was the eldest son of William Carnaby of Halton, Northumberland, and gentleman of the earl of Northumberland's chamber in 1530 and 1532 (but not later). He remained a central figure in the earl's household until the earl's death. (It might be added that he was Wharton's cousin.) He went on to acquire the estates of Hexham in 1538 and was appointed keeper of Tyndale in 1539, but was replaced after he was ransomed by his charges. He died on 17 July 1543.[164]

86 Sir Henry Clifford (later first earl of Cumberland) to the prior of Mountgrace, 12 April [before 1525, possibly 1520].
BL, Althorp B1, fo. 20r-v.

Master Priour, in hertie manner I recommende me unto you and have receyved your lettre and perused the contentes therof. And shewe you that forsomych as the king is grace hath appoynted me to waite uppon his grace in his prefixed journey, it shalbe to me veray chargeablie and costlie at this tyme, fer above myne habilite to susteyn and bere in redy money, the which I wold be loth shuld be oponlie knowen bot to you. And I knowe not howe nei where to make eny shift except your good favor and kindnes. Wherfor Sir, I pray you remember your fermer promes to me and in this my grete necessite helpe me according as my trust is in you and if hereafter it lie in my power, I shall deserve your kindnes and pleasor. And for your suretie herein of repayment, if it like you to come over and bringe such counsell lerned with you as ye shall thinke good, I shall make you such suertie of my londes for the repayment of c marces yerelie to such tyme as the hole summe of dccc markes be payd as your said councell shall devise and thinke resonable. And tho Sir all the londes remembred in your lettre lie profitablie and necessarilie for you, I doubte not bot (all thinges remembred) ye shall opteyn and git as beneficiall a bargan for you hereafter as that is. And if ye helpe me not at this tyme, I knowe not eathlie what remedy. And of your pleasor I pray you sende me worde with this berer to whome I trust ye will gif credence. And thus Jh[es]u preserve you. At my loge of Carlton the xijth day of Aprill.

By yower lover, Henry Clyfford.

Clerk's hand with autograph of Henry 11th lord Clifford. Addressed [fo. 20v], 'To the right trustie and welbeloved the prior of Mountgrace be this lettre delyvered with spede'.

In his edition of *Clifford Letters,* Dickens printed five letters of the early 1520s from successive priors of the Carthusian house at Mountgrace (situated about six miles north-east of Northallerton) to the tenth lord Clifford and his son and established that the tenth lord was a major benefactor of the house.[165] This letter, from the first earl before his inheritance, is the only one extant from a Clifford to a prior. It is not clear when it was written. It cannot be later than April 1525 and the dating from the lodge at Carleton in Craven may offer slender grounds for supposing it to predate the death of the tenth lord in 1523. The reference to the king's 'prefixed journey' may point to the meeting of 1520 with Francis I at the Field of Cloth of Gold. Cumberland appears on a list of those attending, but his name was later struck through and it is far from certain that he ever saw France.[166] Hence 1520 may be adopted as a most tentative dating. There is no extant bond or indenture of mortgage between Mountgrace and Clifford.

The reliance of gentry on monastic houses for loans is often spoken of, but rarely fully described. The prior's concern that an opportunity to buy lands might be lost reflects a preoccupation characteristic of the community's correspondence with the tenth lord.

87 Draft letter from the first earl of Cumberland to unnamed gentry in Westmorland, 12 November 1536.
BL, Althorp B1, fos. 57r-57(bis)v.

xij November.

<Trusty and> welbeloved I recommend me unto you. And where the commons within Westmorland hath not oonly lately without cause made insurrection and congregate theym selfes but also done sundry displeasors to you and every of you which were in mynd to have lyvid in unite and quietnes. Know ye for truth that as now all the causes of ther insurrection ar so pondered by the kynges grace and his honourable councell, that every thyng shalbe brought to good quietnes as by the

[165] Dickens, *Clifford Letters,* 28–9, 62–74.
[166] *LP* iii (1) no. 704 at p. 241.

kynges lettres this day to me address[e]d it doth apper, wherfor I hertly requier you and every of you to let the same be openly and manifest knowen unto aswell the commons as ther capteyns.

Further lettyng you know that every thyng shalbe mercyfully <forgevin> loked upon which was committed and doon befor the appoyntement taken <with> betwyxt the duke of Norffolk and the commons and in case any displeasor or robbery be sens committid, I wold ye advertised theym which have committed the same to make prevey restitucion and that neyther the capteyns, commons ne eny of you gentilmen ther in no wise after the sight herof commit eny manner [of] displeasor to eny person or make eny assemble of the kynges subjectes lest it shall chaunce you for the same to be without the kynges pardon wherof I wold be right sory, for notwith standyng as theis thynges I doubt not but every man wilbe as he is naturally bounde true subjectes unto ther prince and too [fo. 57v] use theym selfes towardes me as ther naturall lord and ruler unto the kyng and for eny thyng past I shall for my parte for your awn welth rejoyce ther good abeyryng herafter; which thynges to gether and my severall former lettres to dyvers of you addressed <by you and every of you> pondyred, I doubt not but ye will every of you in avoydyng the damages expressed, so frome hensford good unite and quietnis and no further attemptates to be committed wherof I wold be right glad. And thus hertly God kep you and every of you. At my castell of Skipton this xijth day of November.

Unsigned draft with some emendations. No endorsements.

The letter dates from the lull in the Pilgrimage after the first Doncaster meeting. Cumberland is able to retail the king's promise to 'ponder' the causes of the movement, but it is not clear on what authority. The king's letters 'this day to me addressed' may be either one or both of those of 1 and 7 November (**18–19**), the first of which includes an instruction to make proclamations, but neither of which contain anything which might be read as offering the possibility of conciliation.

88 Unaddressed, possibly the first earl of Cumberland to William third lord Dacre. Day before Ascension day [late 1530s].
BL, Althorp B1, fos. 70r-71v.

My verey gode lord, in right hertie wise I commend me unto your gode lordship and wher as I and my brother Sir Thomas Clifford ar commanded by the kinges counsell at York to be both by our counsaillours sufficiently auctorised and instructed ther the <xvth> xixth day of this instant monyth of August, sending theder the same tyme our partie of such awarde as my lorde privey seale to his no littil payn and studie did make betwixt your lordship on the one partie and me and my said brother on the oder partie, wich awarde as yit my said gode lord privey seale mensionys not to be performyd nor observyd as the trauthe is so in dede.

My lord, for that purpos becaus my brother is not yit commyn into the cuntre and also that myn audytor who hath my bokes of accomptes in his custode is not so shortly to be found, that I can or may kepe the said day convenyentlie. I wold therfor desire your lordship to respet the matter to a convenyent tyme that my said brother be commyn into the cuntre and that I may have myne audytor and bokes wich I dowt not by the grace of God is like to be shortly. And than upon warnyng convenyently had from you, I and my said brother or counsell shall at convenyent place meyt you or your counsell and com to a rakynyng on our partie as right requireth without trubilling the kinges counsell therwith all oneles it be that in any poynt or condiscon we forton to disagre, in wich cases I shal alway for my part than abide the jugement of the said counsell and as your lordship herwith all is contented, I desire to be certified by your letter agayn. In haste and Almighty God preserve your lordship, this vigil of thassencion.

No subscription or endorsement. Possibly copy or clean draft. Waterstained with small areas of illegibility towards the bottom.

This draft or copy letter offers few immediate clues to either its date or addressee although the writer's reference to his brother Sir Thomas Clifford makes it tolerably certain that its author was the first earl. The letter may be tentatively associated with the dispute between Cumberland and William lord Dacre over Cumberland's purloining of Dacre's goods on his arrest in May 1534. The dispute between them was settled by Cromwell's arbitration of late 1534 although as late as September 1536 Dacre was complaining that Cumberland was failing to keep its terms.[167] A letter printed by Dickens and dated by him (on slender grounds) to March 1535 shows that the lord president, the Council of the North and the assize judges also considered Dacre's grievances and made their own settlement.[168] If the award referred to in this present letter is that made by Cromwell between Cumberland and Dacre, then the reference to the lord privy seal makes it no earlier than May 1537 (Cromwell being nominated to the office in July 1536). Reading the two letters together, it may be inferred that Cromwell had for some reason withdrawn his award and that Dacre had secured a hearing before the Council of the North which Cumberland

---

[167] Harrison, *Pilgrimage of Grace*, 36–7 offers the fullest account. The reference to 1536 is a letter dated 21 September (*LP* xi no. 477) addressed to Cromwell as lord privy seal; it cannot be earlier than 1536 but may be later.

[168] Dickens, *Clifford Letters*, no. 28.

wished to avoid, preferring to negotiate with Dacre. If any such negotiations took place then they failed and the dispute was settled before the northern council reinforced with the assize judges as mentioned in the letter printed by Dickens. It seems likely that the dispute dragged on after 1536 and that both this letter, and that printed by Dickens, should be assigned to dates in the later 1530s.

89 Unknown Clifford correspondent to Sir William Gascoigne, 23 October [   ].
BL, Althorp B1, fos. 74r-75v.

Cosyn Gascoign, after my ryght hertie commendations theise shalbe to advertysse yow that not withstandyng sundry offers by suche as ye wold not shuld have my landes abowt yow, I have spared the partyng therwith at your request and now at the last I have by Thomas Harryson word frome my lady your bedfelow that ye canne ne wyll medle with the same and for that your refusor shall hereafter be no cause off unkyndnes of my parte, in case ye wyll not medle therwith I desyre yaw to advertyss me by <this berour> your lettres so that hereafter it shall appere my forberyng for I muste nedes even now go throwgh therwith, trustyng ye wyll with this berar advertysse me of your full mynd and thus God kepe yow. At my castell off Skipton this xxiijth of October.

Copy, unsigned. No endorsement or subscription. fo. 75r is headed 'Copies of my l[ord's] office' but otherwise blank.

This letter gives few clues as to date or subject. It may be suggested that 'Cousin Gascoigne' was Sir William of Gawthorpe (d. 1551) (for whom see **99-100**). If this is the case, then the only land the Cliffords possessed near his estates was the manor of Bramhope to the north of Leeds, about four miles south-west of Gawthorpe. The first earl acquired this manor (formerly of St Leonard's Hospital, York) with his purchase of the estates of Bolton Priory in April 1542. The second earl sold it to one William Dyneley in late 1546.[169] The evidence is circumstantial, but it might be suggested that the letter is of 1542-6 and concerns Gascoigne's refusal of an offer to purchase Bramhope from the second earl.

---

[169] *LP* xvii no. 283 (11); xxi (2) no. 200 (50).

90 Sir Gervase Clifton to the first earl of Cumberland, [13 October 1536].
BL, Althorp B1, fos. 55r-56v.

Jh[es]us

Ryght honerabull, my speciall and singuler good lord, in the hertyst maner I can I hertely comend me to yow, certefyyng your lordshyp that on Sent Wilfryde day [12 October] my lord stuard [and] my lord of Rotland sent a harod of hermys to the rebellious and thay intercenye hym hely and gave hym a hereward and hasse submyttyd them to the kyng hyf so that he wil grant them all a generall pardon <bot> or ellis no pardon at all. And so <the kyng> the harod hys gon to the kyng ous post with the hanswer of the rebellious and unto he cum a gen I can a certan yow no ferther save at thay wold have gevyn over with owt howe father trobull bot for my lord of Sothefolke. He gave them consell by hys letters not to departe unto thay hade ther pardon. And the rebellious by hys consell hasse sent ther letters to the kyng for ther pardon and thay say thay wil have ther pardon generall or ellys none at all ows knowys God [w]ho ever have yow in hys blesyd kepyng. From Notyngam the moro after Sent Wilfryde day.

By yours at comandment, Gervis Clyfton.

Clerk's hand, signed. Addressed [fo. 56v], 'To the ryght honorabull herle of Cumberland be thes delyveryd dd'.

Gervase Clifton was the first earl's nephew through his sister, Anne, who married Robert Clifton of Clifton and Hodsock in Nottingham in about 1513. Clifton was born in March 1516 and was an infant of 17 months on the occasion of his father's death. In 1530 he married Mary, the daughter of Sir John Neville of Chevet (who wrote in exasperated terms to Cumberland about his son in law, **112** below) and died in 1588.[170]

This letter is written from Shrewsbury's ('my lord steward's') camp at Nottingham retailing gossip about developments in the last days of the Lincolnshire rising of 1536. His information appears to be broadly correct except for his comment that Suffolk had advised the rebels not to depart from Lincoln until they had a pardon from the king. That the Lincolnshire gentry wanted a pardon very much indeed is apparent from other sources, but Suffolk appears to have regarded it as a priority to disperse the rebels. Thomas Moigne reported that the rank and file of the rebels disbanded with the promise that they would reconvene should a pardon not be granted.[171]

[170] For his life, see *HP 1509–1558*, i, 660–1.
[171] Hoyle, 'Thomas Masters' Narrative', 59–60.

91 Sir Humphrey Coningsby to the 10th lord Clifford, 9 September [1514 x 1522].
BL, Althorp B1, fos. 17r-18v.

Right honorable and my right syngler good lorde, with due reverens and with right humble and most hertly recommendacion unto your good lordship. And most herty thankys for your good lordship shewed to me and my poer fryndes at all tymes and specyally for your good lordship and laufull favour lately shewed unto my poer wif and me your dayly oratours yn our rightfull mater betwene us and the lorde Mountegle wheryn and yn all our oder laufull and rightfull causes we besech you to contynewe our good lorde accordyng to indifferent justice, for as yet we can not atteyne eny remedie for not withstondyng your indifferent demeanour theryn, your depute Sir John Louther and Ric' Beanlewe toke full parte ayenst us contrarie to all right and good consciens. And they with oder of there affynyte contrarye to the lawe and yn lett of true justice made all the labour that coude be to stoppe the jure that they shuld not appere yn so mych that dyvers of the jure kept them absent and appered not. And when the jurours that appered shuld have ben sworne to have tryed the trough of the mater, the seid Sir John openly yn the courte contrarie to his dutye to the kyng and to your good lordship gaf open evydences contrary to all trought to the grete hurt and prejudice of the kyng and your lordship to have caused dyvers of the seid jurours to be calenged for to delay the seid mater as it is openly knowen to the grete marvell of many honourable persons that were there present. And by such unlaufull meanes the tryall of the seid mater is differred for this tyme to our grete hyndrans.

And where before this tyme we sued assise ayenst the seid lorde at the last sessyons save one at Appulby and made specyall instans and desire to the seid Sir John to have retorned an indifferent panell, the same Sir John of his parcyalite and for corrupcion of good as it semeth contrary to all trough, retorned such a parcyall panell as he and many oder discrete persons doth knowe mygth not passe yn the mater for v of them were of those that wrongfully and untruely indyted us of forcible entre and the obstans of the residue of the panell be so neyr of kyn and alie to my wif as all the contrey knoweth that they can not passe theryn. And so by the untrue demeanour of the seid Sir John, we were delayd yn the same assise and yet be; which I did at that tyme playnly shewe unto the seid Sir John his demeanour and also shewed hym that if it were not for your sake, whome I will never with Goddes grace offend, I wold have sued for remedie which I coude not doo but if I had made your lordship parte to my compleynt. And theruppon the seid Sir John come home to my wyfes poer hous at Wymmderwath and there instantly labored and desired me to kepe it secrete and promysed on his feith to me before my wif and oder that he wold never after that doo eny thyng to be lett or hurte of our mater, but wold help and avaunce it yn all that he coude <do> or myght doo accordyng to right and consciens. And at my wifes desire I at that tyme lett all thynges passe. And this promyse not withstondyng, he hath nowe doon the contrarie.

And beside all this the seid Sir John, when he was your depute uppon vj yeres past and Launcelett Salkeld undersherif, he caused xxij writtes of recordare which was sued by the lorde Mountegle yn the names of the tenantes of Hutton Ruff uppon a distres that we had taken to be by his parcyalyte unbeceled and kept out and never retourned, wheruppon shuld have insued grete penalties and oder daungers if it had ben persued which I wolde yn no wise doo by cause it coude not be doon but if your lordship had ben made partie to the sute which I wold not ne will doo.

And howe be it that this mater hath ben long yn sute and put us to grete besynes, costes and charges. And ye your self be and ever have ben good and indifferent lorde to us yn this mater. We shall never have remedie but this contynewe yn trouble contrary to all right and good consciens. And so doo and shall doo many moo then we as it is openly knowen for lak of justice, but if your good lordship by advyse of your counsell provyde remedie which I doute not when ye knowe all, ye will so doo, yn such wise as shall be to your honour and plesur to God and discharge to your consciens. Besechyng your lordship that our fryndes yn this contrey may with your favour repare to your lordship for our mater as the cause and tyme shall require. And that it wold please you to contynewe and be good lorde unto us theryn accordyng to right and indifferent justice. And we and our fryndes shalbe ever glad to doo you servyce with the best of our powers with Goddes grace who ever preserve you to his plesur yn honour and prosperous lyf accordyng to your hertes desire. At Kyllyngton the ixth day of September.

Your own assured to best of his litill power, Humfrey Conyngesby J.

One sheet, the address on fo. 17r, the text on the face divided between fos. 17v and 18r. Written in a clerk's hand. Signed. Addressed [fo. 17r] 'To the right honourable and my right syngler good lorde my lorde Clyfforde and of Westmerl[and]'.

The correspondent is the lawyer and justice Sir Humphrey Coningsby, Serjeant 1495, King's Serjeant 1500, Justice at Lancaster 1504-9, Chief Justice there

1509–31 and Justice in King's Bench, 1509–33. He died in 1533.[172] He was thrice married, his last wife being Anne, widow of James Pickering esq. of Killington, Westmorland. She was heiress to the estates of the Moresby family of Asby Winderwath in Asby parish, Westmorland, where she had the house referred to in the letter. The Moresby inheritance also included the manor of Hutton Roof (in Kirkby Lonsdale), the title to which on the evidence of this letter appears to have been challenged by lord Monteagle of Hornby (Lancs.). Coningsby's letter was written from his wife's house at Killington and concerns the defence of her interests in Westmorland. The nature of the dispute is obscure, but an indictment before the Westmorland JPs (and transmitted into King's Bench) of nine men from Hornby, who, with others, disseised Coningsby of his manor and capital messuage of Hutton Roof in October 1512, must bear upon it.[173]

The letter describes at length Sir John Lowther's manipulation of justice in Westmorland (as Clifford's deputy in the shrievalty) in favour of Monteagle and Coningsby's inability to do anything about it.[174] The letter must fall between the creation of the first lord Monteagle in May 1514 (d. 1523) and Anne Coningsby's death also in 1523; it can therefore be no earlier than September 1514 and no later than September 1522. Consequently it may be deduced that it is addressed to the tenth lord Clifford.

92 Christopher Crackenthorpe to the first earl of Cumberland, 7 May [   ].
BL, Althorp B1 fos. 64r-65v.

Most honoraybyll lordshep, advertyssyng yow that after I come from yow to London I was ther vij days after wych tyme [in] the matter in contencion betwyxt Sir Thomas Wharton and me, a grement of metyng was movyd by on M[aste]r Doctor Bellowes wych is gretly twoart my lord privy sell. And so browght us to gether in Stepnay chyrch and then Mr Wharton laid thes artykylles a ganst me; fyrst how good he was in the conclusion of a marag betwyn his cossyng Sandson and me. Item how he put me to the kynges servyce by his wrytyng and instrucion. Item how onkyndly we that longyth to yow was to Gylbert Wharton, his kyn and fre[n]des and that he culd gyt no replevi[n]e nor justes in the cuntry. Item how crowally I delyveryd his servantes wrytynges for Ric' Lame that arranat trator whom ye soltyd sore. And when I had beyn with hym xiiij daies in Scotland and I wold not mak

[172] E. W. Ives, *The Common Lawyers of Pre-Reformation England* (1983), 457–8; J. H. Baker, *The Order of Serjeants at Law* (Selden Soc. Supp. Ser., v, 1984); Somerville, *Duchy of Lancaster*, i, 470, 473.

[173] Nicolson and Burn, i, 249, 509. For Coningsby's interest in the Pickering estates, see PRO, E40/6485. KB9/1063 mm. 16–7.

[174] For Lowther see the notes to **103–5** below.

hym privy to them. Item how the abbot of Holme shuyd hym I occopyed the farmald of Hayll a ganst his wyll and wol gyff hym no gryssom, nor I wold not tak it. Item how he devyssyd the said abbot for to send me word to take it or elles to be dysschargyt off it. And what shuld he doo bot take it when I wold not tak it and so as he says hays done for fowrescore yere and xix. Item how I occopied the said farmyng a ganst his wyll. I[tem] how my lord Clefford wore me as his servand and that I wore his leveray contrayry my othe to the kyng. Item that I shuld say what was he cum of bot oder was as good as he. And that I trystyyd too se hym as lowe as <hys h..> he was hye. And soe I had slanderyd hym a fore the kynges concell. Al this artykylles he laid a ganst me. And soo no forther order or greme[n]t culd we goo to at that tym.

And thene immedyatly I went to my lord of Northfolke who laid at Kennengayll in Northfolke. And with hym I was very well acceptyd in al my byssynes and caussyd me to tarry with hym from Palm Sonday tyll now that he come to London wych was on Sanct Elyng day. And all that space I was in hys howsse very mych maid off and wonderus well intretyd. And not dowttyng by hys good helpe I tryst too procede. Alsso on Setterday last a fore the dait of this I met with Mr Wharton and dyd my dewty to hym and he said he had no god denynges unto me. And thus hettfully and rygorusly he handylles me with owt any causse, bot that is long off hym selff. Alsso as it is said he hays gottyng the ruyll off all the Grames from Sir Wyll[iam] Musgrave. And thus most hertyest I besyche Jh[es]u have yor honoraybyll lordshepe in hys tuyssyon. Wryttyng at London the vijth day of May.

Yours ever, Cristoper Crakanthorppe.

Holograph. One sheet, the text written over fos. 64v-65r. Addressed [fo. 64r] 'To the ryght honoraybyll and my synguler good lord my lord of Cumbreland delyver this'.

Crackenthorpe's letter gives an unique insight into tensions amongst the Westmorland gentry in the aftermath of the promotion of Sir Thomas Wharton to the deputy wardenship of the West Marches in 1537.

Crackenthorpe was head of a family of gentry clients of the Cliffords settled at Newbiggin, three miles north-west of Appleby. Crackenthorpe does not appear as a Clifford officer in the 1534 or 1541 Westmorland accounts probably (as this letter suggests) because he was at that time in the service of Henry lord Clifford. In 1549 he was one of the members of the second earl's household who were attacked by Wharton's tenants while passing through Nateby to hunt in Mallerstang Forest.[175] He was amongst the feed gentry appointed to assist

[175] Nicolson and Burn, i, 368–9; PRO, STAC3/6/46.

Wharton in 1537 and this may explain the reference in the letter to him wearing lord Clifford's livery contrary to his oath to the King.[176]

The letter can be assigned to the late 1530s. The receipient of the letter has to be the first earl given that his son (Henry lord Clifford) is mentioned. The letter is thus no later than May 1541. If the Lord Privy Seal at whose request Bellows tried to arbitrate between Wharton and Crackenthorpe can be identified as Cromwell, then the letter must be dated 1537–40. There are two grounds for believing that this identification is so; the reference to Stepney (where Cromwell had a house) and the fact that the arbiter, Dr Bellows, was a close associate of Cromwell's.[177] In fact 1537 is an impossible date as Norfolk was engaged in the administration of the North throughout the spring.

Beyond this it is difficult to proceed. The abbey of Holm Cultram was surrendered on 6 March 1538 but it is not clear from the context whether the house was still in existence or not. The other dating evidence concerns the report that Sir William Musgrave was to be deprived of his keepership of the border Grahams: I have not been able to trace the grant of the office to Wharton.

The grievances Wharton harboured are deeply obscure. The standard authorities make no mention of a marriage between Crackenthorpe and his cousin Sandson (presumably Sandford) but give him as marrying a daughter of [Thomas] Blenkinsop of Helbeck.[178] Gilbert Wharton was of Kirkby Thore, the next village to Newbiggin, and of a younger branch of the Wharton Whartons. I am unable to gloss the reference to the traitor Richard Lame. The farm at Hale was a grange of Holm Cultram's situated between Newbiggin and Kirkby Thore. I have been unable to trace a lease of the grange to Wharton. The ministers' account for 1539 records a payment of £4 3s 4d in rent for the premises from Crackenthorpe who took the opportunity to purchase the grange and other lands in Westmorland in 1543.[179]

93 Thomas Cromwell to the first earl of Cumberland, 14 October [1536].
Chatws., Clifford Letter Book, fo. 31r.

A lettre from my lord privy seale to the earle of Cumberland.

After my right harty commendations unto your good lordshipp, these shall be to advertize the same that I have receyved your lettre of the 9th day of October and have declared your good advertizementes

---

[176] *LP* xii (2) nos. 249 (6); 250 (i, ii).
[177] Dr Bellows can be identified as Dr Anthony Bellasis, DCL, called by Robertson Cromwell's patronage secretary. He was in Cromwell's service by late 1536. M. L. Robertson, 'Thomas Cromwell's Servants: The Ministerial Household in early Tudor Government and Society' (UCLA Ph.D thesis, 1975), 181–4, 446.
[178] Nicolson and Burn, i, 368.
[179] PRO, SC6/Henry VIII/7348 m. 24d; *LP* xviii (2) no. 449 (17).

therein to the kinges majestie, whoe for your towardnes and good endeavours in the same, his highnes giveth you condigne thancks for the same, like as by his lettres sent unto you at this tyme it doth amongst other thinges more plainly appeare. And touching the annswere of the Abbott of Furneys, I have seene your coppy and mervaile not a little that he hath made no better annswere in that behalfe. Wherefore I have eftsoones written to him and his convent at this tyme by your servant [the] bearer hereof, trusting he will make better annswere thereunto, not doubting but he will satisfye myne expectation therein accordingly, wherein I shall doe all that may be for your satisfaction therein, as I will sembleably doe in any other thing that in my power shall ly. And thus the blessed Trinity preserve you. From Wyndesor the 14 day of October.

Cromwell's letter is the partner to the king's letter of the same date (**16**) both replying to lost letters of 9 October 1536. Cromwell's dissatisfaction with the abbot of Furness can be explained as a reference to the earl's long running attempt to obtain a lease from Furness of their manor of Winterburn in Craven. Cumberland was in fact in possession of a forged lease of the manor, but at this moment was still attempting to cajole the abbot into making him a genuine lease. In his endeavour he had the backing (as this letter shows) of Cromwell. After the fall of the house he had the forgery registered in Augmentations and following Cromwell's death went so far as to claim that the lease was obtained through Cromwell's good offices. The litigation which arose from the lease extended into the 1550s.[180]

94 Christopher Dacre to the first earl of Cumberland, 2 January [1526 or 1535].
BL, Althorp B1, fos. 22r-23v.

My lord in humbull maner I command to yowr lordcheppe. Pleaseth yowr lordcheppe I resowytt yowr wryttyng yesterdaye delyvered to me be yowr servand Thomas Sottell wheyr in yowr sayd lordcheppe wylleth and desyreth me to send to yow the bowkkes of acomppte of the lordscheppe of Peynreth Qwene Hames with the members for ij or iij yeres last past. My lord, of vere trewyth and fydelyte, I never dyd intermell with one maner of the bowkkes of a comppttes of the sayd lordcheppes nor were noyn of the sayd bowkkes of acompptes come to my custodye. In contenement[?] after the resayet of yowr sayd wryttyng, I send to my lord Dacre awdetor for the sayd bowkkes at yowr lordcheppe mygth haffe theym acordyng to yowr sayd wryttyng. The answeyr of the sayd awdetor I send yowr lordcheppe heyr in

---

[180] For the full story, Hoyle, 'Land and Landed Relations', 263-72.

cloysset, besechyng yowr lordcheppe to take no dyspleasor nor thynke no delaye in me for I wyll be glayd to acompleysse yowr lordcheppe desyer in that or ane other thyng at lyes in me to do as owr lord knawes who preserve yowr gowd lordcheppe to yowr herthes most comforth. At Cerlyell the ij daye of Januarij.

Yours at my lytell power, Crystofer Dacre.

Holograph. Addressed [fo. 23v] 'To my synguler gowd lord of Comberland hys gowd lordcheppe'.

Sir Christopher Dacre was the younger brother of Thomas, second lord Dacre (d. 1525) and a prominent figure in the administration of the borders in the 1520s and 1530s.[181] The Queen's Hames formed a part of the Honour of Penrith in Cumberland, the stewardship of which was normally held by the warden of the West Marches as an appendage to his office. In 1525 and 1534 it therefore passed to the first earl of Cumberland who we see here trying to establish his rights and responsibilities in the area.

95 William third lord Dacre to the second earl of Cumberland, 11 February [?1559].
BL, Althorp B1, fos. 79r-v.

My syngler good lord in my most hartye maner I commend me unto your good lordship. And wher as one Mastres Rokeclif is content to shew her favour by the way of matrymonye unto my servant this berer (as I am informed) wherin she wold be glad that it may stond with your lordships pleasour. And so I woll pray your lordship at my request to be good lord unto her in all her besenes. Her frendes takes great displeasour with her therfore. His is one of myne auditors and shall take the rekenynges of the one half of my landes and hathe my wagis, therfore with other profettes wherby he <shall> may be able to live to do me servece for my honour and his profett.

My lord, I beseke you to be good father unto my nevye your son and also to be as his [.....] mother for it hath pleased God (at this tyme) to call her unto his mercy whose sowle God pardon. As for newes upon the west borders, [there] is none worthie thadvertysement. Thus hartely fare ye well, att Langley the xj day of February.

Your awne assuredly at prayer, William Dacre

---

[181] For his life see *HP 1509–1558*, ii, 1–2.

Clerk's hand, signed. Addressed [fo. 79v] 'To my synguler good lord my lord Cumberland his good lordship'.

The present letter, written by William lord Dacre (d. 1563) is one of several soliciting favours for servants (see also **96** and **113**) or thanking Cumberland for kindnesses already granted (**115**). The reconciliation of the Dacres with the Cliffords was accomplished through the mediation of the earl of Shrewsbury and sealed by the marriage of the second earl of Cumberland and Anne Dacre in 1552–3. In the letter Dacre asks after his grandson (later third earl of Cumberland), born on 8 August 1558 and reports the death of his wife, Elizabeth (née Talbot). I cannot trace a reliable date for her death. He makes no reference to his second Clifford grandson, Francis, later fourth earl, born 30 October 1559. The letter may certainly be dated within the four years after 1558 and on the more insecure grounds that only one grandson is mentioned, possibly to 1559.

96 Sir Thomas Fairfax to the (?third) earl of Cumberland, 3 January [?1579 x 1588].
BL, Althorp B1, fo. 83r-v.

Right honourable and my moste singuler gud lorde, my duetie remembred. Pleas yt your gud lordeshipe to be advertised that I have wrytten a lettre unto the right worshipfull Sir Gerves Clyfton knyght by my servantte this berer in the behalf of my said servantte consernyng a fermeholde in the rule of the said Sir Gerves within the lordeshipe of Haitefelde called Gaitehall nowe beyng in thoccupacion of one Jane Hurste wedowe who, as I am enformed, ys mynded to take to hir husbounde this berer. And by the same I have instansed and desired the said Sir Gerves Clyfton to be so gud master unto the said Jane and this berer as to lette them have, continewe and occupie under hym the said fermeholde of Gaite Hall doyng therfore theire dueties and services unto the said Master Clyfton and behavyng them truelie anenste the kynges game there lyke as other fermers therof heretofore have done. Wherfore I shall moste humble desire your gud lordeshipe at this my power instaunce and desire to be so gud lorde unto my said servantte this berer, as that by your lordeshipe ys gud helpe and fortheraunce my said servantte may the rather opteyne and have the said fermeholde at the said Master Clyfton ys handes as I shalbe glad to owe unto your gud lordeshipe acordyng to my duetie, my power service at all tymes. Wrytten this iijde day of Januarie.

Humbly youres with my service acordyng to to my dowtie,
Thomas Fairfax K.

Clerk's hand, signed. Addressed [fo. 83v] 'To the right honourable and my moste singler gud lorde the erle of Cumberlande'.

This letter is probably the latest in the collection. It might be suggested that the author of the letter is Sir Thomas Fairfax of Denton, b. 1521, knighted 1579 and died 1600 rather than his son (knighted 1594) or the earlier Sir Thomas of Gilling, knighted 1513, d. 1520.[182] The steward of Hatfield whose goodwill was sought was Sir Gervase Clifton (for whom see **90** above) who died in 1588, so the letter may be located in the years between Fairfax's knighthood and Clifton's death, 1579 x 1588. The recipient of the letter must therefore be the third earl of Cumberland. The letter could almost certainly be dated more closely by someone familiar with the records of the manor of Hatfield.[183]

As in the previous letter we see a correspondent going to some lengths to commend a servant's needs, in this case using the third earl of Cumberland to address Clifton. The tenants of the manor of Hatfield were copyholders and the letter casts light on the capacity of the manorial steward to influence the possession of tenements.

97 Malcom lord Fleming to the first earl of Cumberland, 21 August [?1534].
BL, Althorp B1, fo. 47r-v.

My lord, in the most hartly manner I commend me to yowr lordschip dwsir and yowr lordschip gwd acqwentans and ar be ony theng to hyr parteys that ma do yowr lordschep plesior I wel be glayd to do it oder awlkys or groundis or ony wder theng that yowr lordschip wel lat me knaw ma do yowr lordschep ony plesior efter my power that I ma do lefwlle and yowr lordschep wel be als homly with me hays I wel be glayd to be with yowr lordschep ane gwd acqwentans over ye yer alkys and growndes or ony wder theng that ma do yowr lordschip ony plesior. Hobeit that the berar be ane sobyr man to beyr maysaigis. I trast he well brein me yowr lordschip wrettyn. Wirtyn at Comyrurld the xxj day of Algwst with nocht illis now bot God haif yowr lordschip in ys kepyn hays I wald be kepyt be yowris yat my utter power[?].

Mawccowm lord Flemyng.

Text, signature and subscription written on one face of the paper only.

---

[182] For Sir Thomas of Denton and his son, see *HP 1558–1603*, ii, 99–101.
[183] Leeds City Archives DB 205.

Sealed. Addressed 'To ane nobyll and worschipfwll lord, my lord ye erll of Comyrland and lord Cleffwrd in England ys be dwliwrit'.

This pleasant letter of introduction comes from the pen of Malcom, third lord Fleming, chamberlain and favourite of James V, killed at Pinkie in September 1547.[184] Fleming is known to have been active on the borders in 1535–7 and served as sheriff of Peebles, 1530–1543. The tone of the present letter and its date in August suggest that it might have served as an introduction to Cumberland when he reentered the office of warden in July 1534.[185]

98 Dr Edward Fox to first earl of Cumberland, 4 May [1533]. Chatsw., Clifford Letter Book, fos. 28v-29r.

A coppy of a lettre from Doctor Fox to Henry first earle of Cumberland.

My lord in my most harty manner I commend me unto your lordshipp and have receaved sundry your lettres and was now utterly determined to have sent unto you by this post such news as be here, which in effect be onely that my lord of Norffolke, and the Controller, my lord of Rochfort and divers others shall be sent now within these twentye dayes into Fraunce, there to meete with the French kinge, and to accompany him unto Nice in Provence where the Pope shall meete with the French king. Albeyt forasmuch as many things may fortune with in twenty dayes and this their voyage is not yet very certeyne I cannot write any thing of certeyntye concerning that matter. And this day arryved here a nuncio from the Pope for to entreat with the kings highnes for a generall councell to be holden in Italye. And this day wee have receaved alsoe lettres from our ambassadors at Rome signifying that the Pope understanding that the kinge is marryed is marvelously discontented therewith, and what he will doe noe man cann tell, and we be utterly determined to sett nought by all that he cann doe, wherein I assure yow my lord, all his nobles be of harty courage and unitye, and soe must you be when it shall come to your part.

To shew you the manner concerning the peace now with the Scottes, it is superfluous, for you be sufficyently instructed therein by the king's

[184] Rae, *Scottish Frontier*, 235, 244: *Scots Peerage*, viii, 537–42.
[185] Cumberland received the grant of the wardenship and the stewardship of Penrith on 24 August and the governorship of Carlisle on 3 September, but Hussey, Lisle's agent, knew of his appointment by 29 July and Cumberland had the lease of the honour of Penrith on 31 July. *LP* vii nos. 1217 (7–9), 1014, 1018.

lettres, which being translated out of French into evill English, yet yee shall well perceave the effect thereof if ye shall call Nicaseus unto you. I thincke ye shall not be sent for upp to the coronation for the king liketh soe well your doeings there that he will not call you from thence. And I assure you my lord, there is noe man that cann or dare hinder you in any thing to the king. And therefore courage your selfe, and thanck God and love the kinge as you doe, for in my opinyon there are few noble men in this realme which be neerer in the kings hart then you be, which I pray God long to contynue with your health and well to doe. This bearer desyred me to [fo. 29r] give you thancks for the goodnes you shewed unto him at his last being with you. At Greenwich in hast for because I must all this night be occupied in annswering our ambassadors lettres at Rome, the 4th day of May.

Edward Fox, bishop of Hereford 1535-8, has long been known as a prime mover in the divorce and a leading figure in Henry's European diplomacy of the early 1530s.[186] In this, the covering letter to the copies of the King's letters to the French ambassador and the commissioners at Newcastle, 11 and 12 above, Fox reviews the diplomatic efforts of the weeks between the announcement of the Boleyn marriage and the news of his excommunication by Clement VII on 11 July. Norfolk, Paulet (the controller) and Rochfort did indeed travel to Nice where Clement met with Francis I in October. The various letters mentioned appear not to survive.[187]

99 Sir William Gascoigne to the first earl of Cumberland, 27 April [1526 x 1533].
BL, Althorp B1, fo. 46r-v.

Right honourabyll and my very good lord my duty to you remembred in my right homble wise I recomend me unto your good lordship even so thankyng your lordship of your goodnes to me shewyd from tyme to tyme. Please yt you to be advertysed that acordyng to my promise I sent my servaunt in to the lordship of Hatfeld for the takyng of suche fesauntes as he ther might come to and ther he e[n]deverid hym self dyligently for the space of viij or ix dayes and cowde not get one but only one fesaunt cock which Mr Hastynges had. Ther had ben takers ther befor and hade taken those that ther were. And after the comyng home of my seid servaunt I sent hym into a nother place of my frendes wher he hathe taken but only ij cockes wyche I here by thes berer do send your good lordship, beyng very sory that I cowde wyn to no more.

[186] For Fox see DNB.
[187] Scarisbrick, *Henry VIII*, 313-320.

Please yt your lordship to understond furder that I sent thes berer my servaunt to the Abbott of Roche to know hys mynd for the fermoll of Marre acordyng to your lovyng mocion made at your last beyng at Donkaster to his brethern ther. And he made answer to my seid servaunt that he wold ther in make no promise ne graunt tyll your plesure therin wer knowen, wyche answer was but a color and delay as I take yt, for your plesure ther in ys well knowen unto hym bothe by your letters and other wise. Wheruppon I shewed the seid Abbot at your request and uppon trust he wold be good to me in thes fermoll, I had movyd and instantid my servaunt Levet for a sessall and stoppel to be made in his accon upon the statut which he hathe comencyd ayense hym and he answeryd he carid not for that; he wold abyd the dawnger of the kynges lawes ther in and this was the Abbot answer to thes berer my servaunt which shall more pleynly informe your lordship therof. My lord, wher as he deferrythe thes mater to your plesure, please yt your good lordship to wryt unto the seyd abbot your full mynd and plesure in the seyd fermoll in your lovyng manner. I ware moche bound to your lordship to thentent then uppon that your plesure knowen I may resort to him for a determynat answer therin, so that uppon your plesure to hym knowen, I shall know wherto I shall trust. And thus I rest at your comandment from tyme to tyme as knowythe Cryst who ever preserve your good lordship in your right noble estat long to indure, thes xxvijth day of Aprile.

At your comandment to the best of my litle power,
William Gascoygyne K.

Clerk's hand, signed. The signature is that of an elderly and infirm man. Addressed [fo. 46v], 'To the right honourabill and my singuler good lord my lord of Comberlondes this be delyvered at Skipton Castell'.

The author of this letter, Sir William Gascoigne of Gawthorpe in Harewood parish (West Riding), must be distinguished from his better known namesake, Sir William Gascoigne of Cardington, Bedfordshire, Treasurer of Wolsey's household. Sir William of Gawthorpe was born c.1465, inherited in 1486 and held estates at Gawthorpe and elsewhere in the East and West Ridings. He was probably the wealthiest West Riding gentleman of his generation, having a subsidy assessment of £533 in 1546 and a rental of £547 earlier in the reign. He died in 1551 having made his will in 1545.[188] The house at Gawthorpe survived until 1770–3 when it was demolished during the landscaping of Harewood Park.

---

[188] Smith, *Land and Politics*, 134, 145–7, 290. G. D. Lumb, *Testamenta Leodiensia, 1539–1553*, (Proc. Thoresby Soc., xix, 1913), 307 prints his will (which is also abstracted in *Test. Ebor.* vi, 234–5).

The letter is addressed to the earl of Cumberland and so cannot be earlier in date than April 1526. If the Mr Hastings mentioned is Sir Brian Hastings of Hatfield (d. 1537), then the letter predates his grant of a knighthood in May 1533. At the broadest the letter must be assigned to the decade or so after 1526.

Gascoigne looked to Cumberland to exercise his influence in securing for him a grant of Roche abbey's grange at Marr, north of Conisborough. The Cliffords were patrons of the house and clearly expected to be of some influence in the disposition of its lands.[189] It appears that Gascoigne was finally left empty-handed, the ministers' account showing that the grange was leased in reversion to one George Handley in August 1533 (which perhaps supplies a further *terminus ad quem* for the letter).[190]

100 Sir William Gascoigne to the first or second earls of Cumberland, 1 March [   ].
BL, Althorp B1, fo. 86r-v.

Right honourable and my synguler good lord, my dutye remembred unto your good lordship. Pleas it you that wher as ye send on John Pudsey unto me for and concernyng one award mayd betwext the sayd John Pudsey and one Thomas Syngylton and Elizabeth his wif, late wif of Henry Pudsey, my lord, the truthe ys that I mayd the seyd award and ther was record Thomas Mershall and William Arthyngton preyst whiche dyd wryt the seid award and the obligacion for the performance of the award and ther was at that same tyme on dede in tayll shewed under seall, the whiche the seyd Wylliam Arthyngton dyd copy word by word, the whiche copy I send unto your lordship by this brynger and also it is wrytten under a notory signe whiche your lordship may se lykwise. And for the more perfyt knowleg in the seyd dede in tayll, I dyd wrytt my letter unto the seyd Wylliam Arthyngton to certefy me if that he dyd se the seyd dede in tayll under seall; whiche letter his answer I likwise send unto yor lordship for to certefy you of the truthe and thus Jh[es]u have your lordship in his kepyng long in helthe and to thencrese of honour. From Gawkthorpe this fyrst day of Marche.

By your kynsman and at your comandement, Wylliam Gascoygne K.

Clerk's hand, signed. Addressed [fo. 86v], 'To the right honourable and his singuler good lord the erle of Cumberland this be dylyv[er]yd with spede'.

It is not certain how the present letter should be dated. The signature is

---

[189] For a letter of Roche to the first earl, Dickens, *Clifford Letters*, no. 11.
[190] PRO, SC6 Henry VIII/4534 m.7.

dissimilar to that of the previous letter and it might be suggested that the letter is from Sir William Gascoigne the younger, son and heir of the last correspondent, who died in 1567. On the other hand, the William Arthington priest mentioned in the letter may be the priest of that name of Adle who died in 1543–4. The letter illustrates the willingness of gentry and nobility to involve themselves in arbitrations, but I have been unable to discover who the parties were or what their grievances concerned. Until this is succesfully done, the identities of author and recipient must remain uncertain.[191]

101 Richard lord Grey to the first earl of Cumberland, 25 November [1525 x 1535].
BL, Althorp B1, fo. 59r-v.

My nown good lord my dewty remembred. I humbuly recomend me unto you. Thys ys to a vertyse you I have receyved of Roger Medoppe your servaunt lx xv powndes dewe to me and my wyffe at the feast of Sent Marten laste past in full contemplacyon of the halfe yere rent. More over he hathe payd me xxxvij pownd xs for the halfe yere dewe at Pentycoste laste paste. Pleasythe your lordshepe to looke apon the qwettonce that I made to your lordshepe at my lord Scroppys place was butt for xxx pownde for the forsayd feast and so remaynes be hynde unpayd vij li xs for the whyche I be syche your lordshepe to be so good lord unto me as to send yt upc by some servauntes of yours to me or elles to mayster Robard Aske at Grayes Enne. And thus I be syche Jh[es]u preserve you. Wrytan at London the xxv day of November.

Rychard Grey.

Text in a rough clerk's hand. Signed. Addressed [fo. 59v], 'To my nown good lord, my lord of Comberlande, thys be delyver[e]d'.

Richard lord Grey (d. 1541–2) was a younger son of Thomas Grey, marquess of Dorset (d. 1530). His connection with the Cliffords arose through his marriage to Florence, second wife and widow of the tenth lord Clifford and step-mother to the first earl. The marriage came late in life for Clifford to a much younger woman, the widow of Sir Thomas Talbot of Bashall (in the West Riding, four miles north-west of Clitheroe). There was a daughter of the marriage (who married Hugh Lowther of Lowther) but there are also signs that the relationship broke down. In 1521 lady Clifford sued at York for the restoration of her conjugal rights and an undated accountant's notebook for the Clifford household

[191] Arthington's will is printed in Lumb (ed.), *Testamenta Leodiensia, 1539–1553*, 83–4. The possibility that Henry Pudsey was of the gentle family of that name resident at Bolton in Bowland proved not to be the case.

contains a note dating it 'after the unkyndnesses and strifes begonne betwixte my lo[rd] Cliff[ord] and my lady about the 12 or 13 of the reigne of Henr' 8'.[192]

The tenth lord's settlement of 20 November 1512 in favour of his wife (by which she had manors in Westmorland for life) was confirmed by her step-son in June 1524 when the lands were leased to Clifford by her feoffees for a term of 50 years (if she survived so long) at a rent of 225 marks. The arrangement broke down after the first earl's death and was the subject of a bill in Chancery before the arrangement was confirmed by the second earl in December 1548.[193]

Dame Florence's third marriage was arranged by Henry VIII. Whitaker saw a letter which instructed her so repair to him at court to know his mind 'wyche sall ryght well satisfye, content and plese yow'.[194] It cannot be discovered when her remarriage took place or when she died. Of Grey little is known. As Suffolk noted in an earlier letter (63), he owed a great part of his income to his wife's jointure. In his will (dated 28 March 1541 and proved the following May), which asked that he should be buried where he died, he left his goods to his wife who he appointed his executrix.[195] The present letter has to be dated before November 1535. The intermediary, Robert Aske of Grey's Inn, achieved a greater notoriety in 1536 and was executed in 1537.

102 Lionel Hamerton to the first earl of Cumberland, 8 July [1525 x 1541].
BL, Althorp B1, fo. 71r-v.

Jh[esu]s

After my dewte remembrt, pleissz your honorable lordship to knaw that we do lak iern as weill for wyndois as for your wyndleisse wherin I besech your lordschip that I may knaw your pleissor herin in all goodle hast after seygth heirof for it liyth of ye haste sped of your warkes. Ferther my lord my [...] your broder did a schew me that your lordship hayth gyffyn hym yerle vj foder hay the whech parson Hogson wyll let me have noyn with owt your warrant or your esspeciall commandment by toykyn as knawyth J[es]hu who ever preserve your honorable lordship to his pleissur and your hertes eisse. Writtyn at Skipton the viijth day of July.

By your servaunt poyr, Lionell Hamerton.

Holograph. Addressed [fo. 71v], 'To the Reygth honorable and my synguler good lord my lord of Cumbrland be thes delyvered in hast'.

It has proved impossible to identify Lionel Hamerton. He was most likely a junior member of the Hamerton family of Hellifield Peel in Craven although his name does not appear in the fullest available pedigree. Hodgson may be the Sir William Hodgson who was a chantry priest at Marton in Craven early in Henry VIII's reign.[196] The letter is dated on the assumption that the earl's brother is Sir Thomas Clifford, captain of Berwick (d. 1541). The hand would suggest a date earlier rather than later in the sixteenth century.

103 Sir Edmund Knivet to the first or second earl of Cumberland, 26 September [1539–51].
BL, Althorp B1, fo. 82r-v.

Right honorabull and my singuler good lorde, my dewety remembred. I recommend me unto youer lordeshippe. And where as your lordeshippe of your gentelnes at my laste beinge here in the countrye with my lorde of Norfolkes grace, gave unto me a guyldinge, at whiche tyme I left hym remaynynge with your lordeshippe. Wherefore I nowe mooste hertely requyre youer lordeshippe to sende hym me by the berer hereof, for at this present tyme I stonde in greate neade of hym by reasone that dyvers of my guyldinges which by mysfortune have myscaryed sethens my comynge to the courte. And in this youer so doinge youer lordeshippe shalle commaunde me with humble servyce to requyte youer goodnes, as knoweth our lorde who preserve youer good lordeshipp. Frome Yorke the xxvjth of September.

By all your homeble to commaunde, Edmunde Knyvet K.

Clerk's hand, signed. Addressed [fo. 82v], 'To the right honorabull and my very singuler good lorde my lorde of Cumberlonde'.

It is impossible to date this letter on the limited evidence it supplies. Its author is most likely to be Sir Edmund Knivet of Buckenham Castle, Norfolk, knighted 1538–9 (providing a *terminus a quo*), died 1551.[197]

104 Sir John Lowther to the first earl of Cumberland, 25 December [1534].
BL, Althorp B1, fo. 50r-v.

My goode lorde in my <hertye> lowlye manner I commende me unto your lordship and to ascertene youe that Cristofer Leighe hase broken

---

[196] Whitaker, *Craven*, 95, pedigree opposite p. 150.
[197] *HP 1509–1558*, ii, 482–3.

Thomas Dalston chamber at Holme and put furthe his depute there with force as breking of the doores, wherupon I advised Mr Thomas to write unto the Abbot, whiche did send hym a symple annswere in writinge againe. Then I advysed this berer Thomas Dalston to come to your lordship hym self, whiche can shew your lordship the hoole circumstance therof. And thus the Holye Trenitie have your lordship in his blissid tuicion. From Lowder this Childermes day at night.

By your servaunt, John Lowther.

Clerk's hand, signed. Addressed [fo. 50v], 'To the Right honorable my lorde of Cumberland'.

The connection between the Lowthers and the Cliffords was one of some antiquity. Sir John Lowther (d. 1553) was a cousin of the first earl in that his mother was a daughter of Margaret, widow of the 9th lord Clifford (d. 1461) by her second husband, Sir Lancelot Threlkeld.[198] The alliance was reinforced in 1528 through the marriage of Dorothy Clifford, the first earl's half-sister (born to his father's second marriage with lady Florence Talbot), with Hugh Lowther, Sir John's son and heir.[199]

The tenth lord Clifford leased the sheriffwick to Lowther for ten years (but during pleasure) on 18 August 1511, Lowther entering a bond in 1,000 marks and receiving a yearly fee of 11 marks. The first earl appointed him deputy sheriff in Westmorland in 1529–30, to hold during pleasure with a fee of 20 marks. He also served as sheriff in Cumberland in 1516, 1542 and 1550. His will was made on 3 February 1552/3 and he was dead by early March.[200]

The stewardship and manrede of the border abbey of Holm Cultram was amongst the offices usually held by the warden of the West Marches. As such it was a Dacre possession, but passed to Cumberland on his appointment as warden in 1534. Dickens has printed the letter in which the abbot offered to draw a grant of the stewardship for Cumberland's use. It would appear that Henry VIII decided late in 1534 to restore the stewardship of Holm to Dacre, but before Cumberland could send word to his man Dalston, Dacre's servant Christopher Leigh evicted him. The King's decision then formed the subject of a complaint to Cromwell by Cumberland, Clifford arguing that he could not serve as warden without the border stewardships. A subsequent settlement of the issues between Dacre and Cumberland by Cromwell assigned the stewardship to Cumberland.[201]

[198] Ms Dodsw. 74, fo. 113r-v.

[199] The text of the settlement survives in the unlisted tracts of Cumbria RO, Carlisle, D/Lons/L but could not be traced in 1989: it is mentioned in D/Lons/L3/1/7 fo. 17v and the marriage has pride of place in the genealogical table on fos. 99v-100r.

[200] Cumbria RO, Carlisle, D/Lons/L/deeds/Lo2/3; Ms Dodsw., 83 fo. 55r. J. Raine jun., (ed.), *Wills and Inventories from the registry of the Archdeaconry of Richmond* (Surtees Soc., xxvi, 1853), 73–5.

[201] Dickens, *Clifford Letters*, no. 4; *LP* vii no. 1589; viii no. 310.

Cumberland's deputy, Thomas Dalston, is a gentleman of the greatest obscurity, but is presumably the Thomas Dalston of Dalston, Cumberland, sheriff in 1540, who had a grant of lands from the crown in 1544 and died in 1550. Leigh may have been of the gentry family of Isel, Cumberland, of which I can find no pedigree; he reappears as the deputy to Richard Dacre when the latter was sworn as Grand Captain at the Broadfield Oak muster of the Pilgrims in November 1536.[202]

105 Sir John Lowther to the first earl of Cumberland, 5 October [?1536].
BL, Althorp B1, fo 53r-v.

Pleas yt your lordship to be advertysit that opon Wadinsday being the fowrt day of October at the shereff turn at Kendall, the constable of Trutbek broght to Kendal fywe prisoners, two men and thre women, for brekyn on hows in Kirkby Stewyn and I wold resayf non of them withowt on warrant from the justice of peace and so thay appontid to go to Ric' Duket that nyght and the constable fest the cariag of the two men with Burse and the thre women with your two balyfs of Kendall and from thens I cawsyt my balyf Leonard Crosby to be redy to hayf resawyt them after the justice of peace had examynyt them to cary them to the gayll and on letter sent to jaler to hayf resawyt them at his hand and after I was departyd the sayd Burse and the balis has lattyn the prisoners depart without caring them to ony justice. Also at the saym turn yowr serwand John Robynson is presentid for marking certayn strayffs his awn mark and to his awn hus.

Newys in this contre is noyn bot the kyng of Scotes serwandes hays mayd on gret fray with French men in Deppe and thus the Holy Trinite kep your lordship. From Lowthis this fifte day of Octobre, by your serwand to his power.

John Lowther.

Clerk's hand, signed. Addressed [fo. 53v], 'To the honorable my lord off Comberland be this deliverytt'.

The letter is difficult to date with certainty although 1536 might be preferred. Wednesday fell on 4 October in that year as it also did in 1525 and 1532, but Lowther's report of a story circulating of an affray between the servants of the king of Scotland and the townspeople of Dieppe may reasonably be connected with James V's landing there on 18 September. The affray is otherwise unrecorded.[203] Otherwise we see Lowther holding the shrieval courts in Westmorland in his capacity as undersheriff with a due regard for the jurisdictions between his office and that of the JPs.

John Robinson, who was accused of converting stray animals to his own use, was bailiff in Kendal ward in 1534.[204]

106 Sir John Lowther to the first earl of Cumberland, 25 April [1537]. BL, Althorp B1, fos. 62r-63v, previously printed in abstract, *LP* xii (1) no. 1038 from a copy (which varies in details) sent on by Cumberland, BL, Cotton Ms, Caligula B III, fo. 216r.

Pleas itt your lordshipp to be advertysyd, that I have resaveyd your letter this Saynt Markes Ewyn wherin I persave the kynges pleasour his that your lordshipp shall fortefy the castell and town with men, veytill and ordinance. There is no perell bot yf ytt be to long in doyng. Yf your lordship hadde vytall to morowe ye have no myln in the castill to grinde with all, nowther hors myln ne hand myln. And yf your lordship had gud ordinanc ye have not on that can shott on gon here for yf your lordship neyd John Wystyng, nother can ne dar schott a gon ne hays ony connyng tharein.

My lorde, I thenke yt goyde ye cause Thomas Byrkbeke to by you som qwet or byg betyme or ony grett noys arys and how so ever yt turn yt wyll gyff you your mony agayn and on hors myln to be mayde, for at the fyrst seteyng of the seyge, the myln damys wylbe pullid doune. And yf your lordship spare the kynges mony to long, ye may soner have blaym tharfor, seyng yowr lordship hays warnyng betym from hys grac for provyssion to be mayde for hoder war of Scotland now qwen the kynges purs is full of the French gold or newer and the comon woys of Scotland hys warr. Also my lorde thys last nyght I sent my man a way to Edenburg qwo shall tary there wyls the kyng land yf he keype his dyett wyche hys assyuytt to hys consell to be on May day at the forthest. I causytt hym goo soner a way by causse I persaveyd the wynde mayd well thes two days past for hys comyng home. The comonty of Scotland preparis contenually for hernes and wepyn. Wherffore, seyng your lordship is put in trust, loyke opon ewerylk thyng betyme and drysse not for a litill that your lordship be not takyn tardy. And thus the Holye Trinitie hayff your lordship in hys blyssitt kepyng. From Carliell this Saynt Markes Evyn by your servant,

John Lowther.

---

[203] *LP* xi no. 512, 631.
[204] Chatsw., BA 8 fo. 19v.

Clerk's hand. Signed. The lower right hand quadrant of fo. 63 torn away. Addressed [fo. 63v], 'To the honorabyll my lorde of Cumberlande be thys d[.....].

In the spring of 1537 there was a general expectation of a Scottish attack on England upon the return of James V from France. Rumours circulated in the borders of musters being held in the Scottish towns.[205] Henry VIII gave orders for the victualling of Berwick and Carlisle on 8 April. Cumberland warned the council on 21 April of the shortage of victuals about Carlisle and the need for a substantial force to defend the castle and reinforced his arguments by sending a copy of the present letter to London later in the month.[206] There was general agreement about the poor state of the defences, with the necessary refurbishments being costed at £1,000. Little was done until after 1541.[207] Thomas Birkbeck was the earl's receiver in Westmorland and Cumberland in 1533–4.[208]

107 John lord Lumley to the first earl of Cumberland, 29 November [1525 x 1530].
BL, Althorp B1, fo. 33r-v.

My va[r]ie good lord, in my harttest manner I recommend me un too youre good lordshippe. My lorde, I hawe resawyde youre letter by youre triste sarwand Mr Blenkynshopp. My lord, I wrott too youre lordshipp too knawe youre ottermest plesur whatt yee wold giff me too girssome for my landdes in Kendall too hawe them too a whitt rentt and as yett I knawe not youre plesur by this berar youre sarwand. My lord, I thynk youre lordshipp wyll bydd me no less and a thowsandd markes consederyng the grett prohettes thertoo belongyn. My lord, I am conttentyd att the instanc and labour off my cosyng Sir Roger Bellyngam and Mr Blenkynshopp for vij howndreth markes, a howndreth yere tak soo thatt I may hawe my money too gether att [the] makyn upp off our wryttynges <too gether> att London and yff youre lordshipp be thus contentydd, I pray you latt me knawe youre plesur by twyx this and Kyrstenmess thatt I may make anser too my layde Par whether thatt shee shall hawe ytt or nay and thus the Holy Gost preserwe you. Wryttyn att my manor, The Broyd Chare in Ne[w]castell,

[205] *LP* xii (i) no. 843 and *passim*.
[206] *Ibid.* nos. 863, 993.
[207] M. R. McCarthy, H. R. T. Summerson and R. G. Annis, *Carlisle Castle, a survey and documentary history* (1990), chs 10, 11; Colvin *et al* (ed.), *History of the King's Works*, iv (2), 664–673.
[208] Chatsw., BA 8 fo. 22r.

on Santt Androw Ewyn, by youre poore kynsman, to the othermest off hys poore.

Jhon Lumley.

Clerk's hand, signed. Addressed [fo. 34v], 'Too my synguler good lord my lord off Comerland by this d[elivere]d'.

John lord Lumley (b. $c.1492$, d. 1544 or 1545) owned an eighth share of the Honour of Kendal. In this letter he invites Cumberland to offer him an entry fine for a 100 year lease of his lands, Lumley suggesting 1,000 marks as reasonable but expressing a willingness to accept as little as 700 marks. He sought a rapid decision as lady Parr (the widow of Sir Thomas Parr of Kendal and mother of William Parr, later Marquess of Northampton) was also interested. Neither Cumberland nor lady Parr became Lumley's tenant. The Lumley fraction of the honour and other lands were exchanged with the Crown for an annuity and added to the estates of the duke of Richmond (who already owned half of the honour, 10 above). This transaction was confirmed by statute in 1531, making the letter of the period 1525–1530.[209]

108 Ninian Markenfield to the ?tenth lord Clifford, 10 April [before 1527].
BL, Althorp B1, fo. 24r-v.

Ryght honourable and my especiall gud lord, in my moste lawly manner I recommend me unto your lordschype, besechyng your lordschype to be so gud lord unto me [th]at ye wold wryte a letter to my lord of Northumberland, [th]at it wold please hym to be so gud lord unto me at your requeste as to relesse me off the reconansanantes [*sic*] that I stand bownd in in the Sterr Chamber. I wold be glad to knawe hys lordschyps pleasour and yours as schortly after Ester as it schall please your lordschype, for me thynke it is verreay dangeros to me seyng that I cannot be herde of my lord of Northumberland in my trouthe. Where fore I besech your lordschype to send a servaunt of yours to my lord to knawe hys pleasour and I schalbe glad to beerr hys costes with the grace of Jh[es]u who have your honourable lordschype in hys blessyd kepyng. At Markynfeld the xth day of Aprell.

Be your awn to hys lyttyll power, Nynyane Markynfeld.

Holograph, sealed. Addressed [fo. 24v] 'To the ryght honorable and my especiall gud lord my lord Clyfford be thys delyvered'.

[209] Statute 23 Henry VIII c.28; *CPR Mary*, i, 157–9.

Sir Ninian Markenfield of Markenfield near Ripon died in 1527.[210] For his second wife he married Eleanor, daughter of the tenth lord Clifford. She survived him, but it is not clear whether this letter is addressed to his father-in-law or brother-in-law. Nor can any litigation between Markenfield and the earl of Northumberland be discovered.

109 Thomas Markenfield to the first earl of Cumberland, 10 October [1530 or 1531].
BL, Althorp B1, fo. 36r-v.

Jh[esu]s

My dewtte dunne wnto youer lordshypp wyth grett thankes for youer grett kyndnes shewyd unto me at all tymes and as yt hayth pleassyd youer good lordshypp to send Thomas Sturke for the rentes of Rommondbe and I only for youer lordshypp pleassur hayth sentt the same rentes unto youer lordshypp wyth thys berrer my serwand George Thakeweray and ony pleassur that I may schew unto your good lordshyppe ye shalbe sur of me at all tymes as knoyth Jh[esu]s who have youer good lordshypp in hys most blyssyd tewyscon now and ewer mor amen.

Thomas Markinfeld.

Pleassyth your good lordshipp yt ys oppenly spokcen in the shyer of Kyrkbe Malsed that youer lordshypp and my lord Clyffurd intendes by the grays of God to keppe the courte at Cyrkebe and all the nabures says that thay wylle take youer lordshypes parte and I for my parte, yff yt plase your lordshypp to take pane to loghe wyth me, I truste youer lordshypp shall hawe a copple of fatt swanes and schyche power loggyng as I hawe. Youer good lordshypp shalbe sure boyth off me and yt or ony pleassur that I may do to my power thys xth day of October.

Perhaps holograph. Addressed [fo. 36v], 'To hys Ryght honourable, syngguler and esspsyalle good lord Henry eyrlle of Comberland del[i]ver thys wyth speid'.

Thomas Markenfield was son of the previous correspondent. He was a minor at his father's death (although it is uncertain whether he was the son of his father's first wife or second) and died in 1550. In this letter he associates himself firmly with the first earl's interest in Kirkby Malzeard. The essential background is that in 1529 Cumberland had the grant from the sixth earl of Northumberland

[210] *Test. Ebor.* v, 232–5.

of the stewardship of Kirkby Malzeard (which Northumberland held from the earl of Derby). At much the same time, John Norton of Norton Conyers had a lease of the manor from the countess of Derby and when Cumberland tried to hold a court at Kirkby in April 1531, he was met by Norton and a party of supporters who forcibly resisted him. The wider significance of these events has been a matter of some recent contention.[211] The letter gives no clue as to whether it was written before this affray or describes plans for a further attempt to hold courts. The manor of Romanby near Northallerton (North Riding), whose rents Cumberland expected to collect, had been granted to Dame Eleanor Markenfield by her husband.[212]

110 Lord Maxwell to the first earl of Cumberland, 25 November [1534]. BL, Althrop B1, fo. 58r-v.

My lord, efter my maist humilie comendation, pleis your l[ordship] to be advertischit my lord capytane your brother and I at owr last meting at Louchmabenstane apoyntit this day off trew to be haldin the last day off November quhilk is on Mounday nixt to cum. We not beand perfytlie advertischit that it is Santt Andrew Day owr patron quhilk said day is nocht leffull till ws till exsersis owr temporell besynes, desiring your l[ordship] the said day be contynewet to the Tuisday on the morn quhilk is the fyrst day off December and to meit at Lowch Maben stane be ix howrs in the mornyng to perfforme sicc besynes as concernis ws.

Alswa your l[ordship] sall ressave the haill tractait off the pece takin betwix bayth the princis quhilk your l[ord] may cawss to dowble and is rycht necessar to you wytht the answeir off ys complaynt giffin in for the slawchter off Mathe Mathow wytht ane small row off complayntis quhilk was nocht giffin in at the last day and ferder God preserve your lordschip in gud heill. At the king owr soveraine lordis castell off Louchmaben this Tuisday the xxv day off November.

youris at comand, Roberd Maxwell.

Written in a rather rough clerk's hand. Signed and sealed. Addressed [fo. 58v], 'To the Ryt honor[a]ble my lord erll off Cumberland wardane off the West Marchis off Ingland for anentes Scotland'.

The letter is a piece of cross-border correspondence dating from Cumberland's second period as warden. In it the warden of the Scottish West Marches, Robert, fifth lord Maxwell of Carlaveroch Castle (d. 1543) informs Cumberland

---

[211] James, 'First earl', 166–7; Hoyle 'First earl', 80–1.
[212] Test. Ebor. v, 232–5.

of his error in arranging with Sir Thomas Clifford a day of truce for St Andrew's Day and asks for it to be deferred to the following day. The conjunction of days and dates reveals the date to be 1534. The treaty referred to is doubtless that signed on 2 August 1534. The castle from which Maxwell wrote was the Scottish king's at Lochmaben between Lockerbie and Dumfries and must be carefully distinguished from the Lochmaben Stone on the north side of the Solway near Gretna, the traditional location of days of truce.[213]

111 Sir William Musgrave to the first earl of Cumberland, 31 July [1536 x 1539].
BL, Althorp B1, fo. 66r-67v.

My lord, as my most assuryd gud lord under the kyng, I have me recommendyt unto your gud lordshyp. And wher as to my puer I have alway intendyt faythfully to be yours, I besych your lordshyp to accompt in me the saym duryng my lyf. And vere gladly wold I see your lordshyp for now my intent is, God willyng, to remeyn as nygh your lordshyp or my lord your son as I may, redy to doy [sic] your servyce and plesur.

For of trewth I had bene with your l[ordship] bi now but for sundry complayntes whych was mayd unto the kyng is hyghnes both agaynst me and Jak Musgrave, the whych the kyng hym sylf opynyd unto me vere sure. Albeyt hys grace sayd he wolld be my gud lord and pardon both Jak Musgrave and me. And therin my sewt was to hys grace to trye me beffor hys counsell, whych hys grace promest me within iij days, wherupon hym sylf cawsyd the counsell to call both Jak Musgrave and me beffor them. Wher as we found my lord privy seall speshall gud lord unto us in our declarasyon, whych I am not able to desserve unto hym wheles I lev. To rehers every manys part her, yt wer to tedyus for your l[ordship], but fynally I am in better favour then ever I was in all my lyf with the kyng and my lord privy seall and all other the kyngs counsell except my lord of Northfolk whych ever will love a Dacre; but therin he can not hurt me now as at my comyng unto your lordshyp ye shall at length perceyv more playnly.

And now the kyng upon the trewth known of my declaracion [fo. 66v] hath commandyt me to mayk my bill of ony resonable thyng and I shall have yt in short tym dyspachyd and that I shuld tary ther for. My sylf and lykwys Jak Musgrave shall have xx li more for term of hys lyf and her ys the cawse of my taryeng all together, but and yt [sic] cum not shortly, I will not tary long her to gyt a mor proffyt. And that our lord knowth who ever kep your lordshyp and all yours in

---

[213] Rae, *Scottish Frontier*, 26, 240, 243 etc. Also *Scots Peerage*, vi, 479–81.

mych honour long to prosper. Wryttyn at my pure howse in London thys Saynt Peter Evyn.

Your lordshyp is assuryd, William Musgrave K.

Holograph. Sealed. Addressed [fo. 67v], 'To my ryght honourable lord the yerull of Cumberlond'.

Musgrave's letter is important testimony to the political infighting of the 1530s on the northern border and offers a rare view of the council in operation. Unfortunately, as the letter is undated and stands alone, it is difficult to assign it a place in the larger history of factional conflict between Musgrave and the Dacre.

Musgrave was the elder son of Sir Edward Musgrave of Hartley in Westmorland and Eden Hall in Cumberland. Sir Edward died only a few months before Musgrave's own premature death in 1544 and because of this, his career was marred by financial weakness which doubtless contributed to his decision to reside in London. Sir William was appointed Constable of the border castle of Bewcastle in 1531, replacing William lord Dacre who had himself been appointed as recently as 1527 on the resignation of one Thomas Musgrave. The office brought him into conflict with lord Dacre and there can be little doubt that Musgrave provided the evidence on which Dacre was tried in 1534. It was his inability to cooperate with Dacre which may well explain his absenteeism, which was the subject of comment as early as 1537.[214] As this letter makes clear, Musgrave was in his own mind a Clifford man (although also a royal servant) and this was acknowledged to be so in the king's reprimand to Cumberland of January 1537 (22). On the other hand, there is little sign that in the manoeuvres against Dacre in 1534, Musgrave was acting on Cumberland's behalf. Rather it seems likely that he was settling scores which had arisen during the war of 1532–3.[215]

The present letter describes how a complaint was made to Henry VIII against Musgrave, how the king raised this with him, promised him a trial before the council and how Musgrave successfully defended himself there to the satisfaction of all except the duke of Norfolk. The letter gives remarkably little evidence as to date. The reference to 'my lord your son' makes the first earl the recipient so the letter cannot be later than July 1541. The hope that the letter might be dated by finding the grants of annuities mentioned proved to be a forlorn one. If the Lord Privy Seal whose advocacy Musgrave so valued can be identified as Cromwell (which is not improbable given the close relationship we see between them at other moments), the letter has to be of 1536–9.

Nor is the letter forthcoming over the nature of the charges brought against

[214] For Bewcastle, see Colvin et al (eds.), History of the King's Works, iv (1), 233–4. Musgrave's career is described in HP 1509–1558, ii, 646–48. Appointments to Bewcastle can be found in LP ii (1) no. 1084; ii (2) no. 3747 (6); v no. 220 (6), 1370 (20).

[215] Harrison, Pilgrimage of Grace, 31–5. The whole question is studied much more thoroughly by Dr S. G. Ellis in a forthcoming paper.

Musgrave, but it is implicit from his comment that Norfolk would ever 'love a Dacre' that they came from within that circle. It may be suggested that the dispute concerns the collection of rents in Bewcastledale which Musgrave claimed to belong to the Crown and to be a perquisite of his constableship but which Dacre took for his own. This dispute had been the subject of a decree in favour of Dacre in Star Chamber in 1531. Sir William was instructed not to collect the rents claimed by Dacre until the matter was settled 'by due force of the [common] law' but in 1535–6 Dacre lodged a further complaint before the council alleging that Musgrave had collected his rents to the value of £104 13s 4d. They asked that Musgrave, 'now being present within your noble court' should appear before the council to justify his breach of the earlier decree. This dispute was still rumbling in the autumn of 1538 when a commission to settle the matter met with both parties at Darlington. After hearing both Dacre's and Musgrave's evidence, the commissioners found that the lands in contention were claimed by Musgrave for the term of his life only with the reversion belonging to the Crown. Considering themselves unable to settle the matter, they referred it back to the Council.[216] The evidence points to Musgrave's letter falling within that general period.

112 Sir John Neville to the first earl of Cumberland, [1530 x 1537]. BL, Althorp B1, fos. 31r-32v.

Ryght honourable and my speciall and synguler gud lord in my lowlyste maner that I can, I humble recommend me unto yower honourable lordshype, trustyng to God that yower lordshype withe my gud lady and all yower lordshypes servandes be in gud helth wyche I pray God long to contynew to the pleasure of God and to yower hertes desyer.

My gud lord, the cause of my wrytyng on to yower honorable lordshype ys humble bescheyng yower lordshype to pardon me that I com nott on to yower lordshyp accordyng to my dewte and promes, butt in gud fathe. My lord I am in case as I was never thys xxx^{ti} yere for be my fathe I have never on nag that wyll cary me x myles a day and my gud lord I am nott in that case butt my son yower neve and all my sarvandes ar in case lyke or els ytt had be come me to have don my dewty on to yower lordshype my selyff. Besechyng yower lordshyp to pardon me.

Ferder more my lord I hertely beseche yower honorable lordshype that I myght have yower lordshype counsell and mynde in a matter consernyng my son in lawe yower neve, for my lord, there ys nothyng to gett a bove butt all to spend as I am sure yower lordshyp knowythe ryght well. And my lord be yower better adwyes, I am moved by hys frendes to lett hym begyn to sett up house in a lytyll corner to se howe

[216] PRO, STAC2/19/127, 20/52, 18/269 (and *LP* xiii (2) app. no. 36).

he wyll frame and my gud lord there ys many of hys frendes that haithe spokyn to me for ytt that wyll gyffe hym many thynges to be gyn wythe all. And my lord, I will for my part se he shall lake no thyng for that porcion that he shall begyn wythe all to he come to hys londes and be that tyme I trust to God he shall loke upon hym selfe, for as yower lordshyp knowyght, ytt goythe as fast from hym as he takythe ytt, for he ys so fre and so kynd that he caryth nott whatt he spendes as yett, bott I trust to God thys wyll make hym knowe whatt a peny coste. Besechyng yower lordshyp that I may know yower lordshyp mynd and pleasure by my serwand thys berar in wrytyng, for I wyll do nothyng butt as ytt shall please yower lordshyp. Howe be ytt my lord, thaye be bothe marvylous sett apon ytt and for my poyer dowghter I trust to God yower lordshyp will lyke her well and I trust she wyll handyll her selfe after that facion that I trust shalbe to yower honore and comfort and to my power hertes ease. In hast from Chete be yowers to hys lytyll power, besechyng yower honourable lordshyp to take credens to my servand thys berar.

John Nevyell K.

One sheet, the address on fo. 31r, text written on the face divided between fos. 31v and 32r. Clerk's hand, signed. Addressed [fo. 31r], 'To the Ryght honourable and my esspeciall and synguler gud lord my lord of Cumberland thys be delivered'.

Cumberland's impoverished correspondent is Sir John Neville of Chevet near Wakefield and although undated, the letter is of the early 1530s. A younger son, Neville came to Chevet through his marriage to Elizabeth, daughter and co-heir of William Bosville of Chevet. He was knighted in 1513 and served as sheriff in 1519, 1524 and 1528. He was executed in 1541 for his inadequacies in dealing with the Yorkshire plot of that year.[217] The present letter describes his parlous financial circumstances and his problems in controlling his son-in-law, Cumberland's nephew. This young spendthrift has to be Gervase Clifton (for whom see **90** above). Clifton was indeed Cumberland's nephew, but he was also Neville's ward and married his daughter Mary in January 1530. The letter must date from before Clifton's majority in 1537 and so describes the practical problems that parents or guardians faced in controlling a married teenage child.

113 William Parr to the first earl of Cumberland, 7 March [1537].
BL, Althorp B1, fo. 60r-v.

Right honorable and my vereye good lorde, in my hartiest maner I commende me unto youre lordeshippe. And where as this bringer my tenante before sufficient witnesse and recorde as George Hilton, Thomas Reyne, Christoffer Dent and others did lende unto John Burrell at Michaellmas laste past iiij oxen, to have the use of the same unto Penticost next ensuynge, for certayn hire betwyxt theym covenanted and agred, that nowe youre lordeshippys offycers amonest Richarde Burrell is goodes (father of the said John) have allso streyned the same iiij oxen appertenyng to this bringer, John Rayn my tenante. Wherefore in consideracon here of, I shall hertely desire youre lordeshippe to be good lorde unto this bringer, that according unto right and good conscence he maye have his said oxen restored agayn. Here in if it shall please your lordeshippe to be good lorde unto him at this my request, you shalbe assured of suche pleasour as I can shew unto your lordeshippe, as knoweth our lorde who preserve your lordeshipp in helth. Frome Newecastell uppon Tyne this vijth daye of Marche.

Yowre owne assurid, Wylliam Parr.

Clerk's hand, signed. Addressed [fo. 60v], 'To the right honorable and my verey good lorde my lorde of Comberlande delyver this'.

On a number of grounds this letter can be associated with the seizure of the goods of rebels in Westmorland after the failure of the attack on Carlisle in February 1537. The author of this letter, William Parr, later Marquess of Northampton (1513–1571) was a Westmorland landowner with estates in the honour of Kendal. In early 1537 he was a member of the duke of Norfolk's retinue travelling around the North, Norfolk especially commending Parr on 24 March.[218] The coincidence that Norfolk was at Newcastle, from where this letter was written, on the day it was written, strongly suggests that it dates from 1537. Furthermore, Richard Burrell of Appleby appears amongst those executed for their role in the February rising.[219] The evidence is not perfect, but this appears to be another instance of a lord trying to secure a favour on the behalf of a tenant. There is no way of knowing whether it was successful.

---

[218] *LP* xii (1) no. 713.
[219] Harrison, *Pilgrimage of Grace*, 139.

114 Brian Rocliffe to the first earl of Cumberland, 5 September [?1534]. BL, Althorp B1, fo. 29r-v.

Right honourable and my mooste espiciall good lorde, pleas yt youe to be advertised, I do sende my bedfellowe and Maister Maunsell my freynde unto your good lordeshippe unto whome I have yeven my full poo[wer] and auctorytie to conclude in suche thinges as I truste shalbe to your contentacion. And the helpe and remedye of my daunger and chargyez that nedes muste be payde aswell to the kinges highnes as to others my freyndes that I am daungered unto. And more over, I am in greate daunger as towchinge one outelagarye that Maister Norton haithe procured a yenste me at the suyte of one Armyn his preste. Whiche matter haithe cooste me xl li as the seid Maister Maunsell can more at large certifye youre lordeshipe. Wherefore my lorde I requyre youe of youre goodnes, consydre myne extremitie at this tyme and what assuraunce so ever ye will have uppon their conclusyon, the same I shall accomplishe in every behalfe as your learnede counsayle shall devise. Thus I besiche Jh[es]u contynewe youe in myche honour. From Colthorpe, this vth daye of Septembre.

Bryane Rouclyffe.

Clerk's hand, signed. Addressed [fo. 29v], 'To the right honourable and his mooste espiciall good lorde, Therle of Comberlande this be yeven'.

This letter provides the occasion to review one of the first earl's major coups, the marriage of the heiress of the Rocliffe family to his second son, Ingram.[220] The correspondent is Brian Rocliffe of Colthorpe near Wetherby who entered into the family estates on the death of his father, Sir John, on 23 July 1533.[221] As early as 1529, Rocliffe had allowed himself to become entangled with the first earl. In return for 200 marks, of which 20 marks was paid in hand, 40 marks on St Luke's day and the balance when Rocliffe required it, he agreed that after his father's death he would make over to the earl the freehold of his moieties of the manors of Steeton and Grassington in Craven. If Rocliffe repaid the earl's advances before his father's death or in the following 12 months, the transaction was to be void; otherwise the earl was to pay such further sums as in total would amount to 16 years' value of the lands for an absolute purchase. Moreover, Rocliffe agreed to appoint the earl steward of his estates within three months of his father's death and conceeded to the earl a preferential claim as future mortgagee or purchaser of his lands.[222]

By the time Brian Rocliffe was in a position to honour these covenants, his

---

[220] For Sir Ingram Clifford, see *HP 1509–1558*, i, 659–60.
[221] Chatsw., Curry 28/1 (copy of his *inquisition post mortem*); *Test. Ebor.* v, 319–23.
[222] Indenture of 25 July 1529, Chatsw., Curry 28/1.

position had changed through the death of his son John on 4 October 1531 leaving a daughter, Anne, aged a year and ten days, as heir to the estates. On 6 October 1534 the earl and Rocliffe entered into a marriage agreement in which Rocliffe consented to the marriage of his granddaughter and Ingram Clifford and settled his whole estate on them, the earl paying 800 marks.[223] No issue of the marriage survived to maturity and the estates were finally divided between the George Clifford, third earl and his younger brother Francis Clifford (later fourth earl).

The urgency of this present letter suggests that it could possibly be dated immediately before the settlement of 1534. Rocliffe's need for money is stated plainly enough although it is less clear how this need arose or why John Norton of Norton Conyers should have behaving with such hostility (although he may have been trying to secure Anne Rocliffe for one of his own children). Mr Maunsell is William Maunsell the lawyer.[224]

115 William St John to possibly the second earl of Cumberland, 12 April [   ].
BL, Althorp B1, fo. 84r-85v.

After most harty recommendacion to your good lordship, I understand by my servant Christofer Blakborne that when he whas last here in the countrey amonges his frindes, it pleased your good lordship to be his good lord and gave hym bothe veneson and mony wiche whas gretly his comfort for the wiche I most hartely thanke you. And shalbe as redy and as willing to do like pleasures to any of yours when it may ly in me. And my lord this bringer being with my servaunt his breder in my house shewed me howe good lord you be to hym wich is his gret comfort and your honour to be so good lord to so poure men, hertely praying your good lordship to contyue your favour and good lordship to them bothe. And I shall do asmoch at your desyres if it may ly in me by Godes grace who kepe you. Writyn the xijth day of Aprell.

Your lordships assured, William Seint John.

Holograph. Sealed. Addressed [fo. 85v], 'To the right honourable and my singuler good lord therle of Cumberland'.

This letter offers no grounds on which it can be dated with certainty. The correspondent may be William St John of Farley Chamberlayne, Hants., (1538–1609) in which case the letter might belong to any part of the second half of the century (although as the recipient is praised for his hospitality, it is more

[223] Copy of the *inquisition post mortem*, Chatsw., Curry 28/3; Curry 28/1.
[224] For whom see *YAJ* xlii (1967–70), 373–4.

likely to be the second earl).[225] Blackburn may be of the family of that name settled at Hetton in Craven.

116 Fourth earl of Shrewsbury to 10th lord Clifford, 6 September [1522].
Chatsw., Clifford Letter Book, fo. 28r.

To my lord Clifford his good lordshipp.

My lord as hartely as I cann I recommend me unto your good lordshipp. And where it hath pleased the kings grace by his most honorable lettres to commaund you to ascerteyne me what nombre of men you will serve his grace with at this tyme against his enemyes the Scottes, which you have not yet doone, whereof I mervaile; and where it is shewed unto me that you be somewhat feeble with sicknes, whereof I am right sorry; I desyre and pray you if you shall thinck yourselfe not able to serve the king in your owne person that you will appoynt your company to attend uppon my cousin Sir Henry your sonn, soe as he with them may advaunce forwardes incontinently upon sight hereof with all diligence to the lord Dacre in the West Marches, where the duke of Albany with the power of Scotland purposeth to enter upon Tuesday next cominge. And further that it may please you to looke upon my cousin Sir Henry your sonne soe as he may the more honorably serve his grace. And soe I doubt not but yee shall deserve speciall thancks of his highnes for the same. And good my lord fayle not to see the premisses with diligence to be accomplished as you intend the kings honor and the weale of the marches there. And our lord send unto you good healthfull lyfe. Written at Yorke in great hast the 6th day of September.

Yours, G. Shrowesburye.

Shrewsbury's letter comes from the campaign of 1522. In a dispatch to Wolsey, written from York on 8 September, he reported that he had written to the sick lord Clifford asking him to allow his son, Sir Henry Clifford, to lead his forces.[226] This is the letter mentioned there. Clifford died the following April.

---

[225] *HP 1558–1603*, iii, 325–6.
[226] *LP* iii (2) no. 2524.

117 George lord Talbot (later sixth earl of Shrewsbury) to the second earl of Cumberland, 21 July 1553.
Chatsw., Clifford Letter Book fo. 27r.

To the right honorable and my very good lord the earle of Cumberland this hast, post hast, hast.

After my very harty commendations unto your good lordshipp, these shall advertize the same, that I and others the Queenes highnes councell in these partes, have receyved lettres from the lordes of the privye counsaile, and one proclamation enclosed in the same, declaringe the Lady Mary Queene of this realme, as of right she ought to be, whoe the lord Elye, the earle of Bedford, the earle of Arundell, my lord my father, and the earle of Pembrocke have proclaimed through the cittye of London; which is the joyfullest news that ever came to England, with whome I will serve duringe my lyfe to the uttermost of my power. And thus I bidd your lordshipp hartely farewell. From Yorke this 21th of July 1553.

Your lord assured, G. Talbott.

The circumstances of Mary's accession in 1553 are well known. Here George lord Talbot, later sixth earl of Shrewsbury, spreads the news of her proclamation by the council on 19 July. In the Chatsworth manuscript the letter is followed (on fo. 27v) by the text of the council's proclamation.

118 Sir Richard Tempest to Sir Henry Clifford, later first earl of Cumberland, 4 October [1513–22].
BL, Althorp B1, fo. 19r-v.

Ryght honourable sir, in my hertelest manner I recommand me un to you, besechyng yowr mastershypp to be gud master to the berer hereof qwyche is my broder Eltoft servant and tenant, qwyche hayth occupiyd the clerkeshypp of Kyldewyke by the space of iij xxx yeres and now by the meanes of Hugo Blakay (as it is said) is putt furth of hys said clerkeshypp. Qwerefor I beseche yowr mastershypp that the said berrer may occupye hys said office accordyng os he hayth don afore tyme by yowr supportacion and helpe and he shalbe yowr daly bedeman and I shalbe glade to doo for you eny thyng that in me lyyth os knawyth Jh[es]u qwom hayth yowr honourable mastershypp in hys blessid tuyssion. From Brasweell the iiijth day of October.

By yowres assured to hys power, Ric' Tempest knyght.

Sir and it plese yowr mastershypp all the hole paresyng is well a myndyth un to the same al only save Hug of Blakay.

Either a copy or holograph. Addressed [fo. 19v], 'To the ryght honourable and worshypfull Sir Henr' Clyfford be thys letter delivered'. Docquetted, 'Sir Ric' Tempest letter'.

Cumberland's neighbour, Sir Richard Tempest (d. 1537), writes from his house at Bracewell on behalf of the unnamed clerk of Kildwick church, a tenant of the Eltoftes family of Farnhill, who had been ejected from his office by Hugh Blakey.[227] Blakey held the capital messuage of Malsis in Sutton in Craven. In the assessments of the early 1520s he appears under the adjacent manor of Silsden.[228] The form of address employed suggests a date between Tempest's knighting in 1513 and the death of the tenth lord Clifford in 1523.

119 George Thompson of Doncaster to the first earl of Cumberland, [1526 or 1527].
BL, Althorp B1, fo. 28r-v.

Jh[esu]s

Ryght honorabyll lord erell of Comberland, I Gorge Tomson sertyfyng yowr lordshep of a sarwand at was my lord P[erse] called Rolland Qwarton wych is departed on Sent Marke day to Almyghty God whose sowlle Jh[es]u hafe mercy a pon. Hys body remanyng in the Whyte Frers cherch in Doncaster. Yowr lordshep sertyfyng my lord Perse of yowr letter that yowr lordshep hasse. Shewyng yowr lordshep that a blake horse with a whyte rake and a whyte tepe of the nose and a whyte saddell of bivfe lether with a blake harnes pertenyng to the sayme wych the proctor of Doncaster hasse resawed for hys mortuary called Master Worrall dwellyng in the parsoneg of Doncaster. I hafe bene with hym shewyng hym that the horse is my lord Perses, the brydell and saddell, he makyng me answere that I shwld hafe the horse yf I wold of my credans, I makyng hym a nanswer I wold not mell with the horse to yowr lordshep mayd a nanswer whether the horse be my lord Perses or no. Sertyfyng yowr lordshep that [ap]perell that was of hys body remanyng in hys oste howse at the Fawcon in Doncaster whose nam is called John Balland beyng in hys purse of money and gold xxiiijs and iijd and on ryng of gold wych remaneth in the handes of Sir John Drenkall the parich prest of Doncaster and

---

[227] For Tempest, see *HP 1509–1558*, iii, 430–1.
[228] Hoyle (ed.), *Early Tudor Craven*, 35, 53, 62.

on bowke called of gold, the wych remaneth in the handes of the pryor of the Whyte Frers of Doncaster. Yowr lordshep sertyfyng my lord Perse yowr brother whether thys ryng and bowke be my lord Perses or no. Wher of is lad forth for his beryall xxs and so the resedew remanyng in the parich prest handes wych as Master Dene beyng vycar of Doncaster hafe comanded hym for to kep it styll and so to make a nynvinytore of the same. Yowr lordshep sertyfyng my lord Perse whether thes persel beyng hys lordshepes or hys awne. No more unto yowr honorabyll lordshep at this tym bot J[he]su hafe yowr lordshepe in his kepyng. Amen.

By your pore bedman, Gorge Tomson.

Holograph. Sealed. Addressed [fo. 28v] 'Thys letter be delyvered unto the ryght honorabyll lord erell of Comberland lyeng at hys lordshep manner of [.....] in Crawen ys letter be dalyvered in hast'.

Trivial in itself, the letter illustrates the problems of dealing with the sudden death of a traveller. The deceased man, Rowland Wharton, was quite possibly a brother or cousin of the future lord Wharton. He was, it appears, a servant of Henry lord Percy's, thus placing the letter before 19 May 1527. That it is addressed to Cumberland places it after June 1525. Wharton died on St Mark's day, 25 April, limiting the letter to late April 1526 or 1527. There appears to be no will or grant of administration for Wharton. I am unable to identify the various clergy named in the standard list of Doncaster incumbents, nor has Thompson left any larger remains.[229]

120 Clement Watson to the first earl of Cumberland, 7 June [1525 x 1527].
BL, Althorp B1, fo. 26r-v.

Right honourable myn esspe[c]all and singuler good lorde, after full humble recommendacion unto your good lordeship, humbly thanking your lordeship for your honourable rewarde sent unto me by my felowe Robert Wharton, undeserved, but with my prayer and poor service. Accompting my self spe[c]ally bounden therunto my life during, withoute that your lordeship at any tyme shulde unto me geve suche rewarde. For it wer but my duety if I couth doe myche moor, beseching your lordeship to take and esteme the same noon otherwise.

Mi lorde, your deligent servantes Mr Blenkensop and Thomas Stirke have not for any payn or laubor to thaym possible pretermitted to avaunce your causes and busynesses her as to thair duetyes doth apperteyne. Howe be it, some parte therof as yet canne nor may take soe breve perfeccion as necessary wer, oonles my lordes grace wer at some better laiser and moor regardeth the same thenne he yet doth. Nevertheles my maister haith remembred his said grace therof, delayed as yet, as other my maisters oune causes be. My maister repaireth to the courte this next wook [*sic*] wher my lordes grace wolbe, as thenne your causes wolbe putte in remembraunce which I shall not faill to call upon my maister for, God willing, whoe ever moor preserve youe myn esspecall and singuler good lorde. At Saint James in the Feilde besides Westmynster the vijth day of June.

Your lordeships daily bedeman and poor servant, Clement Watson.

Holograph in a good secretarial hand. Addressed [fo. 26v], 'To the r[ight] honourable, myn esspecall [and] singuler good Therle of [C]omberlande, warden of the West Marche of Einglande for anenste Scottelande be this deliverde'.

This and the next letter, both from the hand of the otherwise unknown Clement Watson, may be treated together. The date may be deduced from the subscription to Cumberland as warden of the West Marches (**120**) but more specifically vice-warden in letter **121**. Cumberland was warden in his second period of officeholding on the West Marches, but in 1525–7 served as vice-warden to the duke of Richmond. The earlier dating is confirmed by the reference to the lord legate (Wolsey) in **121** which is certainly of October 1525, 1526 or 1527. **120** is likely to be of the same years.

The letters make it clear that Watson held office in a baronial household, most likely that of Henry's bastard the duke of Richmond, established at Sheriff Hutton in 1525 and apparently disbanded around 1530. If the identification is correct, then it would explain the adolescent behaviour of Watson's master upon the receipt of Cumberland's letter which seems fitting for a youth in his early teens.

121 Clement Watson to the first earl of Cumberland, 31 October [1525 x 1527].
BL, Althorp B1, fo. 27r-v.

Right honourable myn esspecall and singuler good lorde, after mooste humble recommendacion unto your good lordeship, pleas it the same to wete, that by your discrete servante, Mr Twhaites, I received youre right honourable letter to me, your mooste humble bedeman, directed, with a riall in goolde therynne cloosed, whiche accoording to the purpoorte of youre saide letter, I received as I have doon many other your bounteous rewardes and charitable dedes to me shewed. Withoute that I am able to deserve the same, but to God for recompence I shall daily pray.

And where ye be desirous to knowe after what soorte my maister received your lordeships letter to hym directed, for notice wherof, truste veraily my lorde, that right thankfully the same was accepted and taken and not a litle to his singuler pleasure and contentacion, wherby ye have bounden hym to shewe mutuell correspondence of kyndenes with suche pleasure as may lye in his power as I doubte not shall and woll evidentely apper in all youre good causes. Immediately upon the receipt of your lordeships saide letter and the contentes therof red and perused, soe farre as touched hym self concernyng your lordeships pleasaunt and honourable writing, he cutte awaye because he wolde shewe the reste therof to sondery of the counsaill, saying 'a man may fare well if he crye it not at the crosse'. The residue of your newes therynne conteynned did marvelously well content and pleas hym with other your doinges upon the bordours, declaring the high service your lordeship have doon, couth and mought doe, wherupon reapoorte wolbe made unto the kingges highnes and to my lorde legates grace in breve tyme. Whiche doon I shall endevour me after knowlege had, to advertise your lordeship of the specalties therof with suche other newes as shall occurre here frome tyme to tyme.

As yet I canne not fynde tyme propice for thattaynnyng of the bookes of accomptes concernyng my lordes graces houshoolde, by reason of our shorte and sklender aboode in any place, remaynnyng here not above vj or vij dayes, being otherwise occupyed as youre lordeship canne consider, having many and sondery busynesses, my maister apt and prone therunto whoe to suche as be ner aboute hym woll make fewe holidayes. Notwithstanding, after oure retorne frome oute of the North partes I shall indevour me with celeritie to depeche the same unto youre lordeship. And eftesoones for your manifoolde benevolence and gratuites to me shewed, I as a poor man may render as unto myn esspecall and singuler good lorde my mooste cordiall and humble thankes and gramerces, daily praying unto Almighty God for the preservacion of youre good lordeship with thencreace of moche honour. At Pountefret the laste daye of October.

Youre bounden bedeman with my humble service, Clement Watson.

Holograph as the previous letter. Addressed [fo. 27v], 'Unto [the ri]ght honourable myn essp[ecal] and singuler good lord [the] erle of Comberlande, vice-warden of the West Marches of Einglande for anenst Scottelande'.

122 Unknown correspondent to Sir Henry Clifford, either tenth lord Clifford or his son, later first earl of Cumberland, n.d. [before 1523]. BL, Althorp B1, fo. 21r-v.

Sir, apon first lonly and hertly promised salutacion unto your goodnes in my tenderest wies, so veraly it is that according unto your advise and my promys, I have taisted both my freyndes and also considered my prise regarding therwith as well all the casuall joperdiez of the byeing of your said wodd as the gret chargez therof both in much more money lieing downe afore handes for thutterance therof besydes your price and the charge and troble for the teith in like caise and whoo wold tak my parte or be my half in the caise. Never the les in good trewth I find noon as yitt that will and darre aventure apon the cause for both the heigh price therof and also for the uncertentye of this [...] dowtfull world and for the said chargez as well of the forsaid teith as of makyng thegez and lieing to to [*sic*] much other money downe afore handes and as frising it long in divers menes handes unto feir and sundre dais of paymentes besides gret carriagez ther of, Godes woill best when it shalbe trewly or fully paid agan ever or never because now all cuntreiz be full of veri pore folkes and because also that every man sellith and uttereth ther woddes riffely and cheiply ynewgh abowt the same cuntre and that ther is in Lincolne and Howll of all such manner stuff pleyntteth lieing as yitt unsold. If all the price therof was is and wilbe easy and reasonable and ynewgh, wherapon of and in so much as your demaund is for to have thole price therof clerely contented yow before handes at once, I therfore can in noo wies assentt therto ne graunt to bargan with your worshipfullnes enence the same except that ye woill both covenant with me for to sell as well all your said wodd with the ringe hegez and dikestalinge and thois few small treiz standing apon the landes or leiz next ther to adjonyng with vj yerez spaice of utteryng therof and to fynd me and our par plaic substanciall surety bownden by men of good landes onygh unto hus in the cuntre for both thuppholding hus of that bargan and for the clerely dischargeing hus therin enence the kynges grace and his officers and we to be att noo ferrther charge bot onely at the price whiche I offered yow therfor and we first for to mak the hole ringe hege abowt and to leif reasonable vaives woddmanlik according unto the custom of the cuntreth as well within your said wodd as in the spring hege and we to dispach or self as well as we can with the vicar or parsonez of the xth the which I fere me will put hus unto gret cost and hyndrance.

Surely Sir noo other man of this cuntre woull undergoo so good a price ne grant to gif it afore handes ne yitt so to venture ther apon with owt som abbey sore and straitly bownden for to warant them the hol bargan and to discharge them in every condition as touching the same. Wherfor Syr I beseich yow apon your favourable answer hereyn and that ye tak noo displeasur with me if I reqire apon yow (as thei[?] wold do) sufficient warantie and good suretie for performyng of our bargan if any be as gud and ye amen.

Letter quite illegible. A very small and cramped signature in the lower right hand corner might be that of J. Bekwith. Addressed, 'To the full much worshypfull knyght Sir Herry Clifforth be this letter delyvered in hast'.

The final letter in this collection is undated and comes from an unidentified writer. The address makes it most likely that it was directed to the first earl of Cumberland in the years before he succeeded his father (and so before 1523). It is possible that it was addressed to the second earl before his inheritance, but the hand would suggest an earlier date. The letter concerns negotiations between Clifford and the writer for the sale of unnamed woods. The writer appears highly sceptical of Clifford's offer, finding it too expensive and seeking acceptance of various conditions.

CLIFFORD LETTERS INDEX

Individual letters are cited in bold type, pages in roman. Counties are those existing before 1972.

II
Patrick Darcy, An Argument

Edited by
C.E.J. Caldicott

CONTENTS

ACKNOWLEDGEMENTS

The compartments of learning represented in the work of a seventeenth-century lawyer and orator are such that they overlap a number of areas of contemporary academic specialization; this edition of Darcy's *Argument* therefore owes much to the encouragement and advice of a number of colleagues. The opportunity arises in my footnotes to thank specifically Professor Kevin Cathcart (Near Eastern Studies), Professor Proinsias NíChatháin (Early Irish), Dr Michael Haren (Medieval History), all of University College, Dublin, and Father Liam Swords (chaplain to the Irish College in Paris). I would also like to record a debt of gratitude to Professor J.P. Casey (Faculty of Law), Professor J. Richmond and Mr V. Connerty (Classical Studies), Mr James McGuire (Modern Irish History), Miss Norma Jessop (Librarian, Rare Books), all of University College, Dublin, and to Miss Mary 'Paul' Pollard, formerly Keeper of Rare Books at Trinity College, Dublin, and Mrs Janet Edgell, Librarian and Keeper of the Records of the Honourable Society of the Middle Temple, London.

The work could not have begun in the first place without the generous interest and advice of Brother Benignus Millett, O.F.M., and the Librarian and staff of Dún Mhuire, the remarkable Franciscan Library of Killiney, Co. Dublin, unswervingly true, throughout the vicissitudes of higher education finance, to their tradition of collection and conservation of Irish archival records. I am most grateful to Miss Carene Comerford, of the secretarial staff of University College, Dublin, and I should particularly like to thank Professor Louis Cullen, of the Department of Modern History at Trinity College, Dublin, who began it all by inviting me to join the delegation of Irish historians at the Franco-Irish seminar on politicization in early modern France and Ireland, organised at Marseille in September, 1988, by the Ecole des Hautes Etudes en Sciences Sociales of Paris. From that encounter and the encouragement of the other members of the delegation, Dr Tom Bartlett and Professor Nicholas Canny (University College, Galway), Dr David Dickson (Trinity College, Dublin), Dr Tom Dunne (University College, Cork), Dr Marianne Elliot (University of Liverpool), and Dr Kevin Whelan (National Library of Ireland), the commitment required to complete this work was born. The background of cross-border support provided by the members of my family, English, Welsh and Irish, deserves its own dedication.

Nobody mentioned here can be held responsible for any mistakes which may survive in my text, but all are warmly thanked for attempting to steer me away from the errors of judgement and fact which have dogged the study of Anglo-Irish relations.

C.E.J. Caldicott,
University College,
Dublin,
29.vii.91

ABBREVIATIONS

The following works have been referred to extensively in this edition; they are identified in the notes in the abbreviated form given here:

Carte — Thomas Carte, *The Life of James, Duke of Ormond*, 3 vols (London, 1735–6); consulted in later edition, 6 vols (Oxford, 1851).

CD — *The Constitutional Documents of the Puritan Revolution, 1625–1660*, ed. S.R. Gardiner (Oxford, 1906).

CCR — *Calendar of the Close Rolls preserved in the Public Record Office* (London, 1901–33), reprint 1972.

CPR — *Calendar of the Patent Rolls preserved in the Public Record Office* (London, 1901–16).

CoInst., or CoLitt.— Sir Edward Coke, *The First part of the Institutes of the Lawes of England, or a Commentary upon Littleton . . .*, 7th edition (London, 1670).

CoRep. — *Les Reports de Edward Coke L'Attorney generall le Roigne*, parts I–XI (London, 1600–15); consulted as *Coke's Reports* in *English Reports*, vols 76–77 (London, 1907). (The Arabic numeral preceding the abbreviation is the number of the report, the numeral following is the original folio number, e.g., 4CoRep.86, folio 86 of Fourth Report.)

ER — *English Reports*, as above.

ESI — *Early Statutes of Ireland*, for *Statutes and Ordinances and Acts of the Parliament of Ireland. King John to Henry V*, ed. H.F. Berry (Dublin, 1907).

FNB — Anthony Fitzherbert, *La Nouvel Natura Brevium . . .* (London, 1567); consulted in edition of 1609.

Fortescue — *De Politica administratione, et legibus civilibus Angliae*, transl. Robert Mulcaster (London, 1599).

HMD — *His Majesty's Directions for Ordering and Settling the Courts within his Kingdom of Ireland* (Dublin, 1622), ed. G.J. Hand & V.W. Treadwell, *Analecta Hibernica*, 26 (1970), 178–212.

JHCI — *Journals of the House of Commons in Ireland*, vol 1, 1613–61 (Dublin, 1753).

Knafla — Louis A. Knafla, *Law and Politics in Jacobean England. The tracts of Lord Chancellor Ellesmere* (Cambridge, 1977).

195

Plucknett   – Theodore F. T. Plucknett, *A Concise History of the Common Law*, 5th edition (Boston, 1956).
Pulton   – Ferdinando Pulton, *A Collection of Sundry Statutes. Frequent in Use, with notes in the Margent*... (London, 1632).
Rastall   – William Rastall, *A Collection, in English, of the Statutes now in force, continued from the beginning of Magna Charta made in the 9..ul yeere of the Reigne of King H.3 untill the end of the Parliament holden in the 4. yeere of the Reigne of our Sovereigne King James* (London, 1608).
Statutes of Henry VI – *Statute Rolls of the Parliament of Ireland. Reign of King Henry VI*, ed. H.F. Berry (Dublin, 1910).
SR   – *Statutes of the Realm*, 4 vols (reprint, London, 1963).
TCIS   – William Molyneux, *The Case of Ireland's Being Bound by Acts of Parliament in England, Stated*, (Dublin, 1698), ed. J. O'Hanlon (Dublin, 1892).

INTRODUCTION

Although it is an important document in the history of Anglo-Irish relations, the text presented here has never yet been produced in a critical edition. It was first published in Waterford in 1643 by Thomas Bourke, printer to the Confederate Catholics of Kilkenny, in conditions of war which were presumably very difficult, and has not been reprinted since its second edition, completed in 1764 by Swift's publisher, George Faulkner.

Expressions of homage to Darcy are, of course, legion; Roy Foster, for example, in his *Modern Ireland, 1600–1972*, says of the *Argument* 'it pre-empted William Molyneux's Case by over fifty years and remained the linchpin of constitutional nationalist thought until the fall of Isaac Butt in 1877' (p.84). Charles Howard McIlwain, the distinguished American constitutional historian, wrote in *The American Revolution: A Constitutional Interpretation* (1958), that Darcy's *Argument* constitutes 'the first definite statement of the central point of the American opposition more than a century later. Patrick Darcy deserves a place in American constitutional history' (p.31). Anticipating, as it were, Blackstone's position against colonial devolution a century later, the *Argument* is the first sustained legal critique of the abuses of English law in Ireland. It appears to be high time, therefore, that the text be made accessible again.

The reasons for the continuing inaccessibility of the text are of considerable interest in themselves; they also illuminate the history of the previous editions and can be summarized as follows:

i) The text was first published in 1643 by Thomas Bourke, printer to the Confederate Catholics, in Waterford. Despite the undoubted difficulties of producing a text of such detailed reference at a time of general rebellion, Bourke's edition is a credit to his craft, with many complex references all reproduced with admirable precision; that being said, it is completely without indulgence for the twentieth-century reader. The production of law books is a highly skilled craft, requiring meticulous attention to an established and detailed reference system, as Richard Tottel's carefully produced *Year Books* show, and yet this little-known Waterford printer produced just such a highly specialised book, in which the overwhelming majority of references have proved to be accurate. On the other hand, nothing is known about the documents upon which the printer's compositorial work was based;

handwritten, and probably in note form, they may not have been revised by Patrick Darcy since the original date of his presentation of the *Argument* in 1641. The period 1641–43, which saw him passing as a lawyer to a position of rebellion in the King's name, was a particularly tense and active one in his life; indeed, it is not even sure whether it was he who commissioned the publication of the *Argument*. The list of *Faults Escaped* at the end of the Waterford edition indicates some revision, but the body of the text remained devoid of any editorial comment; all its references were maintained in a dense and contracted form, and the punctuation is often incomprehensible. In short, the text which George Faulkner re-edited in 1764 was not always easy to understand, which perhaps explains why he contented himself with simply reproducing it (without attending to the list of *Faults Escaped*). The second edition shows evidence of a tendency to tidy up, but the sense of the text is still impeded in the same way and for the same reasons; there is no editorial comment of any kind in the Faulkner edition, and the numerous legal references remained unaltered in style. It has therefore required considerable care and attention to recover the text from its original compositorial difficulties and put it in modern, comprehensible form.

ii) The 1764 text is much more accessible than the 1643 edition, for which Wing's *Short Title Catalogue*... (under D246) lists no copies extant in Ireland. The apparent difficulty of access to the 1643 edition for Irish scholars undoubtedly inhibited the confirmation of the 1764 text as a reliable basis for a new edition. The discovery of a 1643 edition of the *Argument* in the Franciscan library at Killiney, Co. Dublin, in 1988, made the work of collation immediately possible, and it is from that text that this new edition has been prepared. It can now also be added that the 1764 edition introduces almost no changes from the earlier one.

iii) In addition to the doubts caused by unverified states of edition, the question of attribution of the *Argument* has also been a source of anxiety to potential editors. Not all of the material published in the previous editions of the *Argument* is by Patrick Darcy, but there has never been any suggestion that it was; a brief glance at the summary of contents will show that the material habitually assembled under the title *An Argument* includes the message of Sir Richard Blake from the Commons to the Lords and the answers of the judges, in addition to the twenty-one queries and arguments which may more properly be attributed to Patrick Darcy. The famous queries which he carried to the Irish House of Lords for defence and illustration in 1641 were drafted and approved in the Commons on a collective basis some time previously; Darcy himself may have played a part in drafting the queries, but it was essentially in the arguments supporting the queries that he made his contribution. There will perhaps always be a measure of uncertainty about the full extent of his responsibility for the supporting arguments, but a combination of stylistic analysis and circumstantial evidence indicates a highly personal touch in this part of the text, leading to the conclusion that they are the work of one man, who could only have been Patrick Darcy. The *Journals of the House of Commons of the Kingdom of Ireland* (*JHCI*, Dublin, 1753) show that Darcy, M.P. for Bannow (Co. Wexford), was in constant demand as the main co-ordinator and advisor for the presentation of the twenty-one queries. Many of the sources quoted in the text, such as the archives of the Tower of London, would have been either incomprehensible or inaccessible to anyone but a trained lawyer who had spent time in England. Patrick Darcy studied law at the Middle Temple from 1617 to c.1622; he also returned to England for a period of seven months in 1635 with an Irish Parliamentary delegation. As the table of Galway legal family networks shows (p.227), the large and influential circle of Darcy family connections shared a similar background: Richard Blake, Richard Martin, Roebuck Lynch, and Geoffrey Browne all studied at the Temple. By submitting to the expert opinion of his cousins and brothers-in-law most of what he intended to present to the House of Lords in answer to the judges, Patrick Darcy benefited from the support of a uniquely supportive, well-advised and homogeneous professional group. But in the last resort, it was he himself who was required, in the terms of the authenticated extract from the Commons records (published in both previous editions of the *Argument*) 'to declare and set forth, at the said conference, the manifold grievances and other grounds that moved this House, to present the said questions to the Lord's House, to be propounded as aforesaid, and to give particular reasons for every of the said questions' (p.230). A close study of the text shows that he completed his brief in a masterly manner; alternately sarcastic and passionate, contemptuously dismissive or full of ringing conviction, he left an undeniably personal stamp on the text. Like the great tracts of John Milton on divorce and censorship, but arguing from a different perspective, Darcy's work addresses major topical issues with a cogency and style which preclude any possibility of it being composed in committee.

iv) Yet a further cause for earlier hesitation in re-editing the text is the precise date of composition. Historical records confirm incontrovertibly that the *Argument* was commissioned and delivered in 1641; but it was not actually published until 1643. Given that the 1643 edition was part of the Confederate Catholic propaganda campaign, there lingers the fear that the published version manipulated the original.

Once again, there is re-assurance to be found in the substance of the text; there was clearly an attempt to sway opinion in the *timing* of the publication, but within the text itself there are a number of easily verifiable extracts from the Commons records of 1641. Indeed, with their well-known concern for legitimacy and constitutional procedure, *Hibernii unanimes pro Deo, Rege, et Patria* was their motto, it was probably the aim of the Confederates to show that their positions were anchored in the debates of the last legally constituted Parliaments of Ireland. Not only are the certificates of authentic record (issued by Philip Fernely, secretary of the Commons in 1641) reproduced in *copia vera*, but the text of the judges' objections is also included. From an indubitable basis of fact, one may therefore proceed to further tests of consistency; supporting the text of the queries, also published in the *Journals of the House of Commons of the Kingdom of Ireland*, the arguments keep to the point and develop in a full and legally documented manner a series of lucid expositions. That the arguments should at the same time also expose the shortcomings of the judges' objections, also included in the text, is a further confirmation of authenticity: everything coheres.

The issue of the authentic date can thus be seen to be something of a false problem. The date of a given work is habitually taken to be the date of its first printed appearance in the world. Like a great theatrical event, there are aspects of the original performance of 1641 which cannot be entirely recaptured, but the text of 1643, published in the author's lifetime, survives; since the original events lasted several months, from May to July 1641, with a number of different contributions (notably those of Blake and the judges, which are retained here), the text claims authenticity not as an exhaustive record of events, but as a summary of essential points. Lingering uncertainties can thus be answered by evidence from the text and surrounding circumstances, including evidence from the *JHCI*, to show that the hand of Patrick Darcy was dominant in the defence of the twenty-one queries. The conclusion is thus unavoidable, that the text reproduced by George Faulkner in 1764 is sufficiently sustained by the balance between historically verifiable sections and its own inner logic to be considered free from adulteration between 1641 and 1643; the compositorial difficulties and contractions encountered by the Waterford printer lead one to believe, in fact, that it was an original, unrevised manuscript from which he had to work in 1643.

v) A member of the Supreme Council of the Confederation of Kilkenny, Darcy was a catholic royalist and one of the architects of resistance to the excesses of the English Puritan forces at work in the Irish Parliament and administration. His work would thus have been identified in a process of historical telescoping in later years, after his death in 1668 and during the Williamite period, as tainted by the political position of the Jacobites. It would not have been possible, therefore, for Protestant advocates of Irish constitutional issues, such as William Molyneux (1656–98), to allude explicitly to the work of Darcy if they wished to maintain any credibility within the political order of the day. The sanctions visited upon Molyneux after the publication of his *The Case of Ireland's being bound by Acts of Parliament in England, Stated* (1698) were already harsh enough, without the further opprobrium that the use of discredited sources would have brought on him. In fact, Molyneux's justly famous treatise borrows right and left from the work of Darcy, particularly from the later *Declaration* of 1643, but without ever naming him. This is not necessarily to accuse Molyneux of plagiarism, not at least in the orthodox sense; it is just as easy to assume that in his view Darcy's work was politically irredeemable under its own name, but too important to be left out of sight. This view appears to be confirmed by the fact that Molyneux's immediate source of information was the material compiled in 1660 by his father-in-law Sir William Domville, himself a man of the law; Domville's papers, which are preserved in the library of Trinity College, Dublin (ms. 890), reveal an absorbing interest in Patrick Darcy's *Declaration* of 1643. The alternative explanation, which is much harder to believe, is that the records of pre-Williamite constitutional resistance had been so totally expunged that none of the Confederation tracts (including the *Declaration*), nor even the name of Patrick Darcy, had reached Molyneux only fifty years later. The existence of the Domville papers virtually excludes this hypothesis. In fact, the scale of borrowing is such that the ideas, arguments, and the sources originally presented by Darcy remained very much alive in the work of Molyneux and his political heirs, but they were, in a sense, disenfranchised. The price of Molyneux's work of retrieval was complete silence as to the sources used; it was only at the cost of his identity that Darcy's work could surface so dynamically. It is to regain some of that lost recognition, and to restore his voice, that this edition has been undertaken.

All in all, it can be said that the uncertainty which hitherto inhibited the re-edition of Darcy's *Argument* is dissipated by the collation of the 1643 and 1764 editions, and by the well-tried practice of close textual analysis. The reasons for the continuing inaccessibility of the text have now become so many reasons for publishing it.

Written in the wake of Strafford's administration of Ireland, and perhaps also as a contribution to his arraignment, the *Argument* is an astute, combative, legal response to the excesses of a high-handed executive; an edition of such a work thus calls not only for close scrutiny of the text, but for a fuller account of the circumstances in Ireland at the time of its preparation, and for further information on the career of Patrick Darcy.

Patrick Darcy (1598–1668)

The most comprehensive account of the life and career of Patrick Darcy is to be found in the thesis of Liam O'Malley, 'Patrick Darcy – Lawyer and Politician, 1598–1668' (M.A. Galway, 1973); this has been published in considerably reduced form in a collection of commemorative essays, *Galway: Town & Gown, 1484–1984* (ed. Diarmuid Cearbhaill, Dublin 1984), but our purpose here is to illustrate the context and circumstances of composition of the *Argument*, not to paraphrase O'Malley's exhaustive research.

As the genealogical tables show, Darcy's family connections were wide and influential in the province of Connacht. His father's and his wife's previous marriages, and then his mother's second marriage, also within the same merchant-landowner class, accelerated even further the expansion of the family network; it was a network of relations which had the material means and incentive to send its sons to train in English law in London while the opportunity remained open for Catholics to do so. There was no training in law available for any denomination in Ireland at the time.

A further reason which can be advanced for the scions of these Galway merchant-landowners leaving Ireland to complete their education in England is that in their collective mentality, and in spite of their religion, they felt themselves to be part of the English ascendancy; in this regard, they belonged to the group known as the Old English. Aidan Clarke's brilliantly persuasive study of this community, *The Old English in Ireland, 1625–40*, illustrates the strong sense of material, cultural and ethnic interests which held them together. There is little need to comment further on Clarke's work here, except to point out that in his finely tuned synthesis it was not his intention to account for differences of individual family background; thus it is that by indicating that the Galway Darcys came not of Hiberno-Norman stock, but from the Gaelic Dorseys of Partry, Co. Mayo (O'Dorchaidhe, see family tree p.226), the contemporary Gaelic genealogist McFirbis tends to discourage the wholesale assimilation of Patrick Darcy into the Old English group. One of Clarke's conclusions is that Old English opposition to Strafford was fuelled by reactionary self-interest: the point being made here is that, even if Darcy's education in England was due to processes of emulation at work within the Old English community, it becomes difficult to argue that his interventions in the Irish Parliament, and more particularly his *Argument*, were motivated by the material interests of a minority lobby. It would be equally misleading to attribute his work to a sense of nationalist patriotism; there is a grander vision at work here, a more generous interpretation of the law.

The fact remains that the work of McFirbis, a generally reliable source, was published in Patrick Darcy's lifetime and must have been known to him, but there is no record of him refuting it, or reacting against it in any way. The Confederation of Kilkenny was openly critical of the Old Irish (Gaelic)-Old English polarities, dismissing them as artificial and contentious; the term New Irish was, in fact, sometimes used for the Old English. As an eminent leader of the Confederation, Darcy presumably shared this perception of the ethnic mosaic of Ireland. It is true that he acted as legal adviser to a number of Old and New English magnates, including the Butlers of Ormond, the Bourkes of Clanricarde, and the Boyles of Cork, but his writing claims no discrimination before the law in favour of either group.

In none of the correspondence recorded by J.T. Gilbert in his *History of the Irish Confederation and the War in Ireland, 1641-9* or so patiently collated by Liam O'Malley, does Darcy express himself as a firebrand or a rebel ringleader. The tone of his many private letters is endlessly careful, balanced and self-effacing. As a principal negotiator, and counsel to the Confederation, he twice, with painstaking attention to detail, brought negotiations for peace with Lord-lieutenant Ormond to a successful conclusion, in 1646 and 1649, only to have them dashed by circumstances beyond his control. It was also he who was delegated to attempt negotiations with the O'Neill faction when the Confederation finally began to fall apart. As M.P. for Navan (Co. Meath) in the Parliament of 1634, and Bannow (Co. Wexford) in 1640, he fulfilled his obligations conscientiously, undramatically, and very constructively, contributing with distinction to the many Commons committees on which he was asked to serve. It is thus safe to say that, in a wider perspective, the positions of Patrick Darcy and the Old English in the 1640s form part of the history of Irish constitutional opposition, a major confluent in the rising main stream.

The victory of Cromwell in Ireland in 1650 led to the risk of severe sanctions for the Confederate leaders. Under the Cromwellian administration, Darcy was tried, deprived of the right to practise as a lawyer, stripped of his estates and imprisoned. He fared little better under the Restoration: after seven years of service, from 1634-41, as an M.P. in the King's loyal Irish Parliament, nine years subsequently spent on the tightrope of Irish tri-partite division, steering the Confederation on an often-proclaimed policy of legitimate defence (against both royal incomprehension and Puritan aggression), and after waiting ten long years in impotent disgrace for the return of the Stuart dynasty which he had always sought to serve, he was offered very little restitution. The Earl of Ormond was able to help him return to his practice at the bar, but his confiscated property was never returned to him. He died in 1668 and was buried at Kilconnel (Co. Galway) in the friary of the Franciscans, the mendicant order which always remained close to the native people of Ireland and their history. His tombstone can no longer be found in the still-handsome ruins of the friary, but records have been found in France (where his descendants were ultimately to settle) which affirm that it bore the following epitaph:

'Hic misera patria sola columna jacet'[1]

Strafford and Relations at Court

With his appointment as Lord Deputy in 1633, Thomas Wentworth brought an ostentatious display of authority to the government of Ireland. After five years as Lord President of the North, during which he held absolute sway over England north of the Humber assisted by the Council of the North, a prerogative court operating beyond the jurisdiction of the common law, he quickly and inevitably antagonised the Irish Parliament; worse still, leaning increasingly on his executive powers and the Irish prerogative court of Castle Chamber, he finally antagonised both the catholic Old English and the protestant New English representatives in the Parliament. He left Ireland in 1639 to assist Charles I in his difficulties with the Scots, to be elevated to the earldom of Strafford in 1640, subsequently to be brought to trial in March 1641 and executed two months later, on 12 May.

With a similar inevitability, if there was one issue on which Patrick Darcy, the dedicated servant of the law and the Irish Parliament, was certain to challenge the Lord Deputy, it was the latter's plan for the composition of Connacht. It had been Lord Deputy Wentworth's intention to raise more revenue by proving the King's title to the lands held in the province of Connacht, and ultimately to accelerate plantation there; this meant supplanting the claims of existing landowners, many of whom were kinsmen of Darcy. The landowners in the counties of Roscommon and Galway had foreseen the onslaught and sought advice

---

'Here lies the sole support of a suffering homeland'; the source quoted leaves some doubt as to whether this was the epitaph, simply stating that '*la voix publique des Catholiques lui avait destiné cette épitaphe...*' This information is to be found in the Bibliothèque Nationale, *Collection Cherin, Généalogies Classées*, vol. 8, f°14ᵛ; the collection is compiled from material used to verify noble birth for access to office in the service of the King of France. It is a sad irony that one of the most illustrious members of the Darcy family, great-great-grandson of the seventeenth-century lawyer and also named Patrick (1725–79), chose to spend his life in exile. Elected to the Académie des Sciences at the age of 24, he was acclaimed by the French as one of the most brilliant mathematicians of his day. I am grateful to Father Liam Swords, chaplain of the Irish College in Paris, for calling to my attention the fortunes of the Darcys in France. See also *DNB*.

from Darcy and his nephew, Geoffrey Browne, for the hearings to be held at Boyle and Portumna in the summer of 1635. In July, Wentworth swept aside the arguments and legal considerations which impeded his plans for Roscommon, and moved on to the west. The hearing on the Galway estates was held at Portumna from August 13–15; Wentworth was in aggressive mood and his armed troop created a climate of intimidation, but the jury could not be deterred from finding against the claims presented by the Lord Deputy. The result was summarized by one of the commissioners, the Earl of Cork, in his diary: 'the jury would not find the King's title; thereupon Mr Darcy, high sheriff of that county [Patrick's brother Martin] was by us, the commissioners, fined in a thousand pounds sterling; Mr Bourke, for jugging one of the jury £500 and committed to the Sergeant-at-Arms to be carried to the Castle at Dublin, and all the jurors (excepting two) after particular examination, bound in one thousand pounds sterling: each to appear in the Castle Chamber the first of next term'.[2] Needless to say, sanctions against the lawyers who had so ably briefed the jury were also prepared.

Despite the threat of action pending against them, the Galway jurors, landowners, and their lawyers prepared to send a delegation to London to appeal directly to the King. The three-man delegation consisted of Darcy's brother-in-law Richard Martin (a Galway lawyer and landowner), Sir Richard O'Shaughnessy, and Patrick Darcy himself; organising their expedition in secrecy, the three agents arrived in England in early October 1635, hotly followed by Wentworth's letter of 13 October to secretary Coke urging him to treat the delegation as conspirators and then, after granting them a hearing, to arrest them for leaving Ireland without official licence. The Lord Deputy was still unaware of the full background to the Galway jurors' resistance for he wrote of Patrick Darcy as 'a lawyer and in as great practise as any other of his profession. Earnest in the way of his owne religion, but yet to speak truly of the man, that in divers particulars carried himself very well in this last parliament, driven into this business I am persuaded by Mr Martin his brother in law or by some greater persons, for which in truth I am sorry'.[3] By the time Darcy returned to Ireland eight months later to be tried and jailed, he had earned a different kind of respect from Wentworth who now called him 'the principal Boutefeu in that business'.[4]

Although their challenge to the authority of Wentworth seems at this distance to have had little hope of success, the Galway delegation presumably placed much faith in the justice of their cause and in their

[2] *Lismore Papers*, ed. A.B. Grosart, First series, iv. 123–4; quoted in O'Malley thesis, p.55.
[3] Sheffield City Library; Strafford mss. (Wentworth-Woodhouse papers), vol. 9, f° 101.
[4] *Strafford's Letters and Despatches*, ii, ed. W. Knowler, Dublin, 1740, 98.

friends at Court. They pursued their request for a hearing with great persistence[5] and frequented assiduously their principal ally, the ageing Earl of Clanricarde. Thanks to the intervention of Clanricarde and his son, Viscount Tunbridge, the King granted a hearing to the Galway agents before the Committee of Irish affairs in early November. The text of the King's evidence for the Portumna hearing survives in manuscript form, with the notes prepared by the Galway delegation for the London hearing, in Marsh's Library, Dublin (ms. Z3.2.6.), but none of the written material prepared for the meeting carried as much significance as the death of Clanricarde in mid-November; as O'Malley put it, 'any real hope of success died with him'.[6] The King had shown himself in no way prepared to abandon his support for Wentworth; not even the sentencing to death of the Irish Vice-Treasurer, Lord Mountnorris, in Dublin, for opposition to Wentworth's proposals for the customs farm, in December, 1635, appeared to shake the King's confidence in his Lord Deputy. It was at this stage that the Galway agents were ordered to return to Dublin, and 'to make haste to present their account'[7] to Wentworth. At the same time, in the wake of the customs controversy, a number of influential New English dignitaries in Dublin, including Lord Wilmot, the Earl of Cork, and Sir Piers Crosby, came forward with grievances against Wentworth. Openly befriending Darcy and his companions in London, Crosby helped them to win an important concession: Darcy was to be allowed to remain in London to present a report on the Irish customs. This was a major reversal for Wentworth; despite his letters to Archbishop Laud and secretary Coke,[8] with the support that they gave him, the Lord Deputy had not been able to prevent Patrick Darcy from winning some attention in London (whether at Court or elsewhere). In the context of the customs controversy in Dublin, it was more than a blow to Wentworth's self-respect; with New English protestants prepared to lend assistance to an Old English catholic, it was a development which looked even dangerous for him.

Darcy's report on the Irish customs, entitled *Remembrances touching the Revenue of Ireland* (published in Clarendon State Papers, vol. 1), did not attack Wentworth directly, but it did indicate room for improvement. Much of the material assembled for this report, to which English

---

[5] *Propositions humbly tendered to his Majesty, by Sir Roger O'Shaughnessy, Knight, Patrick Darcy and Richard Martin, Esqrs. Agents etc.*, Clarendon S.P., vol. 1, ed. E. Ogle, Oxford, 1872, pp.262–3. This section of the introduction relies heavily on the thesis of L. O'Malley.

[6] L. O'Malley, 'Patrick Darcy, Galway Lawyer and Politician', in *Galway: Town & Gown 1484–1984*, ed. Diarmuid Cearbhaill, Galway, 1984. p.97.

[7] Strafford mss., vol. 15, Laud to Wentworth (27 November 1635).

[8] Strafford mss., vol.9; *Strafford Letters and Despatches*, vol. 1; *The Works of Archbishop Laud*, ed. J. Bliss, Oxford, 1860, vii, *Letters*.

professional associates of Darcy may have contributed, surfaces in the *Argument*; his vision of two kingdoms united by common principles of common law found an economic extension in his advocacy of free movement and trade between England and Ireland. The work on the Irish customs won only a temporary reprieve; anxious to postpone the reckoning with Wentworth, Martin and O'Shaughnessy did not reach Dublin until early March 1636, but this only incited Wentworth to greater efforts to secure the return of Darcy. The return of the third Galway agent to face trial was not only a means of settling the score after Portumna, but it was an essential step in the elimination of the continuing challenge to Wentworth's influence in England. In consequence, Darcy was finally ordered to return to Ireland. In an important and eloquent letter, dated 2 May 1636, to secretary Windebank, he expressed his readiness to comply with the instruction, despite the certainty of the trial and sentence awaiting him in Dublin, and claimed that God and the world would bear witness how hard he had laboured in the King's service.[9] With all the promptitude expected, the Portumna jurors and the three Galway agents were brought to trial in Dublin on 27 May; on 28 May, the Earl of Cork's diary confirms that 'Mr Patrick Darcy the lawyer is now close prisoner'.[10] He was sentenced to jail with his brother Martin (sheriff of Galway); Darcy himself remained in jail for an indeterminate period, but his brother died in jail only one month later, in June 1636. Five years later, Wentworth, too, was dead; the challenge of Darcy's seven-month sojourn in England may have shown the way to that conclusion.

Strafford, Darcy, and the English Parliament
The chronology of events allows no direct connection to be made between Darcy's *Argument* and the execution of Strafford. Darcy began to prepare his presentation of the twenty-one queries after 25 May, the date at which the response of the English judges in the Irish magistrature was first read to Parliament: Strafford had already been executed two weeks earlier on Tower Hill, on 12 May (although it is not clear at what date this news reached Dublin). On the other hand, there is enough overlap in the preceding events to excite speculation and to call for explanation.

The momentum towards the execution of Strafford began in England in 1640; this coincides with the mobilisation of resistance in the Irish Parliament. The twenty-one queries of the *Argument* were first debated and approved by the Irish House of Commons in February 1641, preceded by adoption of a *Petition of Remonstrance* in November 1640, and it was with material emanating from Ireland that Pym prepared the Act of Attainder in May 1641. There is even an identity of terminology between, on the one hand, the legal terms of the third query and Darcy's supporting *ratio*, and, on the other hand, the text of the Act of Attainder itself.[11]

The chain of coincidences is extended even further by the motion approved in the Irish Parliament in February 1641 to impeach Sir Richard Bolton (Lord Chancellor of Ireland), Sir Gerard Lowther (Lord Chief Justice of the Common Pleas), Dr John Bramhall (Bishop of Derry), and Sir George Radcliffe (Strafford's former agent in Ireland). Thomas Carte, the biographer of the Duke of Ormond (an Earl and lieutenant-general of Ireland at the time of these events), reports Ormond's view that the Remonstrance of 1640 was 'part of a conspiracy to cast an odium on the Earl of Strafford and his administration' (Carte, vol. i, 230); it was also Ormond's view that the attempt to impeach the most eminent members of the Irish magistrature was part of the same conspiracy, 'their measures [of the Irish House of Commons] were so exact a transcript of the methods which the others had taken in England, that it is reasonable to imagine that they were suggested and encouraged from thence [from Westminster]' (Carte, i, 303–4). More than that, it was Ormond's considered opinion that the impeachment procedures were designed to prevent the accused from testifying in Strafford's defence in England (Carte, i, 256). There was therefore some collusion between at least some of the Irish M.P.s and some of the English M.P.s, but the role of Darcy in these exchanges remains unclear.

There is no mention of Patrick Darcy in those journals of the Irish House of Commons which report the earlier debates of November 1640, and February 1641; as will be seen in an examination of the text, everything suggests that his brief for the presentation of the *Argument* in May 1641 was to illustrate and defend the ground already demarcated by the Commons in the earlier debates. It is also clear that there would not have been agreement on common ground in the Irish Parliament if the New English M.P.s had not also been discontented with Strafford. The question therefore arises as to Darcy's activity in England at an even earlier stage, from October 1635 to April 1636. Did the opponents of the *Thorough* policy and the Court make themselves known to him at that time? Had he aligned himself in any way with the English

---

[11] Strafford's *Act of Attainder*, (voted in English Parliament, May 1641), includes the passage: '*for having by his own authority commanded the laying and setting of soldiers upon His Majesty's subjects in Ireland, against their consents, to compel them to obey his unlawful summons and orders, made upon paper petitions in causes between party and party*' (S.R. Gardiner, *The Constitutional Documents of the Puritan Revolution, 1625–60*, Oxford, 1906, p.157).

Country party? To what extent had his informed, constitutional opposition suggested further courses of action? There is simply no clear answer available upon such a range of questions, covering both active and passive involvement: active in the sense that he might have collaborated knowingly, as a legal advisor, with New English plans for the downfall of Wentworth; passive in the sense that his example might have attracted attention in England and offered ammunition to a campaign for which he was in no way responsible. It must be pointed out that the hardening of attitudes of the New English Puritan associates in Ireland, and the collapse of the New English-Old English parliamentary alliance, began after the trial of Strafford (which contained essential Irish material, see note 11) and gathered momentum with the Ulster rebellion of October 1641; the implication is that Darcy may well have become in 1635–36 the unwitting trigger or instrument of political forces working for the short-term goal of Wentworth's destruction. Not only the timing but the text of the *Argument*, with all his correspondence, indicate Darcy's own preoccupation with long-term projects for legal reform and specific issues in law. The experience of the Galway delegation to London and the patterns of influence observed further suggest that, within the Irish political community, only the protestant M.P.s of the Irish Parliament could have secured the demolition of Strafford. Darcy himself appears to have been consistent in his role as a lawyer, not as a politician. The extent to which he was manipulated, or to which he manipulated others, remains conjectural.

In the wider context, the *Argument* can be construed as the disillusioned epilogue to the Old English faction's attempt to secure from Charles I the Graces, those concessions which had been under discussion since 1628; in global terms, the disappointment of the 1634 Parliament, when Wentworth dashed any remaining hopes of concessions to the Old English, must have served as a catalyst for further opposition. Significant too, is the collapse of the catholic-protestant, Old English-New English, alliance in the Irish Parliament after the execution of Wentworth; it led to the dramatic marginalization of the Old English. Wentworth is a central figure in all these developments: provoking a coalition in opposition to his policy as Lord Deputy, he released a chain of circumstances which, following his own downfall, led to a New English hegemony in Ireland. The Confederation of Kilkenny, an Old English-Old Irish alliance, was formed only after the English executive in Ireland and the Parliament at Westminster, in an intractable over-reaction to the Ulster rebellion of late 1641, had virtually classified all citizens of Ireland as rebels, and this after the Irish Parliament had formally condemned the rebellion at its outset. Patrick Darcy was among those who condemned the rebellion in 1641. Resistance in Ireland to English legislation, whether from Dublin Castle or from

Westminster, was bound to become generalized in the wake of the odious Acts of Adventurers, passed in series in London from 1642 to 1653; these acts, which put up for sale 2,500,000 acres of Irish land in return for covenanted money to subsidise the levying of troops for Ireland, were passed by the English Parliament without any reference to its Irish counterpart. With the English Parliament increasingly animated by the suspicion that there was collusion between the King and the leaders of the Irish rebellion, and that most inhabitants of the island were associated with the rebellion, the position of Patrick Darcy and other Old English jurists became untenable. They were driven to form a Confederation, based on a formal constitution (drafted by Darcy), which stood for legitimate revolt in the King's name. Irish royalist legitimists were thus branded as rebels by English republican dissidents, and the label has not changed since. Unswervingly loyal to the pen rather than to the sword, Darcy sought for constitutional solutions by legal means, and yet he found himself condemned by the politics of the English Civil War to a path of rebellion. It was in this climate that the decision to publish his *Argument* was taken.

From a degree of cooperation in 1640–41 which made the constricting articles of Poynings' Act (10 Hen.vii, 1494–5) seem even more repressive, the English and Irish Parliaments raced to amalgamation under Cromwell, with the Irish Commons finally represented by no more than 20 M.P.s at Derby House in London. Amalgamation was only achieved, of course, at the cost of catholic representation; it is one of the paradoxes of the time that these deteriorating circumstances enhance the interpretation of Poynings' Law, making it appear to be a better option for Ireland, a legal guarantee that the Irish Parliament should at least exist. Fostered by the New English alliance, Darcy's *Argument* thus transcended and survived the politics of the time to speak for the universal values of Irish constitutional opposition, as expressed by later patriot-lawyers of both religious persuasions.

The chronology of events

The twenty-one queries, which must be distinguished from Darcy's supporting arguments, were first debated and approved in the Irish House of Commons on 16 February 1641, without any known involvement of Patrick Darcy[12] (although he may have given advisory assistance); they are confirmed in the text of the two published editions as *copia vera*, authentic copies of Commons records, by the clerk of the Commons, Philip Ferneley (p.230). At the same time, the House approved the motion to impeach Sir Richard Bolton, Sir Gerard

---

[12] *Journals of the House of Commons in Ireland* (*JHCI*, Dublin, 1753), *passim*, for the years concerned.

Lowther, Dr John Bramhall, and Sir George Radcliffe. The original date of proposal of the queries therefore coincides with a mood of quite explicit hostility towards the judiciary, and it precedes by some months the train of events in which Patrick Darcy was known to be involved. Even before the February vote of the Commons on the queries, many of them had been anticipated by the articles of a *Petition of Remonstrance*, drafted in the Commons in November 1640 (specific points of comparison between the queries and the articles of the Remonstrance are made in the footnotes as they arise).

The constitutional and legal issues raised in the queries were addressed to the Lord Justices of Ireland, but designed as a joint approach from both houses of Parliament; this plan was supported by the Lords who, in the message carried to them from the Commons by Sir Richard Blake, were requested 'to require the judges of this realm [of Ireland] to deliver their opinions unto them [the Lords] of those queries, and that in writing and speedily' (p.238). The Lords complied promptly with the request of the Commons in February, but did not receive their answer from the judges until May. It was not without some coercion that the judges finally responded. Still awaiting an answer from the judges, the Commons sent Sir Richard Blake back to the Lords with a formal enquiry about progress in the matter; he returned to the Commons on 13 May to inform them that the Lords considered that 'matters were of great consequence, and required some debate, but they would by their own messengers give this House [the Commons] a speedy answer'. Further confirmation of the good relations between Lords and Commons came with the supplementary messages borne by Blake: the Commons were also informed that two of the judges, Mr Justice Mayart and Mr Baron Hilton, had acknowledged their obligation to respond; furthermore, the Lords had already made a supplementary order that on 'Monday seven-night the judges shall answer the queries'.[13] In other words, the Lords were doing things their own way, but had already put pressure on the judges to respond to the queries, and had finally given them until Monday, 24 May, to do so. In response to Blake's report, the House of Commons 'was very thankful and did greatly joy that both Houses did so well agree'.[14] It is quite clear from the first paragraph of the judges' eventual answer (p.239) that they had demurred on a number of occasions, but that the Lords had 'overruled them and often commanded their answers to the said questions.' The date given by the text for the judges' answer is 25 May, but this presumably refers to the date of first reading in the Lords, after the arrival of the answer by the stipulated deadline of 24

[13] *JHCI*, 366.
[14] *Ibid.*

May. Since the judges' answer was addressed to the Lords, the Commons did not formally hear the answer until Friday 28 May; the journal of the Commons records that 'this House did not hold it fit it should be called an answer, but absolutely to be refused'.[15] Arrangements were then immediately made to meet with the Lords in joint committee to discuss the matter; the joint meeting was initially planned for the end of the following week, Saturday 5 June, but in the meantime the House was a hive of activity. The next day, Saturday 29 May, the House dissolved itself into a grand committee to discuss the documents received; as recorded in the $JHCI$,[16] the following instructions were agreed:

– 'It is ordered by this House that Mr Patrick Darcy shall be Prolocutor of the committee appointed to meet a committee of the House of Lords on Saturday next [5 June].'
– 'and this House doth strictly charge the said Patrick Darcy carefully to attend that particular occasion and to be prepared for it'.
– it was also ordered that all members of the House, 'especially those of the Long Robe, endeavour to bring in their arguments and objections to that writing [the answer of the judges], and every part thereof, upon Wednesday next [2 June] at ten of the clock in the morning'.
– 'Mr Patrick Besford, Mr Richard Martin, Mr Thomas Tyrell, Mr William Brent and Mr Patrick Kirwan shall immediately have copies of queries and give answers to Mr Darcy by Wednesday at 7 o'clock in the morning.'

Aiming for an agreed plan of action to put to the Lords at the meeting of 5 June, all the talent and energy of the Commons was therefore mobilized to provide Darcy's committee with as full a range of answers as possible by Wednesday 2 June; specialized memoranda from designated lawyers in the House were to be in his hands by 7 a.m. on the same date. Not only did the series of meetings planned for 2 June take place, but a further session was arranged for the Friday, 4 June; at the same time, the Speaker of the House was asked to request the Lords for a postponement from Saturday to Monday 7 June of their scheduled joint meeting. The pressure was clearly mounting, because the previously reserved date of 5 June was used by the Commons to call yet another session of their own, still with the sole subject of the judges' answer on the agenda. The joint meeting of the Lords and Commons of Ireland thus began on Monday 7 June, with the Great Dining Room of Dublin Castle as the appointed meeting place. It was there, after nine days of preparatory work, that Patrick Darcy made his historic presentation, at a session which lasted until Wednesday 9 June.

Whatever the anticipated response of the judges may have been, the answer they actually delivered threw the Commons into a nine-day frenzy, suggesting immediately that there was an element of surprise involved. Could the judges' answer have been less submissive than hoped for? If their response was not unexpected, why such a frenzy of activity? If it was unexpected, Darcy had very little time in which to prepare a very technical and detailed set of answers. He mentions ruefully in the opening remarks of his reply that the judges had had several months to prepare an answer, and that he was bringing forward 'some parts of those reasons and authorities which were gathered and ripened to my hands by the House of Commons' (p.254). This modest disclaimer of more immediate responsibility should be treated with caution. It naturally improved his case to say that it was representative of the House of Commons, but it should also be borne in mind that he could not afford in such circumstances, and in criticizing such eminent authorities, to use any erroneous material; it is a matter of very serious doubt whether, in the limited time available to him, Darcy could possibly have drafted a compendium of all the material submitted during the giant trawl of 28 May–5 June through the Commons, having previously verified the accuracy of all the sources used. Not only are the references of the *Argument* massively correct (and identified in the footnotes), but they relate coherently to each other in a series of clear, cogent theses; the inescapable conclusion is that, apart from some contributions of legal associates, the corpus of material he used was essentially his own. The timetable he faced on 29 May required him to work fast and to rely on his own resources; with sources quoted from the Tower of London, there is every reason to believe that some of the material used in the *Argument* dates from Darcy's early training at the Middle Temple twenty years earlier. This, in turn, suggests that the *Argument* was used as a punctual opportunity to summarize a number of concerns which Darcy had been contemplating for some time.

If it comes as no surprise to learn that Darcy put much more of his own work into his *Argument* than he admits to, it is quite a revelation to discover how fast he had to work. It is generally assumed that, as a seminal document in Anglo-Irish relations, the *Argument* was composed at leisure as the fruit of a long meditation. The reality appears to be somewhat different: meditation there certainly was, spanning the great issues of parliamentary sovereignty and executive authority of the previous quarter century, but the composition was, as another great Irishman might have said, 'a close-run thing'.

The legal sources and issues
Many of the issues in law raised by Darcy were defined by his sources;

the overriding influence in the *Argument*, whether in terms of the number of precedents quoted or of theory, is that of Sir Edward Coke (1552–1633), Lord Chief Justice of England (1613–33) and the first to bear that title. The state inquisitor of Essex, Raleigh, the conspirators of the Gunpowder Plot, and Francis Bacon, but also the champion of the common law and the inspiration of the *Petition of Right* (1628), Coke was a colossus in the heroic age of the common law and parliamentary prerogative. It may seem ironic, but hardly surprising, that Darcy's work should be so strongly marked by the great English jurist; as a student in the Middle Temple from 1617 to c.1622, Darcy would have been subjected to the influence and interest of volume after volume of Coke's *Reports* and *Institutes* as they came off the press – he may even have had the opportunity to meet the great man (himself a former bencher of the Inner Temple), still alive and well during Darcy's student years. Of the fifty-seven cases listed in the *Table of Named Cases*, approximately fifty come from Coke's *Reports*. And Coke's sources, the old *Year Books* (law reports of pre-Tudor times), *Littleton, Fitzherbert, Pulton*, subsequent commentators such as Plowden (1518–85, also a catholic from the Middle Temple), and Egerton on the *Post-Nati* (a text of critical interest for the young expatriate Irishman), became the sources of the young student, just as Coke's theory of the primacy of the common law, before which even Kings had to bend the knee, became the example to follow. The effectiveness of Darcy's position stems precisely from the fact that he berates the English judges of Ireland in terms of English law; it was a particularly well chosen tactic, because the judges were obliged to respond in terms of the law which Darcy appeared to know better than them. In other words, the English administration of justice in Ireland was belaboured not because it was English, but because it was not English enough, failing to reach the high standards that a Coke would have exerted in England. The *Argument* is a critique in English law of the abuses of English law in Ireland; Brendan Bradshaw mentions earlier examples of the kind in his *The Irish Constitutional Revolution of the Sixteenth Century*, and Darcy may have known them, but his was the first sustained work of the kind to be published.

Darcy's originality lies in attempting to apply to the new conditions of post-feudal Ireland this emerging code of law initially designed to protect the common man against abuses of authority in England. Indeed, at one point in the preamble to their answer, the judges attempt to deny the transferability of legal systems, as if the common law was not designed to apply to Irish people (*Argument*, p.243). Darcy himself appears to be in no doubt, 'the law of England, he wrote, it is the best human law, so it is a noble and sociable law, and for the more clear discerning of the truth and equal administration of justice, it refers many cases to their genuine and natural proceedings' (*Argument*, p.271).

The 'law of England', as distinct from civil or Roman law, 'consists', continues Darcy, 'of three parts. First, the common law. Secondly, the general customs of England. Thirdly, statutes here received [. . . .] And yet if any man ask the question, by what law we are governed, there is no proper answer other than by the law of England' (*Argument*, p.269). This 'triangular' analysis comes straight from the first volume of Coke's *Institutes of the Lawes of England*, known as *Coke upon Littleton* (1628): '*Consuetudo* [custom] is one of the main triangles of the laws of England, those laws being divided into Common Law, Statute Law and Custom', (CollInst, f° 110ᵛ).

In the same work, Coke wrote that the sovereign arbiter of the law is Parliament, 'Parliament is the highest and most honourable and absolute Court of Justice in England' (f°, 109); Darcy's view was predictably similar and often repeated, Parliament 'is the supreme Court, nay the primitive of all other courts; to that court belongs the making, altering, regulating of laws, and the correction of all courts and ministers' (*Argument*, p.297). In extrapolating from Coke on the rights of the English Parliament, Darcy assumed that the rights and status of the Irish Parliament were identical and parallel; indeed, he went so far as to present the judges of Ireland, summoned to answer for their negligence before the Irish Parliament, as delinquents, but adding that 'only delinquents of an high nature are defendants in this high court of Parliament' (*(Argument*, p.261). In quoting almost *verbatim* from Coke on the function of Parliament, Darcy leaves himself vulnerable, because he puts himself far beyond the Irish situation. The circumstances in which Coke and the English Parliament found themselves at the time of the *Petition of Right*, for example, were very different from Darcy's situation. 'Look upon the members of it', he writes of Parliament, 'first the King is the head who is never so great nor so strong as in Parliament, where he sits ensconced with the hearts of his people' (*Argument*, p.297). The simple fact of the matter was that the king of England was not in the habit of gracing the Irish Parliament with his presence; the only monarch to have presided over a sitting of the Irish Parliament at the time of the *Argument* was Richard II, to be followed in 1689 by James II. Whether Darcy saw a strategic advantage in taking the work of Coke as his principal source, or whether he really believed in what he was saying, cannot now be determined, but his comments on the role of the Irish Parliament provide some of the more reverberant passages of the *Argument*. He appears to have gained an advantage in the short-term, because the judges, for their part, did not attempt to defend themselves by denying the implicit affirmation of identical and parallel parliamentary rights between England and Ireland.

To defend parliamentary prerogative in Ireland was also a prudent way of attacking conciliar government, that excessive recourse to the prerogative court of Castle Chamber (the Irish equivalent of Star Chamber) which had become habitual under Wentworth; in seeking to defend executive, conciliar government in Ireland, despite the imminent abolition of Star Chamber in England (July 1641), the judges may, in their turn, have been prudently attacking the notion of identical and parallel parliamentary rights. Executive government also meant by-passing Parliament with the reliance on judge-made law. Under the impulsion of Sir John Davies, the Welsh-born Solicitor-General of Ireland (1603–6), and then Attorney-General (1606–19), the English administration had been swift to exploit the collapse of the Irish feudal infrastructure after the flight of the Earls; a corpus of judge-made law was introduced which avoided the need for parliamentary legislation. Identified by Hans Pawlisch as 'legal imperialism' (*Argument*, note 66), it resulted in a tangle of punitive fiscal laws which were further complicated by regional variations; holy water, for example, was taxed in Connaught, but apparently not elsewhere (*JHCI*, 10 June 1640). The strategy of presenting the queries to the judges was designed to remind them of those principles and statutes of law which governed the application of the common law; in other words, the questions were asked not in ignorance, but in full knowledge of the law. Expected to confirm the articles of law asserted in the queries (and having little option but do so), the judges would at the same time expose their own negligence in failing to make the executive answerable to law – and it was in their failure to maintain a legal code of practice for the executive as well as for everyone else that the judges were open to charges of malfeasance. The evidence marshalled against them by the redoubtable Darcy was overwhelming. He was able to quote 28 Hen.VI, c.6 (1450) to show that the jurisdiction of the four courts of King's Bench, Common Pleas, Chancery and Exchequer had been defined in Ireland two hundred years earlier, and he used more recent material to demonstrate that a clear code of practice existed; a frequently-quoted source in the *Argument* is *His Majesty's Directions for Ordering and Settling the Courts within His Kingdom of Ireland* (Dublin, 1622), in which paragraph 1, entitled 'Causes to be heard at the Councell Table', reads 'And that neither the Lord Deputie, Governours, nor Councell Table, do hereafter intermeddle nor trouble themselves with common businesse.'[17] The judges were thus in breach of their own recent manual of proper conduct.

In addition to known and accessible sources, Darcy succeeded in gaining access to the archives of the judicial system in England, at the Tower of London, where the original documents relating to Ireland

---

[17] *His Majesty's Directions for Ordering and Settling the Courts within his Kingdom of Ireland* (Dublin, 1622), eds. G.J. Hand and V.W. Treadwell, *Analecta Hibernica*, 26 (1970), 190.

were also to be found. Needless to say, he did not have time to consult this material in response to the punctual circumstances of May 1641; the information deriving from the Tower archive probably dated from his days at the Middle Temple, and also from his seven-month sojourn in London in 1635–6. His use of this material in the *Argument* is probably the most striking and least appreciated aspects of his work. Its significance lies in the suspicion harboured among the opposition that the chief magistrates of Ireland, almost invariably Englishmen nominated from England, were systematically dilapidating the Irish legal records and parliamentary rolls. The concern surfaced quite explicitly in Parliament immediately prior to the preparation of the *Argument*, on 24 May (the date at which the judges were supposed to have answered the queries), when the Lords and Commons of Ireland drafted a joint petition to Charles I pointing out that, since the Irish parliamentary system had always followed English practice, they required the maintenance of a proper archive and 'pray that the King will not allow this system to be altered. The ancient records of Ireland have mostly gone to England, or been embezzled or destroyed, and the Lord Chancellor and Lord Chief Justice of the Common Pleas had the custody of the few which remained, even after they had been impeached.'[18]

More precise information on the missing material is offered in a later document, also issued in 1643 by the Confederate Catholics of Kilkenny, entitled *A Declaration*, almost certainly written by Patrick Darcy and his circle, it presents the problem as follows: 'But these statutes [of Ireland, from Edward III to Henry V] are not to be found in these parliamentary rolls, nor any parliamentary rolls at that time, but the same are exemplified under the great seal, and the exemplifications were remaining in the treasury of the city of Waterford: and it is most certain that not only these parliament rolls, but also many other rolls and records miscarried in those troublesome and distempered times which have been in Ireland. For in all the times of Edw.3, Rich.2, Hen.4 and Hen.5, which is almost an hundred years, there is not any parliament roll to be found; and yet it is most certain that divers Parliaments were holden in those times.'[19] The concern about the

[18] *Cal.S.P. Ireland, 1633–47* (London, 1901), p.297.

[19] *A Declaration setting forth How and by What means, the laws and statutes of England, from time to time, came to be of force in Ireland* (probably Waterford, 1643), reprinted in W. Harris, *Hibernica*, Part 2, *Two treatises Relating to Ireland* (Dublin, 1770), pp.9–45. The passage quoted is on p.15. One of several passages reproduced in their entirety by William Molyneux in his *The Case of Ireland's Being Bound by Acts of Parliament in England, Stated* (Dublin, 1698), this particular passage can be found in Molyneux, pp.51–3 (edition of J. O'Hanlon, P.P., M.R.I.A., Dublin, 1892). It is here that Molyneux attributes the original reflexions on the missing statutes to Sir Richard Bolton, considered by Darcy and his contemporaries to have been the real culprit in the matter.

missing hundred years of Irish legal archives, from Edward III to Henry V (1327–1422), had certainly been fortified by a similar absence of any Irish statutes, from 3 Edw.II to 7 Hen.VI, in Bolton's *Statutes of Ireland* (Dublin, 1621). One of the few recently published summaries of Irish statute law, this compilation was the work of Sir Richard Bolton, the Lord Chancellor of Ireland who was threatened with impeachment in 1641 and also named in the parliamentary petition to Charles I as a leading culprit in the disappearance of Irish legal records. There was clearly a conspiracy theory in circulation which imputed sinister intentions to Bolton for omitting one hundred years of Irish statute law; by an unfortunate coincidence only those statutes which seemed less clement to the Irish were included in Bolton's work. To add insult to injury, Bolton's son Edward was one of the judges assigned to answer the queries (*Argument*, note 40).

The *Table of Statutes* shows that, of the one hundred and fifty statutes quoted by Darcy in the *Argument*, there are over sixty quoted from the missing century (with more than fifty from the reign of Edward III alone). It is Darcy's great achievement to have recovered the missing hundred years in his *Argument*; where the *Declaration* simply states that the material is missing from the Irish records, the earlier *Argument* makes the same point by recuperating and quoting the material in great quantity. The proliferation of legal references would be a normal feature of judicial procedure, but it is also explained in the *Argument* by an unusual zeal to reveal full knowledge of the Irish legal archive; in the prevailing climate of suspicion, the abundant use of the missing statutes which Darcy had recovered from the Tower of London suggests a coded communication to the judges, in which he sought to stress not only that he knew what they knew, but that he also knew what he was not supposed to know. In recovering so many statutes from the missing century, particularly from the administratively rich 50-year reign of Edward III, Darcy also retrieved a sense of historical existence and continuity for Irish legislation. This was a heroic undertaking, deserving much wider appreciation in the Ireland of today, for the example as much as for any substantive material recovered; his remarkable recovery of the statutes has an added poignancy in circumstances in which his own work stands in need of recovery from the past.

The strategy of retrieval was also a major rebuff for the judges, even if not as explicit as his dismissal of them in the analogy with Hophni and Phinehas, the sons of Levi and unworthy custodians of the Ark: 'the question not being whether the Ark should be rescued from the Philistines, but whether it should be preserved against the negligence of some Hophni and Phinehas in their hands that have the custody of it' (*Argument*, p.262). In a curious codicil to Darcy's recovery of the statutes and his dismissal of the judges, it should be noted that Molyneux's *The Case of Ireland ... Stated* later borrowed wholesale from the relevant passages of the *Declaration* and, in a monument of mistaken identity, attributed authorship to none other than Sir Richard Bolton (see note 19 above). Darcy had, with considerable skill, already transfixed Bolton and his largely Anglican associates with an Old Testament reference to suit the sagest patriarch (1 *Samuel*.i), and cast himself, unconsciously no doubt, in the role of a new Samuel. The image is exemplary; cast in the role of judge and prophet of a new era, custodian of the law, Darcy prefigures a pattern of political conduct which assembles a number of unlikely companions, from the members of the 'Patriot' Parliament in 1689, to Molyneux, to John Philpott Curran, Henry Grattan and even Daniel O'Connell. After the collapse of the old Gaelic order at the start of the seventeenth century, there appears to be no more effective figure of opposition in Ireland than the patriot-lawyer. Brendan Bradshaw's work shows how this pattern even pre-dated the flight of the Earls; the point here is that the number of options available to spokesmen of the opposition in Ireland was even further reduced after the turn of the century.

On introductive and declarative laws
The 'lost' statutes are deployed in a tighter thematic vein in the *Declaration* than in the *Argument*; they are used in the later work to exploit a thesis based on the distinction between *declarative* and *introductive* laws. This thesis surfaces in the *Argument* (p.270), but is not given a full airing; since it is a central feature of Darcy's concept of Anglo-Irish relations, and was also part of his thinking in 1641, it should be examined more closely here. Introductive laws were, in Darcy's terms, those laws which changed the practice of the common law in England or Ireland, which were binding, therefore, in both countries; an obvious example of such a law was *Poynings' Act* (10 Hen.VII), which introduced legislation to ensure 'that no Parliament be holden in this land [Ireland] untill the Acts [proposed legislation] be certified into England [approved by Privy Council].' A declarative law was one which confirmed or clarified the existing corpus of legislation, without 'in any ways altering, adding unto, or diminishing ancient Common Laws' (*Declaration*, pp.14–15). The further point is made in the *Declaration*, greatly expanding on the initial reference in the *Argument*, that no new introductive laws 'have been binding or in any ways of force in Ireland until such time as they have been enacted, allowed and approved of by Act of Parliament in Ireland' (p.15). As confirmation of the point, the text cites a number of examples: *Poynings' Law* under Henry VII, the *Statutes of Marlborough* under Henry III, and the *Statute of Gloucester* under Edward I, were

(amongst others) all passed in the Irish Parliament prior to implementation. This rationalisation of English and Irish statute law was duplicated by Molyneux in his *Case of Ireland ... Stated.*[20] The requirement of approval by the Irish Parliament for introductive laws emanating from England is only implicit in the *Argument*, but there is a lateral line of support in the text for the notion of sovereignty of Parliament in the vast corpus of declaratory law in Ireland which it presents. There is a fine rationalist clarity to the theory, but, for his interpretation of Irish parliamentary sovereignty to be conclusive, Darcy should also have been able to quote an example of the Irish Parliament *refusing* to approve an English introductive law. This is an unfriendly twentieth-century brick to throw at Darcy's constitutional edifice, but within his scheme all introductive laws happen to be English, and by coincidence they all seem to be approved by the Irish Parliament: the approval of *Poynings' Act* by the Irish Parliament is not, in the last resort, a proof of sovereignty. This by no means destroys Darcy's political construct (Poynings' Law was, after all, subjected to a vote in the Irish Parliament before adoption), but it does illustrate how complex and finely balanced the issues were in the constitutional no-man's land which lay between the two kingdoms. In the absence of an English right of conquest, both sides sought solutions without appearing to understand the premisses of the other. In order to illustrate the nature of the balance, it could be said that, from an apprehensive English perspective, Irish declaratory laws could have looked rather more like introductive laws!

There is a bold certitude to Darcy's concept of the law and the constitutional status of Ireland in 1641: 'And yet if any man ask the question, by what law we are governed, there is no proper answer other than by the law of England' (p.270). This presumably meant for him that the Irish Parliament was sovereign within the English legal framework and under the monarch. The situation did not seem as clear two years later when he asserted in the *Declaration* that 'by the resolution of *Calvin's Case*, Coke 51.7.f° *23* [*recte*, 7Co.Rep.23b], it appears that Ireland is governed by laws and customs "separate and divers from the laws of England", which proveth that it is a distinct dominion, separate from the Kingdom of England'. The text of the *Declaration* dates, of course, from the time of the war in Ireland and thus reflects a more sombre mood than the ideas of two years earlier. Even though Lord Egerton took the opportunity to scold the Lord Chief Justice of England for totally confusing the issue on the matter of the Irish constitution, Coke has left in his *Reports* a number of interesting discussions on the status of the Irish Parliament; there are the marginal

---

[20] Molyneux, p.55 and *passim*.

comments in his review of *Calvin's Case* which are mentioned above, but in a full discussion of *Poynings' Act* in 12Co.Rep.110–11 (which Darcy may have heard, but not seen, because it was published posthumously, and after these events, in 1655), Coke himself concludes surprisingly that 'the Acts of Parliament made in England since the Act of 10 H.VII do not bind them in Ireland: but all Acts made in England before the 10 H.VII by the said Act made in Ireland, *anno 10 H.VII cap. 22,* do bind them in Ireland'.[21] According to this interpretation, all acts of Parliament in England which preceded *Poynings' Act* were introductive, and all those which followed, declarative. Fortunately for Darcy, the Irish judges either did not know or want to know this interpretation of Coke's dating from 1604; it would certainly have helped them to counter the exploitation of the 'missing hundred years', but it would also have obliged them to acknowledge that, in the interim, the Irish Parliament had become a sovereign body. The issue of parliamentary sovereignty would not, in any case, have affected Darcy's thesis of 1641 that Ireland was governed by the laws of England.

The judges
It was to the Lord Justices of Ireland that the twenty-one queries of the *Argument* were addressed. The queries covered specific points of law and legal procedure which the Commons deemed to have been neglected in the recent past. Since the answers to the queries were already known, each one was a potential trap for the judges; a denial of the point raised would imply incompetence and provoke supplementary questions, whereas a confirmation of the point would indicate negligence and entail sanctions. It thus hardly surprising that they responded with caution, generally holding their ground but offering a judicious number of concessions; their basic position was conservative, defending recourse to executive authority under the pretext of respect for the royal prerogative. Although attacking the excesses of executive authority in Ireland, the queries carried an implicit accusation of negligence against the judges for failing to impose proper procedure on the executive. The answer of the judges was delivered to Parliament in written form in time for a first reading at the House of Lords on 25 May; as has been seen, their response threw the Commons into a frenzy of activity, apparently fanning the resentment which had been smouldering for some time against executive injustice. If the queries were the first phase of the episode covered by the text of the *Argument*, the judges' response was the second phase, and Darcy's defence of the queries in answer to the judges was the third phase. The deep-seated fear of the Commons was that the judges' answer would be construed

[21] *English Reports*, vol. 77, 1388.

as a legitimization of those procedures of the executive which had provoked the queries in the first place; they needed their best brains to limit the risk.

The seven judges who were given the unenviable task of preparing (or at least signing) an answer to the queries were, in the order of their signatures (*Argument*, p.252):

Sir George Shurley (1559–1647), Chief Justice of the King's Bench, commissioner of the plantation of Ulster.

Sir Edward Bolton (1592–1659), Solicitor-General for Ireland, subsequently Chief Baron of the Exchequer; son of the Lord Chancellor.

Sir Samuel Mayart (1587-c.1646), Second Justice of the Common Bench, treasurer of the King's Inns.

Hugh Cressy (?–c.1643), Second Justice of the King's Bench.

Sir James Barry (?–1673), M.P. for Lismore and Second Baron of Exchequer, later Chief Justice of King's Bench with the title of Lord Santry after the Restoration.

James Donnellan (?–1665), Chief Justice of Connaught and M.P. for Dublin University in 1634; Third Justice of Common Pleas, 1637.

William Hilton, (?–1651), Attorney-General for Connaught, 1626; M.P. for Armagh, 1634; Third Baron of Exchequer, 1638.[22]

Of these, only Barry, Donnellan and Hilton were Irish; Donnellan and Hilton had already been encountered at the time of the composition of Connacht, as had the Crown Clerk Sir Philip Perceval (1605–47) who, besides breaking all records for getting richer quicker than most officers of the Crown in Ireland, is reported as having spent eight successive weeks in Loughrea in 1635 'enrolling titles of the Galway plantation'.[23] Sir Edward Bolton, son of the Lord Chancellor, stood in for his father whose participation was invalidated by the charges of impeachment which were pending.

As far as can be ascertained, the intellectual weight in the panel of judges would have come from Shurley and Mayart. Educated at Cambridge and the Middle Temple, Shurley was the senior signatory, with much experience behind him; it was Mayart who was to provide for the government two years later such an effective response to the constitutional arguments supporting the sovereignty of the Irish Parliament produced by Darcy and his circle under the title *A Declaration*. More information can be found on the judges in the note to the appropriate passage (note 40), but as an assessment of their collective

---

[22] The information on the judges' careers is drawn from F. Elrington Ball, *The Judges in Ireland, 1221–1921* , 2 vols (London, 1926); further material is to be found at note 40 to the *Argument*.

[23] H. Kearney, *Strafford in Ireland: 1633–41: a study in Absolutism* (Manchester, 1959). p.100.

strength, it can be said that they combined experience, knowledge of the law, and exposure to local conditions, with political acumen, mental toughness, and a gift for survival.

The edition of 1643

Against the background of tension and speculation of the months of May and June 1641, following the attainder and execution of Strafford, the *Argument* presented by Patrick Darcy to a joint committee of the Lords and Commons of Ireland emerges, appropriately enough, like the climax to a court-room drama. The subsequent editorial decision of the Confederate Catholics in 1643, set against the even more dramatic circumstances of Civil War, to publish, with the queries and Darcy's supporting arguments, the context of Sir Richard Blake's message to the Lords, and the judges' response, conferred an almost literary life and coherence on the text; this dramatic unity, with its cast of a hero surrounded by villains, was preserved by Faulkner in 1764. The text itself may be compared to a five-act play, with some of the early acts compiled collectively and separated from each other in time, sometimes by as much as several months. The five main divisions of the *Argument* are as follows:

1. The twenty-one queries addressed to the Lords Justices of Ireland, carried by Sir Richard Blake to the Lords to be forwarded by them to the judges (pp.231–8).
2. The answer and declaration of the judges, preceded by a nine point preamble challenging the summons to make answer in Parliament (pp.238–52).
3. Mr Darcy's reply to the answer of the judges – an introductory presentation of the reasons for propounding the queries (253–6).
4. The refutation of the judges' preamble by Patrick Darcy (pp.262–9).
5. A point-by-point refutation of the judges' answer, with a defence of each query (pp.269–309).

There was a sixth and final phase to the original sequence of events, but it is not included here for reasons of economy. This was the vote on the Irish House of Commons in July on the substance of the queries; each of the queries was taken up again individually, rephrased to form a motion, and then voted on. All twenty-one queries, presented as affirmative motions, were voted on and carried by the Commons, *nullo contradicente*, on 26 July 1641. To include the body of queries here, as originally published in 1643 and 1764, with their affirmative versions as motions for debate, would be to create unnecessary duplication. If this final sequence has not been included, it should still be remembered as an important vindication of Darcy's presentation. It can thus be seen that the text of the *Argument* is more than the work of any one man; it is a sequence of inter-related texts which cover a critical three-month period of open debate in the Irish Parliament, from May to July 1641. As generally alluded to in the history of Ireland, Darcy's *Argument* is usually meant to designate sections 4 and 5 above.

The original edition of 1643 bears the title as reproduced on p. 229 of the present edition. Beneath the title, in common with Bourke's edition of *Remonstrance of Grievances presented to his most Excellent Majestie* (also published in 1643), is a half-page woodcut of the British royal arms, with the 'N' of the device 'DIEU ET MON DROIT' reversed. The Dublin edition (not listed in Wing's *Short-Title Catalogue*, which gives the British Library and Bodleian editions under D246) is in quarto, with 148 pages collated A^4 B^4 (B_1 + X^2) C – S^4, 74 leaves, pp.1 2–10 [4] 11 – 144; it is set in ageing Garamond Roman 'Gros texte', alternating with an equally venerable Granjon Cursive 'Gros texte' (italic) and Granjon 'Immortel' (reduced italic). Pages on which new sub-sections begin are decorated by floral bands which are entirely typical of those found on specimen sheets of Dutch printers of the time.[24] The final page carries a list of errata entitled *Faults Escaped*. The edition consulted, at the Franciscan Library of Dún Mhuire, Killiney, Co. Dublin, was bound in the standard sheepskin vellum of the time. The text is handsomely produced for the circumstances in which the printer must have worked, and probably represents as high a material investment as could be afforded at Waterford then; it is an object of considerable interest in the history of Irish printing.

In the preparation of the present edition, all evident and unnecessary forms of archaism in spelling, such as endings in 'ie' or in redundant 'e', have been amended. Punctuation has been completely revised, and the exclamation mark introduced to give range to the author's power of expression; capitalisation, with ligatured 's', has been standardised. There has been no adjustment to the syntax of the original, but the style of abbreviation of legal references has been brought into line with current practice. Where it was felt that the meaning of a passage was obscure in its original form, an articulatory word is sometimes added in square brackets; where words or names were used in error in the original, they are moved to a note at the bottom of the page with an asterisk, and replaced in the text with an asterisked alternative.

It will have become evident from these introductory observations that the *Argument* lives and breathes on the page. Not all of the text, which spans a sequence of events over a number of days, is by Patrick Darcy, nor is everything that was said at the joint hearing from 7–9 June 1641, included in any of the editions; there is material in the text

---

[24]J. Dreyfus, *Type Specimens and Facsimiles* (London, 1963). See also William K. Sessions, *The First Printers in Waterford, Cork and Kilkenny, pre-1700* (York, 1990).

for no more than a few hours' presentation, whereas the joint hearing lasted for two days. What the text does offer is the context of a political debate in which the material and notes of the principal figure have remained intact, giving us the style and wit of the man as well as the weighty documentation which ensures his place in the history of Anglo-Irish constitutional debate.

PATRICK DARCY (1598-1668) – Family Tree*

*See also McFirbis, *Genealogies, Tribes and Customs of Hy-Fiachrach*, 1645, ed. John O'Donovan, Dublin, 1844; M.J. Blake, 'Tabular Pedigrees of the D'Arcy Family', *Journal of the Galway Archaeological and Historical Society*, (1917), 58-66.

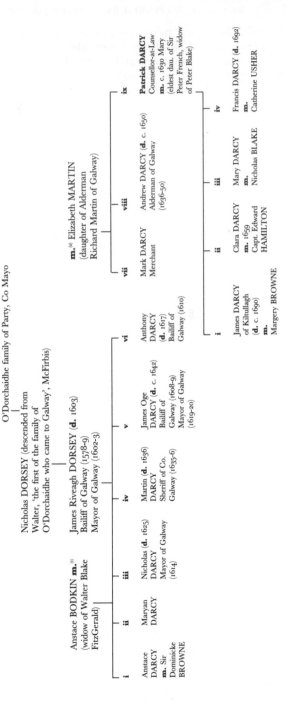

O'Dorchaidhe family of Party, Co Mayo

Nicholas DORSEY (descended from Walter, 'the first of the family of O'Dorchaidhe who came to Galway', McFirbis)

James Riveagh DORSEY (**d.** 1603) Bailiff of Galway (1578-9) Mayor of Galway (1602-3)

m. (i) Anstace BODKIN (widow of Walter Blake FitzGerald)

m. (ii) Elizabeth MARTIN (daughter of Alderman Richard Martin of Galway)

i. Anstace DARCY **m.** Sir Dominicke BROWNE

ii. Maryan DARCY

iii. Nicholas (**d.** 1625) DARCY Mayor of Galway (1614)

iv. Martin (**d.** 1636) DARCY Sheriff of Co. Galway (1635-6)

v. James Oge DARCY (**d.** c. 1642) Bailiff of Galway (1608-9) Mayor of Galway (1619-20)

vi. Anthony DARCY (**d.** 1617) Bailiff of Galway (1610)

vii. Mark DARCY Merchant

viii. Andrew DARCY (**d.** c. 1650) Alderman of Galway (1636-50)

ix. Patrick DARCY Counsellor-at-Law **m.** c. 1630 Mary (eldest dau. of Sir Peter French, widow of Peter Blake)

i. James DARCY of Kiltullagh (**d.** c. 1690) **m.** Margery BROWNE

ii. Clara DARCY **m.** 1659 Capt. Edward HAMILTON

iii. Mary DARCY **m.** Nicholas BLAKE

iv. Francis DARCY (**d.** 1692) **m.** Catherine USHER

NETWORK of LEGAL FAMILIES in GALWAY
(c. 1625-50)*

*See also Donal Cregan, C.M., 'Irish Catholic Admissions to the English Inns of Court, 1558-1625', *The Irish Jurist*, 1970, pp.95-114; John T. Gilbert, *History of the Irish Confederation and the War in Ireland*, 1641-49, 7 vols. (Dublin, 1882-91), reproduced by AMS Press (New York, 1973), *passim*; Liam O'Malley, 'Patrick Darcy, Galway Lawyer and Politician, 1598-1668', in *Galway: Town and Gown, 1484-1984* (Dublin, 1984), pp.90-109.

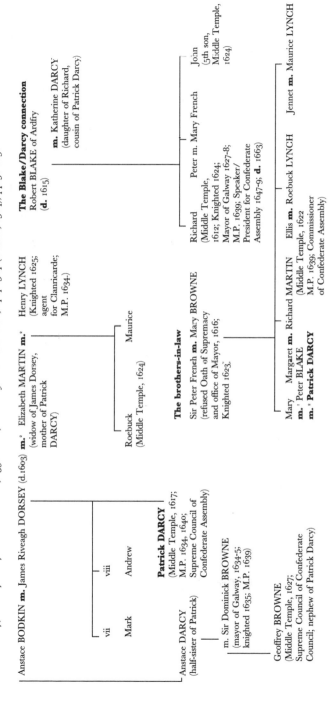

AN
ARGUMENT
DELIVERED BY
Patrick Darcy, Esquire;

BY THE

Express Order of the House of
Commons in the Parliament of
IRELAND, 9. *Iunii,* 1641.

Printed at Waterford by THOMAS BOURKE, Printer
to the Confederate Catholics of Ireland, 1643.

5. Iunii, 1641[1].

By the Commons House of IRELAND
in Parliament assembled.

FORASMUCH *as* PATRICK DARCY, *by a former order of this House, was appointed Prolocutor, at the Conference with the Lords, touching the questions propounded to the Judges, and their pretended answers to the same, it is hereby ordered, and the said* Mr DARCY *is required, to declare and set forth, at the said Conference, the manifold grievances, and other causes and grounds that moved this House, to present the said questions to the Lords' House, to be propounded as aforesaid, and to give particular reasons for every of the said questions.*

Copia vera.

Extract. per Phil. Fern. *Cleric. Parl. Com.*[2]

---

[1] The timetable of events in the Irish Parliament is presented in the *Introduction* (p. 210); 5 June corresponds to the date originally agreed for the joint meeting of Lords and Commons committees, which eventually took place on 7 June; the date of 9 June printed on the title page is not inaccurate, but simply gives the completion date of Darcy's presentation. See *JHCI*, 1, 306–423 (13 Feb.–10 June 1641).

[2] The authentification of the Clerk to the Commons, Philip Ferneley, is a reminder that the preceding text, '*Forasmuch as* ...', is an extract from the Commons' Record.

AN
ARGUMENT
DELIVERED BY
Patrick Darcy, Esquire;

By the express orders of the Commons House of the Parliament of Ireland, at a conference with a Committee of the Lords' House, in the dining room of the Castle of Dublin, *9 die Iunii 1641*, upon certain questions propounded to the Judges of Ireland in full Parliament; and upon the answers of the said Judges to the said questions.

And in the conclusion, a declaration of the Commons House upon the said questions.[3]

THE QUESTIONS

Questions wherein the House of Commons humbly desired that the House of the Lords would be pleased to require the Judges to deliver their resolutions.

Inasmuch as the subjects of this kingdom, are free, loyal, and dutiful subjects to His most Excellent Majesty their natural Liege, Lord and King, and to be governed only by the common laws of England, and statutes of force in this kingdom, in the same manner and form, as His Majesty's subjects of the kingdom of England are, and ought to be, governed by the said common laws and statutes of force in that kingdom, which of right the subjects of this kingdom do challenge, and make their protestation to be their birth-right, and best inheritance[4]; yet, inasmuch as the unlawful actions and proceedings of some of His Majesty's subjects, and Ministers of Justice of late years, introduced and practised in this kingdom, did tend to the infringing and violation of the laws, liberties, and freedom of the said subjects of this kingdom, contrary to His Majesty's royal and pious intentions, therefore the

---

[3] The declaration of the Commons consisted of a vote on each of the queries re-phrased in affirmative form; the queries were approved unanimously in their adapted form on 26 July 1641. Since this re-phrased form of the queries was originally published in the 1643 edition, these preliminary remarks constitute a table of contents rather than a chronology.

[4] The language of the preamble, like the text of the queries, is couched in terms already employed in the Irish House of Commons as early as November 1640, when the M.P.s drafted a *Petition of Remonstrance* addressed to the King (*JHCI*, 1, 279–82).

Knights, Citizens, and Burgesses in Parliament assembled, not for any doubt, or ambiguity, which may be conceived, or thought of, for, or concerning the premisses, nor of the ensuing questions, but for manifestation and declaration of a clear truth, and of the said laws and statutes already planted, and for many ages past, settled in this kingdom. The said Knights, Citizens and Burgesses do therefore pray the House of the Lords may be pleased to command the Judges of this kingdom forthwith, to declare in writing their resolutions of and unto the ensuing questions, and subscribe to the same.

1. Whether the subjects of this kingdom be a free people, and to be governed only by the common laws of England and statutes of force in this kingdom?

2. Whether the judges of this land do take the oath of judges; and if so, whether under pretext of any Act of State, proclamation, writ, letter, or direction, under the Great, or Privy Seal, or Privy Signet, or letter, or other commandment from the Lord Lieutenant, Lord Deputy, Justice, Justices, or other Chief Governor, or Governors of this kingdom, they, may hinder, stay, or delay, the suit of any subject, or his judgment, or execution thereupon? If so, in what case, and whether, if they do hinder, stay, or delay, such suit, judgement or execution thereupon, what punishment do they incur for their deviation and transgression therein?[5]

3. Whether the King's Majesty's Privy Council, either with the Chief Governor, or Governors of this kingdom, or without him or them, be a place of judicature by the common laws? And wherein causes between party and party, for debts, trespasses, accompts, possession, or title of land, or any of them may be heard and determined, and of what civil causes they have jurisdiction, and by what law, and of what force is their order or decree in such cases, or any of them?[6]

4. The like of the Chief Governors alone.

5. Whether grants of monopolies be warranted by the law, and of what, and in what cases? And how, and where, and by whom are the

[5] It quickly becomes evident that there is a strategy at work in the queries: the questions bear on matters to which the answers are already known. Some features appear to be borrowed from the English *Petition of Right* (1628, see note 13), but others indicate a relationship to some of the articles for the *Act of Attainder* of Strafford (voted in English Parliament, May 1641), see Gardiner, *CD*, 157.

[6] Like several other queries, this one echoes a section of the earlier *Petition of Remonstrance* of November 1640 (*JHCI*, 1, 279–82); query 3 corresponds to articles 2 and 3 of the earlier remonstrance. See also *HMD*, paragraph 1 'Causes to be heard at the Councell Table', 190. The terms of this query (originally voted in February 1640) are, in turn, echoed in Strafford's *Act of Attainder*.

pretended transgressors against such grants punishable? And whether by fine, mutilation of members, imprisonment, loss and forfeiture of goods or otherwise, and which of them?[7]

6. In what cases the Lord Lieutenant, Lord Deputy, or other Chief Governor, or Governors, of this kingdom, and Council may punish by fine, imprisonment, mutilation of members, pillory, or otherwise? And whether they may sentence any to such, the same, or the like punishment for infringing the commands of, or concerning any proclamations or monopolies, and what punishment do they incur that vote for the same?[8]

7. Of what force is an Act of State, or proclamation, in this kingdom, to bind the liberty, goods, possession, or inheritance of the natives thereof? Whether they or any of them can alter the common law, or the infringers of them lose their goods, chattels, or leases, or forfeit the same, by infringing any such Act of State, proclamation, or both? And what punishment do the sworn judges of law that are Privy Councillors incur that vote for such acts, and execution thereof?[9]

8. Are the subjects of this kingdom subject to the martial law, and whether any man in time of peace, no enemy being in the field with banners displayed, can be sentenced to death? If so, by whom, and in what cases? If not, what punishment do they incur, that in time of peace execute martial law?[10]

[7] Article 7 of the *Petition of Remonstrance* also complained of the abuse of monopolies; as late as May 1641, Darcy had spoken vigorously in the Commons against the monopoly of the tallow trade, held by Messrs Little and Carpenter. Darcy would also have been familiar with the rousing attacks of Coke against monopolies (see *Case of Monopolies*).

[8] The language used here is that of Parliament rather than of any one man. In the articles of impeachment of the Lord Chancellor and the Lord Chief Justice of Common Pleas presented to the Commons in March 1641 (see *Introduction*, p. 208), it had been alleged that 'many thousands of His Majesty's liege people of this Kingdom have been ruined in their goods, lands, liberties, and lives; and many of them, being of good quality and reputation have been utterly defamed by pillory, mutilation of members, and other infamous punishments' (*JHCI*, 1, 357).

[9] Legislation by proclamation had already been challenged in Ireland in 1606, at the time of the *Report on Irish Gavelkind* which Sir John Davies had instigated. This is one of the many examples of the influence of Sir Edward Coke in the English House of Commons, asserting parliamentary privilege at the cost of the royal prerogative. The exchanges between Coke and Lord Chancellor Egerton on this question would have been studied at the 'moots' of the Inns of Court when Darcy was a student there. See Egerton's *The Speech of the Lord Chancellor of England, in the Eschequer Chamber, touching the Post-Nati* (London, 1608), quoted by Louis A. Knafla, *Law and Politics in Jacobean England* (Cambridge, 1977), 209.

[10] A query which, more obviously than others, indicates prior knowledge of the answer. The basis for the question was the summary sentencing to death of Lord Mountnorris at Dublin Castle in December 1635, on the orders of Wentworth; it was strongly presumed at the time that Wentworth abused his authority in this way simply to appropriate Mountnorris's share of the tax farm.

9. Whether voluntary oaths taken freely before arbitrators for affirmance, or disaffirmance of any thing, or the true performance of any thing, be punishable in the Castle Chamber, or in any other court, and why, and wherefore?[11]

10. Why, and by what law, or by what rule of police is it that none is admitted to reducement of fines, and other penalty in the Castle Chamber, or Council table, until he confess the offence for which he is censured, when as *Revera* he might be innocent thereof, though suborned proofs or circumstances might induce a censure?[12]

11. Whether the judges of the King's Bench, or any other judges of Gaol Delivery, or of any other court, and by what law do, or can, deny the copies of indictments of felony, or treason, to the parties accused, contrary to the laws?[13]

12. What power hath the Barons of the Court of Exchequer to raise the respite of homage arbitrarily to what rate they please? To what value they may raise it? By what law they may distinguish between the respite of homage upon the diversity of the true value of the fees, when as *Escuage* is the same, for great and small fees, and are proportionable by Parliament?[14]

13. Whether it be censurable in the subjects of this kingdom, to repair unto England, to appeal to His Majesty for redress of injuries, or for other lawful occasions? If so, why, and in what condition of persons, and by what law?[15]

---

[11] See *HMD*, article 2: *Oathes in causes betwixt partie and partie, not to be adminstred* [sic] *at the Councell table*. The Council table and Castle Chamber are synonyms for prerogative courts (such as Star Chamber), which were obviously open to the interference of executive authority.

[12] As Darcy will show in a closely argued passage (pp. 291–2), there is no law which can sanction the retroactive justification of executive interference in the course of justice. The term *Revera* is more easily comprehensible as *re vera*.

[13] The claim that a person should know on what grounds he/she is being charged or arrested, relates to clause 4 of the earlier remonstrance which complained that the King's subjects were '*denied princely graces and a statute of limitations*'. The question is also linked to the issue of *habeas corpus*; this had been raised in England in the *Petition of Right*, 3 Car.I c.1 (1628), Gardiner, *CD*, 67–8. Our *Table of Statutes* shows that the *Petition of Right* was quoted explicitly a number of times by Darcy.

[14] See T.F.T. Plucknett, *A Concise History of the Common Law*, 5th Edition, Boston, 1956, p.533. This also echoes concerns expressed in clause 14 of the *Petition of Remonstrance*, 'that by the powerfulness of some Ministers of State in the kingdom, Parliament hath not its natural freedom.'

[15] This query emanates directly from the aftermath of the Portumna hearing of August 1635, when the Galway landowners sent a delegation to England to defend their interests (see *Introduction*, p.205). Clause 12 of the *Petition of Remonstrance* also evoked 'the great and just fears at a proclamation published in this kingdom *in anno domini* 1635, prohibiting men of quality or estates for to depart this Kingdom into England, without the Lord Deputy's licence.'

14. Whether Deans or other dignitaries of cathedral churches be properly, and *de mero jure* donative by the King, and not elective or collative? If so, why, and by what law, and whether the confirmation of a Dean *de facto* of the Bishop's grant be good and valid in law or no? If not, by what law?[16]

15. Whether the issuing of *quo warrantoes* out of the King's Bench, or Exchequer, against boroughs that anciently and recently sent burgesses to the Parliament, to show case why they sent burgesses to the Parliament, be legal. Or if not, what punishment ought to be inflicted upon those that are, or have been, the occasioners, procurers, and judges of, and in, such quo *warrantoes?*[17]

16. By what law are jurors that give verdict according to their conscience, and are the sole judges, of the fact, censured in the Castle Chamber, in great fines, and sometimes pilloried with loss of ears, and bored through the tongue, and marked sometimes in the forehead with a hot iron, and other like infamous punishment?

17. By what law are men censurable in the Castle Chamber, with the mutilation of members, or any other brand of infamy? And in what cases, and what punishment in each case there is due, without respect of the quality of the person or persons?[18]

18. Whether in the censures in the Castle Chamber regard be to be had to the words of the Great Charter, *viz. salvo contenemento, &c.?*[19]

19. Whether if one that steals a sheep, or commit any other felony, and after flyeth the court of justice, or lyeth in woods or mountains upon his keeping, be a traitor? If not, whether a proclamation can make him so?

20. Whether the testimony or evidence of rebels, traitors, protected

[16] Under certain articles of plantation, Anglican church appointees, bishops or deans, could create freeholds and fee-farms on their lands to the detriment of original landowners. Since diocesan grants had usually to be confirmed by the incumbent of the deanery concerned, the mode of nomination of deans was put under scrutiny. *De mero jure* > 'in the strict interpretation of the law'. Patrick Darcy himself sat on a parliamentary committee in 1635, when member for Navan, 'to consider a Bill for the preservation of the inheritance of the rights and profits of lands belonging to the church and persons ecclesiastical' (*JHCI*, 1, 169).

[17] The fear of interference and election-rigging had also been present in clause 13 of the *Petition of Remonstrance*, with concern expressed about the 'Attorney-General querying ancient boroughs' rights to send members to Parliament' (*JHCI*, 1, 282).

[18] The query maintains the thrust of the preceding one, with a challenge to the legal authority of prerogative courts such as Castle Chamber (similar in its functions to the English Star Chamber).

[19] The fining (censuring) of people beyond their means was restricted in *Magna Carta*, c.xiv, by the clause *salvo contenemento*, 'saving to him his countenance'; *SR*, 1, 116.

thieves, or other infamous persons, be good evidence in law to be pressed upon the trials of men for their lives? Or whether the judge or jurors ought to be judge of the matter in fact?[20]

21. By what law are fairs and markets to be held *in capite*, when no other express tenure be mentioned in His Majesty's letters-patents, or grants of the same fairs and markets, although the rent or yearly sum be reserved thereout?[21]

Copia vera.

Extract. per Phil. Fern. *Cleric. Parl. Com.*[22]

---

[20] Article XL of *HMD* had already specified in 1622 that *'the accusations or testimony of condemned persons or under protection, be not used as a convincing evidence; and if opened yet not pressed upon men legally acquitted, or that stand upon tryall of their lives'*, 208.

[21] *'Tenere in capite'*, to hold of the King in chief, therefore tenure *'in capite'* was the holding of land, or specified privileges, of the King subject to a levy. This query challenges the rent levied on fairs and markets held by landowners whose title did not specify such obligations. The resolution finally voted by the Commons on 26 July 1641, was that the said *'fair or market is not held by knight-service* in capite' (*JHCI*, 1, 501–2).

[22] The authentification of Philip Ferneley, Clerk of the Commons, shows this is an extract from the record of the Commons debate of 16 February 1641 (*JHCI*, 1, 306–8). The final vote of approval on the queries as affirmative proposals did not take place until 26 July, *ibid.*, 501–2.

THE
SPEECH
OF
SIR RICHARD BLAKE,
KNIGHT;[23]

Made in the Lords' House, upon presenting
of the said *queries* there, by command
of the House of Commons.

My Lords,

I am commanded by the Knights, Citizens, and Burgesses now
assembled in Parliament to present unto your Lordships certain *queries*,
that by vote were ordered to be entered among the Acts and Ordinances
of that House.

My Lords, it is far from their sense and intention to trench upon
His Majesty's prerogative; they are to their great comfort sensible of
His Highness' most gracious answer to the *Petition of Right* in the third
year of His Majesty's reign, that his prerogative was to defend the
subjects' rights and liberties, and the subject's right to strengthen his
prerogative. No relative is greater than what is between the great
prerogative of the King, and the liberty of the people, none of them
hath existence or being without the other, and the proportionable
temper of both makes the happiest state for power, for riches, and for
endurance. They are cemented and coupled by a gordian indissoluble
knot, which no man ought to cut or untie, and as (like Hippocrates his
inseparable twins) they were born together, so they grew, prospered, and
will for ever by the continued grace of the King of Kings flourish together.

My Lords, those *queries* are but a *compendium* and *epitome* of some
pressures which, under the name and title of law, are practised in a
diametrical opposition to the substance thereof; every *query* is like a
sucker that springs close by the root, and draws the radical substance
from it, to its own nourishment but the plant's destruction. Every *query*
doth tend to discover the *tares* sowed by the enemy amongst the good
corn that over-tops and chokes it.[24]

[23] Sir Richard Blake, who was to become Speaker of the Confederate assembly, was a
member of the circle of Galway lawyers who were educated at the Middle Temple and
related to Patrick Darcy (see *Network of Legal Families*, p.227).

[24] The image of the tares and the good corn comes from *Matthew*, xiii, 36. The spelling
of 'query' has been standardised from the occasional, semi-technical use of the Latin
'*quaeres*'.

My Lords, the House of Commons conceives that the resolutions of those *queries* will bring to light from darkness that hath long involved them, the practises of such under-ground working moles that overturn this our native soil, that they will unmask such licentious spirits, as dare shadow injustice with the cloak and cover of justice. That it will bring a general content and satisfaction to all the subjects of this kingdom, to see that perspective as in a crystalline glass the extent of power, the rules of obedience, and the conformity that the laws expect, and that the consequence will be that justice will be so administered hereafter that the streams of it shall run clear, not crossed, thwarted or diverted by any arbitrary, unlimited or extrajudicial interruptions, and that our laws (which are the fruits and blossoms of justice) will be maintained and exercised in their fundamental and radicative vigour.[25] Your Lordships' interests concentring in this equally with ours, the House hath commanded me to desire your Lordships to require the judges of this realm to deliver their opinions unto them of those *queries*, and that in writing and speedily.

THE ANSWER AND DECLARATION OF THE JUDGES

Unto the questions transmitted from the honourable House of Commons unto the Lords Spiritual and Temporal in Parliament assembled, whereunto they desired their Lordships to require the said Judges' answers in writing forthwith.
May 25, 1641.[26]

---

[25] The central metaphor in Blake's self-consciously eloquent speech was one used by Lord Coke and published nearly forty years earlier: '*Methinks that oftentimes, when I ride by the way, I see the effects of justice rightly resembled when I behold a river with a silver current. Bounded in her equal course, with what just proportion she doth disperse her streams, without bewraying any little rage of intemperate violence! But if the passage of that stream be stopped, then how like a raging sea she overflows her banks!*' (Edward Coke, *The Lord Coke his Speech and Charge*, Norwich, 1607; quoted by Catherine Drinker-Bowen, *The Lion and the Throne*, London, 1957, p.258).

[26] As indicated in the *Introduction*, the deadline stipulated by the House of Lords to the judges was 24 May; the date given here is presumably the occasion of the first reading of the answer in the Lords. The House of Commons did not hear the answer until 28 May. The queries, it will be remembered, were originally drafted and approved in

In all humbleness, the said judges do desire to represent unto your Lordships the great sense of grief that they apprehend out of their fear that they are fallen from that good opinion, which they desire to retain with your Lordships and the said House of Commons in that (notwithstanding their humble petition and reasons to the contrary exhibited in writing, and declared in this most honourable house) your Lordships have over-ruled them, and often commanded their answers unto the said *questions*, although they have informed your Lordships, and still with assurance do aver, that no president in any age can be shown that any judges before them were required or commanded to give answer in writing, or otherwise, unto such general, or so many questions, in such a manner in Parliament, or elsewhere, unless it were in that time of King Richard II, which they humbly conceive is not to be drawn into example. And therefore they yet humbly supplicate your Lordships so far to tender their profession and places, and their relation to His Majesty's service, as to take into your serious considerations the reasons that they have annexed to this their answer, before their answer be entered, or admitted, among the Acts of this high Court, and that if your Lordships in your wisdom shall after think fit to give any copies of their answers, that for their justification to the present and succeeding times, your Lordships will be pleased to require the Clerk of this most honourable House that no copies may be given of the said answers without the said reasons.[27]

*b. *Secondly*, the said judges humbly desire your Lordships to be pleased to be informed that the words of His Majesty's writs, by which they are commanded to attend in Parliament, are, that the said judges shall be present with the Lords Justices or other Chief Governor and

---

February; on that occasion, Ormond's biographer reported that '*it was an hardship on the judges to require them to give a sudden and hasty resolution in matters of such delicacy and moment, and they themselves desired time to answer till the next term; which the Archbishop of Dublin, and the lords Ormond, Moore, and Inchiquin insisted on, as highly reasonable and fitting.*' Ormond went further, and moved that it might be added to the order '*that they may not answer any thing that may trench on the King's prerogative, or that may not stand with the duties of their places*' Carte, 1, 253. The delay of the judges in answering, from February to May, may thus be attributed, in part at least, to the intervention of Ormond.

[27] This general disclaimer of any legal significance in their enforced response constitutes a preamble to eight more points made in protest by the judges before they addressed themselves to the substantive issues raised in the queries. Their expressed desire to avoid any parallel with the reign of Richard II can be attributed to a distaste for the role of the magistrature in the bloody assizes following the Peasants' Revolt, and also to the punitive interference in legal procedure by Richard II; his reign was marked by a long legal debate on the royal prerogative, and by the King's attempt to secure the subjugation of the magistrature to his needs.

*Points lettered b–i in the general preamble of the judges are numbered 2–9 in the original text; the adjustment is made to avoid confusion with the original, substantive questions (numbered 1–21).

your Lordships, at the said Parliament, called, *Pro arduis & urgentibus regni negotiis super dictis negotiis tractaturi & consilium suum impensuri.*[28] And they desire your Lordships to take into your consideration whether any advice may be required by your Lordships from them but concerning such particular matters as are in treaty and agitation and judicially depending before your Lordships, upon which your Lordships may give a judgement, order, or sentence, to be recorded among the records and acts of this honourable House, and whether they may be commanded by your Lordships to subscribe their hands unto any opinion or advice they shall give upon any matters in debate before your Lordships there; and whether your Lordships can conceive any final resolution upon the matters contained in the said *questions.*

c. *Thirdly*, although the said questions are but twenty-two in number,[29] yet they say that they contain at least fifty general questions, many of them of several matters and of several natures, within the resolution of which most of the great affairs of this kingdom, both for Church and Commonwealth, for late years may be included; and therefore the said judges do openly aforehand profess, that if any particular that may have relation to any of those questions shall hereafter come judicially before them, and that either upon argument or debate (which is the sieve or fang of truth), or discovery of any general inconvenience to the King or Commonwealth in time (which is the mother of truth), or by further search or information, in any particular, they shall see cause, or receive satisfaction for it, they will not be concluded by any answer they now give to any of these general questions: but they will upon better ground and reason with their predecessors the judges in all ages with Holy Fathers, Councils, and Parliaments, retract, and alter their opinion according to their conscience and knowledge, and the matter and circumstances of the cause as it shall appear in judgement before them, it being most certain that no general case, may be so put, but a circumstance in the matter or manner may alter a resolution concerning the same.

d. *Fourthly*, the succeeding judges and age, notwithstanding any answer given by the now judges, may be of another opinion than the now judges are, without disparagement to themselves, or the now judges, in regard that many particular circumstances, in many particular

---

[28] In quoting the terms of the royal writs which require their presence at Parliament, 'to examine and concern themselves with the most important and urgent matters for discussion in the King's business', the judges suggest that it is only in answer to a punctual and specific need that they should be required to offer judgement.

[29] There are, in fact, only twenty-one queries printed in the text; the twenty-second had been raised verbally at the Lords on the matter of fees for legal commissioners; the judges' final answer is in response to this question.

cases may fall out, that may alter the reason of the laws, in such a case; which could not be included or foreseen in a general question or answer thereunto. And therefore they desire your Lordships to con sider of what use such answers may be to the present and future times.

e. *Fifthly*, many of the said questions, as they are propounded (as the said judges humbly conceive) do concern His Majesty in a high degree, in his regal and prerogative power, in his government, in his revenue, in the jurisdiction of his courts, in his martial affairs, and in his Ministers of State, so that the said judges considering their oaths, and the duty which by their places they owe unto His Majesty humbly conceive they may not with safety give answer thereunto, without special licence from His Majesty, and therefore they still humbly pray your Lordships (as formerly they did) not to press any answers from them until His Majesty's princely pleasure therein be signified.

f. *Sixthly*, if the matters of these questions which aim at some abuses of former times, were reduced into Bills, they conceive it were the speedy way to have such a reformation which might bind the present times and posterity; and in such proceeding they ought and would most cheerfully contribute their opinions and best endeavours, but in such a course (as they apprehend it) which points at punishment they have reason to be sparing in giving any opinion further than the duty of their places doth command from them.

g. *Seventhly*, although it may be conceived that the answering of such and so many general questions by the now judges may contribute some help to the reformation now so much desired, yet no man knoweth but this new precedent in propounding of such questions to judges in succeeding times (as the judges and frame and constitution of the Commonwealth may be) may fall out to be most prejudicial to the State and Commonwealth.

h. *Eighthly*, most of the matters in several of the said questions are already by your Lordships and the said House of Commons voted and represented to His Majesty for grievances, and therefore no opinions of the judges under favour are needful or to be required thereunto, unless the same shall come in further agitation and discussion in this honourable House.[30]

i. The judges' opinions are not usually called upon in Parliament, but when upon debate great and difficult points in law do arise, where this most honourable House doth think fit to command their opinions, but no resolutions do belong unto the said judges, in Parliament, but

---

[30] As the judges rightly point out, several of the queries had already been incorporated in the *Petition of Remonstrance* submitted to the King in November 1640; their argument is thus that these matters are now *sub judice*.

unto your Lordships. Yet in the front and preamble of the said questions, the resolution of the said questions by the judges, is forthwith desired, to be required by your Lordships in writing, although the first question, *viz. Whether the subjects of this kingdom be a free people, &c.*, be positively resolved by the preamble to the said questions, in which it is likewise declared that the said judges answers thereunto are not desired for *any doubt or ambiguity which may be conceived or thought of, for, or concerning the premises*, nor of the said questions, but for *manifestation and declaration of a clear truth, and of the laws and statutes already planted and settled in this kingdom.*

And they [the judges] say that it is impossible to make any manifestation or declaration of law, or statutes, which may hold or be useful, upon such general questions as most of these are, namely, 'By what law?' 'In what cases?' 'Of what?' 'And which of them?' 'Of what power?' 'Of what force?' 'How?' 'Where?' 'By whom?' 'Why?' 'Wherefore?' 'What punishment?' 'By what rule of policy?' 'In what condition of persons?', in regard that the next succeeding judges may be of another opinion, and that a circumstance may alter the reason of this law, in many particular cases, which the wit of man is not able to foresee, or give a general rule in.

And they say that to give answers unto such questions as might give any satisfaction to your Lordships, or to the honourable House of Commons, would make up a great volume, and require more time than your Lordships have afforded unto the said judges, considering their great toil in their Circuits, the last short vacation, their other employments in the Commonwealth, and their daily attendance on your Lordships in Parliament, and the ordinary courts of justice

And yet least they might seem to come any way short in performance of that duty, which they confess to be due unto your Lordships, or be wanting in promoting or advancing the Commonwealth, which they believe to be aimed at by the said questions, though it may seem to draw damage or prejudice upon their particulars, they do in all humbleness present unto your Lordships, the ensuing answers unto the said questions which is as much as by their Oaths or in the duty they owe unto His Sacred Majesty (before his princely pleasure be therein signified) they can answer thereunto.

1. To the first, they answer that the subjects of this kingdom are a free people and are, for the general to be governed only by the common laws of England and statutes of force in this kingdom. Yet they say that as in England, many statutes are grown obsolete, and out of use, and some particular ancient Laws (as well in criminal as in civil causes) have been changed by interpretation of the judges there, as they found it most agreeable to the general good of the Commonwealth, and as the times did require it, so, our predecessors the judges of this kingdom as the necessity of the times did move them, did declare the law in some particular cases otherwise than the same is practised in England, which the now judges cannot alter, without apparent diminution of a great part of His Majesty's standing revenue, and opening a gap for the shaking and questioning of the estates of many of His Majesty's subjects, and the overthrowing of several judgements, Orders, Decrees, which depend thereupon. For example, if it be found by Office of Record, sufficient for form that a man was killed in actual rebellion, and at the time of his death was seized of lands, hereditaments, goods, or chattels, by the constant declaration of law, and the practise of former times here, the Crown was entitled to such lands, goods, and chattels; and many mens' estates depend thereupon, and yet the law is not so taken in England, so if one or more commit felony, and then stand out upon his or their keeping, and he or they will not submit themselves to be tried by the law, but being in that state do rob or spoil and terrify His Majesty's people, whereby the country is disquieted, this by the constant opinion of our predecessors in this kingdom hath been adjudged a levying of war within the statute 25 Edw.3. and so consequently treason.[31] Also by the commonly received opinion and practise in this kingdom, the wife is to have a third of all the goods, chattels and credits of her husband (the debts being paid) although he disposes of all by his will from her. And yet the constant practice is otherwise in England, and other instances of that kind might be made, so that the words (only) must receive a benign exposition before the first question can receive a general answer in the affirmative.

Secondly, many causes of great weight and consequence in this kingdom are to be decreed and ordered by equity in the proper Courts of Equity, and in course of state at the Council board, and by particular customs, and contrary to law, for which the common law and statutes of force in this kingdom give no remedy.

Thirdly, there are several other laws of force in England, and Ireland, so far as they have been received, which though some would have to be part of the common law of England, yet we find them particularly distinguished from it in our printed books in Parliament Rolls in England, as *Lex est consuetudo Parliamenti, jura belli*, Ecclesiastical or Canon

---

[31] It is suggested that subjects of Ireland are *not* a free people governed only by the common laws of England. The laws themselves are in many cases different and, so their argument runs, 'many causes of great weight and consequence' in Ireland are decided by local custom which is, astonishingly, declared to be 'contrary to law' and 'without remedy'. The twenty-five clauses of 25 Edw.III, Ireland (1351), are a vigorous, far-sighted body of legislation which anticipate the more positive aspects of 40 Edw.III (the *Statute of Kilkenny*, 1366); see Berry, *ESI*, 375–97. They appear to be placed out of context by the judges; it is presumably to the English statute of 25 Edw.III that they advert.

law in certain cases, Civil law in some cases not only in Ecclesiastical Courts, but in the Courts of Constable and Marshall, and of the Admiralty, and upon particular occasions, in the other Courts *lex Mercatoria, &c.*

2. To the second, they say that the judges of this kingdom do take the oath of judges, which oath is specified amongst the statutes in 18 Edw.3 and is after explained by the statute of 20 Edw.3. and that they may not stay, hinder, or delay the suit of any subject, or his judgement, or execution thereupon (otherwise than according to the law and course of the court where they sit) under pretence of any act of state, proclamation, writ, letter, or direction under the Great or Privy Seal, or Privy Signet, or letter, or other commandment from the Lord Lieutenant, Lord Deputy, Justice, Justices, or other Chief Governor of this kingdom, most of which, doth appear by their oath expressed in the said statutes, and the said statute of 20 Edw.3, cap.8, and the statute of 28 Edw.3,cap.2, as to the Barons of the Exchequer. And that as they know no punishment due to judges, for their deviations and transgressions, without other aggravation, so they know no punishment laid down by any law against them for their deviations and transgressions, in hindering, staying, or delaying of justice, contrary to their said oath, other than what is declared in their said oath, and the statute of 20 Edw.3.[32]

3. To the third, they say that it is part of their said oath, as judges, that they shall not counsel or assent to any thing that may turn to the damage or disherison of our Sovereign Lord the King's most Excellent Majesty, by any manner of way or colour. And that they shall give no advice or council to any man great or small in any cases wherein the King is a party, and they shall do and procure the profit of the King and his Crown, in all things where they may reasonably do the same, and that in the explanation of their said oaths, by the statute of 20 Edw.3,cap.1, it is declared that they shall give no council to great men nor small, in case where the King is party, or which doth or may touch the King in any point. And as your Lordships have been honourably pleased by an order of this honourable House, bearing date the first of March, *Anno Dom.* 1641, *annoq. Regni Caroli decimo sexto*, to give way that they should not be compelled to answer any part of those questions which did concern His Majesty's prerogatives or were against their oaths, so they humbly represent unto your Lordships that they conceive

---

[32] The references in *SR*, 1, 303–6, differ slightly from the judges' version: there is no related statute under 18 Edw.III; the oath of the judges is found, with qualifying comment, in 20 Edw.III, c.1–5; for 28 Edw.III, c.2, read c.3. The answer given by the judges remains evasive, because they do not declare precisely what punishment, if any, is prescribed by the statutes of 20 Edw.III for failure to observe the oath. Darcy will provide this information in his reply (see notes 44 & 45).

that the answering of the particulars of this question doth concern both, for that the King's Privy Council as the question terms it, or the Council-board, is a court of His Majesty's high prerogative, where all proceedings are before him and his Council, or before his Governor (who doth immediately, to many purposes, represent His Majesty's person) and the Council, and where the great afffairs of state concerning His Majesty's honour, government, profit, and of great persons and causes concerning the Commonwealth, which, may not conveniently be remedied by the ordinary rules of common law, and many other causes have been treated of, and managed. And as His Majesty is the fountain of all justice within his kingdoms, and may grant cognizance of pleas unto his subjects and Corporations, and may by his commission authorize whom he shall think fit to execute many branches of his authority, so they humbly conceive it doth not stand with their oaths or duties of their places, who are but judges of the ordinary courts of justice, before His Majesty's pleasure signified in that behalf, to search into the commissions or instructions of the Chief Governor and Council, or to give any opinion concerning the limits, jurisdiction, orders, decrees, proceedings, or members of that high Court, and that the King hath a prerogative for the hearing some of the matters in this question specified before his Chief Governor. We beseech your Lordships to cast your eyes on the statute of 28 H.6, cap.2 [recte 6], in this kingdom, where after matters are directed to be sent to the ordinary courts, yet the King's prerogative is expressly saved, notwithstanding all which his gracious Majesty (for whom it is most proper) hath of late been pleased to limit the proceedings of that board by his instructions in print.[33]

4. To the fourth, they answer as to the third.

5. To the fifth, they say that generally all grants of monopolies, whereby trading manufacture, or commerce is restrained, and the profit which should go to many hindered and brought into a few hands, are against law, the liberty of the subject and the good of the Commonwealth, though they carry never so fair a pretence of reforming abuses, and that the pretended transgressors against such grants are not at all punishable by any rule of law that they know of, and yet they say that they conceive that His Majesty, that is the head and father of the Commonwealth, may restrain the use and importation

---

[33]The legislation of 28 Hen.VI, recte c.6, Ireland (1450), was a major piece of legislation emanating from the Parliament of Drogheda under the lieutenancy of Richard, duke of York; at the conclusion of its sweeping proposals there is included, in legal French, the formula 'Save la progatyff le Roy', Berry, Statutes Henry VI, 179–249). This is not a substantial basis for the argument developed here. The argument in defence of Castle Chamber and conciliar justice is equally weak; the assault on prerogative courts had already begun in England, and the Long Parliament was to abolish Star Chamber in 1641.

and exportation of certain commodities, or confine the same into a few hands for a time where there may be a likelihood of His Majesty's profit (which is the profit of the Commonwealth) and no apparent prejudice to the Commonwealth doth appear, and that when time shall discover such prejudice then such restraints ought to cease. So if a man by his own invention at home, or travel, observation, or charge abroad doth introduce a new profitable and useful trade or profession into the Commonwealth, in such cases His Majesty may lawfully grant and licence the only making of such commodity, or teaching or using of such trade for certain time, and the transgressors against such warrantable grants, may be punished by payment of damages unto the patentee, in an ordinary course of justice, or otherwise, as the nature of the offence and matter doth deserve, and as the consequence and importance of the matter may be to the King, State, or Commonwealth. And they say that the matter, manner, restrictions, limitations, reservations, and other clauses contained in such grants or licences, and the commissions or proclamations thereupon and undue execution thereof, and several circumstances may make the same lawful or unlawful, whereof they are not able to give any certain resolution (before some particular comes in judgement before them). Neither are they otherwise able to answer the general in the particulars of the said question, of what, in what cases, how, where, and by whom, or which of them, wherein whosoever desireth further satisfaction he may please to have recourse unto the known cases of monopolies, printed authorities, and written reports, and unto the statute of 21 Ja. in England concerning monopolies, and the several exceptions and limitations therein.[34]

6. To the sixth, they say they can no otherwise answer than they have already in their answer to the third question, for the reasons therein set forth.

7. To the seventh, they say, that a proclamation or Act of State cannot alter the common law, and yet proclamations are acts of His Majesty's prerogative, and are, and always have been of great use, and that the contemners of such of them as are not against the law are, and by the constant practise of the Star Chamber in England, have been punished, according to the nature of the contempt, and course of the said court. And although Acts of State, are not of force to bind the goods, possessions, or inheritance of the subject, yet they have been of great use for the settling of the estates of very many subjects in this

---

[34] 21 Jac.,c.3 (1623–4), *An Act Concerning Monopolies and Dispensations with Penall Lawes and the Forfeyture thereof* (*SR*, 4, part 2, 1212–14). A certain number of exceptions were declared, but the statute is much more clear than the judges' statement: '*Validity of all monopolies and of all such grants & etc. shall be tried by the common law*' (p.1212).

kingdom, as may appear in the *Report of Irish Gavelkind* in print. And further to that question they cannot answer, for the reasons in their answer unto the third question set forth.

8. To the eighth, they say that they know no ordinary rule of law by which the subjects of this kingdom are made subject to martial law in time of peace, and that they find the use thereof in time of peace, in England, complained of in the *Petition of Right*, exhibited to His Majesty in the third year of his reign, and that they conceive the granting of authority, and commission for execution thereof, is derived out of His Majesty's regal and prerogative power for suppressing of sudden and great indolencies and insurrections, among armies, or multitudes of armed men lawfully or unlawfully convened* together (the right use whereof in all times hath been found most necessary in this kingdom). And further to that question they cannot answer, for that as they conceive, it doth concern His Majesty's regal power, and that the answering of the other part of the question doth properly belong to another profession, whereof they have no cognizance.

9. To the ninth, they say that as the taking of any oath before any but such judges or persons as have power to give or demand an oath, for decision of controversies, is by most divines in most cases counted to be a rash oath, and so an offence against God, within the third Commandment, so the prescribing and demanding of a set oath by any that cannot derive power so to do from the Crown, (where the fountain of justice under God doth reside) is an offence against the law of the land. And as for voluntary and extrajudicial oaths, although freely taken before arbitrators or others, they say (as this kingdom is composed in many particulars, as the nature and consequence of the cause, or the quality of the person who taketh, or before whom the same is taken, may concern the Commonwealth, or the members thereof) such taking of such oaths or proceeding or grounding on such oath in deciding of controversies, according to the several circumstances that may occur therein, or the prejudice it may introduce to the Commonwealth, may be punishable by the common law, or (if it grow unto an height or general inconvenience to the Commonwealth or members thereof) in the Castle Chamber. For though such an oath be voluntary, yet in most cases it is received by him that doth intend to ground his judgement thereon, and after the oath is taken, the arbitrator, or he that intends to yield faith to the party that took the oath, doth examine him upon one or more questions, upon the said oath, unto the answer whereof he doth give faith and assent, trusting on the said oath. And whereas oaths by God's institution were chiefly allowed to be taken before lawful magistrates, for ending of controversies, yet

---

*convented

common experience doth teach in this kingdom that oftentimes orders and acts grounded on such voluntary oaths beget strife and suits; and commonly such orders when they come to be measured by rules of law, or equity in the King's Courts become void, after much expense of time, and charge that we say nothing of that, that thereby many causes proper to the King's Courts are drawn *ad aliud examen*, and thereby the King's justice and courts often defrauded and declined.

10. To the tenth, they say that they are not judges of rules of policy but of law, and that they know no certain rule of law concerning reducement of fines. The same being matters of His Majesty's own mere Grace after a man is censured for any offence. And that they know no law that none shall be admitted to reducement of his fines or other penalties in the courts in the question specified until he confer the fact for which he was censured. But forasmuch as the admittance to a reducement after conviction, for an offence, is matter of Grace and not justice, it hath been the constant course of the courts both here and in England, for clearing of His Majesty's justice (where the party will not go about to clear himself by reversal of the censure or decree), not to admit him to that Grace until he hath confessed the justness of the sentence pronounced by the court against him. And that the rather for that commonly the ability and disability of the party doth not appear in judgement before them, but the nature and circumstances of the offence, according to which they give sentence against him or them, *in terrorem*, after which, when the party shall make the weakness of his estate appear, or that the court is otherwise ascertained, that they do, of course, proportion the censure, or penalty, having regard to his estate.

11. To the eleventh, they say that neither the judges of the King's Bench (as they inform us, that are of that court) or Justices of Gaol Delivery, or of any other court, do or can, by any law they know, deny the copies of indictments, of felony, or treason, to the party only accused, as by the said question is demanded.

12. To the twelfth, they say that where lands are holden of the King by the Knight's service, *in capite*, the tenant by the strict course of law ought in person to do his homage to the King, and until he hath done his homage the ancient course of the Exchequer hath been, and yet is, to issue process of *distringas* out of the second Remembrance Office, to distrain the tenants *ad faciendum homagium or pro homagio suo respectuando*, upon which process the sheriffs returneth issues.[35] And if

---

[35] *Distringas* is the first word of the writ served by the sheriff, 'thou shalt distrain'. The Remembrance Office was a debt-collecting branch of the Court of Exchequer; the distraint in question is to render homage (*ad faciendum homagium*) by paying the levy required.

the tenant do not thereupon appear and compound with the King to give a fine for respite of homage, then the issues are forfeited to the King for his contempt, but if he appear, then the Court of Exchequer doth agree with him to respite his homage for a small fine, wherein they regulate themselves under the rate expressed and set down in England by virtue of a Privy Seal in the 15th year of Queen Elizabeth, whereby the rates are particularly set down, according to the yearly value of the lands, which rates are confirmed by act of Parliament in *1 Jacob Regis, cap.* 26, in England, before which time there was not any such certainty; but the same rested in the discretion of the court by the rule of Commonwealth, and so it doth at this day in Ireland, howbeit we conceive that the Court of Exchequer here do well to regulate their discretions by those rates in England, and rather to be under than to exceed the same, which the Barons there do, as they do inform us that are judges of the other courts.

13.   To the thirteenth, they say that they know no rule of law or statute, by which it should be censurable in the subjects of this kingdom to repair into England, to appeal unto His Majesty for redress of injuries, or for other of their lawful occasions, unless they be prohibited by His Majesty's writ, or proclamation or, other command. But they find that by the statute of 5 Rich.2 the passage of the subject out of the realm is prohibited without special licence, excepting noblemen and others in the said statute specially excepted, and some inference to that purpose may be made upon the statute of 25 Hen.6, *cap.* 2 [*recte* 7], in this kingdom.[36]

14.   To the fourteenth, they say that some Deaneries and dignities, not *Deans or dignitaries* (as the question propounds it), are properly, and *de mero jure* donative by the King, some elective, and some collative, according to the first foundation and usage of such churches, and they humbly desire that they may not be required to give any further answer to this question, for that it may concern many mens' estates which may come judicially in question before them.[37]

15.   To the fifteenth, they say that they conceive that where privileges are claimed by any body politic or other, the King's Council may exhibit a *quo warranto* to cause the parties claiming such privileges to show by what warrant they claim the same, and that the court cannot hinder the issuing of process at the instance of the King's Attorney, or

[36]I have been unable to identify the statute of 5 Rich.II quoted by the judges; 25 Hen.VI, *recte* 7, relates to passage between ports of Ireland.

[37]The answer is a pragmatic acknowledgement that there is no one law governing the nomination to deaneries. Appointment may therefore be: i) *donative*, in the gift of the King. ii) *elective*, by election from the diocese. iii) *collative*, in the gift of the patron ordinary, who may be the bishop. The material concerns of landowners involved in such decisions were undoubtedly a further incentive to provide a broad answer.

hinder the King's Attorney to exhibit such informations. But when the case shall upon the proceedings be brought to judgement, then and not before, the court is to take notice and give judgement upon the merits and circumstances of the cause, as upon due consideration shall be conceived to be according to law, in which case the judges or the King's Attorney (as they conceive) ought not to be punished by any ordinary rule of law or statute that they know. But for the particular case of quo warranto, for that it hath been a great question in this present Parliament, and so concerns the highest court of justice in this kingdom, and also concerns two other of His Majesty's courts of justice, and therein His Majesty's prerogative in those courts, they say that they cannot safely deliver any opinion therein before it comes judicially before them and they hear it argued and debated by learned counsel on both sides.

16. To the sixteenth, they say that although the jurors be sole judges of the matter of fact, yet the judges of the court are judges of the validity of the evidence, and of the matters of law arising out of the same, wherein the jury ought to be guided by them. And if the jury, in any criminal cause between the King and party, give their verdict contrary to clear and apparent evidence delivered in court, they have been constantly, and still ought to be, censured in the Star Chamber in England, and Castle Chamber here, for this misdemeanor in perverting the right course of justice, in such fines and other punishment as the merits and circumstances of the cause doth deserve, according to the course of the said courts, for that their consciences ought to be directed by the evidence, and not to be misguided by their wills or affections. And if the jury know any matter of fact which may either better or blemish their evidence, they may take advantage thereof, but they ought to discover the same to the judges. And they say that this proceeding in the court of Castle Chamber is out of the same grounds that writs of attaint are against a jury that gives a false verdict in a Court of Record at the common law, betwixt party and party; which false verdict being found by a jury of twenty-four, notwithstanding that the first jury were judges of the fact, yet that infamous judgement was pronounced against the first jury, which is next or rather worse than judgement to death, and did lay a perpetual brand of perjury upon them, for which reason it was anciently called the *villainous judgement*. And they say that the law to direct the punishment for such offences is the course of the said court, which is a law as to that purpose, and the statute of 3 *Hen*.7, *cap*.1, and other statutes in force in this kingdom.

17. To the seventeenth, they say they can answer no otherwise than they have in their answer to the next precedent question.

18. To the eighteenth, they say that in a legal construction the statute of *Magna Charta*, in which the words *salvo contenemento* are mentioned, is only to be understood of amerciaments and not of fines; yet where great fines are imposed *in terrorem*, upon the reducement of them regard is to be had to the ability of the persons.[38]

19. To the nineteenth, they say that if one doth steal a sheep or commit any other felony, and after flyeth the course of justice, or lyeth in woods or mountains upon his keeping, yet doth he not thereby become a traitor, neither doth a proclamation make him so, the chief use whereof in such a case is to invite the party so standing out to submit himself to justice, or to forewarn others of the danger they may run into by keeping him company or giving him maintenance and relief, whereby he may the rather submit to justice.

20. To the twentieth, they say that the testimony of rebels, or traitors under protection, of thieves, or other infamous persons, is not to be used or pressed as convincing evidence upon the trial of any man for his life; and so is His Majesty's printed instructions as to persons condemned or under protection. Yet the testimony of such persons not condemned, and being fortified with other concurring proof or apparent circumstances, may be pressed upon any trial, and for discovering of their fellows, abettors, or relievers, as the circumstances may offer themselves in their examination, especially if before they confess themselves guilty of the offence in imitation of the approver of the common law, whereof no certain rule may be given. And it need not be made a question here, whether the jurors or judges ought to be judges of the matter of fact, it being positively laid down in the sixteenth question that they are. And though their false verdict doth convince, or not convince, the prisoner, yet they may be questioned and punished for a false verdict, as in their answer to the sixteenth is already declared.

21. To the twenty-first, they say that that question is now judicially depending, and hath been already solemnly argued in His Majesty's Court of Wards, in which court their assistance for declaration of the law therein is already required. And therefore they humbly desire they may not be compelled to give any opinion touching that point until it be resolved there.

22. To the twenty-second, they say that they do conceive that there is no matter of law contained in the said question, yet for the further satisfaction of your Lordships, they say that upon view of an Act of State, bearing date at His Majesty's Castle of Dublin, the twenty-fourth of December 1636, grounded upon His Majesty's letters of the fifth of July then last past, it appeared unto them that four shillings in the pound, as of His Majesty's free gift and reward out of the first

[38] cf. note 19.

payment of the increase of rent reserved to His Majesty, was allowed to the judges that were commissioners and attended that service. And we humbly conceive that the receiving of that four shillings in the pound of His Majesty's bounty stands well with the integrity of a judge. And those judges did inform them that they did not avoid any letters-patents upon the Commission of Defective Titles, but received such to compound as submitted for the strengthening of their defective patents and titles, and such as would stand upon the validity of their grants were left to the trial at law. And that the compositions made after the said grants of the four shillings in the pound were made according to rules and rates agreed upon by all the commissioners before His Majesty's said letters or the said Act of State, and not otherwise.[39]

George Shurley. Edward Bolton. Samuel Mayart.

Hugh Cressy. James Barry. James Donellan.

William Hilton.[40]   Copia vera.

Extract per Phil. Percivall[41].

[39] This is the twenty-second question mentioned by the judges in their opening remarks, see note 29; it bears upon an increase approved by the judges for the Commissioners for Defective Titles. As joint Clerk of the Commission for Defective Titles (among a number of other posts he held) and also clerk to the judges' commission, Sir Philip Perceval may have felt vulnerable to charges of conflict of interest. Since there was general dissatisfaction with the commission's administration of sequestered lands, the increase of remuneration for the commissioners may well have been construed as a further incentive to find defective titles.

[40] In addition to the professional careers of the seven judges, F.E. Ball's *The Judges in Ireland 1221–1921* (London, 1926), offers considerably more information about them. Shurley was educated at Cambridge University and the Middle Temple; he resided at Young's Castle while in Dublin, and left Ireland in 1646. Edward Bolton, son of the Lord Chancellor, was knighted in 1636; he studied at Lincoln's Inn, took up residence at Lissen Hall, near Dublin, and was buried at St Bride's. Mayart, an Englishman of Flemish extraction, was educated at Oxford and the Middle Temple; knighted in 1631, he lived at Oxmantown, Dublin, and was the author of the treatise written in answer to Darcy's *Declaration*. Cressy was educated at Furnival's and Lincoln's Inn. Although active in suppressing recusancy under Strafford, his son Hugh Paulinus joined the Benedictine order and became a servant of Queen Catherine of Braganza. Barry was the son of a former mayor of Dublin; he was educated at Trinity College, Dublin, and Lincoln's Inn, taking up residence at Santry Court and finally buried as Lord Santry in Christ Church cathedral. Donnellan was the son of the Archbishop of Tuam and, like Barry, was educated at Trinity College, Dublin, and Lincoln's Inn, and also buried at Christ Church. Hilton was educated at the King's Inns, Dublin, and Gray's Inn; he became Keeper of the Great Seal on the death of Sir Richard Bolton in 1648, and was buried at St Werburgh's, Dublin.

[41] The Crown clerk, Sir Philip Perceval, was born at Tickenham, Somerset, and succeeded his father as registrar of the Irish Court of Wards; the *Dictionary of National Biography* also indicates that between 1625 and 1641, he became Keeper of Records in

Mr. DARCY'S Reply
TO THE
ANSWER
OF THE
JUDGES

My Lords,

His Majesty's most humble and faithful subjects, the Knights, Citizens, and Burgesses, in Parliament assembled representing the whole Commons of this realm, calling to mind the late invasion made upon their laws and just rights, have heretofore presented unto the the Lords' House certain questions of great weight and moment, to the end their Lordships might thereunto require the answer of the judges in writing, which being long sithence accordingly commanded by their Lordships, the judges have of late delivered in a writing to the Lords' House by them styled *An Answer unto the said questions,* which being sent to the Commons' House to be taken into consideration, and the same and all the parts thereof being weighed in the balance of the grave judgement and knowledge of the said House of Commons, the said answer was upon question voted to be *minus pondus habens,* and not to merit the name of an answer.

This, my Lords, being the occasion of this conference, the House of Commons. appointed me, a feeble organ, to utter part of their sense of the style and manner of this writing, and to declare part of those reasons which satisfied their judgements; that the said writing was short and insufficient, *o utinam,* that were all.

My Lords, The Judges had divers months' time to answer plain questions (plain, I speak of those who would be plain), the House of Commons a few days only, to consider of that intricate writing. My powers are weak, and the infirmities of my body are visible, both in part occasioned by an high hand; I should therefore faint under the

the Bermingham Tower, Clerk of the Crown to the Irish courts of King's Bench and Common Pleas, Keeper of the Rolls, joint Collector of Customs, monopolist (with Sir James Ware) for the granting of licences for the sale of ale and brandy, joint Clerk of the Commission for Defective Titles, and Commissary-General of Victuals for the King's Army in Ireland. It is hardly surprising to learn that in 1641 he was reputed to be fabulously wealthy, with 62,502 Irish acres (99,000 English acres) of Irish land in addition to his estates in England. Through his son John the family became Earls of Egmont.

weight of this burden, but that the task is not great. I do represent to your Lordships, by way of rehearsal only, some parts of those reasons and authorities which were gathered and ripened to my hands by the House of Commons.

My Lords, in matters of importance the course hath been ancient and not yet deserted, to begin with *prologues* or *exordiums*; the work is not mine, I will only *in nomine sanctissimae Trinitatis*, make my entrance upon the matter of this conference which is a general concernment, a great concernment of the whole kingdom: and to that purpose I will declare the causes and reasons which moved, or rather inforced, the House of Commons for to disgest and propound the said questions, and to make appear that none of them is Idea Platonica, none of them circumventing, and all pending*, now or of late.

Preamble to the questions. To maintain the preamble to the questions, viz. that this nation ought to be governed by the common laws of England, that the Great Charter and many other beneficial statutes of England are here of force, by reasoning or argumentation, were to alter a foundation laid 460 years past, and to shake a stately building thereon erected by the providence and industry of all the ensuing times and ages. This is so unanswerable a truth, and a principle so clear, that it proveth all, it needeth not to be proved or reasoned.[42]

Reasons why the questions were propounded.

I.q. I. ratio The reason for the first was the late introduction of an arbitrary government in many cases by some Ministers of State†, contrary to the laws and statutes aforesaid, a government contrary to the just freedom and property of His Majesty's people in their lives, estates, and liberties, whereas the subjects governed by the laws of England are, and ought to be, free subjects; the late disuse therefore of those laws in execution, and the measure of justice being squared by the Lesbian line of uncertainty, as contrary to the laws aforesaid, as any *oppositum* is *in objecto*, produced the first question, and I hope not improperly.[43]

---

* 'depending'
† 'estate'

[42] The anniversary implicit in this remark is presumably that of the naming of Prince John as Lord of Ireland, *Dominus Hiberniae*, in 1177; the first Irish Parliament was held in 1264. The evocation of the 460 years is also to be found in parliamentary debate in May 1641 (*JHCI*, 1, 383).

[43] A Lesbian rule is a pliant principle of judgement which makes clear decisions difficult to reach; the term was used for a mason's rule, made of lead to bend around the curves of a moulding (*OED*). So the clarity of English law was confused by the Lesbian line of execution in Ireland.

2.q. 2.ratio The reason for the second in part ariseth out of the oath of a judge (18 Edw.3), to be found among the printed statutes (Pulton, *fol.*144) and out of the statutes of 20 Edw.3.cap.1, 2, and 3 (Pulton, *fol.*145). This oath is comprehensive and extends to the Judges, the Barons of the Exchequer, and Justices of Gaol Delivery, and their associates.[44]

This great and sacred oath contains several branches. First, well and lawfully to serve the King and his people in the office of a Justice. Secondly, not to counsel or consent unto any thing tending to the King's damage or disinherison. Thirdly, to warn the King of his damage when he knows it. Fourthly, to do equal justice to rich and poor &c., without respect of persons. Fifthly, to receive no reward. Sixthly, to take no fee of any other than the King. Seventhly, to commit such as break the peace in the face of justice. Eighthly, not to maintain any suit. Ninthly, not to deny justice, notwithstanding the King's letters or commandments, and in that case to certify the King of the truth. Tenthly, by reasonable ways to procure the profits of the Crown. Eleventhly, if he be found in default, in any the matters aforesaid, to be in the King's mercy, body, lands, and goods.

The second reason principally moveth from the following particulars: in the King's Bench the major part of the judges denied His Majesty's writ of prohibition to the late court called the High Commission, in a cause merely temporal. The four courts of justice durst not proceed in any cause pending* before the Chief Governor, or at the Council-board upon paper petitions, or rather void petitions, the paper petitions being the oblique lines aforesaid; grave judges of the law were commonly assistants, and more commonly referees, in the proceedings upon these paper petitions. In what causes? In all causes proper for the cognizance of the common law, and determinable by writs of right, and petitions of right, and so to the most inferior action, the like of the Courts of Equity. Whether this be lawfully to serve the King and his people; or whether the King was at loss by the non-prosecuting of the causes aforesaid in their proper orbs by original writs, which might afford the King a lawful revenue, and likewise by the loss of fines, and amerciaments, natural to actions at the common law; or whether the loss aforesaid was made known to His Majesty; or who consented to the King's damage therein; or whether this be a denial of justice, to defer it upon paper orders or commands, or† conformable to that oath, I

---

* 'depending'
† 'be'

44 Ferdinando Pulton, *A Collection of Sundry Statutes, frequent in use...*' (London, 1632), f° 144: '*The Oath of the Justices being made* Anno 18.Edw.3 & Anno Domini, 1344'. This stipulates penalties for breach of oath. Darcy has corrected the judges' reference to 20 Edw.III from c.8 to c.1–3.

will pretermit. Yet your Lordships may even in this mist discern a clear ground for the second question.[45]

3. & 4.q. 3. & 4. ratio. The motive which in part stirred the third and fourth questions was the infinity of civil causes of all natures, without exception of persons, without limitation of time proceeded in; ordered, decreed, and determined upon paper petitions at Council board, and by the Chief Governor alone; the Commons of this kingdom observing the judges of the law who were Counsellors of State,* to have agreed and signed unto such orders, the judges of the four courts, and Justices of Assize in all the parts of the kingdom to be referees upon such proceedings, whereby the new devices were become so notorious that, as all men heavily groaned under them, so no man could be ignorant of them.

5.6.7.q.5.6.7.ratio. By the colour of proclamations more and more frequent, and of the Orders and Acts of State at Council board, which were in a manner infinite, and other proceedings mentioned in these questions, these effects were produced: first, imprisonment, close imprisonment, of such numbers that a great defeat in a battle could hardly fill more gaols and prisons than by these means were surcharged in Ireland; secondly, by seizures made by crews of catchpoles and caterpillars, His Majesty's liege people lost their goods as if lost in a battle, nay worse, without hope of ransome; thirdly, possessions were altered, and that so often, and so many, that more possessions were lost by these courts in a few years than in all the courts of justice in Ireland in an age or two. The fourth effect was this, after liberty was taken away, property altered and possession lost by the ways aforesaid, that was not sufficient; the subject must be pilloried, papered, stigmatized, and the image of God so defaced with indignities that his life became a continuing death, the worst† of punishments. In these feats were advising and concurring some grave and learned judges of the land,

---

* 'estate'

† 'worse'

[45] The oath of the judges reproduced in *SR* (pp. 303–6), under 20 Edw.III, stipulates that '*And in case ye be found from henceforth in default of any of the points aforesaid, ye shall be at the King's will, of Body, Land and Goods, thereof to be done as shall please him (as God you help and all Saints).*' Darcy's summary of penalties incurred for failure to observe the oath is thus accurate. The Courts of High Commission were created to enforce the religious policies of the state; they operated by letters-patent without any recognized judicial procedure. Any deferring by the judges to such courts would have been a source of some concern, and also in breach of 28 Edw.III c.3, which the judges themselves mentioned. Its precise terms are: '*that no man of what Estate or condition that he be, shall be put out of Land or tenement, nor taken, nor imprisoned, nor disinherited, nor put to death, without being brought in Answer by due process of the law.*'

who were Counsellors of State,* as by their signatures may appear.

The House of Commons finding as yet no warrant of precedent, nor countenance of example in the law of England, to bear up the courses aforesaid, have drawn the said questions from the effects aforesaid.[46]

8.q.8.ratio. My Lords, the liberty, estate in lands or goods, the person of the subject, nay his honour and spirit being invaded, altered, and debased in manner aforesaid, there remained yet one thing, his life. See how this is brought into play: nothing must escape. Were not the Gates of Janus shut up, was not the King's peace universal in his three kingdoms, when a peer of this realm, a Counsellor of the King's, a great Officer of State, was sentenced to be shot to death in a court martial? What the cause was, what defence was permitted, what time given, and what loss sustained? I submit to your Lordships, as therein most nearly concerned, were not others actually executed by martial law, at such time as the King's justice in his courts of law, was not to be avoided by any person whatsoever? This was in part the ground of the eighth question.[47]

9.q.9.ratio. This question is plain; a late-introduced practice here, contrary to former use, and no appearing precedent to warrant such prosecution for a voluntary oath, and the great benefit and quiet accrued to His Majesty's people by arbiterments conceived by consent of parties, hath in part occasioned this question.[48]

10.q.10.ratio. Heretofore this confession was not required, for the justness of the judgements was then able enough to bear them up. And if the judgement in some case had been otherwise, what force can the confession of a delinquent add to a judicial act? This is part of the reason for this question.

11.q.11.ratio. A complaint exhibited in the House of Commons touching the denial of the copy of a record, which the complainant undertook to justify, in part raised this question.[49]

---

* 'estate'

[46] The substance of the complaints in his general summary of queries 5, 6, and 7 is also to be found in clauses 2, 3, 5, and 15 of the *Petition of Remonstrance* of November 1640.

[47] See note 10. Darcy was in England with Richard Martin and Sir Roger O'Shaughnessy at the time of the sentencing to death of Lord Mountnorris in December 1635.

[48] See note 11.

[49] All legal courts are courts of record, in which a record of charges brought must be preserved.

12.q.12.ratio. In King James his time, by an order conceived in the Court of Exchequer upon great debate, and warranted by ancient precedents, the respite of homage was reduced to a certainty, *viz.* two shillings six pence sterling. For a manor yearly, and so for towns and other portions of land, this course was always held until now of late the respite is arbitrarily raised as appears by the second remembrancer's **The second** certificate, viz. I find that anciently, before the begin-**remembrancer's** ning of King James his reign, every manor paid **certificate.** three shillings four pence Irish per annum, and every **I. Iunii, 1641** townland twenty pence Irish per annum, as a fine for respite of homage, but cannot find any order or warrant for it until the fifth year of the said King's reign, and there, in Easter Term 1607, I find an order entered directing what homage every man should pay, a copy whereof you have already from me, the preamble of which orders showeth that the matter had been long pending* in the Court undecided; which induceth me, to believe that there was no former precedent or order in it.[50] About three years after, the freeholders of the County of Antrim as it should seem, finding this rate to be too heavy for them, they petitioned to the Lord Chichester, then Lord Deputy, for relief therein, and I find his Lordship's opinion to the court thus recorded:

'I know much of the petitioner's lands is waste, and no part of it improved by any manner of husbandry, other than in grazing of cattle, and in sowing of little oats, and the proprietors of the land, to be for the most part very poor and needy; and the two children of Neal macHugh to be yet under age. Wherefore I think it fit that the Court of Exchequer should consider thereof, and rate the respite of homage accordingly for a time, until the county be better inhabited, and these men made to understand that it is not an imposition, but a lawful duty and payment due to His Majesty. This is my advice and opinion for the present, xxx die April., 1610.
Arthur Chichester.'

Upon this, the said freeholders were admitted to pay but four pence Irish every Twogh of Land, it consisting of sixteen townlands, and according to this rate they still paid until the year 1630 and then the Court, taking notice of the unequality of it, made this order, 5 *February*, 1630:

'After this, I find that all His Majesty's tenants did conform themselves to the

* 'depending'

[50] The remembrancer was a debt-collecting official of the Court of Exchequer. The date of the second remembrancer's certificate (1 June 1641), indicates that there was very little time for this issue to be discussed in the Commons' committee before inclusion in the dossier.

said order of 1607 until Easter term 1637, in which term this ensuing order was made, which is the last that I can find recorded in my office.

Henry Warren:

"*I find by the payments made in the late Queen Elizabeth's time that the rates of homage paid was according to the said order of 1607.*

Henr. Warren." '51

13.q.13.ratio Divers were actually imprisoned, and long kept in close restraint, for none other cause than in dutiful manner and beseeming terms to have made known their particular complaints to His Sacred Majesty. Imprisonment of this kind was frequent, therefore it is not improper to demand by what law it was done.

14.q.14.ratio. Many have lost great estates and possessions by Orders of the Council board, although the Deans elected, or actual Deans confirmed their estates, when* no donation from the Crown was† found upon record to the confirming Dean; and this after that, by verdict at the common law, the Dean was found to be elective. This question therefore is not improper.

15.q.15. ratio. After such time as this Parliament was agreed upon at Council board to be summoned, some persons (having prepared bloody and destroying Bills to be passed as laws, and intending to defeat by Act of Parliament very many of His Majesty's faithful subjects of this kingdom of their estates and liberties, and having obtained some undue elections by threats or entreaties, and mistrusting that all should run clear before them) have caused twenty-four corporations to be seized upon the return of the first summons in several *quo warrantoes* procured by Sir Richard Osbalston, late Attorney General, to show cause why they sent burgesses to the Parliament (the said corporations having formerly sent burgesses to the Parliament, even to the last Parliament), by means whereof the said corporations sent no burgesses in the beginning of this Parliament. From this act being done in a legal court against the high court of Parliament sprung this question which, my

---

*'if'
†'were'
51 *Arthur, Lord Chichester* (1563–1625); Lord Deputy of Ireland, 1604–14, Sir Arthur Chichester was created Baron Chichester of Belfast in 1613. Twogh = tuath, ancient Gaelic unit of land, comparable to, and as variable in area as, the parish, see James Hogan, 'The Tricha Cét and related land measures', *Proceedings of the Royal Irish Academy*, 38c (1928), 148–234. I am grateful to my colleague Proinsias NíChatháin for indicating this reference. *Henry Warren* has not been identified.

Lords, is of consequence, if Parliaments be so as without question they are.[52]

16.q.16.ratio.17.q.17.ratio.18.q.18.ratio. The faith which the common law giveth to verdicts, the jurors being judges of the fact, the late usage of that great court growing to the punishment of jurors and others in greater numbers, by heavier fines and more shameful punishments, without respect to estate, age, sex, or quality, than was or can be observed in all precedent times, and the just sense thereof, moved the House of Commons to propound these questions.

19.q.19.ratio. My Lords, a poor fellow stole, or was accused to have stole, a sheep. Fear, or guilt, or both, brought him to the mountains; another relieved him, the reliever was executed as a traitor, and afterwards the principal submits to trial and judgment, and was acquitted. This example, My Lords, I hope may warrant the question.

20.q.20.ratio. The testimony of such infamous persons have brought men of quality to their trial for their lives, and being acquitted, the jurors being of very good rank, were heavily censured in the Castle Chamber, as well by fines surmounting their abilities, as by most reproachful punishments. Upon these acts the question is grounded.

21.q.21.rat. There being no warrant in the printed law, or otherwise, for ought yet appearing for to make this a tenure *in capite*, the constant course of the Court of Wards taking it to be no tenure in capite since the erection of that court until *Trinity term* 1639, it was then (and not before) certified a tenure *in capite* by the then Attorney of the court, who said that the judges concurred with him in that opinion; by which means counsel did not then argue, and the next term after were denied to be heard, *ne aliquid contra responsum prudentum*. This being done in the Court of Wards, the question did spring from thence.

The two and twentieth question was not yet agitated in the House of Commons, nor brought thither, therefore, my Lords, that may be deferred to a further conference. By this which I have opened, being

---

[52] The boroughs of Newcastle, Naas, Fower, Bannow, Taghmon, Cloghmyne, and Atherdee were initially prevented from returning M.P.s by the Attorney-General's *quo warrantoes*; the Speaker of the House of Commons, Maurice Eustace, intervened with a letter dated 6 October 1640, to the Lord Chancellor, Sir Richard Bolton, to ask why 'the Lord Chancellor made stay of writs to be issued from the High Court of Chancery for the return of M.P.s' (*JHCI*, 1, 265). It will be recalled that Patrick Darcy was M.P. for Bannow. *Sir Richard Osbaldstone*, educated at Gray's Inn, succeeded Sir William Rives as Attorney-General of Ireland in December 1636; he was succeeded on his death in 1640 by Sir Thomas Tempest.

the smaller part of those weighty reasons delivered unto me by the House of Commons yet the best I can for the present remember, I hope your Lordships are satisfied that those questions were not entrapping, feigned, or circumventing, or fantasies, as formerly I touched.[53] In the next place, I will labour to give your Lordships a more clear satisfaction that those questions, grounded upon sufficient and apparent reasons and causes, do deserve clear and satisfactory answers. And to remove all doubts, the questions I will no more call *questions*; I will humbly style them *causes of weight and consequence*, wherein the Lordships and Commons of this realm, on the behalf of themselves and their posterity in after times, are *plaintiffs*, and only *delinquents* of

Hopperus, *de* of an high nature are *defendants* in this high court
vera Juris of Parliament. It is not unworthy your Lordships'
prudentia, consideration [to recall] to whom the questions were
p. 118 put: I answer unto the judges of the land, who are

and, sure I am ought, to be, first *etate graves*, secondly, *eruditione praestantes*, thirdly, *usu rerum prudentes*, fourthly, *publica authoritate constituti*.[54]

The persons unto whom, being thus qualified, the
Lord place where is most considerable is the high court of
Chancellor Parliament, the judges are called thither *circa ardua* and
Egerton, *de* *urgentia negotia regni*, of the whole kingdom, what to do
Postnati, fol. *quod personaliter intersint, cum Rege ac cum caeteris de consilio*
17. *suo super dictis negotiis tractaturi consiliumque impensuri.*

Therefore they are not called thither to be ciphers in augurism, or tell clocks. No, those great causes are mentioned in their writ, and upon the great oath they are to give faithful council and make direct answers to your Lordships in all things wherein *ardua & urgentia regni* are concerned. And whether that concernment do comprehend the matters aforesaid, I do humbly offer to your Lordships' great consideration that most of the matters included in those questions are solemnly voted in both houses as grievances, as may appear by the *Petition of Remonstrance*. The judges could not be ignorant of this, and do take notice of the same in their preamble.[55]

[53] For the twenty-second question, see note 39. It is at this point that Darcy completes his introductory summary of the reasons for presenting the queries; he now turns to a more argumentative and abrasive interrogation of the judges' preamble.

[54] Joachim Hoppers (1523–76), Dutch statesman and jurist, was Privy Councillor to Philip II, Chancellor of the Netherlands, and author of *Seduardus, sive de vera jurisprudentia* (Antwerp, 1590); the criteria he recommends for a judge are a serious disposition, great learning, long experience, and to be established by authority of the state. The argument suggested is that men of such stature should consider it to be their proper place to serve as advisors to Parliament.

[55] Having identified and quoted the judges' own sources (note 32), Darcy expands his citation of Lord Egerton to correct them and to exploit the reference to his advantage. Egerton's text was as follows: 'their oath doth bind them as much in the Court of Parliament, as in their proper Courts: for, that is the Supreme Court of all; and they

My Lords, in the third place no man is more unwilling to discover the nakedness of my fathers, if any be, than I am, yet the question being not whether the Ark should be rescued from the Philistines, but whether it should be preserved against the negligence of some Hophni and Phinehas* in their hands that have the custody of it, therefore I must obey; and as I am commanded, I will offer unto your Lordships how the preamble and answers of the judges might be sufficient, and wherein they are both defective and dangerous.[56]

The judges, in the first reason of their preamble, insist much upon the want of precedent in this kind, only one precedent in the reign of King Richard the Second's time, which they pray may not be drawn into example.

a] 1.ratio. My Lords, this reason requires a more clear explanation which we hope shall be demanded in due time. It urgeth us to this just protestation that, before the least flower in His Majesty's royal garland should wither, we shall be ready to water the same with showers of our blood, even to the last drop in His Majesty's service, and with our lives and substance will maintain the just prerogative of our gracious lord King Charles and his posterity, whom we pray God to flourish on earth over us and ours, until all flesh be convoked before the last great tribunal. Yet, my Lords, that precedent might be spared by the judges; of this no more for the present, I will not exasperate. Had they pleaded, more natural precedents might be stood upon, and easily found. And even in that ill-remembered precedent, if the judges in Richard the Second's time had made direct and lawful answers, they had escaped punishment and prevented many inconveniences which ensued.

My Lords, if precedents be necessary, of many I will enumerate a

---

are called thither·by the King's writ, not to sit as Tell-clockes, or idle hearers: but *quod personaliter interstitis nobiscum, ac cum cæteris de Consilio nostro super dictis negotiis tractaturi, vestrumq.; Consilium impensuri:* And those *Negotia* be *Ardua et urgentia negotia Regni & etc.* And their oath, amongst other things, is, That they shall counsell the King truely in his businesse.' (*The Speech of the Lord Chancellor of England, in the Eschequer Chamber, touching the* Post-Nati, London, 1608, f° 17; quoted by Louis Knafla, *Law and Politics in Jacobean England*, 210). *The Petition of Remonstrance*, also known as the *Remonstrance of Grievances*, of November 1640, can be found in the *JHCI*, 1, 279-82.

·'Ophni' and 'Phines'

[56] Hophni and Phinehas, priests of Shiloh, and the unworthy sons of Eli, make their entrance in 1 *Samuel.*i.4; their exit comes in 1 *Samuel.*iv.2, when the Philistines kill them and capture the Ark. Darcy's allusion is very thinly veiled, and also appears to cast him in the role of the new Samuel. I am grateful to my colleague Professor Kevin Cathcart, of the Department of Near Eastern Languages, University College, Dublin, for pointing out that the original spelling of 'Ophni' and 'Phines' comes from the Vulgate and Douai versions of the Bible.

few: *Deuteronomy, cap.*17, *verse* 8, *si difficile & ambiguum, &c* (Almighty God directs us the way to truth); *Deuteronomy, cap.*32, verse 7, *interroga patrem tuum, &c;* the Romans sent to Greece for a declaration of their laws in causes like to happen, Titus Livius, *decad.* 3, *fol.* 45g; Lancelloti*, *de Ecclesiasticis Constitutionibus, tit. 3, Canonum alii sunt decreta Conciliorum, alii statut', alii dicta sanctorum;* Hotman†, *de Jure Civili, tit.*4, *Praetorum dicta & responsa prudentum,* which cannot be without questions; Venerable Bede, lib.1, cap.27 (St Augustine demanded general questions); J. Selden, *super Eadmerum, fol.*171, William the Conqueror did call to the judges to declare and compile Edgar's laws and St. Edward's laws, which were buried and forgotten by the interruption of the Danish government.[57]

Pulton's Statutes, fol. 6 In the time of King Henry III, certain knights of Ireland desired resolutions in England concerning *coparcenary* and received resolutions according to the laws of England, and this in Parliament, as appears in the statute called *Statutum Hiberniae,* 14 *Henr.*3 in the printed book.

Archivum Turris Londiniensis *Ordinationes factae de Statu Hiberniae* at large in the Roll of 7 *Edw.*2, *parte prima, membr.* 3 & 18; *Rot. Claus., anno* 2 *Edw.*3, *membr.* 17 *(Rex concedit quod ad primum Parliamentum omnes Hiberni qui voluerint legibus utantur Angliae sine Cartis inde fiendis); Rot. Claus., anno* 5 *Edw.*3, *parte prima, membr* 25. The same law in case of wardships.

Ordinationes pro Regimine Hiberniae, 5 *Edw.*3, *Pat., membr. 25; 35 Edw.*3, *parte prima, membr.* 9, which *Consilium* ought to be understood of the Parliament as hereafter I will declare. *Ordinatio facta de ministris Regis in Hibernia, Claus.,* 18 *Edw.*3, *parte secunda, membranes* 9 and 17; *anno* 20

---

*Lancelotus;
†Hotoman.
[57] Titus Livius (Livy, 59/64 B.C.–A.D. 17), Roman historian of whose 140 volumes, 35 survive; Book III, chapters 31–2, relates how the Romans sent a delegation to Athens to consult the Solonian code of laws. *Giampaolo Lancelloti* (1511–91), Italian jurist and compiler of much-edited version of canon law, *Institutiones juris canonici* (Rome, 1555), known as the Tribonian of Perugia. *François Hotman* (1524–1589), French humanist scholar and jurist, also a Calvinist polemicist; the work referred to is probably *Partitiones juris civilis elementariae* (1560). *Venerable Bede* (672/3–735), reference is made to the first book of his *Historia ecclesiastica gentis Anglorum.* John Selden (1584–1654), a legal historian and leading figure in English historical research in the seventeenth century. Editor of the work of Eadmer (c.1060–1128) the biographer of St.Anselm and the Canterbury community *(Historia novorum in Anglia,* c.1115). The title of Selden's edition, *Historia novorum, sive sui sæculi, libri VI, ex bibl. cottoniana ed. Io. Seldenus et notas adjecit et spicilegium* (London, 1623), was abbreviated to *super Eadmerum.* The inventory of sources which Darcy will continue to unwrap should be seen as a strategic answer to his serious concern about the dilapidation of the Irish legal archive.

*Edw.*3, *parte prima,* in dorso; anno 25 Edw.3, membr 29.[58]

My Lords, I have not yet learned how syllogisms can be made, or answers categorical, without propositions. I am as ignorant after what manner ordinances or reformation could be made without questions or propositions.

[58] In no sequence of references is Darcy's concern to verify the Irish legal archive so evident. Quoting initially from his Pulton's *Statutes,* which seems always to be by his side, he goes on to quote directly from sources in the Tower of London. While some of his references no longer correspond to those of current editions of the archives consulted, it is essential to remember that he was compiling his material at a time when contemporary editions of statutes were highly suspect (see *Introduction,* p.217). His notes on sources were presumably several years old, dating from student days, at the time of the *Argument,* allowing further room for error.

Coparcenary: co-partnership, joint share of a heritage. 14 Hen.III, *Statutum Hiberniae, recte* 20 Hen.III (1236), Close Rolls, m.4d (*SR,* 1, 5; Berry, *ESI,* 30). One of Darcy's most careful readers, William Molyneux, summarizes this statute as follows: 'Henry III in this certificate or rescript, which is called *Statutum Hiberniae,* merely informs the Justice what the law and custom was in England, *viz, [. . . .]* that the foresaid customs that be used within our realm of England in this case, be proclaimed throughout our Dominion of Ireland' (*TCIS,* 64).

Ordinationes factae de Statu Hiberniae, 7 Edw.II, Patent Rolls, part 1, m.3 & 18, *recte,* 17 Edw.II (*SR,* 1, 193); Darcy's error is clearly derived from his source, since the footnote in the modern edition of *SR* explains that in the original copies the statute was attributed to 17 Edw.I; this also explains Molyneux's error on the same point.

2 Edw.III (1328), Close Rolls, m.17 (*CCR, 1327-30,* 1, 312), 'that all Irishmen wishing to use the English laws may do so, and that it shall not be necessary for them to sue out of charters for this purpose.'

5 Edw.III (1331), Close Rolls, part 1, m.25 (*CCR, 1330-3,* 2, 203-4), on a dispute of homage relating to wardships, because the custom was contrary to the laws of England, 'the King therefore orders the justiciary to cause the law and custom of the King's realm, and not the custom aforesaid, to be observed henceforth before him.'

Ordinationes pro Regimine Hiberniae, 5 Edw.III (1331), Patent Rolls, m.25 (*CPR, 1330-4,* 1, 84), Mandate to the justiciary, chancellor and treasurer of Ireland, to observe certain articles prepared in the last Parliament for the amendment of the estate of that law, which are set out in the patent.'

35 Edw.III, part 1, m.9; the precise location of this reference causes some difficulty. Of the options available, see 35 Edw.III (1360), Memoranda Roll of the Exchequer (Ireland), on the accountability of the King's officers and officials (Berry, *ESI,* 423-9); also 35 Edw.III, Close Roll, m.40 (Rymer's *Fœdera,* vol.III, part 2, 605, and *ESI,* 420-1, '*Pro clericis de natione Hibernicana*', 'The King to his justiciar and chancellor of Ireland [. . .] and because it is not just, nor was it nor is it our intention, that clerks of the Irish race who have continuously and unswervingly remained in fealty and obedience to us [. . .] should be reckoned as of the condition of our Irish enemies.'

The native Irish were therefore to be considered eligible for office and ecclesiastical benefice in Ireland.

Ordinatio facta de Ministris Regis in Hibernia; this is not be found in 18 Edw.III, but 31 Edw.III (1357): *An Ordinance made for the estate of the land of Ireland* (*SR,* 1, 357-64), the editors' note indicates that in the original archives, the *Ordinatio* of 1357 was found in the documents of 17-18 Rich.II (1394-5). The *Ordinatio* is a comprehensive review of English legislation and administration in Ireland.

20 Edw.III (1351), the reference is incomplete, therefore difficult to identify; it may be intended as a reference to 20 Edw.III, Close Rolls, part 1, m.120, which is an ordinance

It may be objected that the word *quere or question* is new, [but] that word was nothing strange in Edward the Third's time, *Rot. Parliament.*, 21 *Edw.*3, *num.*41.

Camden, The Commons in Parliament prayed that it may be *Anals. Hibern.* inquired how it comes to pass that the King hath no benefit of his land in Ireland, considering he had more there than any of his ancestors. May it not be as lawful to inquire in this Parliament wherefore the King is in debt, and yet his people here gave him more supplies than to any of his ancestors, or wherefore his laws are not observed? I find no difference.[59]

In the printed Year Book, 2 Rich.3, *fol.*9, the King propounded several questions to the judges in the Star Chamber in cases not then pending.*

b] 2.ratio. Their second reason is fully answered to the first; and for more clear satisfaction, the words of the writ which bring them hither are *viz.* to give council *circa ardua & urgentia negotia regni*, the matters now in agitation are *maxime ardua, maxime urgentia*.

The Year Books of law do prove *Provisiones & Ordinationes*, and no cause is said to be pending,† Fitzherbert, *Natura Brevium*,‡ 32d, 39 Edw.3, 7b, *Thorp*; the Lords being assembled can make ordinances as strong as a statute. By the opinion of that judge such ordinances cannot be avoided but in Parliament, an act or statute may be avoided or repealed in Parliament.[60]

c] 3.ratio. Where they say that the questions though in number but twenty-two, yet they include fifty-two questions, that all the affairs of

regulating the conduct of the King's justices, terminating in the text of their oath (*SR*, 1, 305–6).

25 *Edw.III* (1351), Memoranda Roll of the Exchequer (Ireland),m.13f; see note 31. Anticipating the *Statute of Kilkenny* (40 Edw.III, 1366), the twenty-five clauses of 25 Edw.III are a fundamental set of statutes for constitutional historians; among the clauses is the introduction of English law, replacing the Brehon law, for everyone in Ireland (Berry, *ESI*, 375–9).

* 'depending'

† 'pending'.

‡ F.N.B.

[59] 21 Edw.III, n° 41; the reference has not been found, but the substance corresponds to 16 Edw.III (1342), in *Red Book of the Exchequer*, f° 13–20 (*ESI*, 332–64). *William Camden, Britannia*, (London, 1637); the *Annals of Ireland* appear at the end of Camden's work. The subjects' concern for the debts of the King can also be found in England from the reign of James I, in the *Petition of Right* (1628) under Charles I, as well as in article 11 of the *Remonstrance of Grievances* of the Irish House of Commons in 1641.

[60] Anthony Fitzherbert, *La Nouvel Natura Brevium* (London, 1609), cap. 17, '*Assise de Darreine presentment*', p.32d, '*qd' nulla assisa ultime presentationis de cetero capiatur* ...'

Church & Commonwealth may be included in the resolution thereof, and that they will not be concluded by their answers to the same.

My Lords, the House of Commons made the questions so many as they are for the more clear explanation of their candid intentions and not for difficulty (whereas they might reduce them to fewer), but to the end the answers might be the more punctual and satisfactory unto positive points and known law; and the custody of the law, the great treasure of the land, being committed by His Sacred Majesty to their trust, to the end they should declare how, and after what manner, they issued and dispensed that treasure, and discharged that great trust, and not to be bound by their resolutions in Parliament. For judges are, and ought to be, bound by resolutions in Parliament, and not Parliaments by them.

d] 4.ratio. To their fourth reason, what succeeding ages will do, we do well hope they will not do amiss, that no occasion shall be administered hereafter which may enforce the House of Commons to propound the like questions.

e] 5 ratio. That by reason of the King's prerogative and the concernment of his other interests, they cannot answer without His Majesty's especial direction, considering the duties of their places and their oaths.

My Lords, it is manifest that, by their oaths, they are bound to interpret the laws truly between the King and his people, and between party and party; and if in any case granted, it cannot be denied when the Commonwealth desires a declaration of the law in certain points wherein they conceive their just liberties to have been invaded, lest under colour of prerogative (which the Parliament holds to be sacred) some Ministers may presume (as of late they have endeavoured) to destroy the people's just liberties.

In the ordinary courts of justice, the judges upon oath are bound to afford the subject justice against the King and all others, and are appointed by His Majesty for that purpose. All writs are in His Majesty's name in the King's Bench, the pleas are styled *Coram Rege*, letters-patents and writs original are *Teste me ipso*; the King is therefore present in Parliament, being the highest tribunal, wherein truly he sits in the exaltation of royalty and greatness. Therefore, the commands of all his ordinary courts are the commands of the King, [and] much more commands in Parliament, where his presence is more apparent and essential than in all other courts of this kingdom.[61]

It appears copiously by the Great Charter, and by constant practise

---

[61] *Coram Rege*, in the presence of the King; *Teste me ipso* witnessed by me [the King].

of all Parliaments since that time, that all courts and judges were regulated by Parliaments. As for the King's prerogative or revenue, the judges cannot be ignorant but that the Parliament is, and ever hath been, the best maintainer of his just prerogatives, the best overseer of his revenue, which if it fall short, they only are able and willing to supply.

f] 6. ratio. It is true that the abuses of former times might be reformed for the future by Bills to be passed as statutes. Yet that is a way about, and we may not lose the possession of our laws and just liberties, nor by new statutes admit impunity, or give countenance to past offences; statutes of this kind sufficient were already enacted and passed in former ages.

g] 7. ratio. The declaration of a known law, and the manifestation of wholesome statutes already established, well may help the Commonwealth for the present, but cannot in any probability fall out hereafter to be prejudicial to the state or Commonwealth, and there is no precedent or example of any such prejudice.

h] 8. ratio. It is confessed that most of the matters contained in the questions are already voted for grievances in both Houses, and that very justly; but how the law is therein remains yet to be declared as to this present Parliament, which I hope in due time shall be declared, according to law and justice, as in many Parliaments before the same or the like hath been often done.

i] 9. ratio. Where they do again insist upon the want of precedent, and withal that, in the preamble to the questions, the protestation clears the law.

This word 'precedent' sticks close unto us; I have answered it before by precedents, yet some more precedent I will offer as often as they speak of the word precedent: 7, 8 Elizabeth, *Dyer, fol. 241b, placit. 49.* The King's Attorney demanded the opinion of the judges, 9 Elizabeth, *Dyer, 261, placit. 28 Casus Hiberniae,* where the judges of England signed their opinions to questions propounded by the judges of Ireland; 11 Elizabeth, *Dyer, fol. 282b. placit.26, Casus Hiberniae, 19 & 20* Elizabeth, *Dyer, 360.* The case of arraignment of a peer, the like 13 Car. by all the judges of England, the *Earl of Ormond's Case,* and yet in none of these cases the matter was pending* before them.[62] Notwithstanding

---

*depending

[62] These references are all drawn from the reports of Sir James Dyer (1512–82), one of the most important early legal commentators:

7–8 Eliz, Dyer, 241b: 2Dyer 241b, *Brooke otherwise Cobham's Case,* in piracies, the defendant

the protestation may clear the law, yet in all precedent ages laws clear in themselves, for their greater honour and countenance, they have been declared and enacted in Parliament.

The law declared by *Magna Charta* was clear before, yet it was enacted 9 Hen.3 and in thirty Parliaments since, Coke 8, 19b, *Prince's Case*, the statute of *praerog. regis*. And the statute of 25 Edw.3. of **Genesis ch.3** treasons, is declarative and so are many other statutes. **verse 7, & ch. 4,** Adam ate the forbidden fruit, Cain killed his brother; **verse 8.** God demanded whether this was done, yet he could not be ignorant of the fact. The first article in the civil and canon law courts is whether there is such a law. All this is done for illustration's sake.[63]

My Lords, the ground of the questions, and the preamble to the

---

standing mute shall have judgement of *peine forte et dure*. Chief baron and the justice of King's Bench consulted (*ER*, King's Bench Division, vol. 73, 534).

9 Eliz, Dyer, 261: 3Dyer261b, *Casus Hiberniae* (*ER*, ibid., 580); also *Pigot's Case*, 11CoRep.26b. Both cases involve disputed tenure and possession in Ireland referred to the Lords Justices.

11 Eliz. Dyer, 282b: 3Dyer282, *the Archbishop of Dublin vs Bruerton*, on the temporary surrender of the lease of Deanery and Chapter of St Patrick's Cathedral. Judges of Ireland refer to King's Bench (*ER, op.cit.,633*).

19–20 Eliz. Dyer, 360: 3Dyer360, treason committed in Ireland by an Irish peer cannot be tried in England. Referred to the judges of England, who ruled that '*he* [unnamed] *cannot have his trial here by his peers.*'

13 Carol: the reference is not precise enough for accurate location.

The Earl of Ormond's Case: there are three cases to which this reference could apply. First, the attainder brought against the Earl of Ormond by Edward IV following his support of Henry VI at the Battle of Towton (1461); the attainder was removed, and titles restored, by Henry VII. The second possibility concerns the revocation by an Act of the Irish Parliament in 1499 of the *Act of Resumption* as it applied, under Poynings' Law, to the lands of Thomas Butler, Earl of Ormond. The final application possible, and the closest in time to Darcy, was the confirmation by the Irish Parliament in 1641 of the 1537 restoration of Butler titles; divested of their title of Earls of Ormond in 1527 by Henry VIII, in favour of a distant cousin (Sir Thomas Bullen, father of Ann Boleyn), the house of Ormond had their titles restored in 1537.

[63]*9 Hen.3*, too imprecise to locate, but presumably a confirmation of *Magna Carta* as, for example, 10 Hen.III (1226), Patent Roll, m.4: 'the law and customs of our land of England to be kept in our land of Ireland, "as the lord King John enjoined them to be kept"' (*ESI*, 21).

Coke 8, 19b, Prince's Case: 8CoRep.19b (1606–7). This was a case in which royal prerogative was closely challenged in Parliament on the succession of the Duchy of Cornwall. The issue developed on the premature death of Prince Henry, the older brother of Charles I; Coke argued that the succession fell only to the King's eldest son, and that it could not pass to a younger son without the charter being changed by Act of Parliament.

25 Edw.3,5. c.1–2: offers an extended definition of treason (Statutes of the Realm, pp.319–20).

Genesis.iii.7: 'Then the eyes of both of them were opened and they discovered that they were naked'. *Genesis.iv.8*: 'While they were there, Cain attacked his brother Abel and murdered him'.

writing, styled an *Answer,* kept me so long, that I fear much to have trespassed upon your patience; and yet the importance of the cause urgeth me to importune your Lordships' favour a little further.[64]

1 **Question**   This question is short and yet comprehensive; that we
1 **Answer**   are free people, is confessed to my hands. To that part of the answer I do not except; the second part of the question is, whether we are to be governed by the laws of England and statutes of force in Ireland only.[65]

First, though I need not prove it, yet it is clear we ought to be so governed, Matthew Paris, *Historia major, fol. 121;* Sir John Davis, *Discovery of Ireland, fol.100.* King Henry the Second held a Parliament at Lismore in Ireland, in which Parliament, *Leges & consuetudines Angliae fuerunt gratanter acceptae,* by the representative body of this whole nation. *Magna Charta,* and other beneficial statutes of England, are here in the *Red Book of the Exchequer* in, and since King John's time; and so is Gervasius Tilberiensis of the course and officers of the exchequer, in the *White Book of the Exchequer* of Ireland, *leges & consuetudines Angliae,* received in Ireland by Parliament.[66] And otherwise this appears [in] 9 John, *Pat., membr.2;* 1 Hen.3, *Pat., memb. 13; 10.* Hen.3, *Pat., membr. 4;* 12 Hen.3,
Archivum   *Claus., membr.8,* by which words, and by the constant
Turris   practice of all ages since, this kingdom was governed,
Londiniensis   and ought to be so by the law of England, as the law of the land, which law as it was always here received, consists of three parts. First, the common law. Secondly, the general customs of England.

---

[64] Darcy reaches a major turning point in his presentation. He has completed his reply to the judges' preamble and now turns to a detailed defence of the queries.

[65] In response to the temporizing of the judges on this matter (see note 31), a full answer was required; *'the statutes of force in Ireland only'* are the *declarative* laws of the English Parliament from King John to the present, followed by the *introductive* statutes which, in each case, were ratified by the Irish Parliament (see *Introduction,* pp.219).

[66] *Matthew Paris, Historia major a Guilelmo conquestore ad ultimum annum Henrici III* (London, 1571): see also *Matthaei Parisiensis, Monachi Sancti Albani, Historia Anglorum, sive ut Vulgo Dicitur Historia Minor,* ed. Sir Frederic Madden, 1 (London, 1866), 371, *'Sed rex pater, antequam ab Hibernia rediret, apud Lissemor concilium congregavit, ubi leges Angliae ab omnibus sunt gratanter acceptae'.*
Sir John Davies, *Discovery of the true causes why Ireland was never entirely subdued* (London, 1612). Sir John Davies (1569–1626) was Attorney-General in Ireland (1606–19), having been Solicitor-General (1603–6). See also Hans Pawlisch, *Sir John Davies and the Conquest of Ireland: a study in legal imperialism* (Cambridge, 1985).
Leges et consuetudines Angliae fuerunt gratanter acceptae: 'where English law and custom were freely accepted' (extract from Matthew Paris above; duplicated by Molyneux, *TCIS,* 27). *Red Book of the Exchequer (Liber ruber scacarii),* destroyed by fire in the Irish Four Courts, Dublin, 1922; Gervasius Tilberiensis, author of a twelfth-century treatise on the fall of empire, *Otia Imperialia,* is an inexplicable inclusion at this point; *White Book of the Exchequer (Liber Albus* of the Corporation of Dublin). Both collections of these important early statutes have been reproduced in part in *ESI.*

Thirdly, statutes here received. The common law that is cleared already, customs as *tenant* by the *curtesie*. Inn-keepers to be responsible for things within their houses, or the like, when we speak of a custom in the law, it must be intended a general custom over the realm, and no particular custom. And this appears by the Year Books of 37 Hen.6. fol.5; 21 Hen.7, 17-18. Particular customs, as *Gavelkind, Borough, English-tenant right,* or the like, are not to be intended when we speak generally of *custom,* and these customs are warranted by the common law of England, being not contrary to the same, but *praeter legem;* so there may be, and are, particular customs here *praeter legem,* and yet not contrary to law, as in many corporations and countries; so the wife's third of goods is good in England, by the custom of many counties and places, Fitzherbert, *Natura Brevium**, 122, 7 Edward4, 21; 40 Edw.3, 38; 17 Edw..2, *f. detinue 58*. Therefore it is not contrary to law, that such a custom is here, over all the kingdom. And yet if any man ask the question, by what law we are governed, there is no proper answer **Statutum** other than by the law of England.[67] And for the statutes **Hiberniae 67a.** of England; general statutes were received in this kingdom, some at one time, some at another; and all general statutes by Poynings' Act, *anno* 10 Hen.7, but no other statute, or new introducing law, until the same be first received and enacted in Parliament in this kingdom, and this may appear by two declarative statutes, the one 10 Hen.4, the other 29 of Hen.6.[68]

* 'F.N.B.'

[67] *9 John* (1207), Patent Roll, m.2f (*ESI*, 4: '*Irish robbers to be dealt with according to the law of England*'.

1 Hen.III (1216), Patent Roll, m.13, *Magna Charta Hiberniae* (*Red Book of the Exchequer in Ireland,* f° 69–73 in *ESI*, 5–19); as Molyneux expanded on it, 'King Henry the Third came to the Crown the nineteenth day of October 1216, and in November following he granted to Ireland a *Magna Charta,* dated at Bristol in November, the first year of his reign. 'Tis prefaced that [...] *he makes the following grant to Ireland; and then goes on exactly agreeable to the* Magna Charta *which he granted to England*' (*TCIS*, 38).

10 Hen.III, Patent Rolls, m.4; see under 9 Hen.III, note 63.

12 Hen.III (1228), Close Rolls, m.8 (*ESI*, 23–4), 'King John's charter as to observance of English laws and customs in Ireland to be observed'.

The note in the margin indicates that the above documents were verified at source in the Tower of London.

Year Books, 37 Hen.VI, f° 5; 21 Hen.VII, f° 17–18.

Fitzherbert, Natura Brevium cap.57 '*Rationibile parte bonorum*', p.122.

Year Books, 7 Edw.IV, f° 21; 40 Edw.III, f° 38; 17 Edw.II, f° 58.

The general point emerging out of these references is that, even though local custom can vary, that variation (including Irish custom) is itself inscribed in the code of English common law. The concept of a tripartite legal system (common law, custom, and statute) comes directly from Coke: 'Consuetudo is one of the main triangles of the laws of England, those laws being divided into Common Law, Statute Law and Custom', CoIInst, f° 110ᵛ.

[68] *10 Hen.VII, Poynings' Act* (1494–5): *An Act that no Parliament be holden in this land* [Ireland] *untill the Acts be first certified into England*' (Bolton, *Statutes of Ireland,* Dublin, 1621); a facsimile

The law of England, as it is the best human law, so it is a noble, and sociable law, and for the more clear discerning of the truth and equal administration of justice, it refers many causes to their genuine and natural proceedings, as maritime causes to the Courts of Admiralty, Coke *Institutes* 260, 361; Stamford, 57b; Coke 5, 106, 107, *Constables Case*, and there the proceeding is by the civil law, Coke 8, 47b. Matters beyond the seas are determined in the Court of Constable and Marshall, Coke's *Institutes*, 391b; matters of Latin the law refers to grammarians, Plowden, *Commentaries*, fol.122; matters merely ecclesiastical to be tried and determined in the proper courts, Coke 7, 43b; 8Coke 68; 5Coke 57; 1 R.3,4; matters of merchandize to merchants, 34 Hen.8, *Dyer* 52 & 54. Many other cases upon this learning are to be found, Coke 9, fol. 30, 31, 32, *Strata Marcella's Case*. Yet in all these and the like cases, the trial and determination thereof are bounded and controlled by the rules of the common law; they are as rivers which are necessary to run through the land, to help the inhabitants thereof, but if they overflow the banks, the banks are made higher and stronger to suppress their violent current. So in all the cases aforesaid, and the like, the common law hath limited the proceedings; if they exceed their bounds, witness the prohibitions in all our books, and the statutes of *Provision* and *Praemunire*, and the cases thereupon in many ages, by which it is manifest that the supreme and governing law are the common law, common customs, and statutes of the realm, and the rest but ministers and servants unto it; *brevia remedialia* are only by the common law mandatoria, may be in the said other cases, 7 Coke, *Calvin's Case*, *Dyer*,176.[69]

copy can be found in *Facsimiles of the national manuscripts of Ireland*, ed. J.T. Gilbert, vol. 3, plate 53 (London, 1879).

10 Hen.IV (1408–9), summarized by Molyneux as follows: 'And in the 10th of Henry the Fourth, it was enacted in this kingdom of Ireland, that the statutes made in England should not be of force in this kingdom, unless they were allow'd and published in this kingdom by Parliament' (*TCIS*, 51).

29 Hen.VI (1450), following the train indicated by Darcy, Molyneux continues from above 'and the like statute was made again in the 29th of Henry the Sixth'. See also same statute, c.2 'Also it is ordained and agreed that the land of Ireland have and enjoy all its liberties and franchises, good usages and customs, as have been used heretofore.' *ESI*, 251).

Developing the implications of the two statutes above, Darcy later called attention in his *Declaration* to the number of Irish statutes of this period which had disappeared (see *Introduction*, p.219, for this and *introductive* and *declarative* laws).

[69] *Courts of Admiralty*, originally specialised in laws of commerce, trade and the sea; this jurisdiction was transferred to the High Court in 1873 with Selborne's *Judicature Act* (England). At the time of writing, Darcy would have known only of the first volume of Coke's *Institutes* (on Littleton, 1628), known as ColInst., or CoLitt., f° 260, Section 439, Of Continual Claim, 'and yet *altum mare* is out of the jurisdiction of the common law, and within the jurisdiction of the High Admiral'; f° 361 appears to be a mistaken reference since it deals with the distinction between sained and false cases.

So that the answer as to the words (in the general) is short and ought to be positive.

As to the courts of equity, they have been ancient in England, and the courts of equity here ought to be guided by the constant proceedings in England in ages past. I mean not by this or that Chancellor, but by that natural and just equity in the courts there observed. This equity is of absolute necessity in many cases (*ipsae et enim leges capiunt ut jure regantur*) and therefore is included within the law of the land, and not to be divided from it, as out of this writing it may be inferred.

As to the case of killing in rebellion to operate an attainder, if this be no law in England it cannot be law here, **vide** *Dame Hales' Case*,

Stamford, Sir William Stanford, *Les Plees del Coron* (London, 1567); Cap.5, p.57^v, on the functions of '*le Graund Master, ou Seignior Stuard del Hostiel le Roy solement*'.

5CoRep.106–7, Constable's Case: a case brought by Sir Henry Constable, Easter Term 43 Eliz., to defend royal (Admiralty) claim against trespass on *flotsam, jetsam*, and *lagan* and on land between high and low water mark (*ER*, vol. 77, 218–20).

8CoRep.47b, Webb's Case; in the case of John Webb, brought in defence of his claim to income from his office of the King's Tennis plays in Westminster, it was argued that 'Assise lies of the office of the Register of the Admiralty, which the plaintiff had for life. Note that, although the proceedings in that court be according to Civil law, yet the offices are determinable by the Common Law (*ER*, vol.77, 544).

Court of Constable and Marshall, CoLitt., f° 391^v; the court tried cases of treason, crimes committed overseas, and matters touching war.

Plowden, Commentaries, f° 122, the case of Buckley vs Rice Thomas, 'And in order to understand it truly, being a Latin word, we ought to follow the steps of our predecessors, Judges of the law, who, when they were in doubt about the meaning of any Latin words, enquired how those that were skilled in the study thereof took them, and pursued their construction' (*ER*, vol.75, 189).

Matters ecclesiastical; 7CoRep.43b, *Kenn's Case*, if a marriage is below legal age 'the ecclesiastical judge is judge as well of the assent as of the first contract, and what shall be a sufficient assent or not (*ER*, vol. 77, 476); *8CoRep.68*, 'an excommunication must be certified by a bishop' (*ER*, vol.77, 577); *5CoRep.57*, tenure of the manor of Tedcote in Devon, disputed against the Bishop of Exeter, 'that for calling a man heretic, no action on the case lies in our law, for those of the common law cannot determine what is heresy' (*ER, ibid.*, 142).

34 Hen.VIII, Dyer 52–4, 'the King cannot dispense with future acts of Parliament, though he may with things in future whereof he hath the inheritance' (*ER*, 73, 114).

Strata Marcella's Case, 9CoRep.30–2; 'In some cases, as in general bastardy, excommengement, loyalty of matrimony, profession and divers other matters shall be tried by the certificate of the bishop' (*ER*, 77, 777).

For the *topos* of the law as a nutrient stream contained within its banks, see note 25.

Statutes of Provision and Praemunire; these statutes governed and defined the proper jurisdiction of courts in England; in the case of *praemunire*, the restriction of jurisdiction applied to papal and ecclesiastical courts in particular.

Calvin's Case, 7CoRep.1–28. At the conclusion of this long and complex case ascertaining the right of a Scots-born Scot (Robert Calvin) to inherit in England, Coke opined that 'it appeareth that *jurisprudentia legis communis Angliae est scientia socialis et copiosa*' (*ER*, 77, 410).

Dyer, 176, 'If a juror reside within the plaintiff's leet, it is a principal challenge, although no tenure, for he is within the distress' (*ER*, 73, 387).

Plowden, *Comm.* 263a; 8 Edw.3, 20; Fitzherbert, *Dower,** 106; Crompton's *Jurisdiction, fol.* 84a, by which it may be urged that it is an attainder for that he prevented the judgment of law by fighting against the Crown, and by his killing therein, which ensued his unlawful and traitorous act; but I observe to the contrary the books of 7 Hen.4, 32b, & Coke, 4, 57, *Sadler's Case.* I do confess that in England statutes may be obsolete as the *Statute of William Butler,* by which the heir may have an action of wast, Rastell 5, 21. All the books are contrary, and so is the *Statute of Merton* of disparagement as to an action to be brought for the same; so are some antiquated laws, 40 Edw.3, 42; 42 *Ass.*8 & 25; one present and aiding to murder was accessory, but now is principal, 4 Hen.7,18; Plowden, *Commentaries,* 99 & 100. A vicar could not anciently have an action against a parson, 40 Edw.3, 28, Finchden; the law is now otherwise, and so of an entry upon a *feoffe* with warranty *sitț fol.* 13, 24, in the case of disparagement, give the reason, because that those statutes and laws were never used, therefore obsolete. Our case is nothing like, for life, liberty, and property being in debate, but an obsolete law is no law in force. Therefore the answer as to that is defective.[70]

*'fitz.Dower'

†'sit', included in original *Faults Escaped* as correction to 'Lit'.

[70] The general observations on equity entail the equity of the Chancellor, which is a native growth, and equity of the courts, which is more concerned with technical appraisal and correction.

ipsae et enim leges capiunt ut jure reguntur, 'for those same laws govern so that we may be governed by law.

Dame Hale's Case, Plowden *Comm. 263a,* 'those that fly from the law, or that by their acts refuse to be tried by the law, shall forfeit their goods and chattles' (*English Reports,* vol. 75, 404); see also 8CoRep.172a.

Fitzherbert, Dower, 106; this appears to be a faulty reference, corresponding neither to the *Graund Abridgement* nor to the *Natura Brevium*; the section on Dower in the latter work begins at p. 47, the page quoted deals with Attaint.

Crompton's Jurisdiction f° 84a; Richard Crompton, *L'Authoritie et Jurisdiction des Courts de la Roygne* (London, 1594), p. 84.

4CoRep 57; in the case of the commonalty of Saddlers, Coke's summary mentions that '*this Act* [34 E.3,c.14] *extends only where the King was entitled by office only*' (*English Reports,* vol. 76, 1017).

Statute of William Butler, I have been unable to trace this obsolete statute, but f° 521 of William Rastell's *A Collection in English of the Statutes now in Force* ... (London, 1608) does indeed deal with actions of waste.

Statute of Merton, 20 Hen.3, c.6(1235–6): '*And as touching Lords, who have married those that they have in ward to villeins or others, as burgesses, where they be disparaged, if any such heir be under the age of 14 years, and of such age that he cannot consent* [...], *the Lord shall lose his wardship*' (*Statutes of the Realm,* 1, 3; *Early Statutes of Ireland,* p.28).

4 Hen. 7.f° 18, Year Book, see below.

Plowden, *Commentary,* 99–100; in a general discussion of the identity of principals and accessories on charges of murder, Plowden quotes, in fact, 7 Hen. 4 and not 4 Hen. 7.

sit fol. 13,24; this otherwise incomprehensible reference is, in fact, one of the *Faults escaped* of the 1643 edition which were not corrected in the edition of 1764. The text is meant

As to the case of a felon upon his keeping and terrifying of the people, I conceive the answer is uncertain and dangerous; if such a felon raise an armed power against the Crown and terrify that way, no doubt this is treason within the statute of 25 Edw.3 or the equity of it, and by the statute of 10 Hen.7, *cap*.13, in Ireland, *Statuto Hiberniae, fol.* 62. But if such terrifying be without raising arms, or by committing the same or the like felonies, it is no more than the case of purse-takers by force in the highways of England. Many a man was terrified thereby in Salisbury Plain, and yet no treason; and if there be no statute here which is not in England to make it treason, certainly it cannot be treason. Since the Conquest, writs of error have been brought for to reverse judgements given in the King's Bench here, in the Court of King's Bench in England. No course here which is contrary to law, can alter the law of England, therefore to what purpose is a declaration of judges here contrary to the law there? This writ of error is a writ framed in the register and appears by common experience. I will offer a notable case which I saw adjudged in the King's Bench in England, *Pasc.* 18 Jacob for *Stafford* against *Stafford* in a writ of error for to reverse a judgment given in the King's Bench in Ireland when Sir William Jones was Chief Justice here, in an *ejectione firme*, for that in the declaration there was contained among other things *ducentas acras Montani*. Sir William Jones being in England, affirmed the course here to have been so, and vouched many notable precedents; thereupon an order was conceived that Sir James Ley, Sir Humphry Winch, and Sir John Denham, knights (who were formerly Chief Justices here), should certify the course, who made report that the course in Ireland was, and ought to be, in writs original and judicial, to be directed by the register, in pleading to be guided by the books of entries, and thereupon the judgement was reversed. And the Chief Justice Montague said that if they did not proceed in Ireland according to law, they should learn it. And so I conclude that the answer to the first question is insufficient.[71]

to read '**Lit.** fol. ....', as an abbreviation for Littleton, *Tenures* f°13,24. The section quoted deals with fee simple, CoLitt., ff° 1–18ᵛ.

[71] *25 Edw.III, statute 5, c.2(1350–1); a declaration of what offences shall be adjudged treason (SR*, 1, 319). *10 Hen.VII*, this is *Poynings' Act* (1494–5).

Pasc. 18 Jacob, Stafford vs Stafford, recte, *MacDonnogh (ER*, 81, 997), Palmer 100: *Briefe d'Error hors d'Ireland per un Stafford vers MacDonnogh sur Judgement render la in un ejectione firmæ in Banke le Roy la*. The appeal, at which Darcy himself was present, concerned the sale of 200 acres of mountain land, *ducentas acras Montani*, to the plaintiff when he had wanted bogland ('*et ne dit centum acras Bogge*'). Jones, the English magistrate who had presided, argued in defence of his procedure that everyone knew that mountainous land was common in Ireland, '*montaine terre est conuse in Ireland*', and that there was no case for appeal. Scrutiny of the procedure, and consultation with Sir William Parsons, the Surveyor of Ireland, confirmed that the register of deeds was normally used in Ireland, as in England in such transactions, but that it had not been used in this case. The judgement of the English magistrates in Ireland was thus reversed by King's Bench in

Question 2. As touching the second question, which is concerning the oath which these judges do take, the question is, whether the judges of the land do take the oath of judges? And if so, &c.

Answer 2. The answer of the judges to the first part is that they confess they take the oath of judges, which is specified amongst the statutes in 18 Edw.3 and 20 Edw.3 as I said before, and that they may not stay, hinder, or delay the suit of any subject or his judgement or execution thereupon, otherwise than according to the law and course of the court where they sit, under pretence of any Act of State, proclamation, writ, letter, or direction under the Great Seal, or Privy Seal, or Privy Signet, or Letter, or other commandment from the Lord Lieutenant, Lord Deputy, Justice, Justices, or other Chief Governor of this kingdom, most of which doth appear by their oath expressed, expressed in the said statutes, and the statute of 2 Edw. 3, c.8, and the statute of 20 Edw.3 as to the Barons of the Exchequer; and as they know no punishment due to the judges for their deviations and transgressions without other aggravation, so they know no punishment laid down by any law against them for their deviations and transgressions in hindering, staying, or delaying of justice, contrary to their said oath other than what is declared in their said oath, and the statute of 20 Edw.3.

I conceive the answer is not a full and perfect answer to the question. For where the question is, *whether the judges under pretext of any Act of State, proclamation, writ, letter or direction under the Great, or Privy Seal, or Privy Signet, or letter or other commandment from the Lord Lieutenant, Lord Deputy, Justice, or Justices, or other Chief Governor or Governors of this kingdom, they may hinder, stay, or delay the suit of any subject, or his judgement, or execution thereupon?* If so, in what cases? And whether, if they do hinder, stay, or delay such suit, judgment, or execution thereupon, what punishment do they incur for their deviations and transgressions therein?

London; Darcy attaches considerable importance to the judgement of Chief Justice Montague.

Sir William Jones (1566–1640), educated at Oxford and Lincoln's Inn, was sent to Ireland as Chief Justice of King's Bench in 1617 and knighted; he returned to England in 1620 to become a justice for Common Pleas, and subsequently on King's Bench (1624).

Sir James Ley (1552–1629), educated at Oxford and Lincoln's Inn, M.P. for Westbury (1597), was sent to Ireland as Chief Justice of King's Bench in 1603 and knighted; Commissioner for Plantations in Ulster in 1608, he returned to England in 1609, becoming M.P. for Bath (1609) and Chief Justice of King's Bench (England) in 1622, elevated to peerage as Earl of Marlborough in 1626.

Sir Humphrey Winch (1555–1625), educated at Cambridge and Lincoln's Inn, M.P. for Bedford (1593), was sent to Ireland as Chief Baron of Exchequer in 1606 and knighted; returned to England in 1610.

Sir John Denham (?–1639), educated at Furnival's and Lincoln's Inn, succeeded Sir Humphrey Winch as Chief Baron of Exchequer in Ireland in 1609 and was knighted; became Chief Justice of King's Bench in 1612, and returned to England as Baron of Exchequer in 1617, also serving as advisor to Court on Irish affairs (1616–19).

To this they answer, that they may not stay, hinder, or delay the suit of any subject, or his judgement, or execution thereupon, otherwise than according to the law and course of the court where they sit, under pretence of any Act of State, proclamation, writ, letter, or direction, under the Great or Privy Seal, or Privy Signet, or letter, or other commandment from the Lord Lieutenant, Lord Deputy, Justice, or Justices, or other Chief Governor or Governors of this kingdom; whereas they ought to have expressed the particular of this exception, for by that clause it is supposed, or may be strongly implied, that in some cases they *may* hinder, stay, or delay the suit of any subject, or his judgement, or execution thereupon, under pretext of any Act of State, proclamation, letter, or direction under the Great or Privy Seal, or Privy Signet, or other commandment from the Lord Lieutenant, Lord Deputy, Justice, Justices, or other Chief Governor, or Governors of this kingdom, which they ought to have expressly laid down. The question being if they may stay, hinder, or delay the suit of any subject upon any such pretext, then to set forth in what cases, which ought to be particularly answered unto.

In the next place, the question is, if they do stay, hinder, or delay such suit, judgement, or execution thereupon, then to set forth what punishment they do incur for their deviation, or transgression therein? Unto this they answer, they know no punishment due to the judges for their deviation, and transgressions without other aggravation.

This I conceive is an implication that there is a punishment where there is matter of aggravation, and therefore it ought to be expressed what matter of aggravation they intend the same to be.

They further say, they know no punishment laid down by any law against them for their deviations or transgressions in hindering, staying, or delaying of justice contrary to their oath, other than what is declared in their said oath, and the statute of 20 Edw.3.

This I conceive not to be a full answer, in respect the punishment laid down in that oath is in a generality, *viz.* that the judges so offending contrary to their oath, are to be at the King's will, of body, lands, and goods, which they should declare, and express how far that punishment extendeth in their bodies, lands, and goods: whether imprisonment of their bodies, or in their lives, and whether in forfeiture of their lands, goods, or how else?

The breach of an oath is a very high offence, and the higher it is, that the matter it doth concern is the greater, and therefore it is much, *secundum subjectam materiam*.[72] It is to be considered to whom the

---

[72] *18 Edw.III*, and *20 Edw.III*, these statutes have already been encountered in notes 32 and 44.

2 *Edw.III, c.8*, Statute of Northampton, 'It is accorded and established, that it shall not be commanded by the Great Seal nor the Little seal to disturb or delay common

oath of a judge is made, and what matter it doth concern.

To the first, the oath is made to GOD, the King and to the Commonwealth.

For that matter, it is concerning the true and equal administration and distribution of justice to the people.

If the judge do offend contrary to his oath, he commits breach of the trust reposed in him by the King, besides the violation of his oath. Look upon trust between common persons: a man makes a lease for years, the lessee makes a *feoffement*, this is a forfeiture of his estate by the common law, by reason of the breach of trust.

5 Edw.4.2 Lessee for life in an action brought against him prays in aid of stranger: this is a forfeiture of his estate.

A *quid juris clamat* brought against lessee for life, he claims a fee, which is found against him, this is a forfeiture of his estate. So much **36 Hen.6,29** for breach of trust.[73]

14 Hen.7,13. To come unto a false verdict given by a jury, which is a breach of their oath, they being sworn *ad veritatem dicendam*, for this false verdict an attaint lyeth at common law against the petit jury.

The judgement at the common law in an attaint importeth eight grievous punishments: *1. quod amittat liberam legem in perpetuum. 2. quod forisfaciat omnia bona & Catalla sua. 3. quod terrae & tenementa in manus Domini Regis capiantur. 4. quod uxores & liberi extra domus suas ejiciantur. 5. quod domus suae prostrentur. 6. quod arbores suae extirpentur. 7. quod prata sua arentur. 8. & quod corpora sua Carceri mancipentur.*[74] So odious is perjury in the eye of the common law. It followeth therefore that the breach of the oath of a judge, *materia considerata*, in regard it tends to the subversion of justice, is an offence of an higher nature deserving a far greater punishment in his body, lands, and goods, as I conceive.

Right; and though such commandments do come, the Justices shall not leave to do right in any point' (*SR*, 1, 259). Darcy is substantially correct in his summary of the judges' responsibilities here and in preceding statutes; it is a major correction for the judges.

[73] *36 Hen.VI, c.29* (1458), this corresponds to the statute passed at the Parliament of Dublin; article 29 grants livery of the manor of Roche, Co. Louth, to Richard Bellew (*ESI*, 555).

[74] *ad veritatem dicendam*, having been sworn to speak the truth; *quod amittat liberam legem in perpetuum*, the loss in perpetuity of freeman's privileges; *quod forisfaciat omnia bona & Catalla sua*. the confiscation of all goods and chattels; *quod terrae et tenementa in manus Domini Regis capiuntur*, lands and property to be held by the King; *quod uxores & liberi extra domus suas eijciantur*, his wife and children be expelled from their home; *quod domus suae prostrentur*, expulsion from his home; *quod arbores suae extirpentur*, his trees to be uprooted; *quod prata sua arentur*, fields to be ploughed up; *quod corpora sua Carceri mancipentur*, whose person be yielded to imprisonment.

3. question   This question is very short and as plain; it is no more
3. answer   than whether the Council table be ajudicator in civil
causes between subject and subject for lands, goods, or chattles, and
by what law? The answer is wholly *ad aliud*, but it is answered fully by
the Great Charter, *capit*. 11, 9 Hen.3, *Communia placita non sequantur
Curiam nostram* (Common pleas, which are the pleas in question, shall
not follow the King's Court, again cap.29). No freeman shall be taken,
imprisoned, put off his freehold, liberties and free customs, &c., other
than by the lawful judgment of his peers, as by the law of the land.

This great assurance in the 38th chapter of the same statute was
granted for the King and his successors to all his people, and was
confirmed in thirty Parliaments, as I said before, Coke 8, the *Prince's
Case*, by the statute of 5 Edw.3, *cap*. 9; 25 Edw.3, *cap*. 4; 28 Edw.3, *cap*.3;
42 Edw.3, *cap* 1 & 3.[75]

The Great Charter is again confirmed, and not only so, but proceedings contrary to the same (before the King or his Council) are
declared void. The King is to observe and maintain the law, the judge
by his oath, 18 Edw.3, is bound to do right between the King and his
people, and that right strengthens the King's prerogative; precedents
or practice contrary to so many statutes are of no use. In many ages
past, encroachments were made upon these just liberties, which were
always removed by Parliaments. Yet I must confess that of all antiquity
some pleas have been held in the King's royal house, as in the court
held by the Marshal of the King's Household, for things arising within
the Verge, *Fleta, lib.2, cap.2*, but when that court exceeds its due bounds,
declaratory statutes were always made to meet them, as mischiefs in
the Commonwealth, when they meddled with land or the like, as
appears by the statute of *Articuli Super Chartam*, 28 Edw.1; 15.R.2. *cap*.12.
All these statutes, My Lords, and many more to this purpose, are
undeniably of force in this kingdom, and none of them can be with
impunity said to be obsolete or antiquated.[76]

---

[75] *9 Hen.III, c.11*, clauses of *Magna Carta* (*SR*, 1, 23).

5 Edw.III, c.9 (1331), 'that no man from henceforth shall be attached by any accusation,
nor forejudged of life or limb, nor his Lands, Tenements, Goods, nor Chattels seised
into the King's Hands against the form of the Great Charter, and the law of the Land'
(*SR*, 1, 267); *25 Edw.III, c.4* (1350–1), this is presumably a reference to statute 4 of the
Statute of Provisors of Benefices (*ibid.*, 1, 316–8): *28 Edw.III, cap.3* (1354), 'that none shall be
condemned without process of law' (*ibid.*, 1, 345); *42 Edw.III, caps. 1 & 3* (1368); this
statute provides confirmation of the charters and that 'none shall be put to answer
without due process of law' (*ibid.*, 1, 388).

[76] 18 Edw.III is quoted from Pulton in note 44; its successor, 20 Edw.III, is quoted just
as frequently in the same context.

Fleta, Book 2, cap.2 (1368): '*De placitis aule regis*' (Of pleas of the King's Hall), eds. Richardson
and Sayles, Selden Society, vol.72 (London, 1953), pp.110–3.

Articuli super Chartam, 28 Edw.II (1300), *recte, Articuli super Cartas*; confirmation of the Statutes
of Liberty, with punishments introduced to enforce certain articles (*SR*, 1, 136–41); *15*

My Lords, they raise another doubt, viz. that, as the King may grant cognizance of pleas to corporations or the like, and therefore to the Council table. If this need an answer, I will answer it thus: that a grant of cognizance never was, neither can it be otherwise, than to proceed *per legem terrae*, or *per judicium parium*, and in the same manner as courts do proceed at common law, and not upon paper petitions, or summary hearings. Such cognizance was never granted. The King is at loss by such proceedings: he loseth fines upon originals, he loseth amerciaments and fines incident to every judgement at common law. As I said before, the subject undergoeth an inconvenience. First the law will decline, writs original will by disuse be forgotten, clerks who should draw them discouraged to learn, legal proceedings out of doors being the foundation of the law, and instead of regular and orderly proceeding, rudeness and barbarism introduced, the subject will lose the benefit of his attaint and writ of error, by which the law might relieve him against false verdicts or erroneous judgements, he will lose the benefit of his warranty, which might repair a purchaser in case his acquired purchase were not good. Whereas if a judge or juror do wrong, the remedy is at hand, but against the Lord Deputy and Council, who will seek for it? Therefore the countenance of this judicature in Common Pleas is against the King's prerogative and the people's just rights (both which the judges ought to maintain), and likewise against the intent of your Lordships' order.[77]

My Lords, as in England, the said several statutes were made to prevent the inconveniences aforesaid, one good statute was made in Ireland, 28 Hen.6, *cap.2*, *Irish Statute, fol.15*, which directs matters of interest to be determined in the Common Pleas, matters of the Crown in the King's Bench and matters of equity in the Chancery. This law, if there were no more, regulates the proceedings in this kingdom.[78] The judges insist upon the words in the end of that statute, *viz. Saving the King's prerogative*. My Lords this was stood upon at the late great trial in England,[79] and easily answered, for by the common law the King

Rich.II, *cap.12* (1391–2): '*None shall be compelled to answer the private courts for matters determinable by the Law of the Land*' (ibid., 2, 82).

[77] *per legem terrae or per judicium parium*, by the law of the land or the justice of his peers; these phrases are quotations from *Magna Carta*, c.29 (see note 88). On paper petitions, see Strafford's *Attainder*, notes 5 & 6.

[78] *28 Hen.6, cap.2, recte,6* (Ireland, 1449–50), an abridgement of the proceedings of the Dublin Parliament of the same year; the Irish statute, f° 15, offers clear, statutory division of responsibilities of law courts. Matters of personal interest go to Common Pleas; affairs concerning the Crown go to King's Bench; matters of equity were to be dealt with in Chancery. The fourth court, Exchequer, had provisions outlined in the statutes and ordinances of the Parliament at Drogheda in 1450, also 28 Hen.VI (*Statutes of Henry VI*, 169–73 & 189, respectively).

[79] The 'late great trial in England' was presumably that of Strafford, executed less than a month previously.

may, by his prerogative, sue in any of the four courts for his particular interest, although it be contrary to the nature of that court, for he may sue a *quare impedit* in the King's Bench, and the like. Yet so as the **Sir Thomas** said suit be bounded by the rules of law, I will demand **Tempest,** a question: whether the King may bring a *quare impedit* **knight.** in paper at the Council board? The King's present Attorney, I am confident, will answer me [that] he cannot.[80]

The word *salvo* or saving, is in construction of law of a thing in *esse* or *existente,* and no *creative word,* 26*Ass.pla.*66, and cannot in the King's case be construed to overthrow the law, nor many express and positive acts of Parliament.

My Lords, in all humbleness and duty, I will and must acknowledge His Majesty's sacred and lawful prerogative, whereof the King himself is the best expositor: in his answer to the *Petition of Right,* Pulton's *Statutes fol.*1433, he declares that his prerogative is to defend the people's liberty, and the people's liberty strengthens the King's prerogative. The answer was a kingly answer, and (*More majorum*) this is conformable to the Great Charter and to all the statutes before recited. The government of England being the best in the world, was not only royal but also politic; some other princes like Cain, Nimrod, Esau, and the like hunters of men, subverted laws. The Kings of England maintained them, and did never assume the power to change or alter the laws, as appears by Fortescue, that grave and learned Lord Chancellor in King Henry the Sixth's time, *de Laudibus legum Angliae. cap.*9, *fol.*25, and in the same book, *cap.*36, *fol.*84, not to take his people's goods, nor to lay tax, nor tallage upon them, other than by their free consent in Parliament. This appears by the Book cases in 13 Hen.4, *fol.* 14, 15, 16; the great *Case of the Awlnage of London,* and in the *Case of toll-travers and toll-through* (14 Hen.4, 9; 37 Hen.6, 27; 8 Hen.6, 19), all agreeing not* to alter the nature of land as by converting land at common law to *Gavelkind* or *Borough English,* or *e converso*; as to the estate, otherwise as to the person of the King, Plowden, *Commentaries, the Lord Barclye's Case, fol.*246, 247. Yet it is most true that the law of the land gives the King many natural and great prerogatives far beyond all other men, as may appear in the said case, fol.243, but not to do wrong to any subject, *Commentaries,* 246. The person of the King is too sacred to do a wrong in the intention of law; if any wrongs be done, his ministers are authors and not the King, and the King's just prerogatives, by the King's royal assent in

---

*'nor'

[80] Sir Thomas Tempest became Attorney-General to Ireland in October 1640, in succession to Sir Richard Osbaldstone.

quare impedit, 'a writ issued in cases of disputed presentation to a benefice, requiring the defendant to state why the plaintiff should be hindered from making the presentation' (*OED*).

Parliament, were bounded, limited, and qualified by several Acts of Parliament, as if *tenant in capite* did *alien* at common law without licence, this was a forfeiture of his estate, Plowden, *Commentaries, Case of Mines*, fol.332. The statutes of 2 Edw.3, *cap*.14, makes this only finable, and the statute of *Magna Charta, cap*.21, takes away the Kings' prerogative for cutting woods where he pleased: many other cases there are upon this learning.[81]

By this great justice and bounty of the Kings of England, the Kings grew still greater and more permanent. The people became free and wealthy, no King so great as a King of rich and free people. If the Council table may retain cognizance of causes contrary to the law and to so many acts of Parliament, why may they not avoid all acts of Parliament as well? This no man will affirm, nor [do] they intend.

1. Objection My Lords, two objections seem to stand in my way. First, the multitude of precedents countenancing the cognizance of the Council board in the matter aforesaid, some in ancient times, and of late in great clusters and throngs.

2. Objection Secondly, that in Book cases, it appears [that] the judges of law did take advice in their judgements with the King's Council, as 40 Edw.3, fol.34; 39 *Ass., placito primo*, 35 Edw.3,fol.35; 19 Edw.3, Fitzherbert, *Judgement*, 174.[82]

1. Response In answer to the first, as for the multitude of precedents,

---

[81] For *salvo contenemento*, see note 19.

Pulton's *Statutes, f°* 1433, quoting the King in person on 7 June 1628, 'And I assure you, my Maxime is that the People's Liberty strengthens the King's prerogative...'

John Fortescue, *de Laudibus Angliae*, cap. 9, f° 25, and cap.36, f° 84, Mulcaster's translation (London, 1599), 'A King, whose governement is politicke, cannot change the Laws of his realme' and 'Neither doth the kinge there, eyther by himself, or by his servants and officers, levie upon his subjects [...], or alter their Laws [...] without the expresse consente and agreement of his whole royalme in his Parliament'.

Case of the Awlnage of London (Year Book of 13 Hen.IV, f° 14–16), a notable case recorded in the Year Book.

Case of toll-travers and toll-through (Year Books of 14 Hen.IV, f° 9; 37 Hen.VI, f° 27; 8 Hen.VI, f° 19), a notable Year Book case.

Lord Barclye's Case (Plowden, *Commentaries*, f° 246–7, 'for the King cannot do any wrong, nor will his prerogative be any warrant to him to do injury to another' (1Plo.246, *ER*, 75, 355–7).

Case of Mines, 'the King may assign dower to the wife, for this belongs to his prerogative: so that though he has discharged himself of the land, he has not discharged himself of things of prerogative in the land' (1Plo.310–516, *ER*, 75, 503–4).

2 Edw.III, c.14; the precise terms of this statute have not been traced.

Magna Charta, cap. 21, on the King's prerogatives; *Carta de Foresta* deals more explicitly with the matter in hand.

[82] *Year Books*, 40 Edw.III, f° 34; 39Ass., *placito primo*, 35 Edw.III, f° 35.

Fitzherbert, *Judgement*, p.174, *Natura Brevium*, loc. cit., '*Et per le statute de* Articuli sup. chartas cap. 12, *le vic ne doit faire excessive distr. pur det le Roy.*'

hinc illae lachrymae (there is our grief), I find in our book that precedents against law do never bind, there is no downright mischief. But a precedent may be called upon to bear it up: *judicandum est legibus non exemplis*, Coke, 4,fol.33, *Mitton's Case*; Coke, 11, *fol.*75, *Magdalen College's Case*; Coke, 4, fol.94, *Slade's Case, multitudo errantium non parit errori patrocinium.*[83]

2. Response and 2 Object I answer to the second that, in those Year Books of Edward III, it is true that the judges appealed to the King's Council for advice in law, but who gave the judgment? The judges. And what judgement? A legal judgement, and no paper or arbitrary judgment.

If this objection were material, I might answer further that the Council here may be understood [as] the Great Council, viz. the Parliament (*propter excellentiam*), *vide* Coke,6, 19-20, *Gregory's Case*. By the statute of 4 Edw.*cap.*3,14,* and 36 Edw.3, *cap.*10, Rastell, *fol.* 316, Parliaments were then to be held once a year; the book of 39 Edw.3, fol.35, in the case of a formedon, may well warrant this explanation of those books. The Bishops, Abbots, Earls and Barons mentioned in the said books may be well taken to be the Lords' House, which might sit by adjournments in those times of frequent Parliaments. My Lords, I kept you too long upon this question; I will be as short in the next. And so I conclude the answer to this point is no answer, and whether the matters therein comprised be of dangerous consequence [or not], I submit to your Lordships.[84]

---

[83] *judicandum est legibus non exemplis*, judging is from laws and not from examples.

Mitton's Case, 4CoRep.33, 'so the custody of the gaols of counties is inseparable from the sheriff; and therefore if the King grants the custody of such gaol to another, it is void' (*ER*, 76, 966).

Magdalen College's Case, 11CoRep.75, 'the King may sue in what court he pleases, and of this prerogative he is not barred by the general purview of the Act of Magna Charta, cap. 11 *et sic de cæteris*' (*ER*, 77, 1248).

Slades's Case, 4CoRep.94, 'it is to be observed that two or three, or such small number of precedents, do not make a law against the generality of precedents in such case' (*ibid.*, 76, 1076).

*see footnote 84

[84] *Gregory's Case*, 6CoRep.19-20, after judgement was given against exercising of a trade at Ludlow, at the court of Ludlow, error was found, 'because although Ludlow be a Court of Record, yet it is not such a court as is intended by the statute, for several reasons: The Courts intended by the statute, *propter excellentiam*, are the four Courts of Record at Westminster, which are General Courts of Record' (*ibid.*, 77, 283).

4 Edw., cap.3,14, an impossible reference to trace without knowing to which King Edward allusion is being made.

Rastell, f° 316, recte, f° 323, 'A Parliament shall be holden every yeere once, or more often if it need be'.

39Edw.3, f° 35, a *formedon* is 'a writ of right formerly used for claiming entailed property' (*OED*).

4. Question   If the Chief Governor and Council of this kingdom
4. Answer   cannot hear or determine the causes aforesaid, surely
Archivum   the Chief Governor alone cannot do it? All I have
Turris   said to the third I do apply to this question, together
Londiniensis   with one precedent worthy [of] your observation in 25
Edw.I, *Claus.*, *m.*20, where I have an authentic copy, *viz. Claus. vicesimo quinto Edw. primi, m.*20. [*recte* 18].

De comunibus   *Rex dilecto & fideli suo Iohanni Wogan, Iusticiario suo*
placitus per   *Hiberniae salutem; cum intellexerimus quod vos communia*
billas coram   *placita quae totis temporibus retroactis, per brevia originalia de*
Justiciariis   *Cancellaria nostra Hiberniae placitari, deberent, & consueverunt,*
Hiberniae   *per billas & petitiones vacuas iam de novo coram vobis deduci*
nequaquam   *facitis, & etiam terminari, per quod, feodum sigilli nostri quo*
terminandis.   *utimur in Hibernia, & fines pro brevibus dandis ad alia commoda quae nobis inde solent accrescere diversimode subtrahuntur, in nostri & incolarum partium, illarum, damnum non modicum, & gravamen. Nolentes igitur huiusmodo novitates fieri per quas nobis damna gravia, poterunt evenire, vobis mandamus quod si ita est, tunc aliqua placita communia, quae per brevia originalia de Cancellaria nostra praedict. de jure & consuetudine, huiusque visitata habent terminari per petitiones & billas coram vobis deduci, placitari, aut terminari de caetero nullatenus praesumatis, per quod vobis imputari debeat aut possit novum, incommodum, in hac parte.*

Teste Rege aput Shestoniam, xxiii. die Martii.

Convenit cum Recorda,
Willielmus Collet.[85]

[85] *25 Edw.i* (1297), Close Rolls, m.20 *recte*, m.18 (*CCR., 1296–1302*, 22): 'To John Wogan, justiciary of Ireland. Whereas the King understands that the justiciary now causes common pleas, which in all times past have been wont and ought to be pleaded by original writs of the Chancery of Ireland, to be dealt with (*deduci*) and determined before him by bills and blank petitions, whereby the fee of the King's seal in use in Ireland and the fines for giving writs and (*ad*) profits that used to accrue to the King thence are withdrawn in divers ways, to the no small damage of the King and of the inhabitants of those parts: the King, being unwilling that such innovations be practised, orders the justiciary not to presume to cause such common pleas to be dealt with or determined before him by petitions and bills hereafter by means whereof the King's loss of profit (*incommodum*) ought to be imputed to the justiciary. 23 March, Shaftesbury.'
Note that the date and place of the instruction have been adjusted in the translated record; I am grateful to my colleague, Dr Michael Haren of the Dept. of Medieval History, University College, Dublin, for bringing this reference to my attention. John Wogan was Justiciary (an earlier version of Lord Deputy) of Ireland from 1295 to 1308. This record, of which Darcy is at pains to indicate that he has a copy in his possession, was in the circumstances a brilliantly apposite piece of evidence to produce; paper petitions figured in the charges laid against Strafford (see notes 5 & 67), and Darcy happened to have in his possession a copy of a document banning such procedures 350 years previously. He had obviously been reflecting on the matter and gathering relevant material for some time beforehand.

Your Lordships may see that in Edward the First's time the King took notice, first, that the said petitions were void; secondly, that his revenues were thereby impaired; thirdly, that it was against the custom of the land of Ireland; fourthly, that it was to the grievance of the people of Ireland; fifthly, he commanded John Wogan, then Chief Governor, not to presume to deal in the like proceedings thereafter. I marvel not a little wherefore the judges in our time, after so many acts of Parliament since 25 Edw.1, should make any doubt or question to answer this clearly.

5. Question   My Lords, I humbly desire not to be misconstrued in
5 Answer   the debate of this question; my meaning is not to pry into His Majesty's just prerogatives, *Qui enim majestatem scrutatur Principis, corruet splendore eius;* the old saying in English is as good, *he that hews a block above his head, the chips will fall into his eyes.* The question warrants no such scrutiny, I may not officiously search into it. The question is only, whether grants made of monopolies to a subject be good in law? And whether, by pretext of such grants, the King's free people may lose their goods by seizures, or may be fined, imprisoned, pilloried, and papered &c? Those things have been done and acted in many cases where the monopolists were judges and parties, in which case if an act of Parliament did erect such a judicatory, it were void, as against natural justice, Coke,8, 118a, *Doctor Bonham's Case*; I speak to that thing, that odious thing, monopoly, which in law is detestable, Coke,11, 53b, *the Tailors of Ipswich Case*, by which any subject is hindered to exercise his lawful trade, or lawfully to acquire his living, and the condition of a bond being to restrain any man from his trade, the bond is void in law, 2 Hen.5, 5b.[86]

In this case the Judge Hull swore, *par Dieu*, if he who took this bond

---

[86] *Qui enim majestatem scrutatur Principis, corruet splendore eius*, 'For whoever wishes to examine the dignity of the sovereign, may be destroyed by his magnificence'; Darcy offers a more humorous version.

Dr Bonham's Case, 8CoRep.118a, 'censors cannot be judges, ministers, and parties; judges to give sentence or judgement, ministers to make summons [...] And it appears in many of our books that in many cases the common law will control Acts of Parliament, and sometimes adjudge them to be utterly void' (*ER*, 77, 652).

Ipswich Tailors' Case, 11CoRep.53b, 'Resolved 1. At Common law, no man could be prohibited from working at any lawful trade. 2. The Corporation of the Tailors of Ipswich cannot by any ordinance made by them prohibit anyone from exercising his trade...' (*ER*, 77, 1218).

The Case of Cards (Monopolies), 11CoRep.85–7, '*Darcy vs Allen* resolved: A grant by the Crown of the sole making of cards within the realm is void. A dispensation or licence to have the sole importation and merchandizing of cards, without any limitation or stint, is against law, notwithstanding 3Edw.4 which imposes a forfeiture upon their importation' (*ER*, 77, 1260).

were present, he would fine him to the King and commit him to prison, by which case I observe that the consent of the party cannot make it good; that a patent of any such monopolies is a grievance against the Commonwealth, and consequently void in law, the case was of *Cards* which is observable in Coke, 11, 85 - 87 &c., and *Darcy and Allen's Case*. There is a condition, tacit or express, in every grant of the King's, *Ita quod patria magis solito non gravetur vel oneretur*, Fitzherbert, *Natura Brevium, fol. 222, Cod.ad quod damnum*. This learning is so clear as to monopolies thus stated that I will dwell no longer upon them, as I hope they may no longer reside among us. The answer is insufficient, as in the case of a new invention of manufactory or the like. In such cases a patent may be good, they say, for certain years, whereas the years ought to be competent. Ten thousand years are certain, but not competent, and they who offend are to give damage in an ordinary court of justice to the patentee, unto which they add 'or otherwise'. Oh, this arbitrary word! The like arbitrary advice of others, I fear, hath occasioned this question.[87] Where monopolies were clearly void, punishments were inflicted upon the honest man, and the monopolies escaped. They answer nothing to the loss of goods, heavy fines, mutilation of members; the before-recited statutes direct clear answers to these particulars.

My Lords, the statute of *Magna Charta cap. 30, quod omnes Mercatores tam indigenae quam alienigenae* have free passage, *sine omnibus malis tolnetis, & consuetudinibus ex Anglia & in Anglia, nisi antea publice prohibiti fuerunt,* the subsequent statutes declaring many oppressions and grievances occasioned by restraints in trade and commerce, made trade free for victual and merchandises, and in them *Nisi, &c.* is omitted, as the statute of 9 Edw.3, c.1; 25 Edw.3, *cap.*2; 2 Rich.2, *cap.*1; 11 Rich.2, *cap.*7; 16 Rich.2, *cap.*1. These statutes give double damage to the party and the offender to be imprisoned.

The statute of 21 Jacob, c.3, in England against monopolies, in the exception of new inventions limits the time to a reasonable number of years, viz. fourteen years or under; whether the heavy punishments aforesaid can be in this case especially, the private interest of a subject being therein only or mainly concerned, *Magna Charta, cap.* 29, gives me a clear answer and satisfactory: *Nullus liber homo capiatur, imprisonetur, disseisietur vel aliquo modo destruatur, &c nisi per judicium parium & legem*

---

[87] *Ita quod patria magis solito non gravetur vel oneretur*, in the *Case of Monopolies* above, Coke quotes Fitzherbert and adds '*Illa quod patria per donationem illam magis solito non oneretur seu gravetur (therefore every grant made in grievance or prejudice of the subject is void)*'; Fitzherbert, *Natura brevium*, pp.221ᵛ–226ᵛ, c. 140, *Briefe de Ad Quod dampnum*, offers corroboration in less explicit form. A printing error at this point was one of the original *Faults escaped* of the 1643 edition.

terrae, if this be law or a lawful statute, as no doubt it is, the question is soon answered.[88]

My Lords, by this time you know how the innocent was actually punished in these cases. Now it is time, and not improper, to show how the nocent ought to be punished, who took unlawful monopolies and seized the subjects' goods by violence, imprisoned, fined, mutilated, and destroyed the King's people, and caused all the evils that depended thereupon. For that, my Lords, it is not within my charge, yet I hope it shall not remain unrepresented by the House of Commons, nor unremembered by your Lordships in due time.

6. Question   To this the judges answered nothing, but with a
6. Answer   reference to their answer to the third, whereas in truth this comprehends two matters besides, of great weight and consideration. First, whereas the third question concerneth the decision at Council board of matters of interest only, this question is of matters of punishment in an extrajudicial way; secondly, this question demands knowledge of the punishment due to such as vote for such extrajudicial punishments. To these main matters there is no answer at all.

My Lords, the statutes and authorities before-mentioned upon the third and fourth questions against the determination at Council board, or before the Chief Governor in matters of interest, do clear this business as to the punishments depending upon those interests, although not *é converso*. And as for such as voted and acted therein, if they be sworn judges of the law, the before-recited oath of 18 Edw.3 declares enough.

His Majesty at his coronation is bound by oath to execute justice to his people according to the law. This great trust the King commits to his judges, who take a great oath to discharge this trust; if they fail

---

[88] *Magna Charta*, cap.30, '*quod omnes Mercatores tam indigenae quam alienigenae*', all merchants, whether native or foreign'; '*sine omnibus malis tolnetis, & consuetudinibus ex Anglia et in Anglia, nisi antea publice prohibiti fuerent*', without prejudice, and within and without the custom of England, unless they were previously prohibited.
9 Edw.III, c.1, recte, statute 1 c.1 (1335), *SR*, 1, 269–71); *25 Edw.III, cap.2* (1351), *statutum p. hiis qui nati sunt in partibus transmarinis* [for those born in foreign parts], *ibid.*, 1, 310. The following statute (25 Edw.III,2.c.7) has further recommendations relative to the point, *ibid.*,313. *2 Rich.II, c.1* (1378), reiteration of foregoing statutes, *ibid.*, 2,6. *16 Rich.II, c.1* (1392–3), reiteration of above and preceding statutes. Darcy is undoubtedly well briefed on the matter of monopolies and free movement in trade; this is probably due to the time spent in England in 1635–6 during which he prepared a paper for the King on customs revenue (see *Introduction*, p.12).
21 Jacob.I, c.3 (1623–4): *An Act concerning Monopolies and dispensations with Penall Lawes and the forfeyture thereof* (*SR*, 4, part 1, 1212–4).
Magna Charta, cap.29, *Nullus liber homo*... No free man may be seized, imprisoned, expropriated, nor by any other means reduced, unless by the justice of his peers and the law of the land.

therein, Sir William Thorp in Edward the III's time, for breaking this oath in poor things, was indicted thus: *Quia praedictus Willielmus Thorp habuit Sacramentum Domini Regis erga populum suum, ad custodiendum, illud fregit malitiose, false & rebelliter, quantum in ipso fuit,* this extends to a judge only who took that oath, & *habuit leges terrae ad custodiendum.*

The trust between the King and his people is threefold; first, as between sovereign and subject; secondly, as between a father and his children, *unde Pater Patriae*; thirdly, as between husband and wife, this trust is comprehensive of the whole body politic. And for any magistrate or private person to advise or contrive the breach of this trust in any part, is of all things in this world the most dangerous (*vae homini illi*).

7. Question First, I do conceive that an Act of State or proclamation
7. Answer cannot alter the common law, nor restrain the old, nor introduce a new law, and that the same hath no power or force to bind the goods, lands, possessions, or inheritance of the subject, but that the infringing thereof is only a contempt, which may be punished in the person of the delinquent where the proclamation is consonant and agreeable to the laws and statutes of the kingdom, or for the public good, and not against law, and not otherwise punishable.

I do conceive that a proclamation is a branch of the King's pre-rogative, and that the same is useful and necessary in some cases where it is not against the law, wherein the public weal is interested or concerned, but that any clause therein containing forfeiture of the goods, lands, or inheritance of the subjects, is merely void. Otherwise this inconvenience will ensue, that proclamations or Acts of State may be made in all cases, and in all matters, to bind the liberty, goods, and lands of the subjects. And then the courts of justice that have flourished for so many ages may be shut up, for want of use of the law, or execution thereof; and there is no case where an offence is committed against law, but the law will find out a way to punish the delinquent.[89]

Natura Br., The King by his proclamation, may inhibit his subject
fol.85, in le that he shall not go beyond sea out of this realm
Briefe, de without his licence; and this without any writ or other
securitate commandment to his subject, for perchance the King
inveniend., may not find his subject, or know where he is. And if
quod non se the subject will go out of the King's realms contrary
divertat ad to this proclamation, this is a contempt, and he shall

---

[89] A number of the preceding and following examples are drawn from Egerton's *The Speech of the Lord Chancellor of England, in the Exchequer Chamber, touching the* Post-Nati (*cf. note 9*); mention is made in Egerton's text, f° 14–15, of the Justice William Thorp who failed to respect his oath (13 Edw.III); justice of *oyer & terminer* in Somerset, he is indicted in Darcy's quotation, for 'maliciously, falsely and rebelliously breaking the oath of the Lord King to his people', but there is no information as to what exactly he did or what his sentence was.

partes exteras, 'pars extera' cannot be intended the King's dominions.

be fined to the King for the same. [But] as saith Fitzherbert, such a proclamation cannot prohibit the King's subjects to repair into England, for England is our mother, and though the sea divide us, that sea is the King's, and therefore it is not *pars extera* in this sense.[90]

Fol.12 and 13.

It seems by the Lord Chancellor Egerton's argument upon the Case of *Post-Nati,* that a proclamation cannot bind the goods, lands, or inheritance of the subjects.[91]

Natura Br. fol.32, 19 Hen.3 Fitzherb., *darrein presentment*

A provision was made in *haec verba, Provisum est coram Domino Rege, Archiepiscopis, Comitibus, & Baronibus quod nulla assis. ultimae praesentationis de caetero capiatur de Ecclesiasticis praebendatis, nec Fitzherb., praebendis,* but I do not find any forfeiture or penalty upon the liberty, goods, or lands of him that would bring an assize of *darrein* presentment* for a prebendary.[92]

4Hen.3, Fitzherbert, *Dower,* fol.179

I do find that a provision was made in *haec verba Provisum est à Consilio Regis quod nullus de potestate Regis Franciae respondeat in Anglia antequam Anglici de jure suo in terra Regis Franciae, &c.* Yet by that provision no forfeiture upon the lands or goods of him who sued a Frenchman in England at that time.[93]

35Hen.6, c. 26 It is true that a custom may be contrary to law, and yet allowable, because that it may have a lawful commencement, and continual usage hath given it the force of a law, *Consuetudo ex certa rationabili causa usitata privat communem legem,* but no proclamation or Act of State may alter law.[94]

*'Darien'

[90] *Fitzherbert, Natura Brevium, p.85,* the marginal note is the title of chapter 45 in the *Natura Brevium,* under the general heading *'Suertie de non aler ouster le mere.'*

[91] *Case of the* Post-Nati, f° 12-13, taken from the speech mentioned above in note 9, where Egerton quotes *'a learned gentleman of the lower house'* who said that *'Proclamations can neither make nor declare Lawes'.* Egerton's view was slightly different, and it does not fully support the claim made here by Darcy.

[92] Fitzherbert, *Natura Brevium,* 32, see note 60; Darcy has abbreviated Fitzherbert's text in his quotation.

Darrein presentment, a reference also taken from Egerton; the term means a case of last resort in the law of tenure. Plucknett quotes the example of the assize being asked to say 'whether the plaintiff was the last patron in time of peace who presented a parson to the church in dispute' (*A Concise History of the Common Law,* p.360).

[93] Fitzherbert, *dower,* p.179, also taken from Egerton; the quotation, which does not come from Fitzherbert at the passage indicated, shows that no subject of the French King is subject to English law in precedence to his own oath in France.

[94] *35 Hen.VI, cap.26* (1456-7), the quotation from the statute states that 'from the use of custom and certain reasonable causes, the common law is drawn'. An illustrative case is to be found under the same statute in the *Statutes of Henry VI,* p.475; 'It is granted and ordained by authority of said parliament, that the said act or ordinance made against

For example's sake, at common law a proclamation cannot make lands devisable which are not devisable by the law, nor alter the course of descent.

37Hen.6, c.27; The King by his letters-patent cannot do the same, **49Edw.3, c.4** nor grant lands to be ancient demesne at this day, nor make lands to be descendible according to the course of *Gavelkind* or *Borough English*, unless that the custom of the place doth warrant the same, nor Gavelkind land to be descendible according to the course of law. A *fortiori*, an Act of State, or proclamation, which I hold to be of less force than the King's patent under the Great Seal, cannot do it.

And in the case of *Irish Gavelkind*, it is not the proclamation, or Act of State, that did abolish or alter it, but the very custom was held to be unreasonable and repugnant to law.

11. Coke, 86 If an Act of State be made that none within the kingdom shall make cards but John-at-Stile, this act is void, for the King himself cannot grant a patent under his Great Seal to any one man for the sole making of cards. So it is of all proclamations, or Acts of State, that are to the prejudice of traffic, trade, or merchant affairs, or for raising of Monopolies, or against the freedom and liberty of the subjects, or the public good, as I said before.[95]

Also, if proclamations, or Acts of State, may alter the law, or bind the liberty, goods, or lands of the subjects, then will Acts of Parliaments be to no purpose, which do represent the whole body of the kingdom, and are commonly for creating of good and wholesome laws.

Therefore I conceive that all proclamations made against law are absolutely void, and that the infringers thereof ought not to lose, or forfeit their liberty, goods, or lands.

And for the punishment of such judges that vote herein, I refer to the sixth; they deny to answer to this question.[96]

8. Question This answer is general, and dangerous withal it is **8. Answer** general, *viz.* they know no ordinary rule of law for it, they ought to declare the law against it. The right use of it here they commend, and yet they do not describe that right use. Therefore they commend two things: the one the life of a subject to be left to martial law in time of peace, the other they leave it likewise discretionary when

the said Richard [Tame, gentleman] be repealed, revoked, annulled, made of no effect and held for nothing in law, and cancelled'.

[95] *37 Hen.VI, c.27; 49 Edw.III, c.4*, passages from the Year Books which support Darcy's interpretation of custom, *11CoRep.86*, another reference to the *Case of Monopolies*, see note 86.

[96] The sixth question asked what sanctions would be incurred by the Lord Lieutenant, Lord Deputy, or other Chief Governor, if they were found to have enforced decisions not sanctioned by law.

they describe not the right use. Their last resort is to the King's prerogative.

I have said before that lawyers write [that] the King can do no wrong, and sure I am our King means no wrong. The Kings of England did never make use of their prerogative to the destruction of the subject, nor to take away his life nor liberties but by lawful means. I conceive this advice should become the judges; other advice they find not in their law books. The statute of *Magna Charta, cap*.29, and 5 Edw.3, *cap*.9, the *Petition of Right*, the third of King Charles in full Parliament declared, [all] tell them, nay do convince them, that no man in time of peace can be executed by martial law.[97]

9. Question   My Lords, I could wish the judges had timely stood
9. Answer   in the right opposition to the drawing of the causes proper for the King's courts to an *aliud examen*, [and to] the improper and unlawful examen thereof on paper petitions whereby the King's justice and courts were most defrauded, whereas an arbitrament being a principal means to compose differences arising between neighbours, and to settle amity between them, without expense, of time or money, was a course approved by law. All our books are full of this.

[If] it is by consent of parties by arbitrators indifferently chosen, bonds for performance thereof are not void in law, but* [in] *judgements* given upon arbitraments and such bonds in our books, without question or contradiction to the lawfulness of an arbitrament or bond in proper cases, the principal good wrought by them was the hindering of suits and debates at law; therefore that exception falls of itself. Then I am to consider how far an oath in this particular is punishable; I will not speak of an oath exacted or tendered, that is not the question. The question is of a voluntary oath which the arbitrator cannot hinder. I speak not to the commendation of any such oath (nor do I approve of any oath other than that which is taken before a magistrate, who derives his authority from the King, the fountain of justice), but only how far this oath is punishable by the late statute, 10 *Car., fol.*109: a profane oath is punished by the payment of twelve pence and no more, *vide* **Statute of Marlborough** *cap.* 23, 52 Hen. 3, *viz. Nullus de caetero possit distringere libere tenentes suos, &c. nec jurare faciat libere tenentes suos contra voluntatem suam, quia nullus facere potest sine praecepto Domini Regis*, which

---

*'and'

[97] This is a roll-call of the Statutes of Liberty, all of which have been already quoted by Darcy: 'that the King can do no wrong', comes from Plowden, *Lord Berkeley's Case*, note 81; *Magna Carta*, c.29, '*Nullus liber homo capiatur* ... see note 88; *5 Edw.III, c.9*, is a confirmation of *Magna Carta*, see note 75; the *Petition of Right*, which is an assertion of parliamentary prerogative master-minded by Coke, has already been invoked several times by Darcy, sometimes disingenuously as proof of the King's great bounty.

statute teacheth us that [if] an exacted or compulsive oath is by the King's authority [only], a voluntary oath is not reprehended (19 Edw.4, 1a); [although] it was not reprehended in the case of an arbitrament, this voluntary oath is punishable in the Star Chamber, as the judges would affirm, which I conceive to be against the law. First, for that we cannot learn any precedent in England for it; it was but lately introduced here, therefore the House of Commons is unsatisfied with the answer to this question. In *Boyton and Leonard's Case* in the Star Chamber in Ireland, Boyton was dismissed in a case to this purpose about the year 1630 or 1631.[98]

10. Question   It hath been the late introduced course of the Castle
10. Answer   Chamber and Council table not to admit the party censured to the reducement of his fine before he acknowledged the justness of the sentence pronounced against him, and that for divers reasons. First, the course of a court being as ancient as the court, and standing with law, is *Curiae lex*, as appeareth by our books, 2Coke,16b, *Lane's Case*, 17 *Long*, 5 *Edw.* 4, 1; but if it be a course introduced *de novo* in man's memory, or a course that is against law, it cannot be said to be *lex Curiae*, for *consuetudo licet sit magnae authoritatis numquam tamen praejudicat manifestae veritati.*[99]

Let us therefore examine the course alledged here, in both those points, and if it be found to fail in either of them, it is to be rejected.

As to the first, I cannot find or read any precedent of it until of late, and the usage of it for a few years cannot make it to be *cursus Curiae*, which ought to be a custom used time beyond the memory of man.

As to the second, it is confessed by the judges that they know no law to warrant this course. Let us see then, whether it be against law or standeth with the law; and I conceive it is against law for divers reasons.

First, by the common law, if a judgement be given against a man after a verdict of twelve men, which is the chief and clear proof which the law looketh upon, or upon a demurrer after solemn argument, he shall in the one case have an attaint against the jury, and in the other a writ of error to reverse the judgment; but in this case by the confession of the justness

---

[98] *aliud examen*, other forms of scrutiny. *Statute of Marlborough*, 52 Hen.III, c.23, *recte*, 22 (1267), translated as 'None from henceforth may distrain his freeholders to answer for their freeholds [...] nor shall cause his freeholders to swear against their wills; for no Man may do that without the King's commandment' (*SR*, 1, 24).
Boyton and Leonard's Case; Darcy's own information is imprecise and it has not been possible to find further reference to this case.

[99] *Lane's Case*, 2CoRep.16b, 'for the course of every court is as a law, of which the common law takes notice, without alleging it in pleading' (*ER*, 76, 423).
5 *Edw.IV*, 1, 17*Long*, The text from the Year Book states that 'custom [precedent] is allowed if it is of great authority, but never to the detriment of the establishment of truth'.

of the sentence, all the means to reverse the sentence is taken away, and therefore contrary to law and reason.

[Secondly], whereas, by the common law, fines ought to be moderate, *secundum quantitatem delicti in reformationem & non in destructionem*, of late times the fines have been so high in destruction of the party in the Castle Chamber as his whole family and himself (if he did pay the fine) should be driven to beg; and without performance of the sentence he could not be admitted to reverse the sentence. In respect of all which, howbeit in his conscience he is not guilty, yet to gain his liberty and save part of his estate, he is necessitated to acknowledge the justness of the sentence, so that the confession is extorted from him, and consequently is against law.

Third reason: if the fine were *secundum quantitatem delicti*, as it ought to be, without danger of destruction, the reducement of the fine had not been so necessary, and therefore no just ground for this confession.

Lastly, the confession of the party after sentence doth rather blemish the sentence than any way clear it, for the confession coming after the sentence, which ought to be just in itself, can add nothing to it but draw suspicion upon it. And in that respect, a confession is strained; the rack used by the course of the civil law in criminal causes, to clear the conscience of the judge to proceed to sentence, is intolerable in our common law.

And therefore this course, being an innovation against law and without any reasonable ground, the said judges ought in their said answer to declare so much, to the end a course might be taken for abolishing the same.

11. Question   This answer I will not now draw into question; I could
11. Answer   wish the rest were answered no worse.

12. Question   What power have the Barons of the Court of the
12. Answer   Exchequer to raise the respite of homage arbitrarily, &c?

Unto this they answer that, until the King's tenant by knight's service *in capite* hath done his homage, the ancient course of the Exchequer hath been, and still is, to issue process to distrain the tenants, *ad faciendum homagium* or *ad faciendum finem pro homagio suo respectuando*, upon which process the sheriff returns issues; and if the tenant do not appear and compound with the King to give a fine for respite of homage, then the issues are forfeited to the King. But if the King's tenant will appear, the Court of the Exchequer doth agree with him to respite his homage for a small fine.

Vide **5 Hen.7,9,**   They say further that it resteth in the discretion of the
a prescription   court, by the rule of the common law, to lay down a

to impound fine for respite of homage, according to the yearly
Cattle until value of the said lands; which I conceive to be to very
amends be unreasonable and inconvenient, that it should lie in
done according the power of any to assess a fine for respite of homage
to his will not such as to him shall be thought meet in discretion.
good For if so, he may raise the fine to such a sum as may
exceed the very value of the lands. Neither hath the same been the
ancient course, for it appears by several ancient records, and by an
order of the Court of Exchequer made *termino pascae* 1607, that there
should be paid for respiting of homage for every township xx pence*
Irish, and for every manor xxxx pence* Irish, and that such as hold
several houses, acres, or parcels of land, which are not manors nor
townships, shall pay for every hundred and twenty acres of land,
meadow, and pasture, or of any of them, xx pence* Irish, and no more;
This appears and according to that rate and proportion if a greater
by several or lesser number of acres, and for every house without
records in ground iiii pence* Irish. And of cottages, or farm-
Hen.6 & Hen.7 houses which be upon the lands, no fine to be paid
time in the for them solely alone. And I conceive where a man
Second holdeth several parcels of land of the King by several
Remembrancer's homages, that in such case he is to pay but for one
Office in respite of homage only and no more, for that man is
Ireland, to do homage but once, and consequently to pay for
24Hen.8; B. one respite of homage only.
Fealty, & The late course in the Exchequer here hath been
homage 8. contrary; whereas in their answer they go in the
Exchequer according to the statute of *primo Jacobi, cap.26,* in England,
under their favour, they go clear contrary. For that statute was made
in confirmation and pursuance of former orders in the Exchequer,
whereas the barons here go directly contrary to the ancient course and
order of the Exchequer in this kingdom; more of this is my reason or
ground for this question. So I conclude their answer to this is short.[100]

13. Question. My Lords, the question contains two points. First,
13. Answer. whether the subject of this kingdom is censurable for
to repair into England to appeal to His Majesty for redress of injuries,

---

* 'd'

[100] *in capite,* see the definition in note 21.
The second remembrancer, see note 35; a debt-collecting agent of the Exchequer.
24 Hen.VIII; B. Fealty and homage, 8, untraced.
I Jacob., cap.26 (1603–04), *'An Acte for the continuance and due observation of certaine orders for the Exchequer, first set downe and established by vertue of a Privie Seale from the late Queene Elizabeth'* (*SR,* 4, part 2, 1052).

or for his lawful occasions; secondly, why, what condition of persons, and by what law?

The first part of the judges their answer is positive and full, viz. they know no law or statute for such censure (nor I neither and could wish they had stayed there). In the second part of their answer, they come with an *if*, *viz.* unless they be prohibited by His Majesty's writ, proclamation, or command, and make mention of the statute of 5 Rich.2, *cap.*2, in England, and 25 Hen. 6, *cap.*2, in Ireland. I will only speak to the second part of this answer.

My Lords, the House of Commons in the discussion of this point took two things into consideration. First, what the common law was in such cases. Secondly, what alteration was made of the common law by the statute of 5Rich 2, *cap.*2. in England, and 25 Hen.6, *cap.*2, in Ireland, as to the subjects of Ireland. As for the first, the Register hath a writ framed in the point, *viz.* the writ *De securitate invenienda quod se non divertat ad partes exteras sine licentia Domini Regis*, Fitzherbert, *Natura brevium, fol.*85. The words of this writ clear the common law in the point. It begins with a *datum est nobis intelligi, &c.*; the King being informed that such person or persons in particular do intend to go, whether *ad partes exteras*, *viz.* foreign countries, to what purpose, to prosecute matters to the prejudice of the King and his Crown, the King in such a case by his writ, warrant, or command under the Great Seal, Privy Seal, Privy Signet or by proclamation, may command any subject not to depart the kingdom without the King's licence. This writ is worthy to be observed for the causes aforesaid therein expressed; the writ extendeth only to particular person or persons, and not to all the subjects of the kingdom. No man can affirm that England is *pars extera* as to us, Ireland is annexed to the Crown of England and governed by the laws of England; our question set forthe the cause, *viz.* to appeal to the King for justice, or to go to England for other lawful causes, whereas the said writ intends practises with foreign princes to the prejudice of the King and his Crown.[101]

At the common law, if a subject in contempt of this command went *ad partes exteras*, his lands, and goods ought to be seized, 2 & 3 Philip & Mary, *Dyer*, 128b, and yet if the subject went to the parts beyond the seas before any such special inhibition, this was not punishable before the statute of

---

[101] 5 *Rich.II*, *cap.*2, *recte*, statute 1, cap.2 (1381–2), 'None shall depart the realm without the King's licence' (*SR*, 1, 18); this underpins the point made in Fitzherbert's *Natura Brevium*, p.85 (already quoted at note 90).

25 *Hen.VI*, *cap.*2 *(Ireland)*, 1447, 'that the land of Ireland have and enjoy all its liberties and franchises, good usages and customs, as have been reasonably used heretofore' (*Statutes of Henry VI*, 55). There is no immediately evident connection between this and the preceding statute, but it seems to be Darcy's purpose to develop the evidence for the islands of Britain and Ireland as an integrated whole within which freedom of movement, as well as equality before the law, are legitimate expectations.

5 Rich.2, *cap*.2, as appears, 12 & 13 Eliz.*Dyer*, 296a. So that before the inhibition the law was indifferent, now the question is at common law, whether the subject of Ireland having no office, can be hindered to appeal or go to the King for justice. The King is the fountain of justice, and as his power is great to command, so the sceptre of his justice is as great, nay the sceptre hath the priority, if any be, for at his coronation, his sceptre is on his right side, and his sword on his left side; to his justice he is sworn, therefore, if any writ, commandment or proclamation be obtained from him, or published contrary to his justice, it is not the act of the King, but the act of him that misinformed him. Then will I add the other words of the question, *viz.* or other his lawful occasions, as I said before in the case of a writ of error in the King's Bench of England, or in the Parliament of England, which are remedies given by the law, therefore the common law doth not hinder any man to prosecute those remedies which are given to every subject by the same. A *scire facias* may be brought by the King in England to repeal a patent under the Great Seal of Ireland of lands in Ireland, 20 Hen.6, *fol.a*.

An exchange of lands in England for lands in Ireland is a good exchange in law, 8ass., *placit.* 27, 10 Edw.3, *fol*.42; *tempor*.Edw I, Fitzherbert voucher 239*. What law therefore can prohibit any subject for to attend this *scire facias* in England, or to make use of his freehold got by exchange?[102]

The law being thus, then it was considered what alteration was wrought by one branch of the statute of 5 Rich.2, *cap*.2, by which the passage is stopped out of the kingdom (Lords, notable Merchants, and the King's soldiers excepted). I conceive this statute doth not include Ireland; I never heard any Irishman questioned upon this statute for going into England, nor any Englishman for coming into Ireland, until the late proclamation by the statute 34 Edw.3, *c*.18; in England all persons which have their heritage or possessions in Ireland may come with their beasts, corn, &c., to and fro, paying the King's dues. The

---

* '*Fitzvoucher*'

[102] *2 & 3 Philip & Mary, Dyer, 128b*; in *Mansell and Herbert's Case*, it was confirmed that 'if a subject refuse to return into the kingdom upon the King's mandate, his lands and goods shall be seized for the King's use' (*ER*, 73, 280).

5 Rich.II, cap.2; as above, note 101.

12 & 13 Eliz.,Dyer, 296a; in *Mannocke's Case*, it was affirmed that 'departing the realm for the sake of living out of due obedience to the laws, is no offence, unless there has been express restraint by writ or proclamation' (*ER*, 73, 664).

scire facias, a *scire facias* is 'a judicial writ served by a sheriff requiring the party concerned to show cause why a patent such as a charter should not be revoked' (*OED*).

20 Hen.VI, f°ᵃ, this reference is incomplete, thus not traceable.

Year Book, 8ass., placit 27, 10 Edw.III, f°42.Fitzherbert, *voucher*, p. 239, *Natura Brevium*, cap. 149, '*Supersedeas*', *voucher in Court baron*'; 'voucher' is 'the summoning of a person to court to warrant the title to property' (*OED*).

statute of 5 Rich.2 did never intend by implication to avoid the said express statute of Edw.3 between the King's two kingdoms, being governed by one law, and in effect the same people.[103] The words of the statute of 5 Rich.2 are observable, the principal scope of it is against the exportation of bullion; in the later part there is a clause for licences to be had in particular ports, by which I conceive that the customers of those ports may grant a let pass in such cases.

It is therefore to be considered whether that branch of the said statute of 5 Rich.2 was received in Ireland. I think it is clear it was not, for by the statute 10 Hen.7, *cap.* 22, in Ireland, all the general statutes of England were received in Ireland with this qualification, *viz.* such as were for the common and public weal, &c. And surely it cannot be for the weal of this kingdom that the subjects here be stayed from obtaining of justice, or following other lawful causes in England?

The statute of 25 Hen.6, *cap.*2, in Ireland, excuseth *absentees* by the King's command, and imposeth no other penalty; so that upon the whole matter, this question is not answered.

14 Question For so much as they do answer of this question, the
14 Answer answer is good, for there is no doubt to be made but deaneries are some donative, some elective, and some may be presentative, according to the respective foundations.

I will only speak of a Dean de facto; if a Dean be made a Bishop and hath a dispensation *Decanatus dignitatem in commenda* in the *retinere*, the confirmation of such a Dean is good in law. This was the case of *Evans and Acough* in the King's Bench in England, *ter.*3 Car., where Doctor Thornborow, Dean of York, was made Bishop of Limerick with a dispensation to hold in the *retinere* after his patent, and before consecration it was adjudged his confirmation was good; and yet if a

Vide 2 & Dean be made a Bishop in any part of the world, this
3Phil. & Mary, is a cession, Coke 5, 102a, *Windsor's Case*, Davies,
123b. Reports,42,43 &c. The Dean of Ferns his case, & 18 Elizab., *Dyer*, 346, the confirmation of a mere *Laicus* being Dean is good, though he be after deprived, 10 Eliz., *Dyer*, 273. 12 & 13 Elizab., *Dyer*, 293, although the Dean be after deprived by sentence declaratory, yet his precedent confirmations are good.

So I conceive that a Dean, who hath *stallum in Choro & vocem in Capitulo* during all the time of his life, and never questioned, and usually confirmed all leases without interruption, is good. And to question all

---

[103] *5 Rich.II, cap.2*, see note 101 above. *34 Edw.III, c.18* (1360–1), 'English landowners in Ireland may import and export from and to England' (*SR*, 1, 368). Once more, the idea of 'one law, one people' is implicit behind the details of free movement and trade, as in notes 88 & 101.

such acts, 40, 50, [or] 100 years after, is without precedent, especially in Ireland, until of late years. And in this kingdom few or no foundations of bishoprics or deaneries can be found upon any record, therefore I conceive the judges ought to answer this part of the question.[104]

15 Question   My Lords, I know you cannot forget the grounds I
15 Answer   laid before for this question, nor the time nor the occasion of the issuing of *quo warrantoes*, nor what was done thereupon in the Court of Exchequer.

Now remaineth to consider of the answer to this positive question, the answer is too general, *viz.* the Parliament is concerned therein, and so are two other courts of justice, and likewise the King's prerogative is interested therein, wherefore they cannot answer till the matter come in debate and be argued before them.[105]

The consideration of the Court of Parliament will much conduce to the clearing of this question, Coke, preface to the *Fourth Report*, the exposition of laws ordinarily belongeth to the judges, but (*in maximis difficillimisque causis ad supremum Parliament' judicium*) Coke, preface to the *Ninth Report*, describes that Supreme Court in this manner, (*si vetustatem spectes est antiquisssima, si dignitatem, est honoratissima, si jurisdictionem, est capacissima*). Of this enough, the learning is too manifest that it is the Supreme Court, nay the primitive of all other courts; to that court belongs the making, altering or regulating of laws, and the correction of all courts and ministers. Look upon the members of it,
Coke 4   first the King is the head, who is never so great nor
***Inst.,* 109.** so strong as in Parliament, where he sits ensconced

---

[104] *Commenda* in the *retinere* refers to the specific recommendation (from the King) that a bishop may, after his nomination, hold a benefice of a Deanery previously granted.
Windsor's Case, 5CoRep.102a; in the case of a disputed benefice 'if two have title to present by turns, and one presents a parson, who is admitted, instituted, & etc., and afterwards is deprived, he shall not present again, but it shall serve his turn, for it was but voidable' (*ER*, 77, 213).
Dean of Ferns, I have been unable to trace further details of this case.
18 Eliz.,Dyer,346, *Bacon vs the Bishop of Carlisle and Another*, 'if the incumbent be deprived for not subscribing the articles, the ordinary must give personal notice to the patron' (*ER*, 73, 778).
10 Eliz.,Dyer,273, in *Walrond vs Pollard*, 'the deanery of Wells is a spiritual and not a temporal promotion, nor is it donative, therefore leases made by the dean need not the confirmation of the King, nor even of the Bishop...' (*ER*, 73, 610). See also note 37.
12 & 13 Eliz.,Dyer,293, in *Bedinfield vs the Archbishop of Canterbury*, 'tho' the presenter to the church be a mere layman, still if admitted, instituted and inducted, there must be a sentence of nullity before any other presentation, and the ordinary must give notice to the patron of such sentence before any lapse can incur' (*ER*, 73, 657); the recommendations of one who is incumbent *de facto* rather than *de jure* are therefore to stand.
[105] The court of Parliament being the principal one concerned here, the others being King's Bench and Exchequer. See also notes 17, 52, 78.

with the hearts of his people; the second are all the Lords spiritual and temporal; the third the Knights, Citizens and Burgesses. These three do represent the whole Commonwealth. Look upon the causes for which they are called (*Circa ardua & urgentia negotia Regni*), look upon the privileges of it: if any member or members servant thereof be questions, or any thing ordered against him in any other court sitting [besides] **Stat. Hib.** the Parliament, or within forty days before or after, **3Edw.4, cap. 1.** all the proceedings are void by the laws and statutes of this realm. The not clearing of this question is against the King's prerogative, which is never in greater splendour or majesty than in Parliament, and against the whole Commonwealth therein concerned as aforesaid. The King hath four Councils, the first is *commune concilium*, which is this Council; secondly *magnum concilium*, which is the Council of his Lords; thirdly the Privy Council for matters of State*; fourthly, the judges of his law, Coke, *Institutes*, 110a.[106]

Then by what law or use can the inferior of these four Councils question the first supreme and mother Council? I know not. The state of the question considered, which is of *Boroughs*, which* anciently and recently sent to the Parliament, by the same law, that one member may be questioned, forty-eight members may be questioned (as was done in our case in one day); six such days may take away the whole House of Commons, and consequently Parliaments, especially as this case was, for upon the return of the first summons four-and-twenty Corporations were seized. The learning therefore is new, that it should rest in the discretion of the sheriffs, who might make unfaithful returns, and of three Barons in the Exchequer, who have no infallibility, to overthrow Parliaments, the best constitutions in the world. Search hath been made in the two books of *Entries*, in old *Natura brevium*, and in all the Year Books that are printed; there is not one precedent that in any time ever so bade. Such a *quo warranto* was brought in, Coke *Entries*

---

* 'estate'

* 'who'

[106] *Coke, preface to the Fourth Report* (1604), '*maximis difficilimisque causis ad supremum Parliament' judicium*', 'The expounding of Lawes doth ordinarily belong to the reverende judges, and Sages of the Realme: And in case of greatest difficultie and importance, to the high Court of Parliament', no page number.

CoLitt., f°109, The First Part of the Laws of England, or a Commentary upon Littleton (1628), Section 164, '*Of tenure in Burgage*', 'Parliament is the highest and most honourable and absolute Court of Justice of England'.

Statutum Hiberniae , 20 Hen.III, see note 58; *3 Edw. IV, cap. 1* (1463), *recte*, cap. XLVII: 'the privilege of every Parliament and Great Council within the land of Ireland is that no officer of said Parliament should be impleaded, vexed or troubled' within forty days of sitting, *Statute Rolls of the Parliament of Ireland. First to the twelfth year of the Reign of King Edward the Fourth* , ed. H.F. Berry (Dublin, 1914), 41–265.

CoLitt., f° 110a.

527a, against *Christopher Helden*, and others, to show cause why they claimed such a *Borough, & etc*, which is nothing to our purpose. The *quo warrantoes* in the question, and those which were in the Exchequer, did admit them *Boroughs* and yet required them to show cause why they sent burgesses to the Parliament. This is *oppositum in objecto*, to admit them burgesses, and to question their power to send burgesses, which were formerly, both anciently and recently, so admitted in Parliament; *Master Littleton*, the first book we read, clears this question, *sectione* 164. There are ancient towns called boroughs, the most ancient towns of England; all cities were boroughs in the beginning, and from them come burgesses to the Parliament, so that in effect if an ancient borough, *ergo*, they sent burgesses to the Parliament; all these ancient towns in England did remain of record in the Exchequer, 40 *ass., plac.* 27. In Ireland they do remain of record in the Parliament Roll, the trial of them is by the record itself, and not otherwise. If a Town send burgesses once or twice, it is title enough to send ever after, 11 Hen.4, 2. So, if a peer called once by writ, and once fitting as a peer, Coke *Institutions, fol.*9b, he is a baron ever after.[107]

In the four ordinary courts they have privilege for the meanest of their members, or servants, why not the Parliament? It was the custom of the ancient grave judges to consult with Parliaments in causes of difficulty and weight; a Parliament was then to be at hand, they did not stay to advise with them in a point which concerned the Parliament so nearly, and which was of the greatest weight of any cause that ever was agitated in the kingdom. In our books and all the entries, it is true and clear that *quo warrantoes* are brought, and ought to be brought, against such as claim privileges, franchises, royalties, or the like flowers of the Crown; but to question burgesses in this nature is to question the King's prerogative in an high degree. Privileges take from the King, Parliaments add and give unto him greatness and profit; in Parliaments he sits *essentially*, in other courts not altogether so, but by representation. What greater disservice could be done the King than to overthrow

---

[107] In appreciation of the arguments reviewed here, it should be remembered that Darcy's own seat of Bannow was jeopardized in 1640 by the Attorney-General's *quo warrantoes*, note 52.

Coke, *Entries, A Booke of Entries: Containing perfect and approved Presidents of Courts, Declarations, Informations, Pleints, Inditements, Barres, Replications, Rejoinders, Pleadings, Processes, Continuances, Essoines, Issues, Defaults, Departures in Despite of the Court, Demurrers, Trialls, Judgements, Executions, and all other Matters and Proceedings* [... & etc] (London, 1614), f° 527ᵛ, a case of *quo warranto* against Christopher Helden.

*11 Hen.IV, c.2, recte,*1 (1409–10); this statute refers back to 7 Hen.IV, c.15, but it does not go beyond description of procedure for election, appearing not to say quite what Darcy attributes to it (*SR*, 2, 162).

CoLitt., f 9b, Section 3, '*Of fee simple*', 'for when a man is called to the Upper House of Parliament by Writ he is a Baron and hath inheritance therein without the word (heirs)'.

Parliaments? How shall subsidies be granted, or the kingdom defended? How shall *ardua Regni* be considered? Oh, the Barons of the Exchequer, I wot, will salve all these doubts!

I may not forget, my Lords, how the law of the land and the whole Commonwealth is herein concerned, and upon that I will offer a case or two. If a statute be made wherein the private interest of a subject, **Coke 4,3.** or the general interest of the Commonwealth, be **Bozoon's case.** enacted, the King by his letters-patent cannot dispense with this statute, Coke 8, 29a, *Prince's Case,* though they be with a *non obstante,* nor make any grant *non obstante* of the common law; therefore I conclude this question:

First, that it is against the King's prerogative to issue such a *quo warranto,* as is here stated. Secondly, it is against the Commonwealth, as destructive of Parliaments, and consequently of government. Thirdly, this is no privilege, but a service done to the King and whole Commonwealth which cannot receive so much as a debate but in Parliament. Fourthly, all the proceedings in the Exchequer touching this Parliament were *Coram non judice,* as was already voted in both Houses. As for the punishment, we come not to urge your Lordships to punish other than with reference to that which I said before, *viz.* the Oath.[108]

16. Question These two questions have so near a relation, the one **16. Answer** to the other, meeting in the centre of the Castle **17. Question** Chamber, that I will speak to them at once or as to **17. Answer** one question.

My Lords, if that golden mean and mediocrity which regulated the power of that great court in former times had not been of late converted and strained unto that excess we saw, these questions had never been stirred, but many things being extended to their uttermost sphere, or I fear beyond the same, enforce me, although unwillingly and slowly, to look upon our laws and just rights.

The answer to the sixteenth, *viz.* whether jurors giving their verdicts according to their conscience, may be punished in the Castle Chamber by fines excessive, mutilation of members, &c:

I find in my *Lord Barclaye's Case,* Plowden, *Comm.* 231, [that] from the beginning the usual trial at common law was divided between the judges and the jurors; matters of fact were and are triable by the jurors, and matters in law by the judges. The antiquity of this trial appears,

---

[108] *Prince's Case,* 8CoRep.29a; see note 63.

Bozoon's Case, 4CoRep, 3, *recte, Bozoun's Case,* 4CoRep, 34b; 'when the Queen by the common law cannot in any manner make a grant, there a *non obstante* of the common law will not, against the reason of the common law, make the grant good' (*ER*, 76, 972). *Coram non judice,* not before a proper court.

On the sanctions incurred by judges for not respecting their oath, see note 45.

Glanvill, *fol.* 100b, in Henry the Second's time, Bracton, 174; Britton, *fol.* 130a; Fortescue, *De laudibus legum Angliae, fol.*54 & 55. So much being cleared, they being *jurati ad dicendum veritatem*, are judges of the fact, Coke 9, 13a, *Dowman's Case*, & 25 &c, *Strata Marcella's Case*, and infinite other authorities; they are so far judges of the fact that, although the parties be estopped to aver the truth yet these judges of the fact shall not be so estopped, because they are upon their oath, Coke 2, 4b, *Goddard's Case*, Coke 4, 53a, *Rawlins Case*, 1 Hen. 4, 6a &c. They are so far judges of the fact that they are not to leave any part of the truth of the evidence to the court, Coke 1, 56b, *Chancellor of Oxford's Case*;[109] nay they may find releases and other things of their knowledge not given in evidence, 8 *ass., plac.* 3; Coke 10, 95b, *Doctor Leyfield's Case*. What is done by judges shall not be tried by jurors, Coke 9, *Strata Marcella's Case* 30, *ergo è converso*, but if any doubt in law ariseth upon the evidence, there is a proper remedy by bill of exception by the statute of W.2, *cap.*30, which Coke 9, *Dowman's Case, fol.* 13a, saith to be in affirmance of the ancient common law. As to this point of law, the judges of the law are judges of the validity of the evidence, but under favour not of the truth of the fact, as it is set forth in the answer; if the judges of the law do err in matter of law, the party grieved hath

---

[109] *Lord Berkeley's Case*, see note 81.

Glanvill, f° 100b, Tractatus de Legibus et Consuetudinibus Regni Angliae qui Glanvilla vocatur, 1187–9; there being only 54 folio sheets in this text, the reference is taken to mean f° 50ᵛ, '*Sumone per bonos sumonitores duodecim liberos et legales homines*' (summon by good summoners twelve free and lawful men); ed. G.D.G. Hall (London, 1965), p. 165.

Bracton, f° 174, Henrici de Bracton, *De Legibus Angliae*, 1569; Cap. XII, *Cui fieri debet querela*' (To whom complaint ought to be made); ed. Sir Travers Twiss, 6 vols., Rolls series (London, 1878–83), iii, 103.

Britton, f° 130a, John T.P. Britton, *Britton* (London, 1540; O.U.P., 1865).

Fortescue, De Laudibus legum angliae, pp.54–5, c.25, '*How jurours must be chosen and sworne*'.

Dowman's Case, 9CoRep.13a, 'that in all pleas, as well of the Crown as in Common Pleas [...] the jury may find the special matter, which is pertinent, and tends only to the issue joined upon which, being doubtful to them in law, they may pray the opinion of the Court' (*ER*, 77, 750).

Strata Marcella's Case, see note 69.

Goddard's Case, 2CoRep.4b, 'for though a party to a deed cannot aver that it was delivered before the day on which it bears date, yet the jury are not estopped to say the truth' (*ER*, 76, 396).

Rawlyns's Case, 4CoRep.53a, 'that estoppels conclude the parties to say the truth, but cannot conclude the jurors because they are sworn *ad veritatem de super praemissis dicendam*' (*ibid.*, 76, 1011).

Chancellor of Oxford's Case, 1, *recte*, 10CoRep.56b, 'and although the jury have found circumstances and presumptions to incite the jury to find fraud, yet it is but evidence to the jury, and not any matter upon which the Court could adjudge fraud; and the office of jurors is to adjudge upon their evidence concerning matter of fact, and thereupon to give their verdict, and not to leave matter of evidence to the Court to adjudge' (*ER*, 77, 1011).

his remedy by writ of error, but he is not punishable if malpractice or misdemeanor do not appear, 2 Rich. 3, *fol.* 9-10; Fitzherbert, *Natura Brevium*,* 243; E.27, *ass.*18, 4Hen.6, and other books. By the same reason, the judges of the fact, if they go according to their conscience as our question is stated, if the jury in this case go contrary to their evidence, the common law gives a full remedy by attaint wherein the judgement is most heavy if the jurors have done amiss, as I said before to another question. Yet in this action the law gives credit to the verdict before it be falsified, for if a judgement be given upon this verdict and after an attaint is brought, no *super sedeas* can be in this writ to hinder the party who recovered from his execution, 5 Hen. 7, 22b; 33 Hen.6, 21, otherwise [than] in a writ of error.[110]

Your Lordships therefore may see what faith is given to verdicts at common law. I observe the notable case of 7 Hen. 4, 41b, where Gascoigne answereth the King, that would give judgement contrary to his private knowledge.

As for the next part of these two questions, it was the late height of punishments,[111] and the drawing of more causes to that court than in former times, moved this debate, out of the statute of 3 Hen.7, *cap.*I, concerning this court. I make these observations: first, that the judges of that court, according to their discretion, may examine great offences; **Verba Statut.** secondly, that they may punish according to the demerits of delinquents after the form of the statute thereof made; thirdly, in like manner and form, as they should or ought to be punished if they were convict by the due order of the common law. For the first, what discretion this is, we find in our books, Coke 5, *fol.*100, *Rooke's*

---

*'Fitz Natur. br.'

[110] *Dr Leyfield's Case*, 10CoRep.95b, *recte*, 88a, 'but when the law creates the estate, the deed doth not belong to him, nor ever was in his power then shall he not shew it as in the said case of guardian in chivalry' (*ER*, 77, 1069).

Strata Marcella's Case, see note 69.

W.II, c.30, see note below, *Dowman's Case*.

Dowman's Case, 9CoRep, 13a (see also note 109), 'and therefore the law will not compel neither the jurors, who have not knowledge of the law, to take upon the knowledge of points in the law, either in cases which concern life or member, or inheritances, freehold, goods, or chattels, but leave them to the consideration of the judges; nor the Justices of Assise nor any other judges, be it in Pleas of the Crown or Common Pleas, to give their opinion of questions and doubts in law upon the sudden [...]And therefore it was resolved that the said Act of W.2, c.30 was but affirmance of the common law' (*ER*, 77, 750-1).

Fitzherbert, *Natura Brevium*, p. 243, c.52, '*Brief de Certiorari*', '*Pour remouer ass. en bank le Roy*'. *super sedeas*, a writ commanding the stay of legal proceedings.

[111] *7Hen.4, f° 41b*, this particular Year Book has, with the details of the case, remained inaccessible.

'the late height of punishments' is a reference to the severity of Strafford's administration; 'this court', alluded to a little later, is the Castle Chamber.

Case, discretion is to proceed within the bounds of law and reason; at common law a man in a leet is fined but in ten groats for a light bloodshed; in the Castle Chamber a nobleman for an offer of a switch to a person inferior to him, upon provocation perhaps given, was fined **Lord Viscount** in four thousand pound, committed to long impris- **Clanmorris** onment, and low acknowledgements were imposed on him. For the second and third observations, if men of quality and rank were pilloried, papered, stigmatized, and fined to their destruction in cases where, if they had been convicted by due order of law, they could not be so punished by any law or statute, I humbly offer to your Lordships sad and grave consideration.

And whether these courses be warranted by the said statute of 3Hen.7, *cap*. I, or by any other law or statute of force in this realm, and if all jurors be brought to the Castle Chamber, what shall become of that great and noble trial, by which all the matters of our law regularly are triable? And so I conclude that the answers to these two questions are not satisfactory.[112]

18 Question Whether in the censures in the Castle Chamber, regard **18 Answer** is to be had to the words of the Great Charter, *viz. salvo contenemento, &c.*

I conceive that in the censures in the Castle Chamber, regard is to be had to the words of the Great Charter, *viz. Salvo contenemento*, &c. although in the Great Charter, and in the *Statute of Westminster* I, *cap.* 6, *amerciamentum* and *misericordia* are expressed and not fines or *redemptio*, because a fine and an amerciament are in the old Year Books used promiscuously as *synonyma* for one and the same thing, and therefore in 10Edw. 3, fol. 9 and 10. The jurors of the Abbot of Ramsey's leet, being sworn, and refusing to present the articles of the leet, were amerced and there it is resolved, because all did refuse to present, all shall be amerced, but when the same shall be imposed or affeared, shall be imposed severally upon each of them *secundum quantitatem delicti salvo contenemento suo*, yet the sum there imposed was *revera à fine*, and

---

[112] *3 Hen.VII, cap.1* (1487), '*An Acte giving the Court of Star chamber authority to punnyshe dyvers Mysdemeanors*' (*SR*, 2, 509); a specific reference was made in these statutes to murderers, a far worse category of offender than Darcy had alluded to in the Dublin Castle Chamber. *Verba statut.*, quoting from the statute.
Rooke's Case, 5CoRep.100, 'for the statute of 6Hen.6, cap.5, on which the commission of sewers is formed and specified, has precise words in the said commission, that no person of any estate or commission shall be spared. And if the law should be otherwise, inconvenience might follow' (*ER*, 77, 209).
Lord Viscount Clanmorris, another Galway man; Thomas Bourke, recorded as in the Irish House of Lords in 1634, was related to the Clanricardes and went to jail with Patrick Darcy in 1636 in the wake of the Portumna hearings. The particular incident alluded to here is another episode about which no details have been discovered.

not an amerciament as an amerciament is now taken, and herewith agrees 4 Eliz., Dyer, 211b, in these words (if the jurors of a leet refuse to present the articles of the leet, according to their oath, the steward hall assess a fine upon every of them), and *Godfrey's Case*, 11 *Rep. fol.*42b, 43a.[113]

Secondly, if by intendment of law, as the law was conceived at the time of the making of the statutes of *Magna Charta* and *Westminster 1*, fines and amerciaments had not been, or taken to be, *synonyma*, the feazors of those acts would not have so carefully provided remedy in case of amerciaments, which were always moderate, and wherein *à moderata misericordia* did lie for all men, *ab enumeratione non partium, viz. Comites & Barones non amercientur & miles & liber homo amercientur & salvo contenemento suo, mercator salva merchandiza sua, Villanus Salvo Wainagio, Clericus salvo Laico, Feoudo, &c.* and have thought of no redress or moderation of fines, which are more grievous, and of late times infinitely swollen above amerciaments, for in 19 Edw.4, *fol.*9, and 21 Edw.4, *fol.*77, the amerciament of an Earl Baron, *&c.* is but five pounds, and of a Duke ten pounds, yet a Baron's ancient fee or livelihood consisteth of four hundred marks land per annum, an Earl's of four hundred pounds, a Duke's of eight hundred pounds per annum.

Thirdly, amerciaments imposed upon those that have the administration of justice or execution of the King's writs, for their commission or omission contrary to their duty, are out of the letter of *Magna Charta* [and] are indeed fines, and to be imposed and taxed by the judges; yet are they called *misericordiae*, because great moderation and mercy must be used in taxing of them; *Grisley's Case*, 8*Rep., fol.* 48a-b.[114]

---

[113] *salvo contenemento*, a clause from *Magna Carta*, see note 19.

Statute of Westminster 1, cap.6 (1275), '*Amerciaments shall be reasonable*' (Extract from the *Red Book of the Exchequer*, Dublin, *SR*, 1, 26).

Abbot of Ramsey's leet see *Cartularium Monasterii de Rameseia*, ed. Hart & Lyons, 3 vols, Rolls series (London, 1884–93).

4 Eliz.,Dyer,211b, 'A leet jury refusing to present according to their oaths, the steward may set a fine upon them. Or if it be a jury or homage of copyholders in a court baron, it is a forfeiture of their tenures' (*ER*, 73, 467).

Godfrey's Case, 11CoRep.42a–43, 'Two of the jury of a leet refused to make a presentment that they paid 10s for the certainty of leet; the steward imposed a fine of £6 upon them, and the lord distrained for the fine, and pro certo letae [...] *Resolved – the fine imposed upon the jurors jointly is not lawfully imposed; it ought to have been severally assessed*' (*ER*, 77, 1199).

[114] *ab enumeratione*..., penalties were not equal, but proportionate; Earls and Barons were not amerced, the soldier and the freeman were amerced *salvo contenemento* (according to their station), the merchant according to his merchandize, the villein according to his serfdom, the clerk according to his lay or feudal condition.

19 Edw.IV, f° 9; 21 Edw.IV, f° 77, Year Book references for evidence of inflation of amerciaments.

Griesley's Case, 8CoRep.48a-b, *recte*, 38a-b, 'for a fine is always imposed and assessed by the Court, but an amercement which is called in Latin *misericordia*, is assessed by the country. And this word (*afferer*) is as much as to say *ponere in certitudinem seu taxare* to assess

Fourthly, in case fines be not within these words of *Magna Charta*, *amercietur salvo contenemento, &c*, yet ought they by law to be reasonable and not excessive, for every excess is against law, *excessus in re qualibet, jure reprobatur communi*, as excessive distress is prohibited by the common law 41 Edw.3, fol.26. So is excessive and outrageous aid, as appears by the *Statute of Westminster 1, cap.35*, and by Glanvill l.9, *fol.*70, an assize lies for often distrayning because it is excessive, and therefore against law; an excessive fine, at the will of the Lord, is an oppression of the people, 14Hen.4, *fol.*9. If *tenant* in *Dower* have rich *villains* or *tenants* at *will* and he by excessive taxes or fines make them mendicants, it is waste in the eye of the law, 16 Hen.3, Fitzherbert* , waste 135; *Register Judiciale, fol.*25. If the fines of copyholders be uncertain, the lord of the manor cannot exact unreasonable and excessive fines, and the unreasonableness of the fines shall be determined by the judges having respect to the value of the copyhold, 4Rep., *fol.*27b. The King, before the making of *Magna Charta*, had *rationabile relivium* [*recte, relevium*] of noblemen and it was not reduced to any certainty, yet ought it to have been reasonable and not excessive, Coke, *Institutes*, 83b.[115]

They say that in a legal construction, the statute of *Magna Charta*, in which the words *salvo contenemento* are mentioned, is only to be understood of amerciaments and not of fines, yet where great fines are imposed *in terrorem*, upon the reducements of them, regard is to be had to the ability of the persons.

Now whereas they allege that upon the reducements of fines, regard is to be had to the estate of persons, I humbly conceive [that] that

or tax, and the afferance is as much as to say assessment or taxation' (*ER*, 77, 532–3).
* 'Fitz.'
[115] *excessus in re qualibet, jure reprobatur communi*, excess in whatever thing is condemned by common law.
Statute of Westminster cap.35, see note 113. 'Excess of jurisdiction in franchises' (*SR*, 1, 35).
Glanvill 1.9, f 70, see note 109. The reference here is to f° 35ᵛ, '*Breve de summonenda magna assisa inter dominum et vassallum*' (The writ for summoning the Grand assize between Lord and Vassal), ed.Hall, p. 111.
Fitzherbert, *Natura Brevium*, p.135; Darcy's purpose is not clear here. There is no reference to 'wast' at the quoted passage (which deals with the guarantees of the Great Charters); 'wast' is to be found at pp. 55–59ᵛ. *Register Judiciale*, untraced.
4CoRep.27b, in *Hobart & Hammond's Case*, 'The non-payment of an unreasonable fine, where the custom is uncertain, is no forfeiture of a copyhold. Whether a fine be reasonable or not shall be determined by the justices either upon demurrer, or upon evidence to a jury, or confession or proof of the yearly value' (*ER*, 76, 942–3).
rationabile relevium, > relevy, 'a payment, varying in value and kind, according to rank and tenure, made to the overlord by the heir of a feudal tenant on taking up possession of vacant estate' (*OED*); CoLitt, f° 83ᵛ, '*Of Knight's Service*', 'Before the making of the statute of *Magna Charta*, the King had *rationibile relevium* of Noblemen and it was not reduced to any certainty'. Spelt 'relivium' in the 1643 edition, and signalled as a *Fault escaped*, this is another correction which the 1764 edition ignored.

makes but little, either for the ease or security of the subject, or the providence or wisdom of the law, for that such reducements are not grounded upon any rule of law, but rest merely in the King's grace and bounty which, if the prince should withdraw and leave the subject to the law, in what case he is in I leave it to your Lordships. If there be no rule in this case, it may rest in the arbitrary will of four or five persons in that court to destroy any man, and in their will to reduce as they please, but never to reduce before confession of the sentence which is destructive, wherein perhaps there is no infallibility, *Magna Charta, cap.*29. *Nullus liber homo aliquo modo destruatur, &c.* and so I conclude as to this answer.[116]

19 Question　This answer as it is here is sufficient, yet contrary to
19 Answer　　 their answer to the first question upon the same point, and so contrary that both are incompatible.

20 Question　　My Lords, I am come to the life of man, after that
20 Answer　　　God concluded the work of the whole world saying to
Genesis,　　　　 every particular *& erant valde bona*, to make the work
cap.I v.31.　　 complete *creavit hominem ad imaginem & similitudinem suam.*
Genesis　　　　　Aristotle in his treatise *De natura animalium saith that*
cap.1,v.27.　　 *unum vivens est magis dignum*, which is man, that creature alone is more perfect and noble than all the world besides. The common law of the land hath three darlings, life, liberty, and dower. The former-recited statutes give protection to three things, to life, estate, and liberty; the life of man is the eldest child admitted to the favour of the law, and the first and chief within the protection of these statutes, the other two are but ministers and servants unto it. The trial of this life by the law and statutes aforesaid is regularly *judicum parium*; to multiply cases upon so plain a learning were but [to] pass time, or waste time. Your Lordships have other business of weight and consequence: the proof which taketh away this life with infamy, which corrupts the blood of him and his posterity, defeats the wife and innocent children of their fame and substance, surely ought to be clear and convincing proof.[117]

---

[116] *Magna Carta,* cap. 28, see note 88.
[117] *Genesis.*i.31, 'and God saw all that he had made, and it was very good. Evening came, and morning came, a sixth day'; *Genesis,*i.27, 'So God created man in his own image; in the image of God he created him'.
Aristotle, *De natura animalium*; this is probably an allusion to *De historia animalium*; in the absence of a specific reference, and given the generality of the idea proposed, one may suppose that the quotation has a basis in Aristotle's work.
judicium parium, the justice of equals; a quotation from *Magna Carta*, see notes 88 and 97.

The case of an approver is the only case we find in our law where a person infamous may accuse another for his life; this accusation cannot take away the life of any man otherwise than by a legal trial, *viz.* by a trial of jurors, who ought to have other good proof before they find a subject guilty, or by both, wherein the approver hazards his own life, which is sacred unto him by the law. This approver is not received in another felony, or treason, than he himself is guilty of by confession of the fact, nor for his relief after he commits the crime confessed, Stamford, *Pleas of the Crown, fol.* 142, 143, for notorious rebels or malefactors. I find not any book in law to give countenance unto such testimony. I find in the fourth article of the King's printed book of instructions that such testimony shall not be pressed when any man stands upon trial of his life. The judges do answer well to one part, *viz.* that such testimony is not convincing, but they go further: that the testimony of such persons, not condemned, concurring with other proof or apparent circumstance, may be pressed upon the trial of a man for his life; the said article in the instructions saith it shall not be pressed at all. No law warrants such pressure.[118]

It is quite different from the case of an approver who confesseth himself guilty and who is limited to the crime whereof he is guilty; a rebel is left at large to prove any crime, nay the relief of himself.

The testimony mentioned in the question differs in all things from the approver, therefore they cannot be resembled; the concurrence of such testimony with other proof is not material, for other proof will do the deed without this bad concurrence, and so will a violent pre-sumption; as if two go safe into a room, one of them is found stabbed to death the other may suffer, this presumption is inevitable. The law of God, the laws and statutes of the realm, protect and preserve the life of man; it were therefore hard to take away by circumstance such a real and noble essence. This concurrence mars the evidence, it helps it not. If one gives false testimony once, by the ancient law his testimony shall never be received again, Leges *Canuti Regis*, Lambarde, *Saxons laws, fol.* 113, p.34, much less where they are notorious ill-doers. This and the reason and ground of this question already opened, will, I hope, give your Lordships satisfaction.[119]

---

[118] Stamford, *Pleas of the Crown*, pp. 142–3, Sir William Stanford, '*Des queux offences home approuvera*'; see note 69.
Unless Darcy is quoting from an unidentified source, 'the fourth article of the King's printed book of instructions', should be the fortieth; *HMD*, Article XL, '*Against the testimony of persons condemned or in protection*' eds. Hand & Treadwell, 208.

[119] Lambarde, *Saxons laws*, f° 113, p.34; Darcy has vulgarized the title of William Lambarde's *APXAIONOMIA, sive De priscis Anglorum Legibus Libri* (London, 1568). The reference is to p.34 of *Leges Canuti Regis*, which is on f° 116ᵛ of the 1644 edition of Lambarde, '*De falsi testimonio accusato*'.

21 Question For this question, I will state it, without any tenure **21 Answer** reserved by express words, as the question is put, whether the reservation of rent, or annual sum, will raise this to be a tenure *in capite*; I conceive it will not for sundry reasons. First, from the beginning there have been fairs and markets, and no precedent, book-case, or record, to warrant the new opinion in this case before *Trinity term*, 1639, in the Court of Wards. Secondly, the practice of that court was always before to the contrary, in the same and the like cases. Thirdly, it is a thing as the question is of new creation, and never *in esse* before, for this see the Book of 3 Hen.7, 4; 12 Hen.7, 19; 15 Edw.4, 14; 46 Edw.3, 12; 21 Hen.6, 11; Stamford, *Prerogative* 8.

48 Edw.3,9, Therefore there is no necessity of a tenure thereof; **33. Hen.6,** upon the Conquest it was necessary that all lands **7-8,Hen.7,** should be held by some tenure for the defence of the **12.Coke 6,6.** kingdom.[120]

Coke 9,123. 1. The statute of *Quia emptores terrarum, &c.,* *praerogativa Regis,* speak of *Feoffator, Feoffatores, &c.,* therefore a tenure (I mean this tacit or implied tenure) was originally only intended of land.

2. The King may reserve a tenure in all things not mainerable by express reservation or covenant, 44 Edw.3, 45; Fitzherbert, *Natura brevium,* 263, &c., but that is not our case.

3. Here it is left to construction of law, which is *aequissimus judex,* and looks upon the nature of things, and therefore in cases that include land, or where land may come in lieu thereof, a tenure may be by implication, as a mesnalty, a reversion expectant upon an entail and the like, 10 Edw.44a [*sic*]; 42 Edw.3, 7; Fitzherbert, *Grants,* 102, and divers other books.

4. No tenure can be implied by reason of a rent, if the rent be not distrainable by some possibility of its own nature upon the thing granted, as appears by 5 Hen.7, 36; 33 Hen.6, 35; 40 Ed.3, 44; 1 Hen.4, 1, 2, 3; Fitzherbert, *cessabit,* 17.

5. The distress upon other land is the King's mere prerogative, like the case of *Buts,* Coke 6, 25, a distress may be for rent in other land by covenant.

6. This is no rent because it issueth not out of land.

7. If the patentee here had no land, there can be no distress in this case.

---

[120] Stamford, *Prerogative 8*; Sir William Stanford, *An Exposicion of the Kinge's Prerogative; collected out of the great abridgement of Justice Fitzherbert* (London, 1567); as the final cluster of Year Book cases on this page will indicate, this work is a selective compendium of the statutes gathered together in Fitzherbert's three-volume summary of the Year Books, entitled *La Graund Abridgement* (London, 1565).

8. This is a mere privilege, it issueth out of no lands, and participates nothing of the nature of land; all the cases of tenures in our books are either of land or things arising out of land, or some way or other of the nature of land, or that may result into land, or that land by some possibility may result into it. Therefore I humbly conceive that new opinion is not warranted by law or precedent.[121]

These, my Lords, are in part the things,
which satisfied the House of Commons
in all the matters aforesaid;
they are now left to the
judgement and justice of
your Lordships.

[121] *6CoRep.6b*, in *Wheeler's Case*, 'If the King grants lands in fee, and reserves nothing, the patentee should hold by knight's service *in capite*. The same law, if the King grants lands by express words *absque aliqua inde reddendo*; or if he grants lands without any reservation, the tenure should be of the King by knight's service for the incertainty, and so it is held in 33 Hen.6,7a' (*ER*, 77, 262–3).

9CoRep.123, in *Anthony Lowe's Case*, 'And the King cannot by his charter alter the law, but it shall be expounded as near the King's intent as may be, and that is to extinguish all services, but that only which is an inseparable incident to every tenure, and that is fealty, for that the King may do by the law, and *id Rex potest de jure potest*. Vide 8 Hen.7, casu ultimo. And as to the cases which have been put out of the book in 33 Hen.6, they were agreed affirmed for good law' (*ER*, 77, 910).

Fitzherbert, *Natura brevium*, p. 263, c.170, '*Briefe de Dote Assignanda*'.

Fitzherbert, *Grants*, p.102; the 1609 edition of *Natura Brevium* (which is not in-folio) offers no corresponding information at this reference, and 'grants' are found at pp.152–5.

Fitzherbert, *cessabit*, p.17, *recte*, 'Briefe de cessavit' to be found in Fitzherbert, pp. 208–10.

Butts Case, 6CoRep.25, recte, 7CoRep.23a, 'If a man seised of Black-acre in fee, and also possessed of White-acre for years, by his deed grants a rent out of both to A to have and perceive to him for the term of his life, with clause of distress in both; A may distrain in White-acre, for rent arrere; and resolved, [...]: If the manor of D, out of which the rent is granted, be recovered by eigne title, all the rent is extinct; but if the manor of S, in which the distress is limited be evicted, the whole rent remains' (*ER*, 77, 446).

It is appropriate that the last word should be with Sir Edward Coke to whose example Darcy's work owes so much. Here ends Darcy's argument in defence of the queries, refuting the objections raised by the judges. The editions of 1643 and 1764 do not, however, end here; they include in a final section a reformulation of the twenty-one queries in affirmative form, as they were voted and approved, *nullo contradicente*, at the Irish House of Commons on 26 July 1641.

TABLE OF STATUTES

In the rare cases where statutes are marked with an asterisk *, it has not proved possible, for one reason or another, to verify them at the reference given; this does not necessarily indicate an error on Darcy's part. There is undoubtedly room for confusion in the lack of identification of *editions* of sources (such as Fitzherbert's *Natura Brevium*). Other references are simply incomplete; in such cases it has not always been possible to summarise the contents of the statute concerned.

(The statute attributed wrongly to 7 Edw.II above appears to be attributed by Molyneux to 17 Edw.I.)

(The above-mentioned statute, 31 Edw.III, was originally listed in the archives under 17 Rich.II).

TABLE OF YEAR BOOKS

Produced annually by the Stationers' Company until 1535, the *Year Books* were an indispensable guide to the corpus of English statute and case law. They were superseded by the reports and commentaries of a new generation of specialist observers of the law such as Dyer, Plowden, Coke *et al.*, but for legislation prior to the reign of Henry VIII, the *Year Books* provided the most convenient means of access, although not replacing consultation of the records themselves. The majority of the following references come not from source, but from Darcy's utilisation of them as legal dates in the cases reported by Dyer, Plowden, Coke, and Fitzherbert; this list is therefore presented as a record of the range covered by Darcy, but will not be given the same coverage in the footnotes as the statutes and law reports.

TABLE OF NAMED CASES

The sources of information for these cases are for the most part in the reports of Dyer, Coke, and Plowden, where they have been verified in the *English Reports*.

DARCY'S ARGUMENT INDEX

III
The Diary and Speeches of Sir Arthur Kaye, 1710–21*

Edited by
D. Szechi

*I am deeply indebted to Clyve Jones of the Institute of Historical Research Library and Dr Eveline Cruickshanks of the History of Parliament Trust for their help and advice in preparing this edition of Kaye's diary and speeches.

INTRODUCTION

Written 'to supply the defect of an ill memory', Sir Arthur Kaye's manuscript diary is one of the few early eighteenth-century accounts of Parliamentary politics that have survived to the present day.[1] It is also one which scholars in the field have found very useful. As Geoffrey Holmes, the doyen of early eighteenth-century British history, has put it: 'no contemporary material illustrates more vividly the negative side of the country member's prejudices'.[2] The Parliamentary speeches also preserved amongst Kaye's papers are less well known but in their own way are just as valuable, hence the publication of the two in conjunction.[3]

Kaye was a High Church Tory from a wealthy Yorkshire family with a distinguished Cavalier pedigree. His grandfather, the first baronet, raised a regiment for the king in 1642–3, incurring large debts in the process, and was obliged to compound with Parliament in 1645. Kaye's father, Sir John Kaye, stood for the county against the Exclusionist tide between 1679 and 1681, and was active in harassing conventiclers in the early 1680s. Finally returned for Yorkshire in 1685, he soon disgraced himself with the court by rebuffing their attempts to persuade him to support the repeal of penal legislation directed against Roman Catholics. Nonetheless, Sir John steadfastly refused to join the earl of Danby's pro-Williamite rising at York in 1688. Returned for Yorkshire again in 1689, Sir John settled into a long and undistinguished Parliamentary career as a moderate, solid Tory backbencher until his death in 1706.[4]

Kaye seems to have spent the years 1706–10 getting the family's affairs in order before launching himself into Parliamentary politics. He was first returned for the county in 1710 and represented it in every Parliament thereafter until his death in 1726.[5] Though there is no direct evidence that he was a leader among the backbenchers, because he

[1] The diary is interspersed among the Dartmouth MSS held by Staffordshire County Record Office. Years 1710–14 are in D.1778/V/200, years 1715–20 are in D(W)1778/V/202 and years 1720–1 are in D(W)1778/III/156. I am grateful for their kind permission to publish Kaye's diary and speeches.

[2] G. Holmes, *British Politics in the Age of Anne* (2nd edn, 1987), p.123.

[3] All Kaye's speeches are located in Staffs R.O., Dartmouth MSS, D(W)1778/III/156.

[4] *The House of Commons 1660–1690*, ed. B.D. Henning (3 vols, 1983) ii. 668–9. The estate was valued at £2,109 *per annum* in 1722: Dartmouth MSS, D(W)1778/I/ii/580.

[5] *The House of Commons 1715–1754*, ed. R.R. Sedgwick (2 vols, 1970), ii. 183.

was a Knight of the Shire Kaye's support would automatically have been sought amongst his peers, and his views would have carried weight in any association of backbenchers of which he was a member, which makes his testimony particularly valuable. Moreover, though his politically active years were 'interesting times' in general, the first session of Kaye's first Parliament (1710–11), when his notes were fullest, was an unusually turbulent one even for that period. Between 1710 and 1713 the Tory Harley ministry was plagued by a series of Parliamentary revolts generated by backbench irritation with what they saw as its lack of a sufficiently partisan party spirit.[6]

Kaye was an early member of the main source of these backbench thorns in the Harley ministry's flesh, the 'October Club'. This launched its first Parliamentary offensive early in January 1711 and Kaye's account of its activities is one of only a handful of sources that deal with the Club's exploits from the point of view of an insider. Its aims were simple: to 'drive things on to extreams against the Whigs, to call the old ministry to account, and get off five or six heads'.[7] Goals with which Kaye seems to have been happy to be associated for the next two Parliamentary sessions. Greater political experience, and growing disillusion with the October Club after it struck a bargain with the ministry late in 1711, seem to have cut Kaye adrift from his former friends and associates by 1713. He joined Sir Thomas Hanmer's backbench revolt against ministerial legislation enacting the French Commercial Treaty in June 1713 (which led to the bill's defeat), and, returned for Yorkshire once more in the general election of that year, seems to have drifted uncertainly during the battle for political supremacy between Harley, by then earl of Oxford, and viscount Bolingbroke that erupted early in 1714.[8] Bolingbroke's decisive move in his struggle with Oxford came in May, when his partisans introduced the schism bill in the Commons. A measure designed to draw all factions of the party together in a joint effort (under Bolingbroke's aegis) to crush religious dissent, the bill exactly served Bolingbroke's purpose with respect to Kaye. He committed himself wholeheartedly to the bill, and thereby moved de facto into the pro-Bolingbroke camp.[9] Kaye's and the Tory party's triumph over the schism bill, and their hopes of future measures designed to isolate and eliminate the dissenting

[6] D. Szechi, Jacobitism and Tory Politics 1710–14 (Edinburgh, 1984), pp. 75–84, 98–9, 123–4; G. Holmes and C. Jones, 'Trade, the Scots and the Parliamentary Crisis of 1713', Parliamentary History, i (1982), 47–78.

[7] Quadriennium Annae Postremum; or the Political State of Great Britain, ed. A. Boyer (8 vols, 1718–19), iii. 117–21; Jonathan Swift: Journal to Stella, ed. H. Williams (2 vols, Oxford, 1948), i. 195.

[8] Szechi, Jacobitism and Tory Politics, pp. 104–5, 106–10, 137, 161–70.

[9] Ibid., p. 174.

interest, religious and political, were, however, rudely shattered on 1 August 1714 by the death of Queen Anne. For many Tories a conflict of loyalties ensued. The last of the Protestant Stuarts was dead, but a Catholic Stuart lay over the water, and his attractiveness increased by leaps and bounds as the Hanoverian dynasty unequivocally attached itself to the Whig cause. A good many Tories, more or less reluctantly, correspondingly became involved in conspiracies aimed at overthrowing the Hanoverians in favour of James Francis Edward Stuart, the Old Pretender. Kaye, however, was not one of them. Despite Whig accusations that Kaye distributed Jacobite pamphlets in 1715, there is no evidence that he ever inclined towards Jacobitism. On examination it appears that the Whigs' charges rested on his dissemination of the Tory party's *de facto* manifesto, Bishop Francis Atterbury's, *Advice to the Freeholders of England*, in support of his election campaign.[10] There is no other indication that Kaye ever wavered in his support for the Hanoverian succession, and he was not listed among the potential supporters of a Jacobite rising in 1721.[11] Right up to his death in 1726 Kaye nevertheless stuck loyally with his party as it was driven ever deeper into the political wilderness by Whig proscription and royal hostility.

Kaye's diary is an invaluable source for the day-to-day ebb and flow of the party battle, but his speeches have a more general value for all working on the politics and political thought of the first age of party. Most of them concern issues and debates mentioned in the diary, and consequently give an unusual insight into contemporary Tory thought. Studies of political polemics and 'high ideology' in general are undoubtedly necessary, but without some indication of what practising politicians made of the work of the political theorisers it is difficult to gauge their impact. Kaye's speeches are the kind of historical evidence that enables us to assess their influence.

The abiding concerns of Kaye's speeches perfectly reflect those of his backbench Tory peers. Corruption of the electorate by the ministry, the threat to constitution and social order posed by a standing army, and, most of all, the threat posed by religious dissent to the Church of England. The speeches Kaye preserved for posterity are overwhelmingly dominated by this last concern, and, taken together, eloquently confirm the revisionist thesis that the Tory party never did accept the permanence of the religious settlement of 1689 and were determined severely to cut back the latitude it allowed for religious dissent.[12] As Kaye's speech in support of the notorious schism bill (designed to

[10] *House of Commons 1715–54*, ii. 183; W.A. Speck, *Tory and Whig. The Struggle in the Constituencies 1701–15* (1970), p.41.

[11] *House of Commons 1715–54*, i. 112.

[12] G. Holmes, *The Trial of Dr Sacheverell* (1973), pp.35–46; Szechi, *Jacobitism and Tory Politics*, p.174. Cf. L. Colley, *In Defiance of Oligarchy. The Tory Party 1714–60* (1982), p.13.

prevent dissenting parents bringing up their children in their faith) illustrates, he wanted, if at all possible, to eliminate religious dissent entirely. The idea of religious uniformity retained a strong attraction for Kaye, and given the solidity of the Tory vote on such subjects after 1704, it seems likely that his fellow backbench Tories were drawn in the same direction.

Kaye's diary and speeches have been widely quoted but never published before. In this edition the diary is presented chronologically with the individuals and issues mentioned therein elucidated in the footnotes, and Kaye's speeches interpolated in italics following the appropriate diary entries. The diary is at its best in the 1710–11 session, while he was still finding his way through the maze of contemporary politics. Thereafter it rapidly becomes sporadic and abbreviated. Since most of the information the diary contains after 1712 merely duplicates the daily entries in the *Journals of the House of Commons*, diary entries from 1712 onwards have only been left in the text where a speech survives to illustrate Kaye's thinking and political position. In one case, the 1721 speech on the standing army, I have had to reassemble the speech from a mish-mash of notes and jottings left by Kaye. In the case of all the other speeches, the text Kaye left has been published with only minor emendations. Abbreviations have been silently expanded throughout the text.

THE DIARY AND SPEECHES OF SIR ARTHUR KAYE

Remarkables in the Parliament begun the 25th of November 1710. Design'd to supply the defect of an ill memory.

Mr Bromley[1] was chose Speaker without any opposition, to the great satisfaction of the honest part of the whole kingdom.

December the 21st [1710]. The first division of consequence was upon the commitment of the place bill. The ayes who went out upon the question for committing it, were 239. The noes who staid in against it were 76. These were chiefly those who had been lately in places[2] which some of them yet held. And amongst the first were the present ministry. This bill was committed to a committee of the whole house for the 16th of January [1711]. And the qualification bill for the 18th.

Sir, I should not have troubled you at this time had I not been surprised to see a bill of this nature have so few advocates. How often Sir, has such a bill been wish'd for & the want of it complain'd of? And shall it now meet with the same success & without any reasons given, I speak of myself, that gives me any satisfaction why it should not pass? I have heard it said without doors that the country gentlemen were not let into the secret. I shall never be much sollicitous for that matter, & truly Sir, if there are reasons against the passing [of] this bill which must not be made publick to convince gentlemen I think there is a secret wee are not to be let into. It may be said, that you have now less occasion for such a bill since the happy change of the administration, Sir, I am [as] very pleased with that change of hands as any body is, but I cannot forget the ill effects too many placemen within these walls were once thought to have upon the public. And tho you are now in hands which wee believe will not follow ill examples or make an ill use of their power, yet the affairs of England have seldom been so steady but that in a few years there have still been changes in the ministry, & tis against such changes that I think wee ought in a good Parliament to provide against the ill consequences of a bad one. I am sure there is nothing more expect[ed] from us by the country, in this Parliament, when you have more landed men of it, who are yet independent, then

[1] William Bromley of Baginton, M.P. for Oxford University and a leading High Church Tory. His election as Speaker probably went uncontested by the Whigs because, following the Tories' landslide victory at the polls, they were loth to highlight their weakness in the Commons so early in the session.

[2] I.e. they were Whigs. Place bills traditionally united courtiers and civil servants from both parties in opposition to the measure as much as they united backbenchers from both parties in their favour.

has been in any one Parliament for some years past & if you don't pass such a bill as this now, when can wee hope for it? And therefore Sir, I am for the bill.

January the 10th [1711]. Upon a motion that the committee for the Bill for preventing bribery and corruption in elections have power to receive a clause to save to the Quakers the liberty they now have of their affirmations instead of oaths, it was carried in the affirmative by a 100. The meaning of the Gentlemen [Tories] being to continue [the Quakers' right to affirm], which was but to answer, and to take off, the jealousy of designing any thing against the Toleration which the faction [Whigs] wou'd have insinuated, and leaving [it] to the Parliament to let it fall or still prolong it upon its expiring; as a properer time.[3] The ayes went out.

[11 January 1711. Speech by Kay during consideration of a petition against the sitting M.P.s for East Retford[4]] *Sir, I am called up to give you an account of a place which has made some noise in the country for which I have the honour to serve. I confess I was never within their walls, or if I had, I might have given a blacker history of it. 'Tis a dissenting seminary, a publick nursery of schism & sedition, where youth is educated in a notorious disaffection to the Church & State. Yet from this place & another of the same sort, they have pick'd out as I am inform'd, the vilest wretches to be made what they call Honorary Freemen at Retford. To whose honour this laudable design may turn, I won't say, I am sure not to that of the place from whence they came, nor I hope to its advantage, for being so dangerous to the constitution, if suffer'd to continue, being illegal in its self. And I hope this Parliament will amongst other good things they may take in hand to answer the wishes & expectations of those that sent us hither, take a proper time to take further notice of it.*

The 26th of January [1711]. Wee had a strugle about a duty upon inland coal.[5] But the inconveniencys appear'd so great, & the advantage to the publick so small from the difficulty of collecting it, & the multitude of officers it would require, that the last appearing impracticable, & the Ministry coming in to us, for that reason wee carried our point by a Majority of 157 against 61. This was in the committee for ways & means. The noes divided to the left, the ayes to the right.

Mr Speaker, I did not presume to trouble you upon the long debate you had lately upon this subject in the committee & won't take up much of your time now, but I

---

[3] The Quakers' privilege of affirming to, rather than swearing, public oaths was one many Tories bitterly opposed. Clawing back that particular concession to religious Dissent was seen by many Tories as a necessary first step in a complete overhaul of the religious settlement of 1689. See: Szechi, *Jacobitism and Tory Politics*, pp.98–9, 122, 159.

[4] Two Whigs: Thomas White and Thomas Westby.

[5] With the ministry.

can't but wonder to see this so much insisted on by gentlemen for whom I have all the respect that can be paid by one who has sat so little a while in this House, as believing them as much in the interest of the nation as any gentlemen here, where private interest does not interfere, as I find it does in this case.

I can't but wonder Sir I say, to see this duty so much press'd, when I can't believe the gentlemen can have any other meaning than to endeavour to evade one duty by pressing another. Or, if they are in earnest, I must ask leave to say, that I am confident they have not sufficiently consider'd the consequences of it in general, nor the great prejudice it must necessarily bring upon our woollen manufacture in particular, which 'tis alwaies the interest of an English Parliament to encourage.

Gentlemen can't but know that our wooll can't be wrought up without coals, but they may not know the hardships the poor manufacturers at this time lye under. Whose wages are so low, that to my knowledge they scarse get bread for their familys. I speak for the country I have the honour to serve for, & if there be a duty upon inland coal, whatever that duty is, I will say, it takes off so much from the support of these poor people, who already subsist with difficulty.

Their coal serves them to a double purpose, for warmth & for light, for they work hours by fire light, & if they can't have these at a reasonable price, pray Sir what must become of them? What must the consequence be but the utter ruine of thousands of them, & the increase of the necessitous poor, without any prospect of maintaining them but with the ruine of whole countrys where they are settled, & in time must bring a ruine upon the trade itself.

I hope Sir, the duty upon water born coals will be no example for you in this case; nor the hardship that is complain'd of bringing upon some, be any argument for laying greater hardships upon many. And therefore hope Sir it will never have the concurrence of this House.

[January] the 29th [1711]. The place bill was read the 3d time & pass'd after long debate, by a majority of 235 to 143. All who have had, or now have, or are in hopes to have places, dividing against it, except Sir William Drake[6], Mr Benson[7] and Mr Aislabie[8]. The reason I believe why the Ministry divided for the commitment [of the bill] & against the passing [of] it being either from the opinion that as it was drawn it would upon further thought be disliked, leaving too great a number of great offices, which might have too much influence; or from the hopes of persuading gentlemen, that it would be unacceptable to the Queen, & therefore if this was dropt, they would come in to the Qualification Bill to make it more effectual then this cou'd be; or from

[6] Tory M.P. for Honiton and a lord of the Admiralty.

[7] Robert Benson, Tory M.P. for York and at this time a lord of the Treasury. Subsequently Chancellor of the Exchequer and 1st Lord Benson.

[8] John Aislabie, at this time a Tory (he went into opposition with the earl of Nottingham in December and by degrees mutated into a Whig by 1714), M.P. for Ripon and a lord of the Admiralty.

a belief that it would be in their power either to clog it more or throw it out by force, whenever they pleased.[9] But Harley[10] had the mortification to see what the country gentlemens' interest may do, if they don't suffer themselves to be trick'd out of that union they ought to preserve inviolable.

The chief objections were, its lessening the interest, the power & as some improperly call'd it, the prerogative of the crown if it inferr'd, which wee ought not to suppose, the Crown and people to have different interests, as if gentlemen in places cou'd not serve both at the same time. That it would be ill taken by the Queen, that such a Bill shou'd now pass, in such a ministry & such a Parliament, which wou'd never be allowed in the late administration, & that it would give the Whigs an opportunity of making their court again by opposing it here & throwing it out in another place.[11] But those who were for it said, the bill shew'd sufficiently the respect the House bore to the crown by allowing so many exceptions. That it cou'd be no inconvenience to it [the crown] under a good prince, who having no other view than the true interest of the subject, wou'd not stand in need of any corrupt partie in the house, when he wou'd have the united hearts of all; nor with a good Ministry, who shou'd act upon right reason with honour & integrity, who wou'd not want [i.e. lack] to be supported. But as so great a number of people so influenced might lift their heads up against the crown as well as against the liberties of the subject, & might support a faction in a ministry to the lessening the power & prerogative of the prince, as wee had seen in a late instance[12], it cou'd never be for the true interest of either to have the House liable to such corruptions as might have so fatall consequences. And tho tis true, it would not prevent private pensions, yet as the making that a reason was a tacite confession there might be such, it would at least take off part of the inconvenience, by stopping the current at least of one evill, which at present flowed upon you in two channels.

February the 2^d [1711]. The Lords threw this bill [the place bill] out at the first reading, in a thin house, being 45 against 28, with some reflections made by Lord Pawlet[13] upon those who had supported it in our House, as the dregs of all the discontented parties.

---

[9] See diary entry for 21 Dec. 1710.

[10] Robert Harley, M.P. for New Radnor and premier minister. Subsequently earl of Oxford and Mortimer.

[11] I.e. the Lords, where the Whigs retained a slight majority (when they could persuade Court Whig placemen to vote with them) until January 1712.

[12] A reference to the former, Whig, administration.

[13] John Poulet, 4th Lord (and subsequently 1st Earl) Poulet, a High Church Tory with Jacobite proclivities who was nonetheless a devoted follower of Harley.

[February] the 3^d [1711]. Upon the report of [the] Tavistock election, where bribery & corruption had appear'd as flagrant against Sir John Cope[14] who was not petition'd against, as against Mr Manaton[15] who was & [was] thrown out; it was moved that a day might be appointed him to answer to that charge which might be brought against him from those proofs that appear'd upon the report from the committee, & was seconded: but the question [was] not put, tho there were two precedents quoted. The only argument against it was that no gentleman's seat there ought to be call'd in question after the time directed for presenting petitions, & then of those only of whom the petition takes notice. And the debate dropt tho against the opinion of most of the experienc'd members. I believe upon the reason of being willing not to be thought too severe [sic].

March 26 [1711]. A duty upon leather being proposed in the committee, it was rejected upon a division. Ayes 95, noes 136. It was computed in gross at £120,000 per annum, but no perticulars open'd.

But what was now rejected, was the next day allow'd upon raw hides.[16] And the ministry had that influence upon the good natures of gentlemen, who were told there could not be any other fund thought of that could so effectually answer the present occasions, & that if it was not pass'd the armies could not take the field, the campaign would be lost, & their credit, which was now reviving, would be entirely sunk, [so] that wee the noes were but 75 to the ayes 181.[17]

My reasons were the heavyness of the duty & the vexation I fear'd in the collecting [of] it. And that I did not see such a necessity for it because I verily believ'd they had other projects in peto [sic], but would admit no proposals but what came from themselves.

The bill to prevent bribery etc. in elections was thrown out by 148 against 98.[18] For tho there were many good things in it, yet the making gentlemen so liable to actions from any villain whose single oath was

---

[14] Sir John Cope of Bramshill, a Whig, a director of the Bank of England and a Commissioner of the Equivalent.

[15] Henry Manaton, unseated in favour of James Bulteel, a Tory who subsequently joined the October Club.

[16] Henry St. John, Secretary of State, later Viscount Bolingbroke, was at this time managing affairs in the Commons for the ministry due to Harley's enforced absence while he recuperated from wounds he had received during the Abbé Guiscard's attempt on his life in February. Bolingbroke's abilities as a Parliamentary manager were thrown into question by the loss of the leather duty to the October Club's raid on the 26th, and he only retrieved his reputation by persuading enough of the Octobermen to relent to let the duty pass under another title next day. H.T. Dickinson, *Bolingbroke* (1970), pp.81–2.

[17] Kaye's figures suggest that Dickinson was incorrect in stating that St. John's hide tax 'met little opposition'. Dickinson, *Bolingbroke*, p.82.

[18] This actually occurred on 17 April not 26 March. *CJ*, xvi. 600–603, 17 Apr. 1711.

a conviction, swayd with me as well as others. And I believ'd wee were not in such hast [as to have] to take it with its faults in the first session, when a better bill might be prepared the succeeding meeting.

[March] 21st [1711].   The qualification bill for Justices of [the] Peace was tied down to £200 per annum by 129 against 76. Which being above incumbrances, I thought higher than £300 would have been at large.

April the 6th [1711].   That in the suburbs of London & Westminster fifty new churches are necessary, computing 4,750 persons to each church.[19]

I think it appear'd that in the parish of Stepney, where there is only the parish church, there are 22 meeting houses of several sects.

[April] 14th [1711].   Resolv'd, that the petitioners[20] have fully prov'd their allegations, & had just reason to complain.

Resolv'd, that the inviting & bringing over into this kingdom the poor Palatines, of all religions, at the publick expence, was an extravagant & unreasonable charge to the kingdom & a scandalous misapplication of the publick money, tending to the increase & oppression of the poor of this kingdom, and of dangerous consequence to the constitution in church & state.

Resolv'd, that whoever advised the bringing over [of] the Palatines into this kingdom, was an enemy to the Queen & kingdom.

The clause offer'd to the post bill, was a perticular exception of the disabling which by this bill, excluded the commissioners & others of the post office from Parliament.

[April] 24th [1711].   Resolv'd, that it appears to this House, that of the moneys granted by Parliament & issued for the publick service to Christmas 1710, there are £35,202,107:18:9 for a great part whereof, no accounts have be[en] laid before the auditors, and the rest not prosecuted by the accountants, & finish'd.

[April] 26th [1711].   A clause to prevent the exportation of bark was offer'd to the Hide Bill, & rejected.

[April] 28 [1711].   Resolv'd, that the not compelling the several accountants to pass their respective accounts, has been a notorious breach of trust, in those, that, of late years, have had the management

---

[19] The substance of the report that led to the Fifty New Churches Act of 1711.

[20] Petitioners against measures taken to relieve the sufferings of Protestant (but Calvinist) refugees from the Palatinate. See: H.T. Dickinson, 'The Poor Palatines and the Parties', *EHR*, lxxxii (1967), 464–85.

of the Treasury, and an high injustice to the nation. Ayes 181. Noes, 119.[21]

Resolv'd, that the several accountants who have neglected their duty in passing their accounts ought no longer to be entrusted with the receiving [of] the publick money.

Memorandum: the leather duty Lowndes computed at £130,000 per annum, but [this] was certainly too lowe, & the additional post duty at £30,000, total £156,000 of which £140,000 was appointed a fund for the increase of the annuities.

May the 3^d [1711]. The Lords threw out the bill for enquiring into the grants in a thin House.[22] Several of the Tory Lords absenting.

Resolv'd, that a fund be granted, redecmable by Parliament for paying the interest at 6 percent, of the debts for which a supply was voted the 18th of March. From Christmas 1711.

This fund to be raised from the impositions & additional impositions by the act of the 8th [year] of the Queen, an act for continuing several impositions upon goods imported, for the service of the year 1710, & from the first duty upon candles, clerks & apprentices, and in case of a deficiency, to be supplied annually out of the first Aids given by Parliament from time to time.

Resolv'd, that the Proprietors of the said debts be incorporated to carry on the trade to the south-seas, & a fishery here, as it was open'd, tho not mention'd in the votes.[23]

May the 5th [1711]. Upon consideration of the report of the arears of taxes.

Resolv'd, that there was in arrear of 8th of December 1710 of the land tax for 5 years, ending the 24th of March 1709, £272,596:08:08, of which there was standing out the beginning of April 1711, £180,439:07:06.[24]

Resolv'd, that the not obliging the receivers of the land tax & other receivers of the publick revenues to pay the money by them received

[21] Kaye's figures conceal a split in the October Club revealed by the presence of prominent Octobermen as tellers on both sides of the division. *CJ*, xvi. 28 April 1711.

[22] The grants resumption bill. This was a measure designed to resume all royal grants of land and pensions since the accession of William and Mary. Many Tory peers enjoyed such grants and were correspondingly loth to support the bill. Scottish Record Office, Register House, Dalhousie Papers GD 45/14/352/8: Lord Balmerino to Henry Maule, 1 May [1711].

[23] I.e. the proprietors were to be shareholders in Harley's new South Sea Company, for details of which see: B.W. Hill, *Robert Harley. Speaker, Secretary of State and Premier Minister* (1988), pp.144–5.

[24] The overwhelming bulk of these missing monies, as with the allegedly 'missing' £35 million noted by Kaye on 24 April, had not been embezzled (as the Octobermen feared) but were instead enmeshed in the toils of the snail-like accounting procedures used by the Treasury at the time of the Commission of Accounts' investigation.

into the Exchequer, as required by law, has been a great loss to the publick & one cause of the debts of the nation.

May the 15ᵗʰ [1711]. Upon consideration of the report of the public debts of the Navy & other offices, for which no provision is made by Parliament.

Resolv'd, that the increasing [of] the public expences beyond the supplies annually granted by Parliament has been the chief occasion of the debts of the nation, & an invasion of the rights of Parliament. Ayes 141, noes 70.

Resolv'd, that it appears to this House, that the sum of £606,806:7:7 has been paid out the moneys issued to the service of the Navy, for provisions supplied to land-forces sent to Spain & Portugal & for the garrison of Gibraltar, for which no deductions have been made from the pay of those forces, nor any part of that sum assign'd to the victualling; notwithstanding the severall letters & representations made to the Treasury in that behalf.

Resolv'd, that such diverting of moneys issued to the service of the Navy, to the land forces, has lessen'd the credit of the Navy, discourag'd the seamen, occasion'd the paying [of] extravagant rates on the Navy contracts and was a misapplication of the public money.

Resolv'd, that the applying any sum of unappropriated money or surplusages of funds to uses not voted or address'd for by Parliament has been a misapplication of the public money.

[December 1711]. The Parliament met in that 2nd session [on] the 7th of December, when upon a motion of an address of thanks to the Queen for her speech, the following words were offer'd by the Whigs as an addition to the resolution on which the address was to be drawn up, viz, 'not doubting but effectual care will be taken to prevent the kingdom of Spain & the West-Indies from remaining in the possession of a prince of the house of Bourbon, which must be destructive to the safety of her Majesties person & government, the Protestant succession in the house of Hanover & the liberties of Europe.' Which being intended to express the sense of the House for not having peace without Spain & the Indies, tho at the same time they knew the conquering [of] them impracticable. The clause was thrown out by a majority of 232 against 106. On the 8th [of] December the engross'd bill from the Lords, entituled, 'an act for preserving the Protestant religion, by better securing the Church of England as by law establish'd; & for confirming of the toleration granted to Protestant Dissenters, by an act entitled, an act for exempting etc, & for supplying the defects thereof, etc, was read a first time, & the 2nd time on the 19th & committed, & went thro the Committee [on] the 20th, reported and pass'd. Thus this bill flew through both Houses in a very few daies without any opposition, which had before been espoused & opposed by both parties with the greatest zeal, & which remains a mistery to me on the part of the Whigs.[25] And their dependents without doors were very much allarm'd at it & disatisfied.

If gentlemen have nothing to propose, I have had something in my thoughts to offer, which I hope may not be altogether undeserving their thoughts; and that is the taking notice of that great abuse of the act of indulgence in the publick dissenting seminaries[26] maintain'd amongst us. But I would not be understood to offer any thing of this nature to be pursued in [a] Parliamentary way, which I think there can be no occasion for, because I believe every gentleman here will agree with me that those seminaries are in no wise comprehended in that Act of Indulgence granted to those scrupulous consciences who are so unhappy [as] to differ from us. But if gentlemen will reflect on the evident inconveniencies & dangers to our constitution from those nurseries of faction & schism, which I believe was never the intention of the makers of that law to encourage, much less to perpetuate, I hope gentlemen will think fit to take notice of them in any way which may seem most proper, and whether that may not be by indictments at our severall assizes, and that the prosecutions may be general. I must submit to them and I hope this may be so far from being an unseasonable time to take notice of them, when you are in expectation of a bill which by report may confirm that act of indulgence, that I hope gentlemen may think it the more proper time to give some hopes, by such a proceeding, to the friends of our establish'd Church that you have no intentions [sic] to perpetuate our divisions by continuing that connivance, which they take as an encouragement.

But as I only offer this to gentlemen I shall be very glad to hear their thoughts of it.

January 17th [1712]. Upon the first resolution concerning Walpole, for which see the notes, the numbers upon the division were, yeas 205, noes 148.[27] Upon the motion made to leave out the words, 'notorious corruption', noes 207, yeas 155. Upon the 2nd, no division. Upon the

---

[25] The 'No Peace Without Spain' clause and the occasional conformity bill which followed it were in fact two halves of a political bargain. In return for the support of the High Church Tory earl of Nottingham and his friends in the Commons and (more importantly) the Lords, where Nottingham's defection gave the Whigs the crucial one vote extra they needed to pass the 'No Peace Without Spain' amendment to an address of thanks to the Queen, the Whigs in the Lords finally allowed an occasional conformity bill to pass after having successfully blocked such legislation for the previous nine years. H. Horwitz, *Revolution Politicks. The Career of Daniel Finch Second Earl of Nottingham* (Cambridge, 1968), pp. 185–7, 189–90, 197, 232–4.

[26] I.e. Dissenting Academies (later the principal target aimed at in the Schism Act).

[27] Robert Walpole, Whig M.P. for King's Lynn (the future premier minister), was accused by the Commission of Accounts of having taken bribes from a syndicate of army contractors in return for the allocation to them of a contract to supply forage to troops stationed in Scotland in 1708. *The Lockhart Papers*, ed. A.A. Aufrere (2 vols, 1817), i. 359–61.

motion for adjourning, ayes 168, noes 156.[28] Upon the 3rd, no division. On his being expell'd, ayes 170, noes 148.

January 24th [1712]. Resolv'd, that the taking several sums annually from the contractors for bread as a perquisite to the [Captain-] Generalship (words moved to be added, 'as has been usually & customarily done by the Commander in Chief', rejected; noes 270, ayes 165) is illegall & unwarrantable, ayes 265, noes 155.[29]

Moved to adjourn, noes 233, ayes 142.

An act to repeal the naturalization act, agreed to by the Lords, without opposition, & pass'd, February 9th.[30]

February 7th [1712]. A bill to prevent the disturbing those of the Episcopal communion in Scotland in the exercise of their religious worship & in use of the liturgy of the Church of England, & for repealing an act of the Scots Parliament entituled, 'an Act against irregular baptisms & marriages', pass'd the Commons, ayes 155, noes 17.[31]

A clause offer'd in the committee to oblige all persons in Scotland, who have any office, civil or military, or any salary or place of employment of profit under the Crown, to attend divine service according to the law of Scotland, & to restrain them from going to Episcopal meetings, was rejected without a division.

February 9th [1712]. A petition from the Quakers, praying [that] the sacred name of God may be left out of their affirmation, was rejected. Ayes 80, noes 101.[32]

February 14th [1712]. In the committee upon the barrier treaty dated November 1709, resolv'd,

That in the treaty between her Majesty and the States-General for

---

[28] Kaye confused the Ayes and Noes on this occasion. *CJ*, xvii. 30: 17 Jan. 1712.

[29] The Captain-General was John Churchill, 1st Duke of Marlborough, and the Commission of Accounts condemnation of his levying a fee from the army's bread contractors was connived at by the ministry with a view to discrediting him and thereby driving him out of politics. *Lockhart Papers*, i. 352–9; Szechi, *Jacobitism and Tory Politics*, pp.107–8.

[30] By this time the Queen had at a stroke created 12 new Tory peers so as to give the ministry a majority in the Lords (E. Gregg, *Queen Anne* (1980), pp.349–50). Consequently the Whigs there did not see any point in straining their new alliance with Nottingham and his friends by futilely opposing something their allies were likely to be in favour of.

[31] The Scottish Episcopalian Toleration Act was another measure allowed to pass unopposed by the ministry as part of its effort to keep on good terms with the Country Tories in general and the October Club in particular. See: D. Szechi, 'The Politics of "Persecution": Scots Episcopalian Toleration and the Harley Ministry, 1710–12', in, *Toleration and Persecution, Studies in Church History*, ed. W.J. Sheils, xxi (1984), 275–89.

[32] A further token of the October Club's determination to cut back the Dissenters' civil and political rights, starting with the Quakers.

securing the succession to the crown of Great Britain & for settling a barrier for the States against France, under colour of securing the Protestant succession, there are several articles destructive to the trade & interest of Great Britain & therefore highly dishonourable to her Majesty. Ayes 279, noes 117.

Resolv'd, that it appears that the lord Viscount Townshend had not any order or authority for negociating or concluding several articles in the said treaty. No division.

Resolv'd, that the lord Townshend who negociated & sign'd, & all those who advised the ratifying of the said treaty, are enemys to the Queen & kingdom. Ayes 226, noes 75.

Upon the report of these resolutions, the House agreed to all, but with a division upon the first. Ayes 238, noes 104.[33]

February [1]5th [1712]. Resolv'd,

That the first proportion of three fifths, to two fifths, agreed upon between his late Majesty King William & the States-General, for the service of the war in Flanders, has not been observ'd by the States-General.

The ayes for the question upon the report were 217, noes 54.

Moved in the committee to add these words, viz, 'other proportions having been agreed to by the Queen & Parliament'. Noes 235, ayes 90.

Resolv'd, that the States-General during the course of this war have furnish'd less than their proportion in Flanders, [by] 20,837 men.

Resolv'd, that the condition for prohibiting all trade & correspondence between Holland & France, on which the troops of augmentation were granted in 1703, & afterwards continued, has not been observ'd by the States-General.

Resolv'd, that her Majesty has not only furnish'd her proportion of 12,000 men, according to the treaty enter'd into for the service of the war in Portugal, but has taken upon her the Emperor's proportion, by furnishing two thirds, when the States-General only furnish'd one third for that service.

Resolv'd, that by the treaty with the King of Portugal[34], there was to be furnish'd 12,000 foot & 3,000 horse, at his own expence; & in consideration of a subsidy to be paid him, 11,000 foot & 2,000 horse

---

[33] This series of resolutions and those of 15 Feb. were designed to empower the ministry to ignore its obligations to the Dutch republic under the Barrier Treaty of 1709 during forthcoming peace negotiations with France. The Tory backbenchers, who virtually uniformly loathed the Dutch, were more than happy to support the ministry on this issue. Szechi, *Jacobitism and Tory Politics*, pp.108–9.

[34] The military alliance and commercial treaty negotiated by John and Paul Methuen with Peter II of Portugal in 1703.

more; notwithstanding which, it appears that the King of Portugal did not furnish 13,000 men in the whole.

Resolv'd, that since the year 1706, when the English & Dutch march'd into Castile & return'd no more into Portugal, h[er] Majesty has replaced more than her share, according to her proportion, & the States-General have not had any troops in Portugal.

Resolv'd, that towards carrying on the war in Spain, in order to reduce that monarchy to the house of Austria, neither the late Emperors[35] nor his present Imperial Majesty[36] have ever had any troops on their own account there till the last year, & then only a regiment of foot, consisting of 2,000 men.

Resolv'd, that the forces supplied & paid for by her Majesty for the carrying on [of] the war in Spain, from the year 1705 to the year 1711, inclusive amounted to 57,973 men, besides 13 battalions & 18 squadrons, for which her Majesty has paid a subsidy to the Emperor.

Resolv'd, that the forces supplied by the States-General for the service in Spain, from the year 1705, to the year 1708, both inclusive, amounted to no more than 12,200 men, & that from the year 1708 to this present time, they have sent thither no forces at all.

Resolv'd, that at the beginning of this war, the subsidies were paid in equal proportions by her Majesty & the States-General, but her Majesty has since paid more than her proportion, 3,155,000 crowns.

Resolv'd, that the States-General have been deficient in their quotas for sea-service, in proportion to the number of ships provided by her Majesty, some years two thirds, & generally more than half of their quota.

Memorandum, that instead of the Queen's proportion of 2 fifths for the army in Flanders, she had 157,000 men to the Dutch 93,000. That instead of 5 eighths which ought to have been her proportion she had furnish'd 387 ships more than her proportion, which computed at a medium of 70 gun ships for the line of battle, amounted to £9,057,000. That she had paid more in Portugal, which[?] was £850,000, & in Spain of £330,000 ... more than she ought to have, the Dutch being so much defective, & had paid for subsidies more than her proportion £759,000, which in the whole amounted to £1,930,000 more than ought to have been the Queen's proportion.

February 18th [1712].   Resolved,

That it has appear'd to this committee, that the charge for transport service, in carrying on the war in Spain & Portugal, from 1702 to 1711, inclusive, amounted to £1,336,719:19:11.

Resolv'd, that it has appear'd to this committee, that there has been

---

[35] Leopold I and Joseph I.
[36] Charles VI.

paid by her Majesty for contingencies, bread, & bread waggons, forrage, & all other extraordinaries, both for the English & foreign troops, in Savoy, Piedmont, Italy, Spain, Portugal & Flanders, since June the 24th 1705, so far as the same has been return'd from abroad, several sums, amounting in the whole, to £3,487,002:00:11.

Resolved, that it has appear'd to this committee, that the charge of victualling the land forces for the service of the war in Spain and Portugal, has amounted to £583,770:08:06.

Resolved, that it has appear'd to this committee, that if the charge of her Majesty's ships & vessels, employed in the service of the war in Spain & Portugall, reckon'd after the rate of £4 a man a month, from the time they sailed from hence till they return'd, were lost, or put upon other services, amounted to £6,540,966:14:00. Total – £11,948,457.

February 25th [1712]. The reason of discharging the committee of elections of the petition referr'd to them from Lyn-Regis [King's Lynn], was grounded upon the vote of the House expelling Walpole, which the committee could not properly take cognizance of, & then the merits of the whole was likewise to be consider'd.[37]

PARLIAMENT WHICH MET 16th OF FEBRUARY 1713/14

March 18th [1714]. A debate arising upon the method of proceeding upon Mr Steel's[38] defence to the accusation of publishing severall seditious pamphlets, it was order'd after two hours arguing, that he shou'd not answer paragraph by paragraph, but make his whole defence at once, the particulars of which he was charged, having been read at the table some days before, & this time appointed for hearing him; being also the day [he] himself had agreed to, & consequently could not be supposed to be unprepar'd.

The next query was, whether he shou'd first make his defence, being apprised of the charge, or shou'd hear his accusation again open'd. But order'd he shou'd make his defence in the first place. For which a precedent was quoted in Mr Prinn's[39] case for publishing a seditious

---

[37] Despite Walpole's expulsion from the Commons and imprisonment in the Tower for corruption, the borough of King's Lynn persisted in re-electing him until 6 Mar., when the Commons finally declared that there were to be no further by-elections to replace him.

[38] Richard Steele of Llangunnor, Whig M.P. for Stockbridge, the famous essayist and playwright.

[39] William Prynne of Swainsrick, M.P. for Bath, the pamphleteer whose attacks on the government of Charles I cost him his ears in 1637, but who zealously supported the restoration of Charles II in 1660. In 1661 he was forced to admit his authorship of a pamphlet accusing borough M.P.s who had voted for the Corporation Act (a measure designed to exclude Dissenters from municipal office) of perjury, and was lucky to escape with a tearful, grovelling apology to the Commons and a severe reprimand from the Speaker.

paper in 1661, who after being heard in his place, then withdrew, which precedent was follow'd in this case, being a paralel.

The resolution after ten hours debate was, that a printed pamphlet entituled *the Englishman*, being the close of the paper so call'd, & one other pamphlet intituled *the Crisis*, written by R. Steel Esq. a member of this House; are scandalous & seditious libels, containing many expressions highly reflecting upon her Majesty, & upon the nobility, gentry, clergy & university[ies] of this kingdom, maliciously insinuating, that the Protestant succession in the house of Hanover is in danger under her Majesty's administration, & tending to alienate the affections of her Majesty's good subjects, & to create jealousies & divisions among them.

That he be for his offence in writing & publishing the said scandalous & seditious libels, be expell'd the House.[40]

[Speech on the schism bill, May–June 1714] *I shall ever think it my duty whilst I sitt here to add to the security of that excellent Church of which I profess my self a member by any good law which may prevent the teaching & the propagating any principles disagreable to those excellent doctrines taught in her. And I hope Sir, I shan't be understood to intend the weakning [of] the Toleration, let that be enjoyed which with convenient restrictions may lessen evill & remove some inconveniencies; but all can never be taken away without another sort of education. And as the Toleration was first intended for those unhappy scrupulous consciences only, who had then the misfortune to dissent from us, I believe no gentleman here will believe it was intended to propagate the schism.*

If it be a natural right to chuse what religion he will profess, there is yet no right of nature which I know of but what is limitable to the public good & forfeitable by the abuse of it. And when the public peace is hasarded, the safety of the government endanger'd, when 'tis apparent religion itself is damnified, [by] the persons professing those doctrines, the propagating [of] those doctrines ought to be restrained.

[Speech proposing bill to augment clergy stipends, May 1715] *Sir, you had the last year a bill brought into Parliament for the augmentation of poor vicarages & chapelries.[41] But being brought in late in that session, it drop'd rather for want of time to perfect it, then from any dislike shew'd to the bill.*

And when gentlemen reflect on the low condition of many of our clergy who are really men of learning & merit, who might appear with great advantages, & be much more capable of doing that good they really wish to do, was their support in

---

[40] Kaye was clearly present at the debate, and as he does not figure in the lists of those who spoke or voted in Steele's favour (W. Cobbett, *Parliamentary History of England* (36 vols, 1806–20), vi. col. 1282–3), it seems reasonable to assume that he voted for Steele's expulsion.

[41] I have been unable to find any record of the introduction of such a bill.

any degree equal to their office, I am confident there is not one gentleman here who will not encourage such a bill.

And, that no gentleman may suppose there is more design'd then what will provide for a reasonable & indeed a necessary maintenance for 'em, & that nothing is intended that shall be a force upon the majority of the people, I will open the substance of the bill as I presume it may be drawn. And that is by inclosing such common grounds as may be proper for it; & which I take to be the interest of England in gentlemen to do, if wee had hands to cultivate 'em, but in this case, not to exceed a reasonable number of acres with the consent of such a proportionat number of those who have freeholds, & with the consent of the lord of the manor, so that there will be no constraint upon the majority, no force upon the land.

[Speech urging Commons to proceed with bill augmenting the stipends of poor clergymen, July 1715] *Sir, I hop'd a Bill of this nature, which is providing maintenance for the poorer clergy, for which there is so great an occasion, would have mett with no opposition from this House of Commons.*

I hope gentlemen will allow me to know something of my own country. And I will take upon me to say, that the small endowments of several vicarages & many chapelries there are so far from giving an envied plenty to their ministers, that [they] scarse afford a competent substance.

Gentlemen say 'tis giving away part of the people's properties without their consent. Sir, is not every new law allmost you make, an alteration of property in some kind or other? But Sir, this [is] not compulsive upon the lord of the manor, but gives it in such a way, as the people themselves are the doers of it, as well as the petitioners for it.

And I hope it is a design so well becoming this House that I shall take the liberty to move you that the bill may be committed.[42]

[January] 9th **[1719].** Upon the motion for an instruction for a clause, that every person in order to his qualification [for office], shall acknowledge that the holy scriptures of the Old and New Testament were given by divine inspiration, & shall acknowledge his firm faith & belief in the ever blessed trinity.[43] Upon the previous question, ayes 136, noes 234.

Upon a amendment in the committee, to divide the two Bills, repealing the Schism, but retaining the Occasional Bill. Ayes 170, noes 221.

I shoud not have troubled the House so early in this debate, had I not reason to believe that this opportunity may, perhaps, be the last I may ever have of speaking in the defence of our constitution, & of that church, wich has been so long the bulwark against popery & atheism ['and preserver of the true religion, taught as

---

[42] The bill appears to have lapsed at this stage.
[43] A Tory attempt to exclude Deists and anti-Trinitarian Christians from office.

derived from the gospel in its greatest purity', erased]. And I wish it may not be for that reason, that it is now attack'd. For, when wee are told that there is no occasion for any directors of our consciences in the explanation of its doctrines, or any occasion of canons or discipline, but that every man is to go his own way to heaven or to perdition, & is justified in good meaning,[44] however averse to admitt a better information, or however erroneous; I can look upon the influence of such positions in no other light then that formerly exploded doctrine of the Church of Rome has taught, of an equivocation & a mental reservation; which as they can never be explain'd without a liberty of extracating themselves by one or other new invented system of divinity; so the ill consequences of 'em can never be provided against; but by the laws which the establish'd government has an undoubted authority of prescribing. That such a power in government is necessary, will not I believe be disputed. That this was the design of the Act of Uniformity and afterwards of the Corporation & Test Acts, will I believe be as little question'd. That the confirming these by what is commonly call'd the Occasional Act is undoubted. And shall wee now think ourselves so much wiser then our forefathers, to do that at once which shall destroy the fabrick they have built & have been so many years endeavouring to strengthen? And shall wee do this at a time, when wee have such open declarations of attacking the establish'd church, when an herald from the enemy shall publickly declare they rejoyce to see the foundations shaken, & the fabrick sinking?[45] Have wee not reason to be upon our guard? When no concession whatever were or are, & from thence wee may reasonably conclude, ever will be satisfactory, without giving up the whole. Which to me, implies the same thing as to say, 'tis not the liturgy, 'tis not the discipline, but 'tis the power wee contend for; tho it be at the expence of religion itself.

But there is another argument used, that 'tis not only a natural law, which is unchangeable, but a natural right every man has to chuse what religion he will profess.[46] It may be so to a natural savage, bred without any other light but that of nature. But there is no right of nature, that I know of, but what is limitable to the public good, and forfeitable by the abuse of it.

And tho toleration with convenient restrictions might lessen the evil & remove most of its inconveniencies, tho all can never be taken away without another sort of education then the next generation may have; and even under good limitations may increase the licentiousness of the age both in doctrine & practice; yet when 'tis apparent that religion itself is damified, the safety of all government endanger'd, & the publick peace subject daily to be broken, by any of the many new doctrines taught amongst us; the persons professing those doctrines have forfeited their natural

---

[44] Possibly a reference to Bishop Benjamin Hoadley's controversial Erastian sermon on the theme, 'my kingdom is not of this world', preached before George I on 31 Mar. 1717 (and subsequently published as *The Nature of the Kingdom of Christ*), which sparked the Bangorian controversy. See J.C.D. Clark, *English Society 1688–1832* (1985), pp.300–1.

[45] Possibly a reference to the anti-episcopal pamphleteers Thomas Gordon and John Trenchard.

[46] A reference to the writings of Thomas Chubb the Deist pamphleteer.

freedom, so far as not only to be subject to the laws, but to be for ever unqualified & incapable of bearing any trust in the execution of 'em.

October 31 [1721]. 14,294 men voted for Guards & Garrisons. A division. Ayes 121, noes 37.

Memorandum: 2,200 of these are in Scotland, & there are besides 5,546 men abroad.

Estimate of the debt of the Navy given in now was before this reign [£]151,705, & since this £1,874,158.

Memorandum: the expence of 40,000 men in Flanders[47] cost at first no more than £700,000 tho afterwards it swell'd to near a million.

Hints about a standing Army

Those considered disaffected: sure it must not be to the antient limited legal monarchy, it must be a French fashion'd monarchy, where the king has all power & the people no security. If by it all princes have not become absolute? If without it [a standing army] any? Whether our enemies shall conquer us is uncertain; but whether an army will enslave us, reason will not suffer us to doubt.

I had rather pay double to any charge in improving our militia from whom I fear nothing, then half so much to those from whom our countreys [i.e. counties] must fear every thing.

No fear of invasion in a vacancy of Parliament during the septennial bill.[48]

The freedom of this kingdom depends on the people's choice of the House of Commons, who are a part of the legislature & have the sole power of giving money. Were this a true representative & free from external force or private bribery, nothing could pass but what is thought to be for the publick good. For their own interest is so interwoven with the people's that if they act of themselves, they must act for the common interest, & if a few should think it their present interest to abuse their power, it will be the interest of the rest to punish 'em for it.

[Alternative version of paragraph above:] As the model of the constitution of England is adapted to every part of the constitution acting agreably to its own interest, the abuses [that have] crept into it, ought to put us upon our guard against encroachments in any part of the constituents, & as the freedom of this kingdom depends on the people's chusing the House of Commons, were this a true representative, free from external force & secret bribery, nothing could pass there, but what they thought was for the publick advantage. Their own interest is so interwoven with that of the people, that if they act of themselves, they must act for the common interest and if they can be preserv'd free from corruption, they will keep every body else so.

Our constitution seems to have provided for it; for when the civil offices were possess'd by the Lords, the Commons were severe inquisitors into their actions. But if the crown by increase of [the number of] offices, disposed amongst the Commons

---

[47] During the War of the Spanish Succession.
[48] The act of Parliament passed in 1716 extending the maximum life of a Parliament to 7 years.

to engage 'em – I won't say to corrupt 'em – & had the power of adding the military interest in Parliament to it, what is to be expected, from the behaviour of such who may accept 'em, in one capacity? Or from the others, whose declared honour, according to the modern notion of the army, is to obey all orders without any distinction, whether those are for, or destructive to the fundamentals of their government.

When they distort their reason to find arguments, & make the abuses they had been complaining of precedents to justify their proceedings, [it] must be regardless of reputation. But there is nothing so extravagant wee may not expect to see, when early patriots become servile flatterers, old Commonwelths men declare for prerogative & Admirals against a fleet.[49]

[A lengthy, reign by reign, enumeration of the growth of the standing army probably followed at this point]

Read the history of Louis the 11th of France, who notwithstanding his extravagance & lewdness, severely forbade his soldiers to do any injury; [and ordered them] to behave peacably in quarters; & punished the disobedient with the utmost rigour. And this was the reason his kingdom flourish'd prety well, tho sufficiently loaded with taxes.

Thus, sometimes, the ill qualities of a monarch are compensated with others which may make the people happy . . .

AN ARGUMENT SHOWING A STANDING ARMY IS INCONSISTENT WITH A FREE GOVERNMENT & DESTRUCTIVE TO THE CONSTITUTION OF THE ENGLISH MONARCHY.

The force to consist of the same persons as have the property, such cannot act to the disadvantage of the constitution, unless one could suppose 'em felons de se, which is a violence against nature.

Patriots for liberty who would hardly afford the crown its due prerogative, apostates, excused by saying, 'if you don't comply, others may & will be caress'd & wee turned out', as if arbitrary government was different in their hands from what it is in others.

Miserable examples of too credulous generosity.

[A] colony giving their slaves their arms to carry were cut off by 'em.

An army different in a free monarchy from a Commonwealth, where the people nominate, discard & punish the Generals. But the King is perpetual & however he may model it, it would be call'd treason to oppose him.

If a few in an invasion can oppose the King, nobility, & people, & militia united, what may it not against the last, supported by the former, now as well as ever. The continuation now an establishment for ever. The very discontents they may make, an argument for continuing 'em [the army].

---

[49] This may be a jibe at Sir Robert Walpole, the earl of Sunderland and Sir George Byng respectively.

Charles the 2nd has the first Guards besides the Pensioners & Yeomen.

Has not he the power of raising money to whom no one dares refuse it?

All methods to make the militia more serviceable discouraged, why may not the nobility, gentry & such be as well trusted & be capable as their meanest servants, who hires into the service?

Army and militia together incompatible.

Did either York or Lancaster do it?

The Pensionary Parliament[50] address'd against the Guards.

The capricious humours of the soldiery have produced more sudden Revolutions than in unarm'd Governments.

Of 26 Roman Emperors, 16 deposed by their own army.

In 1629 3,000 foot only, in the 1st project of [creating] an army.

The Parliaments [who are] the keepers of English liberties, can ill perform that office when they have parted with their power into other hands.

If wee contribute to our ruine by our own folly & for seeming but a false interest, it will hereafter carry a severe sting with it.

England can never be destroy'd but by it self, not the constitution, but by Parliament.

The Romans well knowing such men & liberty to be incompatible, & yet being under a necessity of having armies, made frequent changes of the men, permitting 'em after some time in the army to return to their possessions & trades. How true this judgement was; observe the [men] who subverted that government found themselves obliged to continue the same soldiers alwaies in constant pay.

[50] The Cavalier Parliament of 1661–79.

KAYE DIARY INDEX

IV
Letters of Bolingbroke
to the Earl of Orrery
1712-13

Edited by
H. T. Dickinson

INTRODUCTION

Henry St. John, Viscount Bolingbroke, was one of the Secretaries of State in Queen Anne's Tory administration of 1710–14 which sought to bring an end to the increasingly burdensome War of the Spanish Succession. Employing somewhat dubious means, he and his ministerial colleagues eventually made peace with France by the Treaty of Utrecht in 1713; a treaty which paid more attention to the interests of Great Britain than to those of her allies, the Dutch and Austrians. In seeking peace at almost any price Bolingbroke and his colleagues faced a particular problem with the former Spanish territory of the Southern Netherlands (or Flanders). The Dutch were particularly interested in this territory because they hoped to secure possession of strong fortresses there which would provide them with a secure barrier against a sudden attack by the French. The Austrians, for their part, hoped to gain this territory as part of the Emperor's inheritance of former Spanish possessions. Britain herself was concerned to serve her allies in this territory at least. She also had commercial interests in Flanders and had long sought an effective barrier to French efforts to expand into the Low Countries. These concerns were reflected in Bolingbroke's correspondence with Charles, Earl of Orrery, one of his Tory friends, who was appointed in 1711 as the Queen's envoy-extraordinary to the States General in The Hague and to the Council of Flanders in Brussels. Orrery served in this capacity for most of 1711. In late 1712 he returned to these duties and served there for a further year.

A few of Bolingbroke's letters to Orrery, during his two periods of service at The Hague and in Brussels, were published nearly two hundred years ago in the *Letters and Correspondence of Bolingbroke*, ed. Gilbert Parke (4 vols., London, 1798). In 1927 and 1933 the Bodleian Library at Oxford purchased two letter-books containing copies of some fifty-three letters written by Henry St. John (before he became Viscount Bolingbroke) to Orrery between 1709 and 1711. I edited these letter-books (MS. Eng.misc.e.180 and MS. Eng.lett.e.4) for the Royal Historical Society and they were published in *Camden Miscellany*, 4th series, volume 14 (1975), 137–99. Early in 1989 the Bodleian Library acquired a third letter-book containing copies of twenty letters sent by Bolingbroke to Orrery during his second period of service in the Low Countries from 1712 to 1713. Sixteen of these letters were apparently unknown to Gilbert Parke and are missing from his edition of 1798.

This newly-acquired letter-book, catalogued as MS. Eng.lett.e.214, has 'Orrery 1732' written on the inside cover and notes in pencil which suggest that it was once owned by W.J. Armytage of Halston, Co. Westmeath, Ireland, was in the library of Dr. T.P.C. Kirkpatrick up to 1955 and was purchased by a Mr. Figgis in a Sotheby's sale in 1956. The letters copied into it are written only on the odd-numbered pages. The even-numbered pages were left blank. The contents of this letter-book are printed here by kind permission of Mary Clapinson, Keeper of Western Manuscripts, and of the Bodley's Librarian.

LETTERS OF BOLINGBROKE
TO THE EARL OF ORRERY

[p.1] Copies of Mr Secretary St. John (afterwards Lord Bolingbroke)'s Letters to the Rt Hono^{ble}: Charles Earl of Orrery written in the years 1712 & 1713.

I.

Whitehall. 30th: April 1712

My Lord,

I send your Lordship for yor information the enclosed extract of the Earl Strafford's letter of the 3^d of May concerning the garrison which remaines at present in Ostend.

I am, My Lord,
Your Lordship's most faithful
humble servant
H. S^t: John

[p.3] Here follows the extract of a letter from his Excellency the Earl of Strafford[1] dated at Utrecht the 3^d May 1712; (mentioned to be inclosed to Earl of Orrery in the preceding letter.)

I am informed that Monsr: Wrangle[2] who now commands the Walloons in the Spanish Low Countryes, has lately order'd the only battalion of Walloons that was in Ostend to march from thence to the army; so that there now remaines none but Dutch in that garrison. The Pensionary[3] pretended to me to know nothing of it, & to make slight of it. I told him, tho' I was assured it was done without reflection, being we were able to make reprisal in other places, if we found it was other ways; yet at this time this had better have been let alone, because it may give a handle for malicious people to make reflections, that this was done at the time when the Queen had insinuated she thought she

[1] Thomas Wentworth (1672–1739), 3rd Earl of Strafford, was a soldier and diplomat. He was made British Ambassador Extraordinary at The Hague and one of the two British plenipotentiaries at the peace negotiations at Utrecht in 1711.

[2] Fabian, Count van Wrangel (d.1737), was a Swedish-born professional soldier who served first with the Dutch, then with the Imperial, forces. He was subsequently an Imperial Field Marshal and Governor of Brussels.

[3] Anthonie Heinsius (1641–1720) was Grand Pensionary of Holland from 1689 and first minister of the States General.

might reasonably [p.5] expect, for the security of the trade of her subjects that Ostend should be garrison'd with troops: & especially since Wrangle was one known to be extreamly favour'd by them, & was at the Hague att the time Prince Eugene[4] was last there, as if he was to have taken instructions from thence.

2.

Whitehall. 8th May 1712

My Lord,

I am sorry I disappointed yor: Lords^p before you went into the country; at your return I must endeavour to make you amends.

I shall have this week ready those instructions, which her Majesty has order'd to be prepar'd for your Lordship; of which you are besides your general orders to act upon; so that if you are delay'd for no other reason [p.7] your Lordship may soon be on your way to Brussells.

It is certainly true, my Lord, that our affairs are & have been in great confusion. Those, who are most employ'd, feel sufficiently the load & burthen of it. But this ought to be the less surprizing, when it is consider'd what an entire change has been wrought this winter in the system of the war, & in the measures of all our foreign negotiations.

I hope, we see daylight, & I make no doubt but we shall extricate our country from the difficultys which she groans under. After that is done, I shall be of your Lordship's mind; & chuse to retire, much rather than to act in a publick station.

I have done Mr Cecil[5] all the good offices in my power; but I must say, that the Duke of Ormonde[6] & my Lord Lansdowne[7] must be helpfull in matters of the army, w^{ch}: are entirely out of my province. I do not know what [p.9] he means by complaining he cannot get his commission out of my office. I remember, I got one sign'd for him, but I remember too that it was stopp'd on his Colonel's application; &

---

[4] François Eugène, Prince of Savoy-Carignon, was French in origin, but was the greatest general serving in the Imperial forces.

[5] William Cecil, a kinsman of the Countess of Orrery, had fought at Malplaquet. Formerly a Captain in Orrery's regiment of foot, he was eventually made a brevet Lieutenant-Colonel on 1 July 1712. He was sent to the Tower in 1744 as a Jacobite conspirator.

[6] James Butler (1685–1745), 2nd Duke of Ormonde, commanded the British forces in Flanders after the dismissal of Marlborough. In May 1712, he was given the notorious 'restraining orders' not to attack the French army.

[7] George Granville (1667–1735), Baron Lansdowne, was made Secretary at War in 1710 and was one of the 12 Tory peers created at the end of 1711 to ensure that the peace negotiations were accepted by the House of Lords. An ally of Bolingbroke's, he became Comptroller of the Household in 1712 and Treasurer of the Household in 1713. He was later arrested as a Jacobite.

therefore it would have been proper whilst Sybourg[8] was here, to have stirr'd in this affair.

As to Mr Fenton[9], I will do him all the service I possibly can; & I dare say, my Lord Treasurer[10] will bestow some employment on him.

I am ever, my Lord,
Your Lordship's obedient
& most humble servant
H. S^t: John

3. [p.11]

Windsor Castle. 25 Octo^r: 1712

My Lord,
I have acquainted my Lord Treasurer, as you desired me to do, that you cannot goe over unless the arrear so often promis'd be paid you. He commands me to let you know that 2000 l. shall be paid the next week; and that the remainder you shall have the week after. I thought it proper to lose no time in giving you this account, because I know that the publick service, of which only I can judge, requires your presence instantly abroad.

I shall not return from hence till Tuesday. Could you not be here to morrow, or Monday, to take your leave of the Queen?

Adieu; I am in great hurry, but with the utmost truth, my dear Lord
Your ever faithfull
Bolingbroke

4. [p.13]

Whitehall. 14 Nov^r: 1712

My Lord,
Finding by the last letters from Holland, that a deputation of the States of Brabant are gone to the Hague, & intend to stay there till your Lordship's arrival, in order to discourse you upon the inauguration of the Emperour[11], & some other matters relating to the Spanish Low

---

[8] William Cecil had served as a Major General in Charles de Sibourg's regiment of foot since December 1710. Sibourg, said to be an illegitimate son of the Duke of Schomberg, had fought at Blenheim, Ramillies, Oudernarde and Malplaquet. He had replaced Orrery as Colonel in the Duke of Argyll's regiment of foot in 1710.

[9] Elijah Fenton (1683–1730) was secretary to the Earl of Orrery in Flanders. He later gained some fame as a poet and as the headmaster of Sevenoaks grammar school.

[10] Robert Harley (1661–1724), 1st Earl of Oxford, was Lord Treasurer and head of the Tory ministry 1710–14.

[11] Charles VI (1685–1740) succeeded to the Imperial throne in April 1711 on the death of his brother. He was the Austrian claimant to the throne of Spain.

Countryes; I thought it proper to acquaint your Lordship with her Majesty's sense upon those points, that you may be prepared to answer accordingly.

As to the inauguration of the Emperour, which they seem to insist so much upon, your Lordship will please to say, that we are now coming to a conclusion of the peace, & by consequence to a general settlement; so that their government will be soon establish'd as they [p.15] themselves desire; that therefore they are a little too precipitate in their measures, since if the inauguration be a work of some time (as her Majesty is inclin'd to think it will prove) it cannot be done so soon as these Deputyes urge to have it; & if it be not a work of time, they are still in the wrong to insist so rashly on a thing, which will be a natural consequence of the approaching peace. In the mean time, should they neglect to make a regular provision for the subsistance of the imperial troops that are to remaine among them, their country would be in a very miserable state.

As to the proposal of giving the government of Gand[12] to Monsr: D'Audigne[13], your Lordship will say to the Dutch ministers; that if the Queen consents to that disposition, she will insist that Mr Devenish shall be Governour of Bruges, & that some establishment shall be found for the Marquis de Paleotti[14] which her Majesty thinks may very well be done by dividing D'Aubigne's regiment (in case he be made Governour of Gand) & by forming one [p.17] out of it for the Marquis de Paleotti.

I am, my Lord,
Your Lordship's most
obedient humble servant
Bolingbroke

The new project of a Treaty of Succession & Barrier[15] is herewith sent to your Lordship, w^{ch}: compleats the papers I am order'd to put into your hands.

---

[12] Ghent.

[13] Mons. Dodigny and Mons. Davenish became governors of Ghent and Bruges respectively in 1713. Both were regarded as political upstarts with poor reputations. See John Drummond's letter to the Earl of Oxford, 30 Nov./10 Dec. 1713 in HMC, *Portland Mss*, v, 366.

[14] Ferdinando, Marquis de Paleotti, an Italian adventurer, was the brother of the Duke of Shrewsbury's wife. Despite his poor reputation Orrery secured him the command of an Imperial regiment in British pay serving in Flanders.

[15] For the prolonged negotiations on the Dutch Barrier see Roderick Geikie and Isabel A. Montgomery, *The Dutch Barrier* (Cambridge, 1930).

5.

Whitehall. 9th Decem^r: 1712

My Lord,

I have two letters from yor: Lordship to acknowledge, the last whereof is of the 13th of this month N. S. and both which I have had the honour to lay before her Majesty who your Lordship may be sure, was very glad to find that our new project of a Treaty of [p.19] Succession & Barrier is likely to be accepted by the Dutch; & that the Council of State promise, at least, to conform themselves to whatever you desire. The same consideration will, I believe, in the end determine both the governors in Holland, & the governors in Flanders, to submit to the Queen's measures: & that is plainly this; their perverseness & obstinacy may create to us trouble for a time, but must necessarily conclude in their own ruine.

The Queen, my Lord, approves of your going to Brussells[16], according to the resolution which you had taken, & which, I suppose, you have before this time executed. If you had continued at the Hague, you could not have arriv'd at a certainty concerning their resolution on the grand affair in less than a fortnight: & as your Lordship observes, your other business would not allow so long a delay. Besides which, as your Lordship has, I make no doubt, in very explicite termes laid open to the Dutch [p.21] ministers what your orders are, & upon what conditions only they can expect your assistance, & as your Lordship will not fail strictly to pursue that measure, your being at Brussels may, perhaps, have even a greater influence on the deliberations of the Provinces of Holland, than your continuance at the Hague.

Your Lordship has now in your hands an affair of great importance & delicacy to manage; &, I am very sure, it will be supported with all the spirit, & negociated with all the address, which it deserves.

I know that you are so much inclin'd to serve the Duke of Shrewsbury[17], that I need not recommend the Marquis Paleotti's interest to you. Allow me to put you in mind of poor Capt. Platt[18], who has really some merit, & I fear, no fortune.

I am with very great truth, my Lord,
Your Lordship's most faithfull

---

[16] Orrery went to act as joint governor of the Southern Netherlands, together with a Dutch diplomat.

[17] Charles Talbot (1660–1718), 1st Duke of Shrewsbury, was married to Adelaide Paleotti. He was on good terms with Orrery.

[18] An experienced professional soldier Captain John Platt served in Orrery's own regiment of foot (as did his son of the same name). On 1 January 1712 he had been promoted a brevet major, but by 1713 he was on half-pay after his regiment had been disbanded.

& most humble servant
Bolingbroke

6. [p.23]

Whitehall. 2d Jan'ry 1712/3

My Lord,

I am to acknowledge your Lordship's letters of the 28th: & 31st of Decem^r:, & of the 4th: & 7th: instant; to which I have not troubled you with regular answers, since no alteration has happen'd in the state of affairs, to make any instructions necessary besides those you carryed with you.

The behaviour of the Council of State[19] is, indeed, very extravagant, & is in this respect the less justifiable, that for some years past the Queen has employ'd her authority as a screen for them against those hardships which they apprehended from another quarter, & even in the project for a Treaty of Succession & Barrier lately sent to the States, the interest of the Emperour & of the Netherlands has been so much consider'd, that it is for the most part agreeable to those remarks [p.25] which his Imperial Majesty's own ministers made on the former Barrier Treaty.

I think, there can be no doubt of the Emperour's being willing to accept the Spanish Low Countryes, & as he cannot but be sensible, that the manner in which he will have them depends on the good harmony between him & Her Majesty; so by our last letters from Holland, & from the language of his minister here, I find, he now takes the turn of desiring to be reconciled to the Queen, as well as the States, & thereby to procure something more than the empty name of sovereignty; &, I hope, the people of the Netherlands will be of the same mind, & not give your Lordship & the Dutch minister[20] any occasion to apply violent remedies, which must, however, be made use of, if mild ones prove ineffectual.

The project for reestablishing commerce betwixt Great Britaine, Ireland, & Flanders, is sent to the Lords Commissioners for Trade to see what observations they may have to make upon it. I don't pretend to be master of [p.27] that matter myself but, I think, I can see upon a cursory view that several of the points contain'd in it are such as are rather to be wish'd, than hop'd for; which is generally the case of all representations from merchants relating to trade, wherein they are concern'd.

[19] The official governing body in the Southern Netherlands.

[20] The Dutch governor, serving in the Southern Netherlands as joint governor with Orrery, was Johan van den Bergh. See note 37.

The Duke of Argyll[21] arriv'd here this day.
I am, my Lord, with very great truth,
Your Lordship's most humble
& obedient servant
Bolingbroke

7.

Whitehall. 20 Jan'ry 1712/3

My Dear Lord,

I shall not be able till Friday's post to say anything to you either of publick business, or of your own affairs. In the mean [p.29] time I thought proper not to lose this opportunity of sending two blank proxies[22], for fear of accidents, to you.

Our parliament certainly meets the 3^d of February[23]; &, I believe, we shall have a battle the first day.

Ever yours most faithfully,
Bolingbroke

8.

Whitehall. 3^d Feb'ry 1712/3

My Lord,

I am to acknowledge the receipt of your Lordship's letters of the 26th: & 30th: of January, & of the 6th: instant, N. S.

I have by her Majesty's command sent all the papers concerning commerce, which came enclosed, to the Board of Trade, that by considering thereof they may be the better [p.31] enabled to form instructions for her Majesty's commissaries, who are by the 13th: article of the Barrier Treaty to meet, in fifteen days after the ratification of it at Brussells, in order to adjust & settle all points relating to the trade of the Netherlands. It is her Majesty's intention, my Lord, that these gentlemen should proceed upon the general principle of reducing everything in the Spanish Low-Countryes to the foot on which it stood

---

[21] John Campbell (1680–1743), 2nd Duke of Argyll, who had fought with distinction in Flanders, was jealous of Marlborough and had drifted temporarily towards the Tory ministry. He was also on good personal terms with Orrery.

[22] The Tory ministry's majority in the House of Lords was still insecure, and Tory peers who could not attend the House were asked to fill in proxies allowing political allies to vote for them in their absence.

[23] Delays in the peace negotiations in fact resulted in parliament not being summoned until as late as 9 April 1713.

in the time of Charles the Second late King of Spain[24]. And as to those places, which are now to be yielded to the Emperour, & were not in possession of the aforesaid King, the Queen's sense is, that consideration should be had of the manner, in which the trade has been carried on, whilst they were under the dominion of France; & that it should be continued in the same, or altered, as shall be found most convenient.

The Queen is sorry to find, that matters in the Netherlands continue in so great perplexity; but entirely approves your Lo$^{p's}$: resolution [p.33] of avoiding extremityes; for since the Emperour is now shortly to become master of these provinces, & her Majesty to rid her hands of an invidious government, which the scituation of affairs made it necessary for her to hold some time, it is certainly most eligible that everything should be amicably compos'd.

Your Lordship having dated your last proxy, & the Queen's gout having occasion'd a further prorogation of the parliament to the 17th: of this month, I would not take upon me to alter the date, but chose to send you another; (which comes here enclosed,). Your Lordship will please to return it sign'd, leaving the daye in blank, which is fix'd for opening the session, & likewise the day of your Lordship's signing.

I am ever with true respect, my Lord,
Your Lordship's most humble
& obedient servant
Bolingbroke

9. [P.35]

Whitehall. 6th Feb'ry 1712/3

My Lord,

I have her Majesty's commands to write to all her ministers abroad to endeavour to get Mr Maccartney[25] secured, who, we find, by information on oath is escaped beyond the seas; & was met at Hanover in his way to Vienna. My Lords the plenipotentiaries at Utrecht[26] have

---

[24] Charles II of Spain had died without a direct heir in 1700 and this had precipitated the War of the Spanish Succession.

[25] General George Maccartney (1660?–1730) had been dismissed from his military command after the fall of Marlborough in 1711. He acted as second to Lord Mohun in the fatal duel with the Tory Duke of Hamilton on 15 November 1712. Fearing arrest he fled to the continent and did not surrender himself for trial until after the fall of the Tory ministry. See H.T. Dickinson, 'The Mohun-Hamilton Duel: Personal Feud or Whig Plot?', *Durham University Journal*, lvii (1965), 159–65.

[26] The British plenipotentiaries at Utrecht were Strafford (see note 1) and John Robinson (1650–1723), who had been abroad for many years. He was made Bishop of Bristol in 1710 and Lord Privy Seal in 1711. A loyal supporter of Robert Harley, Earl of Oxford, he became Bishop of London in 1714.

directions to apply to the Imperial ministers upon this occasion. I hardly think, that Mr Maccartney will ever come into the country where your Lordship is; yet, in pursuance to her Maj$^{ty's}$: general orders, I am to acquaint you with her pleasure on this subject; & I doubt not but that, if an occasion offers, your Lordship will use your utmost endeavours to have a criminal of so black a dye seized & delivered up to justice.

I am, my Lord,
Your Lordship's most obed^t:
humble servant
Bolingbroke

10. [p.37]

Whitehall. 3^d Mar. 1712/3

My Lord,

Your Lordship's letter of the 6th: instant N. S. is come to my hands.

Her Majesty, upon considering several of your Lordship's former dispatches, had begun to think it was impossible for her to expect any good effects from continuing to keep that share in the government of the Low Countryes, w^{ch}: she has hitherto held; since those people seem to have shaken off all obedience both to her & the States. The Queen, therefore, my Lord, had thoughts of directing your Lordship to leave Brussells, & come to Ghent, & after a short stay there to execute some orders, which she would have sent you, her Maj^{ty}: intended to have call'd you home.

The Declaration lately made by Count Sinzendorff[27] (whereof your Lordship has without doubt been inform'd by the Queen's plenipotentiaries) that the Councill of State at Brussells has [p.39] not the least authority from the Emperour to act in that station, gives the Queen some hopes that these gentlemen will become as tractable as to carry on the publick service till the country is deliver'd up to the Emperour, & all matters adjusted with her Majesty & the States; which cannot now be vary far off, since (as your Lordship must have heard,) the great bottom of the peace is at last wound up, & there remaine only a few loose threads to be put in order.

As to Messrs: D'Audegnie, Paleotti, & Devenish, her Majesty thinks your Lordship judges very right; & that such a provisional clause as you propose would be very proper to be inserted in the treaty with the Emperour for the delivering up of the Netherlands; not only to secure

---

[27] Philipp Ludwig (1671–1742), Count Sinzendorff, was the Imperial ambassador at The Hague and was involved in the negotiations over the Dutch Barrier.

these gentlemen the full effect of the orders given by her Majesty, & the States, in their favour; but also on account of any other things which ought to have been done, & w^{ch}: have been neglected.

I find by my Lords the plenipotentiaryes letters, that both the Imperialists & Dutch are ready at Utrecht to treat about those points, [p.41] which by the Barrier Treaty are to be referr'd to commissaryes, and if they could be settled there, it might probably prove as usefull, & a more expeditious method than the other. In a very few days one of the two will be resolv'd upon, & yor: Lordship shall not fail of hearing from me upon that subject.

I am, my Lord,
Your Lordship's most humble
& obedient servant,
Bolingbroke

11. [pp.41–45] This letter, dated 6 March 1712/13, is printed in *Letters and Correspondence of Bolingbroke*, ed. Gilbert Parke (4 vols., London, 1798), iii, 491–2.

12. [pp.45–49] This letter, dated 24 March 1712/13, is printed in Parke, iii, 518–21.

13. [p.51]

Whitehall. 26 Mar. 1713

My Lord,

I am to acknowledge the receipt of your Lordship's letters of the 20th:, 23^d:, 27th:, & 30th: instant N. S.

The Queen very much approves the method which your Lordship & the minister of Holland[28] took, of removing those members of the Council of State from their employments, who had continued to behave themselves in so turbulent & seditious a manner. The answer, which these gentlemen return'd to the requisition given in by your Lordship, & the Dutch minister, was an aggravation of their former behaviour: & the regard for the Emperour w^{ch}: used to be the pretence of their mutiny, could be now no longer urg'd in excuse, since his Imperial Majesty has entirely disavow'd their conduct. Her Majesty therefore thinks, the chastisement, which was given them for their disobedience, was the least that could be done for the vindication of her honour, & that of [p.53] the States General, as well as for the peace of the country.

Your Lordship may very easily imagine, that, by the accounts w^{ch}: the Queen receives from you, she is very desirous to rid her hands of

[28] Johan van den Bergh. See note 37.

all concern in a government, which has only expos'd her to indignities, & from whence the interest of others is all she has to hope for. Her Majesty is therefore determin'd, as soon as possible, to put this country into the Emperour's hands; which nothing can retard, but the obligation she is under by the Barrier Treaty to see the interests of Holland, with respect to their Barrier, previously adjusted with his Imperial Majesty. And these, the Queen thinks, are in a fair way of being settled, since the great article of the upper quarter of Guelder has been compounded between the Imperialists & Dutch at Utrecht, as her Maj$^{ty's}$: ministers there inform her.

Your Lordship will see, by an extract of my letter to the pleni-potentiaries, on this head, (which comes inclos'd) more fully what the Queen's intentions are; & your Lordship will accordingly please to prepare for your return [p.55] home; and to consider whether any form, or what sort of one, must be observ'd upon the Queen & States resigning the administration of the government of the Low Countries to the Emperour.

Your Lordship may expect by the next opportunity such letters as are necessary for you to have upon your quitting your post.

    I am, my Lord, with much respect & truth,
        Your Lordship's obedient &
           most humble servant
           Bolingbroke

Here follows the extract of a letter from my Lord Bolingbroke to the Lords Plenipotentiaries, dated at Whitehall the 26th: of March 1713; mention'd to be inclosed in the preceding letter.

The Queen, my Lords, is very uneasie to be longer concern'd in so troublesom & unprofitable a matter, as the government of the Spanish Low Countries. My Lord Orrery is desirous to return home, & [p.57] her Majesty is equally so to recall him; but then she would at the same time give up to the Emperour her share of that authority w^{ch}: she exercises for him. A commission is preparing for Mr Drummond[29] to be the Queen's commissioner for regulating & securing our commerce in those countryes. He is to proceed in this business under your Lo^{ps}: at Utrecht; & the Treaties of Commerce, w^{ch}: now subsist with Spain, & w^{ch}: must, I suppose, be made wth: the Emperour, will be likewise your Lordships' care: so that, upon this account, my Lord Orrery's longer continuance at Brussels is unnecessary, & British garrisons, remaining

---

[29]John Drummond, a Scots merchant who had lived many years in Amsterdam, acted as an unofficial agent for the British government from 1710. Fluent in Dutch, he later negotiated at Utrecht to secure British commercial interests in the Southern Netherlands. For his role, see many of his letters to the Tory ministers in *Letters and Correspondence of Bolingbroke*, ed. Gilbert Parke and HMC, *Portland Mss*, iv–v.

in Ghent & Bruges, are sufficient securities that matters of trade will be adjusted to satisfaction. The agreement between his Imperial Majesty and the States General, as to the Barrier of the latter, we suppose to be as good as finish'd; since the great dispute about Guelder is accommodated. The Queen would therefore have your Lordships earnestly press the States to finish this matter, that so she & they may jointly give up to the Emperour [p.59] what is to belong to him. The result of these applications, & the judgement which you shall make of the time at which the Emperour may be put into possession of the government of these countryes, your Lordships will be pleased to communicate to the Earl of Orrery, to whom I shall send in a day or two all the dispatches necessary for him to have before he leaves that post; and in the easing of which he will govern himself by what he shall hear from your Lordships.

14.

Whitehall. 27th: Mar. 1713

My Lord,

The enclosed petition of Mr Gatchell[30], a merchant at Tiverton, complaining of very hard & unfair usage from one Mr de Wulfe at Ghent, having been laid before the Queen, I am commanded to transmitt it to your Lordship wth: a signification of her Majesty's pleasure, that you should countenance and assist the petitioner as far as you shall find the justice of his cause deserves [p.61]

I am, my Lord,

Your Lordship's most obedient
humble servant
Bolingbroke

Here follows the copy of the petition, mention'd to be inclos'd in the preceding letter.

To the Queen's most excellent Majesty in Council assembled.

The humble petition of Edward Gatchell of Tiverton in the county of Devon, merchant, humbly sheweth,

That your petitioner having corresponded with Ludovicus de Wulfe of the city of Ghent in Flanders, merchant, from the year 1680 to the year 1701, during which time they carefully closed their accounts, & with that exactness, that in the year 1701, they had no accounts unbalanced. Shortly after w^{ch}: time, the said De Wulfe order'd [p.63] your petitioner to bye for his account goods to the value of about 400

---

[30] Edward Gatchell was head of one of the foremost cloth merchant families in Tiverton, where he had considerable political influence.

l. sterling; w^{ch}: merchandise your petitioner accordingly bought, & sent to the said De Wulfe, & which he acknowledg'd to have received, & to have made himself debtor for on his books to your petitioner for the value of the same; & withall writ him, that he had sent him in part payment the value of 160 l. sterling in gold specie, promising to remitt him speedily the remainder of the value of such goods: but far from so doing, writ your petitioner a letter a short time after, advising him, that, instead of paying yor: petitioner the value of his goods, which he had received, he would arrest all your petitioner's effects wheresoever he found them; and he failed not of putting his threats in execution, having shortly after made arrests of your petitioner's goods in the hands of several of your petitioner's correspondents in Holland & Flanders to the value of about 2000 l. sterling; & this under pretence, that he the said De Wulfe had been serv'd by your petitioner during the 20 years aforesaid in quality of factor; & that your petitioner had overcharged [p.65] him during such time of their trade & correspondency both in the price & freight of the said goods, w^{ch}: he had bought for him.

While proceedings, so unjust & irregular of the said De Wulfe, appeared altogether surprizing to your petitioner; & the more, because he had no accounts undecided or open with the said De Wulfe (except for the last parcell of merchandize above mentioned) all their former accounts being closed & adjusted, as appeared plainly by the said De Wulfe's sending your petitioner 160 l. sterling on account of such goods, & promising him to remitt the remaining value of such goods first as above mentioned; from whence it is manifest, that your petitioner was far from being any way indebted to him.

Your petitioner's effects being so unjustly arrested by the said De Wulfe (who was indebted to your petitioner as aforesaid) your petitioner was forced to send his son John Gatchell into Flanders to take off such arrests, & to procure justice there against the said De Wulfe for such base practises, & to recover what was justly due [p.67] from him to your petitioner as aforesaid:– Where your petitioner's said son, on the behalfe of your petitioner, commenced his action for the same against De Wulfe, before the magistrates of the Keure [Curia?] of the City of Ghent aforesaid the 25th: of February 1710; where such cause continued depending until the month of August 1711: and since that time (by virtue of an appeale) before the Council of Flanders to this present time, where little progress has been made in order to the decision thereof, by reason of the said De Wulfe's delays & obstacles thereto; in hopes your petitioner would have quitted his just demands against the said De Wulfe, rather than expose himselfe to the vast charges of the continuance of such a tedious law-suit for so many years in a foreign country.

This being a matter of account & trade, & proper to be left to the determination of merchants, your petitioner's said son has several times in your petitioner's behalfe offer'd to submit the same to the judgement & determination of any indifferent merchants; which the said [p.69] De Wulfe utterly refuses to doe, in hopes to weary & ruine your petitioner, there having been no sentence made or given in the said cause, but what creates fresh disputes; in so much that the same is not likely to be ever concluded, where its now depending; & to embarrass your petitioner the more, doth endeavour to procure his books of account to be transported from this kingdom into Flanders, to be inspected by him, in order & under pretence to raise fresh scruples & delays from thence.

Which proceedings & delays not only tend to your petitioner's utter ruine, but to the destruction of the commerce of Great Brittaine, & there will be no end in trade, if accounts (after so long time fairly stated & closed), should be ravell'd into;

Wherefore your petitioner humbly prays your most sacred Majesty to take the same into your most serious consideration, the same being expressly against, & contrary to the third & thirty first articles of the Treaty of [p.71] Commerce, made & ratified the three & twentieth of May 1667, between your Majesty's kingdoms & his most Catholick [Majesty][31]; that the same may be rectified; & your petitioner relieved in such manner, as your Royal Majesty in Council shall think proper; and your petitioner shall ever pray &c

Edward Gatchell

15. [This letter is quite different from that dated 1 May 1713, printed in Parke, iv, 84–5.]

Whitehall. 1st: May 1713

My Lord,

I have put into Sr William Wyndham's[32] hands, to whose Department of Business those affairs belong, your Lordship's last letter, & the papers which came inclosed. He will consult the Duke of Ormonde, & communicate to the officer commanding her Majesty's forces in the Netherlands, such orders as shall be judg'd proper; whereof your Lordship shall have notice at the same time from me.

By the Earl of Strafford's letter from [p.73] the Hague, I find, the Dutch were extreamly pressing to have your Lordship take a journey thither, as they were a little before extreamly alarm'd on the report of your revocation.

The ministers at the Hague were ready to propose several matters

---

[31] Charles II of Spain, king 1665–1700.

[32] Sir William Wyndham (1687–1740) was a close friend and political supporter of Bolingbroke's. He became Secretary at War in June 1712 and Chancellor of the Exchequer in 1713.

relating to their Barrier & other interests; but I tell the Lords at Utrecht & am to tell your Lordship, that these gentlemen must have a little patience. The Barrier Treaty is, indeed, sign'd with the Queen, but an agreement must be made with the Emperour before that Treaty can have its full effect: & in the mean while the administration of all parts of the government of those provinces must hobble on, as it has hitherto done.

One thing, her Majesty thinks, carryes reason with it. The Dutch represent, that to guard all those great towns, which are not included in their Barrier, nor garrison'd by the Queen's forces, the Walloons have but seven battalions; & they therefore propose that three battalions of Leige, which were in the service of [p.75] the States, & which are now to be dismiss'd, may be taken into pay by the Spanish Provinces for their own defence; in which case, the oath of the States must be discharg'd & a new one taken.

The Queen, as I said before, My Lord, does not think this proposal unreasonable; especially when she considers, how great an expence is sav'd by the retreat of the Imperial Army, & the ceasing of the war on that side. Yo^r: Ld^p: will therefore, please, unless you have some particular objection w^{ch}: does not appear to us, to concurr w^{th}: the Dutch Minister in bringing this matter to bear; but, at the same time, you are to let him know, that he must concurr with you in procuring the regiment of Waleff[33] to be provided for in like manner. This is a Leige regiment; & their behaviour last year entitles them to the Queen's patronage & good offices.

I am, my Lord,
Your Lordship's most obedient
humble servant
Bolingbroke

16. [p.77]

Whitehall. 5th: May 1713

My Lord,
The Act of Cession of the Spanish Netherlands given by the Elector of Bavaria[34], pursuant to the 9th: Article of the Treaty of Peace between

---

[33]Blaise-Henri de Corte (1661–1734), Baron de Walef, commanded the dragoons of Liège which were in the Queen's pay. He was the only mercenary commander to follow the Duke of Ormonde on the separation of the British army from the allies in 1712. He was awarded a pension on the Irish establishment by the Queen.

[34]Maximilian II Emmanuel, Elector of Bavaria, fought on the French side in the War of the Spanish Succession. The French had hoped to reward him with the cession of the Spanish Netherlands.

France & Holland, has been delivered to the Queen's ambassador at Utrecht, & is now in her Majesty's hands. It is therefore out of dispute what disposition is to be made of these provinces or to whom they are to belong.

I told your Lordship in my last letter, that the Queen thought it reasonable the country should take upon themselves the charge of as many troops as are necessary for the garrisoning such places as are neither included in the Barrier of Holland, nor possess'd by her Majesty's troops: which orders your Lordship will please to pursue and endeavour to execute them in such manner as to answer the end the Queen proposes by them. [p.79] I am now directed further to acquaint your Ld^P: that as the Queen has Ghent, Bruges, & Nieuport in trust for his Imperial Majesty, to whom they are already declared to belong, & into whose possession they are to be put as soon as he shall think fit to accept of them; she thinks it highly reasonable, that the expense of these garrisons should not be upon her. This my Lord Ambassador at Utrecht[35] will represent to the ministers of Holland; and in this style your Lordship is to speak to the Council of State, others whom it may concern in the Netherlands. If the garrisons, which are in these places, shall be thought too great, the Queen is willing immediately to reduce them to such a number as they themselves shall judge to be necessary, in order to make the charge as light as possible. The Queen can't but imagine, this proposition must be agreeable enough to the people of the Netherlands, since the Imperialists being gone, & they not having Walloon troops enough to supply these garrisons, there remaines no choice but between British or Dutch forces: and she imagines it more [p.81] agreeable to their inclinations, as it certainly is to their interest, to have these towns during the intermediate time in the hands of her troops; since she can have no intention of retaining them absolutely, or of making any use of this possession, w^{ch}: may be disadvantagious, to the country, whilst she does retaine it. This matter your Lordship is to push to the utmost, & to demand the concurrence of the Dutch ministers in it: the point is of consequence, & your Lordship will easily see, that if you succeed entirely, or in a great degree, you will perform a very acceptable piece of service to the Queen; & very much add to the reputation of your own ministry. It is proper, for your Lordship's private information, I should acquaint you, that the Queen cannot think of maintaining these garrisons during the latter half of this year, without running herself into a greater expense than she intends; & without demanding a larger supply of parliament than the estimates have been calculated for; which would break thro' the whole system of the session, & render such taxes necessary [p.83] as she is determin'd

---

[35] The Earl of Strafford. See note 1.

not to have laid. In confidence to your Lordship I may tell you, that if this point cannot be carryed, I believe, her Majesty will resolve to leave a battalion in the castle of Ghent, & one or two with the Holsteiners in Nieuport; which latter body of forces she will peremptorily insist that the country should pay, & then call all the rest of her troops out of the towns of Ghent and Bruges home; in order that they may be broke or reduced; & the growing charge of them cease. I believe, it is necessary that your Lords^P: should, by the first opportunity, give me an acco^t: how the duties in the towns possess'd by the Queen are collected, & to what uses they are apply'd; because I am not certain whether, if the Queen find herself unreasonably oppos'd in this matter, she may not think fit to seize on those revenues; and apply them to the payment of the troops during the time they shall continue there.

The peace was proclaim'd here yesterday, & if there remaine any persons either at home or abroad, who are in doubt concerning the bent & disposition of people towards the Peace, & her [p.85] Majesty's measures in order to obtaine it, the unprecedented, universal, & frantick joy, which appear'd on this occasion, may serve to settle such in their opinions. But, I believe, all are convinced; tho' many will persist in speaking, & acting, as if they were not.

    I am with truth, my Lord,
     Your Lordship's most humble
      & obedient servant
       Bolingbroke

17. [pp.85–89] This letter, dated 9 June, 1713, is printed in Parke, iv, 156–8.

18. [p.89]

        Whitehall. Thursday [no date]

My Lord,

Having been prevented from waiting on you this morning, as I intended to have done, I give you the trouble of this note to acknowledge the receipt of your Lordship's of the 14th:, which came to my hands just before I went last to Windsor.

When your Lordship return'd from the Netherlands, her Majesty resolv'd to employ in that country no body above the character of Secretary, or Resident, for the future. [p.91] It is with great truth that I can assure your Lordship, that, as I always have in my little sphere endeavour'd, so I always shall to contribute to promote whatever may be agreeable to your Lordship either at home, or abroad.[36]

---

[36] Orrery had hoped to secure another diplomatic appointment after his services in the Southern Netherlands. Disappointed in his ambitions he began to drift into opposition to the Tory ministry in late 1713.

When I return from Windsor, I will wait on you, & be ready to receive any commands which you may have for

> My Lord,
> > Your Lordship's most humble
> > & obedient servant
> > Bolingbroke

19. [pp.91–95] This letter, dated 18 September 1713, is printed in Parke, iv, 287–9.

20. [p.95]

> Windsor Castle. 5th: Oct^r: 1713

My Lord,

I have not been able to answer your letter till this evening; the leave, which her Majesty has given me of going tomorrow for some days to my house in Berkshire, having made such numbers press to speak w^{th}: me, that not one moment of my time this day has been pass'd [p.97] alone.

I should be glad to send your Lordship so positive an answer, as that you might take your measures upon it; but my Lord Treasurer is not here. I have writ to his $Lords^p$: on the occasion, &, I believe, if you speak to him, he will give you satisfaction. As to an employment here I do not think your Lordship will be disappointed, but her Majesty has approv'd of two schemes of establishments of foreign ministers, for the Northern & Southern Provinces, by which no ambassador is allow'd for the Hague; so that the Earl of Strafford being recall'd, an envoy only will be order'd to succeed him. I take the Queen's intention to be, in other instances as well as this, to reduce her civil list expence to a certainty; & on no account to depart from the rule she setts.

As to the Netherlands, I believe, the Queen thinks, the less she is concern'd, the better: and the lower the character of her minister there is, the more on a levell she is with Vanderberg.[37]

[p.99] I shall return to this place in ten days or a fortnight, in the mean time, & at all times,

> I am, my Lord, faithfully
> > your most obedient
> > Bolingbroke

[pp.101–165 are blank.]

---

[37] Johan van den Bergh (1664–1755), burgomeister of Leiden, a Dutch Field Deputy and, with Orrery, joint governor of the Southern Netherlands.

BOLINGBROKE LETTERS INDEX

V
A Leicester House Political Diary, 1742-3

Edited by
R. Harris

INTRODUCTION

This political diary forms part of the Holland House papers, which were purchased from the trustees of the fifth Earl of Ilchester in 1960 and 1963 and deposited in the British Library.[1] J.B. Owen, author of the fullest modern account of the politics of the early 1740s, did not have access to these papers, so was unaware of the diary's existence.[2] However, two other historians of the period have used it: the sixth Earl of Ilchester, who of course had good reason to be familiar with the contents of the Holland House papers, and Linda Colley.[3] Neither appears to have been aware of its significance.

The manuscript comprises a single quarto volume. It contains 56 folios. The inside front cover has pasted on to it a key to a code for the leading political personalities who appear in the diary. Most are given numbers: George II is 30; Frederick, Prince of Wales, 29; the Duke of Cumberland, 28; Princess Augusta, 27; Prince George, 26; Prince Edward, 25; and Thomas Pitt, 6000. William Pitt and George Lyttleton, however, appear respectively as 'Brutus' and 'Cassius'. There is little consistency about the usage of the code in the body of the diary. Thus, although 30 is often used to denote George II, on other occasions he is simply referred to as 'the K.'. This inconsistency may be in part explained by the fact that the manuscript appears to be a copy of part of an original covering a broader chronological span. The entries cover most of 1742 and 1743. Yet on the key, there is a reference to passages concerning 1746.

Who made the copy is not clear, although internal evidence suggests that it dates from sometime during the reign of George III, after 1772.[4] Nor is it clear why it was made or when and how it found its way into the possession of Holland House. It seems unlikely, however, that it was in the Holland House papers before 1822. This was the year in

---

[1] Now Add. MS 51437.

[2] J.B. Owen, *The Rise of the Pelhams* (1957).

[3] Pencil notes in the sixth Earl's hand appear throughout the manuscript. It also seems likely that he used it for his study of the political career of Henry Fox, *Henry Fox, First Lord Holland; His Family and Relations* (1920). Linda Colley drew from it evidence that the Prince of Wales provided subventions to induce some reluctant or poor Tory M.P.s to come up to London for the beginning of the crucial 1741–2 parliamentary session (see L. Colley, *In Defiance of Oligarchy: The Tory Party 1714–60* (Cambridge, 1982), p.351, n.12.).

[4] The key refers to Prince George, 'now G: the 3d'. It also notes that in entries for 1746 the number 20 occasionally denotes 'the late Princess of W[ales]'.

which John Murray published the first edition of Horace Walpole's *Memoirs of King George II*, edited by the third Lord Holland.[5] Holland had been given the manuscript, together with a manuscript of the memoirs of the second Earl Waldegrave – which he also edited and guided through publication – by the sixth Earl Waldegrave. Walpole's jaundiced account of the politics of the 1750s raised a number of controversial issues. One of these was whether Sir Robert Walpole's fall from power in February 1742 was caused by treachery on the part of the Pelhams. The diary would have furnished Holland with additional evidence on this question. Yet he appears to have been unaware of its existence. So does his librarian and collaborator on historical projects, John Allen, who reviewed his patron's book for the *Edinburgh Review* in June 1822. Allen made copious notes for this review.[6] These indicate that he closely scrutinised Archibald Coxe's *Memoirs of the Life and Administration of Sir Robert Walpole, Earl of Orford* (1798) and Richard Glover's *Memoirs of a Celebrated Literary and Political Character* (1813) before putting pen to paper; but not the diary. Allen's interest in the fall of Sir Robert Walpole did not end here. A few months later, he made copies from transcripts of letters from Horace Walpole to Sir Horace Mann then in the possession of the sixth Earl Waldegrave, probably for a life of Henry Fox. The copies are contained in five quarto volumes.[7] The first of these contains letters relating specifically to, as Allen put it, 'the fate of Sir Robert Walpole'. One possibility (although I have found no evidence to support this hypothesis) is that the diary was sent to Allen or the third Lord Holland sometime afterwards. In this context, it is worth noting that in his review of Walpole's *Memoirs*, Allen observed that it was 'remarkable' that so few contemporary accounts of politics during the reigns of the first two Georges were yet in the public domain. He also expressed the wish that Lord Waldegrave's example of offering material in his possession for publication, together with the 'acrimonious strictures of Lord Orford on the characters and conduct of his contemporaries', would induce others to follow suit.

There is no direct evidence about the original authorship of the diary, although the entries point overwhelmingly to one candidate: Dr. Francis Ayscough. Little is known about Ayscough, although he appears to have possessed sufficient intelligence and personal qualities to overcome considerable obstacles to advancing his career.[8] His principal

---

[5] Holland's edition was entitled *Memoires of the Last Ten Years of the Reign of George II*. For the circumstances surrounding its publication, see Horace Walpole, *Memoirs of King George II*, ed. John Brooke (New Haven and London, 1985), i, xv–xvii.

[6] *The Edinburgh Review*, lxxii (June 1822), 1–46. For Allen's notes, see Add. MS 52236 (Holland House papers) ff.94–1056.

[7] Add. MSS 52234 A–E (Holland House papers)

[8] See the opinions of Ayscough expressed by Lord Camelford and Horace Walpole

routes of advancement were, first, the Pitts and Lyttletons and, then, the Prince of Wales. He owed his first preferment to Thomas Pitt, who presented him to the living of Boconoc after he was forced to leave Oxford, where he had been tutor to George Lyttleton between 1726–8.[9] In 1730 he made an unsuccessful attempt to secure the hand in marriage of one of Pitt's sisters, Ann. A few years later he seems to have entered into an understanding with Ann Lyttleton, George Lyttleton's sister, which was eventually to result in their marriage in 1745. George Lyttleton entered the Prince's service in 1732, and it was through Lyttleton and William Pitt that Ayscough seems to have been introduced into the Prince's circle.[10] As with so much about Leicester House in the mid to late 1730s, the timing of this is unclear. However, what does seem certain is that at least from the early part of the next decade Ayscough was playing an important if shadowy role in Leicester House politics, a role which was to cost him easy preferment in the Church and earn him the enmity of George II.

Between 1740 and the Prince's death in 1751, Ayscough held two official positions in the Prince's household: clerk of the closet, to which he was appointed in 1740, and, from 1744, preceptor to the future George III and his brother Edward, duke of York. Horace Walpole claimed that Ayscough was responsible for managing the Prince's privy purse and his electoral affairs.[11] About his close involvement in the latter, at least before 1748, there can be no doubt. During the general election of 1747 he acted as the Prince's election manager, conducting a detailed correspondence with Thomas Pitt about the Prince's wishes for the disposal of various Cornish boroughs.[12] With regard to the privy purse, the evidence of the diary suggests that Ayscough often found himself at the heart of the Prince's always stretched finances.[13] Because of his close relationship with Lyttleton and the Pitts, Ayscough also found himself on occasion playing a key role in important political negotiations. During 1742–3, he was employed to carry messages from the Prince to William Pitt and his older brother, Thomas Pitt, primarily

quoted in Maud Wyndham, *Chronicles of the Eighteenth Century, Founded on the Correspondence of Sir Thomas Lyttleton and his Family* (1924), i, 248–9, 258.

[9] Ayscough appears to have run into considerable problems at Oxford because of his Whig and latitudinarian inclinations. His election to a fellowship at Corpus Christi was initially blocked by the president and fellows of the college; and it was only after an appeal to the visitor, Richard Willis, bishop of Winchester, that Ayscough finally secured his fellowship (see *Memoirs of a Royal Chaplain, 1729–1763*, ed. Albert Hartshorne (1905), pp. 281–3.)

[10] Horace Walpole, *Memoirs of King George II*, i, 56.

[11] ibid.

[12] See *Historical Manuscripts Commission, Fortescue*, i, 107–32.

[13] For the Prince's heavy borrowing, see A.N. Newman, 'The Political Patronage of Frederick Lewis, Prince of Wales', *Historical Journal*, i (1958), 70–71.

aimed at either silencing William or bringing him into the administration.[14] In 1750 he was again at the heart of an extremely sensitive political negotiation, acting as an intermediary between Pitt and the Prince as they explored the possibility of Leicester House allying with the Pelhams against the Duke of Cumberland and the Bedfords.[15]

Ayscough's political career ended abruptly with the death of the Prince, when he found himself fully exposed to the King's animosity; he was immediately dismissed as preceptor, being 'proscribed to the Princess in the first meeting with her and the King'.[16] He had, moreover, to wait several years before gaining long-desired preferment in the Church. When this came it was not through the agency of the court. Ayscough appears to have been on the latitudinarian wing of the Church; certainly Horace Walpole suggests that his fellow clergymen suspected him of heterodoxy.[17] Not surprisingly, given Ayscough's theological bent, it was Benjamin Hoadly, then bishop of Winchester, who finally advanced Ayscough's clerical career further, appointing him to a prebend of Winchester which became vacant on the death of Arthur Ashley Sykes in 1756.[18] Court favour only came with a new King. In 1761 he became Dean of Bristol. He died in 1763.

The main subject of the diary is the repercussions which the fall of Sir Robert Walpole had for the opposition and the court. Ayscough's comments and observations are important for at least two reasons. First, there are very few sources for the political settlement which emerged in the weeks and months following Walpole's departure from office. This is especially true of contemporary sources. On the ministerial side, the Newcastle and Hardwicke papers remain conspicuously silent between February and March. On the opposition side, the only contemporary sources, apart from the diary reproduced below, are the diary of John, first earl of Egmont and material in the Secker papers.[19] The other relevant sources date from years after the event. The value of these is also reduced by the fact that they are, for the most part, attempts by various of William Pulteney's intimates – such as Thomas Newton, the Bishop of Bristol – to vindicate Pulteney for his role in

---

[14] See below.

[15] See 'Leicester House Politics, 1750–60', ed. Aubrey Newman in *Camden Miscellany, XXIII* (Fourth series, vii, 1967), 193–4.

[16] 'Leicester House Politics', 211. See also Horace Walpole's comments on Ayscough's dismissal in *The Yale Edition of Horace Walpole's Correspondence*, ed. W.S. Lewis (New Haven, 1937–1983), 20, 239.

[17] Horace Walpole, *Memoirs of King George II*, i, 56.

[18] Ayscough's appointment to the prebend may also have been influenced by the fact that Hoadly's son was the Princess of Wales' chaplain (see *Memoirs of a Royal Chaplain*, pp. 281–3).

[19] *Historical Manuscripts Commission, Egmont Diary*, iii, 247–64; Add. MS 6043 (Secker papers).

the political settlement of 1742.[20] Secondly, the diary sheds new light on the negotiations and manoeuvring which were such a prominent feature of politics throughout 1742–3. Ayscough had a good vantage point. For long periods during 1742–3, but especially in the first half of 1742, a steady traffic of opposition politicians passed through Leicester House, conferring with the Prince, seeking to enlist his support, lay down their demands, and ventilate their grievances. Because of his position in the Prince's household, and as one of the Prince's confidants, Ayscough was privy to much that went on. He also held discussions himself with a number of the leading opposition politicians.

Walpole was forced from office on 2 February 1742; the entries in the diary commence on 6 January when Walpole was fighting to save his political life. It was on 5 January that Walpole was to make his final significant bid to retain power – the offer to pay the Prince's debts and increase his allowance from the civil list in return for his support. The Prince refused to countenance any deal which would have left Walpole in office, a refusal which finally prised free Walpole's grip on power.[21] Yet the Prince may have been prepared at this stage to put his weight behind a deal which would have secured Walpole a safe withdrawal from office. As part of his efforts to vindicate his coming to terms with the administration after Walpole's fall, William Pulteney was to claim afterwards that Lyttleton, the Pitts and Grenvilles had entered into negotiations with Walpole and the administration before 2 February. He was to receive belated support for this contention from Richard Glover. Glover asserted in his memoirs that the Prince of Wales had informed him about a letter written by Lyttleton and passed to Walpole by George Augustus Selwyn in which Walpole was offered a safe retreat in return for favour at the court. He was also to assert that the truth of this deal was confirmed to him by Ayscough and Richard Lyttleton.[22] Recent historians appear to have either dismissed or passed over Glover's claims, no doubt because of Glover's unreliability. The entries in Ayscough's diary for 6 and 7 January suggest, however, that Glover may, in this instance, have been reporting the truth. The first of these entries indicates that Walpole had in fact been

---

[20] Thomas Newton, *The Works of . . . Thomas Newton with some account of his Life and anecdotes of several of his friends, written by himself* (1782), i, 28–41. Newton's *Works* also quotes relevant comments from the autobiography of another of Pulteney's intimates, Zachary Pearce, bishop of Rochester. Archibald Coxe's discussion of the political settlement of 1742 is informed by discussions he held with John Douglas, bishop of Salisbury. Douglas was groomed by Pulteney over a number of years to write his political apologia. However, this project was never brought to fruition. Richard Glover sketches the main events of early 1742 in his memoirs.

[21] See Owen, *Rise of the Pelhams*, p.29.

[22] Glover, *Memoirs of a Celebrated Literary and Political Character*, p.3.

offered 'security and protection'. It also suggests that Lyttleton was at the heart of the negotiations, and was acting with the Prince's knowledge, possibly even with his approval. The second entry reveals the cause of the negotiations' failure: George II. The existence of these negotiations only underlines the confusion and divisions which pervaded the opposition on the eve of what was widely regarded as a great victory. It also underlines the dislocation between the manoeuvring and battle for places which dominated politics at Westminster and St James's at this time and popular expectations. Popular hopes that Walpole's fall would see the dismantling of Walpole's system of corruption and a new era of patriot government were hopelessly unrealistic.

If the Prince was instrumental in bringing Walpole down, he also played an important role in the reconstruction of the ministry between February and July. The Prince's support helped the reformed ministry negotiate the early months, when the rivalries and ambitions of politicians jostling for power and advancement, together with alienation of some of the Walpolian whigs (the so-called old corps), threatened to destroy it. This support was not, however, unwavering. In early February the Prince showed signs of vacillating. The timing and extent of this is very clearly illuminated by Ayscough. On 12 February, William Pulteney came under concerted attack for the tactics which he had adopted in negotiations with the court at a meeting of opposition peers and M.P.s held at the Strand Tavern.[23] As the entry in the diary for 13 February discloses, the following day the Prince joined in the attack on Pulteney. Three days later, however, Pulteney regained the Prince's support at a conference at Leicester House also attended by various opposition peers. The diary provides ample evidence of the cause of the Prince's vacillation: his susceptibility to manipulation by stronger political personalities and intelligences. For much of the time, the Prince appears to have been pushed along by forces and pressures over which he had little or no control. The unpredictability surrounding the Prince's continued support for the ministry was a source of considerable uncertainty throughout the first half of 1742. It was also a factor in the ministry's willingness to provide places in July 1742 for Lords Gower, Cobham and Bathurst, despite the lukewarm nature of particularly Cobham's attachment to the administration. The Prince, as the diary emphasises, had been very active between February and July in pushing for the three peers to be readmitted to court favour.

A further source of strain in early 1742 and indeed throughout 1742–3 was the difficult relations between George II and the Prince. The

---

[23] For this and the meeting on 16 January referred to below, see the then Solicitor General, Dudley Ryder's comments which are reprinted in *The History of Parliament: The House of Commons 1715–1754*, ed. R. Sedgwick (1970), i, 51–2.

mutual hatred between the King and his son had manifested itself for over a decade when Walpole was ousted from office. The Prince's role in forcing his father to part with his favourite minister, however, only exacerbated the friction which existed between father and son. As the diary discloses, George II made no effort to disguise his repugnance for Frederick and those politicians who were closely associated with him. Again and again, Ayscough records snubs which the Prince and his household were subjected to at court, the most flagrant being the reluctance with which the Prince's allocation from the civil list was raised to £100,000, the price of his reconciliation to the court. The diary also makes it clear that George II's hostility towards his son was a crucial limitation on how far the Pelhams and Lord Carteret were able (or perhaps prepared) to meet the Prince's wishes concerning the disposal of relatively minor places. Certainly, Ayscough was to find his path to preferment blocked by his close identification with the Prince.

Another who found himself excluded from the political settlement in 1742 was William Pitt. His response was to launch a series of rhetorical onslaughts in the winter of 1742-3 in the Commons against Lord Carteret and the taking into British pay of 16,000 Hanoverian troops in August 1742. These speeches and their impact are well known, although the diary provides an interesting additional commentary on the latter, particularly in respect of their impact on the King. Less well documented is the story of Pitt's relations with the ministry in this period. Partly this reflects the paucity of relevant evidence: surviving references to the halting negotiations between various opposition figures and the Pelhams throughout the early 1740s are scarce and often cryptic. Underlying a major part of the diary, however, is the dilemma which confronted the Prince because of the prominence in the opposition after February 1742 of Pitt and, to a lesser extent, Lyttleton, both of whom remained members of the Prince's household despite his reconciliation with the court.[24]

Efforts to bring Pitt and Lyttleton into the administration appear to have begun at least as early as the summer of 1742, and not in the summer of the following year as has hitherto been assumed.[25] These efforts entered a new phase of intensity in November 1742, which lasted until the following March. The timing is significant. It was in November that William Murray was brought into the administration as Solicitor-General and found a place in the Commons. The driving force behind this move was the Duke of Newcastle. Newcastle was anxious to increase the ministry's debating strength in the Lower House for the

---

[24] George Lyttleton remained the Prince's secretary until late 1744; while William Pitt retained his position of Groom of the Bedchamber until early 1745.

[25] See Owen, *Rise of the Pelhams*, p.194.

next parliamentary session, an imperative which was widely recognised among his colleagues. The Prince and Ayscough played a prominent part in the overtures made to Pitt and Lyttleton between November and March, although they appear to have been acting under pressure from St James's. This partly reflected the fact that both Pitt and Lyttleton were, as referred to above, still part of the Prince's household. But it also reflected the lines of communication which existed between them and Ayscough. There was much posturing on both sides. As throughout his career, Pitt hid behind a masque of 'Honor and Connection'. The Prince's stance, meanwhile, suggested ambivalence. Although he was obviously irritated by Pitt's outspoken attacks on Hanoverian influence, he handled him with kid gloves. On one occasion, he even suggested paying for Pitt to travel abroad, a suggestion that foundered on Pitt's notorious sensitivity about money. He also indicated that even if he were to dismiss Pitt and Lyttleton from his service, he would keep them on his payroll. Throughout 1742–3, the Prince also made a protracted effort to detach Thomas Pitt from the opposition in order to deflect the pressures created by his brother's anti-Hanoverian phillipics. This effort appears to have reached a successful conclusion in late 1743, when Thomas Pitt agreed to support the ministry in return for additional financial remuneration.

The final part of the diary is overshadowed by a new crisis which threatened to undermine the ministry in late 1743. The basic cause of this crisis was the wave of intense anti-Hanoverianism unleashed by the military campaign of the summer of 1743. As far as politics at home was concerned, the campaign was dominated by the victory over the French at Dettingen in June, the favour which George II showed the Hanoverian troops in the Pragmatic army (and also in British pay) from the time he joined it in May, and the resignation in September of the army's commander-in-chief, the Earl of Stair. Dettingen created hopes that the allied army would advance into France, capturing outlying provinces and shackling French military might once and for all. These hopes were not to be realised; the campaign ended in a series of desultory and ineffective manoeuvres on the French border.[26] This, together with Stair's resignation in protest against his lack of influence and reports of George II's favouritism towards the Hanoverians, which flooded London in late 1743, created an intense popular outcry.[27] This gave great heart to the opposition, who galvanised

[26] The best narrative of these events is contained in Rohan Butler, *Choiseul: Father and Son 1719–1754* (Oxford, 1980).

[27] For the popular and press dimension to the intense anti-Hanoverianism of the winter of 1743–4, see R. Harris, *A Patriot Press: National Politics and the London Press during the War of the Austrian Succession, 1740–48* (Oxford, forthcoming).

themselves to attack vigorously the conduct of the war in the new parliamentary session.

The ministry survived this new challenge, at least in the short term. Despite losing the support of a number of M.P.s who usually voted with the ministry, its majority held up in the crucial Commons motions of that winter. However, the outcome was attended with uncertainty right up until almost the last minute, the ministry only deciding finally to ask parliament to renew the grant for payment of the Hanoverian troops after the opening of the session. The diary highlights the atmosphere of rumour and speculation which prevailed in London in late 1743. It also focuses attention on a number of the factors which were helping to create uncertainty. Three of these stand out: the division which had opened up in the course of 1743 between Lord Carteret and the Pelhams; the presence in the capital of officers who had returned from the continent bursting with stories about missed opportunities and slights allegedly suffered by the British troops at the hands of the King and the Hanoverian soldiery; and negotiations between the Pelhams and various opposition politicians aimed at ousting Carteret from office. Although, the broad outlines of the latter are fairly clear, it is not certain just how many of the opposition whigs were involved. The situation is also complicated by the fact that, as the diary makes clear, there was little internal coherence amongst this group; the independence of politicians such as William Pitt, George Lyttleton, Lord Cobham and the Earl of Chesterfield constantly threatened to dissolve any sense of group identity. The talks seem to have broken down at the beginning of December, a fact signalled by the resignation on 8 December of Lord Gower as Lord Privy Seal and Lord Cobham's resignation of the command of his regiment. One of the difficulties which the ministry encountered in this context (apart from differences of attitude amongst the opposition whigs) was the Prince's continued support for Lords Carteret and Bath, something which is also clearly disclosed by Ayscough. As the price of his factions's support, Lord Cobham was calling for the dismissal of Bath's supporters from the administration. This would have placed at risk the Prince's continued support, something which the Pelhams could ill afford at this juncture.[28]

The diary entries are in an abbreviated, often cryptic, style, probably because they were originally written contemporaneously or near-contemporaneously with the events behind described. Transcription has also been complicated by the fact that a later hand has gone through the manuscript, making interpolations, extending abbreviations, and attempting to identify persons referred to in the entries. I have made no attempt to expand the entries, except to translate the numerical

[28] Owen, *Rise of the Pelhams*, p.195.

code. This is partly because to do so would have overburdened the text with critical apparatus. But it also because what the entries lack in clarity is compensated for by the sense of immediacy which they convey. Where the code is translated, this is indicated by means of an asterisk. The later hand is indicated by use of square brackets and, in a number of places, textual notes. In several places words are in a third hand, almost certainly near-contemporaneous with the original copyist's hand. These are indicated by the use of two carets ('. . . .'). The odd word or phrase has defied transcription either because of ink blots or, more often, simple illegibility. Where this is the case, this is indicated by means of angled brackets (<? . . .>).

In preparing the diary for publication, I have been greatly assisted by the help of the staffs of the British Library Department of Manuscripts and the Bodleian Library. I have also benefited greatly from the comments made on various drafts of the diary by Dr. Paul Langford, and advice on ecclesiastical questions from Dr. Stephen Taylor. I also wish to acknowledge my thanks to the British Library Board for permission to publish this edition.

A LEICESTER HOUSE
POLITICAL DIARY
1742-3

1742

Jany 6. Conversation with (*words scored out*) [Lyttleton, – the Prince] That Sr. R.[ober]t could not stand it – Terms offered, viz – Security & Protection; might be had now; could not perhaps a Week hence.

7th. Terms refused – The King* [The King] would not be dictated to.

23d. With Lord Cob.[ham] – It would do, but he did not like it – What would be done afterwards for the Country?

25th. With the Prince* [The P of W] very warm – That unless all people could be gratified at once, it was very hard upon him – That he had taken up the Opp.[osition] a Dying Bird, and it would now pick his Eyes out. On one side was called undutiful – on the other a mollifier; and having views desirous of running in. He could retire and [live] like a Country Gent. – and would – would come no more to Town – & where would (*word scored out*) [they] be then? – The King* [The K.] might live to 70 [years of age] – The Prince* [The P] would never forgive them – not even /f. 2r/ when He came into power – Every Man was said to belong to Him that came to his Court – Somebody had been too witty, why was He so?

$$\begin{array}{r} £6000 \text{ as I knew} \\ \underline{2780} \\ 3220 \end{array}$$

Rem.[ark] –   3220– which Sum since Xtmas has been expended to keep some People (some Tories) ready.

Feby 3d. The P.[arliament] adjourned.

Sir R., Ld. O. to be succeeded by

With the Prince* [The P] – The strongest Assurances – when opportunity served – Thomas Pitt* (*identified by later hand, hereafter* a, *as* 'Pitt the Elder Brother': f. iv) to have 1000 – Eliott[29] Nephew 200 & to succeed Thomas Pitt* [Pitt][30] – Sands and Sir John Rush.[out] went in without participation.

[29] Richard Eliot, M.P. for Liskeard and Receiver General of the duchy of Cornwall.
[30] Pitt was appointed Lord Warden of the Stannaries, relinquishing his position as Assay Master of the Stannaries.

13th. With Pult.[eney]; Withdrew into another Room: He declared he meant nothing more than the Publick. The Prince* had railed at him – No, I hoped he was mistaken – 'No, he was sure of it' – T'was necessary to do it by degrees – The K. would not let Lord G.[31] into /f. 3r/ the Privy Council at this time, no more than he would thrust his head into that fire. How would the Prince like it – Were He King it might be done by degrees; and not otherwise.

Feb. 15th – Never did Week begin with more confusion and uncertainty in regard to publick affairs. Gone over without participation to the Court, Lord C.[32], Sands, Rushout, Winchelsea – Going, Gibbons[33]. Pulteney, Rushout, yesterday at Court – when 'twas reported that Lord Win.[chelsea] and D. of D.[orset] would [go] into the King and say that they could not serve him on the broad bottom – Qre? – Bludworth said he had it from Lord George Sack.[ville]. Can the Opposition stand it without those who have left them? Qre –

Quere about the Prince* – Drax very violent – left him with the Prince* – Bootle waiting e contra –

A.[34] to be Com. of the Customs.

Elliot will follow Carteret, sans Doute –

The past Conversation betwixt the Prince*, and me – Much to be inferred from that.

16th. With the Prince* [The P.] – Every thing extremely bad – all over. /f. 4r/ Mr [Pulteney] said to be with him at 2 [o'clock] – The same Evening a Conference; and every thing settled – Deo Laus – The next Morning His R.H. waited on the K. at St. James's.

18th. With the Prince* [The P.] at 6 o'Clock in the Evening – Conversation about Pitt – non pro vitâ –

To see Lord F.[almouth][35] tell him that his Brother should have Mr Pitt's Place of (gap left in MS) of the (gap left in MS) with 100 more added. To tell Retzau[36] to make out the Patent, 'ad morem Schutz[37]'

Ch. Bootle –

---

[31] Lord Gower.
[32] Lord Carteret.
[33] Phillips Gybbon, M.P. for Rye.
[34] Not identified.
[35] Hugh Boscawen, 2nd Viscount Falmouth. The brother referred to here is probably Edward Boscawen, future victor over the French at Lagos (1759).
[36] Fred Ritzau, Clerk of the Privy Seal and Council Seal in the Prince's household.
[37] Presumably John Schutz, Groom of the Bedchamber and Master of the Stannaries.

Carlisle, Admiralty – Douglass[38] – When there would be a Place vacant in the family – Not a word of myself –

To offer to St James's Church –

Mad Carew[39] [to the] Admiralty at Lord G[ranville]'s[40] desire. The letter to the K. – forgiveness & favour.

Would not have spoke to him – asked him how the Pss. did –

19th. Ly.[41] had wrote to the Prince* – who would ('not' *scored out*) ask for nothing under <? ...> [Episcopacy] – The present were disposed of to Clag. and Hut.[ton].[42] /f. 5r/

With Ld. Cob[ham] – advised pro parvis –

March 6th. Fresh quarrels – K. refused – The Admiralty Board, viz. Lord Winc., Granard, Sir J.H. Cotton, Lymerick, Jefferies, Chetwynd, Lee.

8th. A new Board – viz Trevor, Winchelsea, Granard, Cavendish, Sir H. Lyddell, Lee, Baltimore.

Duke of Argyle would act no longer with them – Sr. John Norris threw up – All confusion – With the Prince* – Grieved at what Ld. Cobham said – but must act as a Son – Tout va mal – Lord Baltimore.

Carey[43] had wrote to Holsworth[44] – His wishes the same with mine – but Turbeville (Alderman of Plympton), Edgecumbe[45] & Clutterbuck[46], Executor[47], had wrote – The whole depended on Hollsworth. Connections betwixt him & Treby still subsisting.

9th Champernowne Esq[48], at Darlington near Totness or Ashburton – Just going out of Town – Would /f. 6r/ go to Hollsworth, nomine principis, & let him know how agreeable it would be to His R.H. to

[38] James Douglas, M.P. for St. Mawes and Clerk of the Household to the Prince.
[39] Thomas Carew, eccentric Tory M.P. for Minehead.
[40] G here refers to Lord Gower and not the Earl of Granville.
[41] Possibly George Lyttleton.
[42] Nicholas Clagget and Matthew Hutton. Clagget was elevated to the Bishopric of Exeter in August 1742. Hutton succeeded Thomas Herring at Bangor in 1743, when the latter was translated to York.
[43] Walter Carey, M.P. for Dartmouth. The following two paragraphs concern the vacancy created at Dartmouth by the death of the constituency's other sitting M.P., George Treby.
[44] Arthur Holdsworth, governor of Dartmouth Castle and manager of the borough for the government.
[45] Richard Edgecumbe, the government's chief election manager in Cornwall.
[46] Thomas Clutterbuck, M.P. for Plympton.
[47] Not identified.
[48] Arthur Champernowne, who unsuccessfully contested Totnes in 1732 and 1734.

have a Man elected – To let me hear certainly from him.

At Kew – The Prince said he would by G-d take the first opportunity etc. – was only sorry for Ly.[ttleton] & Pitt – That he loved P.[itt] most sincerely – Qre. De Ln. – The K. had made Ld. Bal.[49] and Ld. Arch.[50] Lds. of the Admiralty – He had wrote to the K. to thank him for it – They should be able to go on – Should carry 25 with him – Qre. –

Erskine etc – was for the Enquiry – had sent up 2 of his Servants – & Sr. Wm. I.[rby] in his own Coach. The same Day the Enquiry lost, 244 – [against] 242 – absent Erskine, Bootle, Montague, Baltimore, 6 Scots –

10. The D. of A.[rgyll] threw up all his Employments. In the Evening with Lyttleton* (*identified by a as* 'Lyttleton': f. 5v) – said Lady Archibald [H] was not in it.

20th. With the Prince* at Kew – Lord Carteret had been with him – 3 lists – much interested for Balt.[imore] – The Clamours about him would soon be absorbed.[51] L.[yttleton] had talked / f. 7r / to the Prince* [The P] about Balt.[imore] – all things going into confusion again.

With G. G.[renvill] heard that the K. had refused the Prince* his Allowance – 80000 at most – and stay for that, some time.

– The Enquiry to go on. –

23d. The Enquiry carried 252–245 – 2 of the Court Side, 1 of the other shut out.

$$\begin{array}{rr} & 245 \\ & 252 \\ & 3 \\ \text{Tellers} & 4 \\ \text{Speaker} & 1 \\ & 505 \end{array}$$

24th. With the Prince* [P o W] – pleased with what had passed – would bring them to comply.

'Sr' Whistler 'W' – Balt.[imore] might make an Impression on them – about a month –

[49] Lord Baltimore, Gentleman of the Bedchamber and Cofferer of the Household to the Prince.

[50] Lord Archibald Hamilton. Hamilton's wife was the Prince's mistress.

[51] Baltimore's reelection for Surrey, following his elevation to the admiralty board, became a focus for popular disgust about the lack of substantial political change in the aftermath of Walpole's fall (see N. Rogers, *Whigs and Cities: Popular Politics in the Age of Walpole and Pitt* (Oxford, 1990), pp. 197–204).

25th. Ld. K 1726 Wood — 1702 (*whole line crossed out*)

26th. The B[ishops][52] for the Committ: lasted till the 27th / f.8r/ 3 o' Clock — 16 out of 21 —[53]

31. With Pulteney — Carlton — Grant — Would mention it to Night — when there would be a Meeting to settle and provide for their friends; — Sr. R.'s Tools must go out — Some Tories would be brought in, not as pledges for the rest, but to try whether the ('K.' *scored out by a and replaced with* 'Prince') would take those who were willing to serve him — Agreed with me that the Prince* could not do it now but when he was in when the Reconciliation was more cordial — Would press it — I should hear from him soon. /f. 9r/

Ap 3d. With Mr Pulteney — had mentioned it at the Meeting — Ld. Chanr., D. of Newcastle, Ld. Carteret, Mr Sandys — D. of N.[ewcastle] said that Ld. Cowper[54] had wrote to the K.[ing] claiming a promise ('of the' *crossed out*) from the late Q. at whose desire his Bro.[55] took orders — Mr Sandys [said] — that Cowper was too young — many competitors — Cowper will have it — Ld. Chanc [said] that all these things abated from the great Point for the P.[rince] — Pulteney said — that as Matters now stood — would not do — When the Recess was more perfected — [They] Would never be cordial: Jealousy on the K.[ing]'s side — [who] Called his Son's Spirit turbulent — That I stood very well with the Ministry — Would not give it up — but still it might be better for another time — my being Chaplain might shock and be against me.

<6>th. With Ld. Cob.[ham] would not do for Ld. Gow[er] —

9th. With Bris[tol] — Every thing in an exceeding /f. 10r/ bad state — The Prince* had disgraced himself.

Ap. 10th. [was] Sent by the Prince* to Lord Cob.[ham] — Pulteney had been with the Prince* [The P] that Morning — It would do for Ld. Gow[er] to be Privy Seal, and in the Cabinet. Ld. Bathurst to have the Band of Pensioners, or the Stag Hounds — Ld. Cob. to have his Rank before Ld. Stair, and the 1st Reg of Horse that should be vacant — Ld. Cob. received the Message with good humour — ordered

---

[52] B is here incorrectly extended. From the context, it obviously refers to ballot and not bishops.

[53] This refers to the Commons vote on the composition of the committee of enquiry into Walpole's administration. Only 5 members on the Court list were elected to the committee (see Owen, *Rise of the Pelhams*, pp.106–8).

[54] William, Lord Cowper, eldest son of William Cowper, the former Lord Chancellor (d. 1723).

[55] Hon. Spencer Cowper. Cowper was appointed to a prebend of Westminster in May.

me to thank the Prince* for what he had done for him – He would not refuse the Rank if it was offered him – and would serve his K.[ing] and Country when called upon to do it – It might be 7 years before a Regiment of Horse became vacant – Should not stay in long – would be at liberty to vote – for which he supposed he should be turned out again – Lord Westmoreland had been offered his Rank, and would take it /f. 11r/ – Ld. Gower would accept – Ld. Bathurst Q? – With the Prince* – something [as] in praesenti – Constable of the Tower –

Lord Carlisle satisfied if he could be in the Cabinet – aliter non –

Edgecumbe to be succeeded by H. Vane[56] –
Harris[57] to go out – Sr. Rob. Browne – Do.[58] –

Jefferies, by Pulteney – renewed all his protestations to me – The Revenue at Hanover £600000 per ann. –

Carteret [said] of Lyttleton* (identified by a as 'Lord Ln': f. 10v) – Let me but have him – I'll do any thing [with him: &] – make him an obedient Politician.

17th Ap. With the Prince;* would do – should have 100,000, had been offered 85000 – refused – could carry it in Parliament – Go[wer] & Bath[urst] would be made – had proposed to Cart. to make Cob[ham] Cap. Gen of all the Troops to be left at home – 'twas design'd for Wade – but Cart. would try for Cob. and /f. 12r/ believed 'twould do –

20th. With Cob.[ham] – There was a stop put to 100000

29. With the Prince* – to Morrow the Affair of the 100,000 to be brought on the tapîs –

Not pleased with the Debate [of] yesterday about the 4000. (extra zero scored out).[59] Lyttleton* had done well – nil de Pitt* – Pitt* et Credo (Lyttleton*). Both Parties joining in one Interest would carry everything. Sir J.H. Cot[ton] had now done for ever –

30th. The Prince's Affairs settled – The whole 100000 granted – H. Pelham to assure the Prince* that he was no obstruction to Ld. G.[60] and Ld. B.[61] but would further it.

---

[56] As Vice-Treasurer of Ireland.
[57] John Harris, M.P. for Ashburton. The rumour that he was to be replaced as Master of the Household was false.
[58] M.P. for Ilchester. Brown was displaced as Paymaster of Works.
[59] 4000 troops were brought over to the mainland from Ireland to replace a similar number which had been sent to the continent.
[60] Lord Gower.
[61] Lord Bathurst.

May 1st. With the Prince* – That the B.[ishop] of S.[arum].[62] had been employed in settling this matter –

Hammond had promised him – viz, assented to what he said in the Morning about the 4000 (extra zero scored out). Wondered how any one could oppose it and then voted against it – It looked as if he was Ld. /f. 13r/ Ch.'s Son – After he left him, had met with, and been influenced by Lord Ch.[olmondeley] –

The Hessians to come on; 6000 – to go to Flanders – How his family would vote –

H. Pelham had changed his language much – 'twas their interest to oblige the Prince* [The P.] – beg'd him to save them – etc.

The A[rch]B[ishops][63] Conversation with the Prince* – was ordered by the late Queen to come to him as soon as ever the Reconc.[iliation] should be brought about, to offer his & the Clergy's Service to him – About Sawyer[64] – Yes he had merit to the Government – for he had the disposal of a Borough – was Lord of the Manor where Parsons[65] –

May 3d. Conversation with the Prince* – who had been that Day at Kensington – An appearance of concord in the younger part of the family – The D.[uke] could not come to the Prince* without leave – Some of them always expected to be in the way – The Duke of Cumberland* [The D. of Cumberland] had desired leave to go Abroad – Proposed /f. 14r/ being at the Hague in Ld. Stair's House – The King* [The King] in a violent Rage with Newcastle – and not better with Carteret – What was the B. of S[arum] to be put upon him again – they had been meddling in his family – had made one Son Rebellious, i.e. independent of him, and now were meddling with another – Difficulties about the Warrant – but would be got over Wednesday next – Impractible Pride – No one could manage him but the Q.[ueen] and she with Tears and fits – Carteret said he was tired –

The King* nec amat, nec amatur –

Passed the 100000 – but in the most disobliging way – ordered that it should be paid last from the Exchequer – Ld. Cholmondeley – Ld. Carteret – etc would bring in the 4 Lords[66] – Time will shew –

[62] Thomas Sherlock.
[63] John Potter.
[64] Probably Dr. George Sayer, son in law of Potter and Archdeacon of Durham. Potter was pushing the ministry very hard for a bishopric for Sayer (see Add. MSS 32700 (Newcastle papers) f. 100; 32701. ff. 278–9, 314–15; 32702, ff. 3–4).
[65] Not identified.
[66] Gower, Bathurst, Cobham, and Chesterfield.

May 16. Bludworth said that Pulteney told him that they had deceived the P.[rince] and every /f. 15r/ one else – With the Prince* – very zealous for Union – That His Lords might – but that Pulteney was angry at the thought of their coming in before his Friends in the H. of C. were come in – It was all a scramble for Employments – Lyttleton* (identified by a as 'Lord Ln': f. 14v) [said] there plainly & honestly – What should they come in for only to go out again? – Affairs both foreign and domestick look very ill – The Dutch will not receive our Troops, or join with us – This Ministry founded on screening, and made up of 9 out of 10 of the last – Can that stand? – Pitt* & Lyttleton* would leave in less than a year – Q.

June 6. The Prince* sent to me – resolved to set up Dr. L.^{67} at Tr^{68} bid me to go in his name to Ld. F.[almouth] that his Brother should be Equerry, etc. – Ld. Scarbor had told him so – Ld. F[almouth] obstinate – would set up the Capn.^{69} – Wrote by the Command of the Prince* – and as he said by the approbation of Ld. Cart. to Lemon.^{70} – Friday Evening the messenger returned – Lemon said that he should be sorry /f. 16r/ that any disturbance should be made in the Corporat[ion] but if desired would exert himself for Dr. L if there was a prospect of succeeding. The Prince* insisted still on choosing Dr. L. instigated by Ld. Bal[timore], Bootle, etc – Wrote again strongly by Saturday Night's Post, & to Hussey^{71} – Lord Edge.[cumb] wrote to 2 Foots, & Ennys^{72}, & Thomas^{73} – Lord Cart[eret] said that had not yet mentioned it to the King* [The K] – Great clamor about it – Know not how 'twill turn out – The Prince* full of acknowledgments and professions to me.

15. Married Mr. L.[yttleton] to Miss F.^{74} – bene facit Deus – Present the Prince – Lord and Lady Cobham and Sr. John Norris.

July 15th Returned to London –

16. With the Prince* – The 3 Lords had kissed Hands – tho' after long delays – Ld. Cob.[ham] would have gone out of Town without it, would Lord G[ower] have consented –

---

^{67}Dr. George Lee. Following his appointment to the admiralty board, Lee's re-election at Brackley was opposed by the borough's patron, the Duke of Bridgwater. Lee was eventually found a place at Devizes.

^{68}Truro.

^{69}i.e. his brother, Captain Edward Boscawen.

^{70}William Lemon. Lemon was again encouraged by the Prince to run against the Boscawen interest at Truro in 1747 (see Historical Manuscripts Commission, Fortescue, i, 109).

^{71}Almost certainly Richard Hussey, son of John Hussey, town clerk of Truro (1722–37).

^{72}Not identified.

^{73}Possibly Sir Edmund Thomas, M.P. for Chippenham.

^{74}Lucy, daughter of Hugh Fortescue, M.P. for Devon.

The Prince* very warm for the Court – would have me tell P.M.[75] that he must serve for his Place/f. 17r/ or lose it – Would say the same to all his Servants except Pitt* & Lyttleton* (*identified by a as* 'Pitt & Lyttleton': f. 16v). Their continuing in Opposition must be very disagreeable to him – No one knew what Messages might be sent – The 15th the P.[arliament] prorogued – State of Affairs – the Nation dissatisfied extremely – The Bottom not much enlarged – Those who have places not at all in humour – Ld. Cob[ham] would act as be pleased, and have the G[renvilles] to do the same – The Prince* has neither Power, Influence, or Credit – His interfering for any one is the sure way of ruining their Interest – Undone with his own Party – neglected by the Court – The King* jealous of him to the last degree, and uncivil to him – He has intimations given him to go into the Country – to Clifden the 20th – where he is to stay a Month – Lyttleton* has received Messages from the Ministers – would have an Office & not a Place – if any thing – talk of for Secretary of War, if Waller & Sr. J. Cotton /f. 18r/ were satisfied –

What force the Opposition will have the next Session uncertain Glover[76] said he would raise the City – perhaps other Corporations may petition for Justice – The Prince* says the Court will have a Majority of 75 next Session.

Augst. 1st. Carried by the Prince* to the Forest – From that time till the 4th of October backwards and forwards betwixt Bristol and London – on the affair of the Tin Contract, which is not like to succeed with the Bristol Merchants.

October 23. With the Prince* at Clifden – The Jealousy still subsisting betwixt the Prince* & the King* – The Prince could not make his Page Mill.[77] an Ensign – forced to put both him & Scot[78] on the Irish [Establishment] – Lyttleton* & Pitt* – Lyttleton* had been more gentle than Pitt*. Ld. Bath[urst] laughed at the Opposition & would bring all in – told the Prince* that Pitt* would retreat – which he much wondered at – had but 100 – <?...> 300. /f. 19r/ The Prince* had spoke very warmly of me to Ld. Cart – but it would not yet do – Jealousy still continued – The Prince's* great point was the Campaign, which the King* had refused him – Lyttleton* told me at Stowe the Affair of his

[75]Who is being referred to here is uncertain; none of the M.P.s with places in the Prince's household at this time has the requisite initials.
[76]Richard Glover, Hamburg merchant and poet. Glover was very active in City politics throughout the late 1730s and early 1740s.
[77]Not identified.
[78]William Scott, Equerry to the Prince.

going in – Conversation at Ldy. Arch [H. W.] – If they were called together and it was proposed to them whether he should go in comme un fils – no one could say a word against it – it must be so, but could he go in as a Son, and not as a Courtier – As to his own part he believed that he himself could not – The Prince* paused some time, then laid his hand on Lyttleton's* Shoulder & said by God he could – The Prince's* illness followed – nurse Balt[imore] – He then entered in to Engagements to cooperate with the Court – Cryed when he saw Ld. Cob. said that he would force none – Ld. Cob. told him that he would force all that he could – that there were some he could not –

Novr. 12. With the Prince* – Lord Bathurst – had been just /f. 20r/ before me – Complaint from the Prince* that Lds. Cobham and G[owe]r had refused to attend the Cab[inets] – Had declared that they did not like measures, and would not (*word scored out*) concur. – The Prince* expressed great Concern – This was Waller's doing – Pitt* & Lyttleton* – What could he do – Would give his Finger to bring them in for the Hanoverian Troops – Where else could the King hire them? They were 25 per cent cheaper than any other – Hume would – That the name Hanoverians would be given to all who voted for them – which might ruin the family – He should be called shuffling if his Servants did not follow him; if they would not what – a pause – D. of A.[rgyll] had wrote that he would concur.

Novr. 14th. With the Prince* – Had heard that T. P.[79] was as far as Oke[hampton] – on his way to Town – What had I done – Shewed him T. P.'s letter in which he said he would not come till Xmas. /f. 21r/ The Prince* well satisfied – would tell H. Pelham about it – had mentioned me already to him – He said he had heard that I was a sensible Man – Ld. Gower came out from the Prince* very red, and hot – D. of New. – Alderman Heathcote – very loud – Ld. Bat would bring in his (word scored out) Son in Law[80], and Champ – 'ness'[81]

17 Nov. P.[arliament] met – Majority for the C. 109 – all the Prince's family but Pitt & Lyttleton who spoke against the Address – particularly the Hanov[erian] Troops –

Novr. 29th With the Prince* 2 Hours – Conversation chiefly on P.[itt] and L.[yttleton] had been very angry with them, particularly P. yet still loved them – was in great pains for their behaviour next Friday – Not

---

[79] Thomas Pitt.

[80] Probably James Whitshed, who married Bathurst's eldest daughter, Francis, in 1738. Before the general election of 1747, Whitshed was included by Ayscough in a list of persons to be brought into Parliament by the Prince (see *Historical Manuscripts Commission, Fortescue*, i, 108).

[81] Possibly Arthur Champernowne.

so much concerned for the Enquiry − They might do as they pleased, but did not know the consequences − on what Messages might be sent if P. should quit his service − yet he would [give] him his Allowance /f. 22r/ secretly. The 20th a Meeting of about 30 of Mr S[a]nds. friends in Downing Street − to oppose any further Attack in any shape against Ld. O.[82] − of the Pces. family − Present Bootle, Hamilton, Sr. E. Thomas, Eliot. −

To tell the Prince* from P.[itt] that − I found him very unhappy − but determined − That the late turn of Affairs had put him in a most hopeless situation, but that he was still resolved to go on where his Honor and his Engagements lead him − As to the money − I durst not mention it to him − I know him and durst not.

Furnese resigned[83] − succeeded by Jefferies. The King* [The King] civil to the Duke of Cumberland* [The D of Cumberl.], still otherwise to the Prince* [The P] − but the Prince* still thought it would wear off − He had points to manage (the Campaign the great one) and would give, to receive − Thomas Pitt's* [Mr Pitts Elder Brother] Affair should be managed to some such purpose − The B[ishop] of L.[ondon][84] desired an Audience − He guessed what he wanted, but had other Clergymen to take care of − P. and L.s behaviour was /f. 23r/ placed to Ld. Cobs. account, and not to his −

Decr. 1st. With the Prince* − told him that I had tried P.[itt] that I found him determined − that he was very unhappy, but that he was determined. The Prince* held up his hands − seemed very much concerned perfidium ridens − That P. said my pressing him made him still more unhappy. − The Prince* said he had received mes[sages] from the King* [The King] − that the King* was in a great rage − said that People would sh-t on his nose − He always said it would be so − That formerly Jeremy Pelham was kicked out of the Doors to make room for L.[85] and now he saw how they served him − That the Ministry had told him that as long as they had such a Majority as 70, they would protect the King* [The King] from violences − by this they meant turning out Ld. Cob. or Ld. Gower − but if matters should come nearer, Examples must be /f. 24r/ made − That he (the Prince*) would have made examples of any but P. & L. that I might be convinced of that from what he said to me about T. P. That he had a particular kindness for L. and P. I said that I knew <?...> had the same for

---

[82] Lord Orford.
[83] As Secretary to the Treasury.
[84] Edmund Gibson.
[85] Pelham had been dismissed as the Prince's secretary in 1737 to make way for Lyttleton.

him – That I had spoke only to P. – He (the Prince*) said that was the same thing – L. would follow P. I told him that P. had no particular prospect that he said the late turn of affairs had put him in a hopeless Situation, but that still he was determined to go on where his Honor and his Engagements led him – Why did he enter into those Engagements – It was what he had warned him against in the Summer – That this would end in a new quarrel with the King* – That he had a most disagreeable time of it – That he was told by the old family that they were loved – and why should not they P. & L. – That the King* had said to Ld. Cart. these are your Recommendations, /f. 25r/ viz. Ld.s Cob. & Gower – That they the King [The King] & Ld. Cart. must eat some more salt together before he could admit of his Recommendations – That he, the King* [The King], knew mankind better than Ld. Cart. did – and always told him how it would be – That P.[itt] had attacked Sands with great spirit, and genteely, but that did Sands' Business and made him still dearer to the King* [The King] – That the King* had said, since they piss upon you, I will stand by you – Did I think that Lady A[rchibald] H[amilton]'s speaking to him would have any effect? – Ans. That I knew he, P.[itt] had the highest opinion of Lady A. H.'s Heart & Head – had often heard him speak of her as of a Woman of a most superior Understanding, and of the honestest Heart – but believed he was still determined – The Prince* said he had been peremptory in saying he would have no Messages from the King* [The King] – but knew not what he could do – (word scored out) The Prince* overacted /f. 26r/ his part – seemed to be in a rage – but still smiled – P.[itt] could not blame him if he drew up to him – The Prince* said I could do no more – I had done every thing – He could not blame me –

The Prince* said that Waller & Ches.[terfield] were gentle enough. That Ches. would get something; and leave them, P. & L., in the lurch –

Decr. 1st – The motion for a new Committee made by L. seconded by W.W. W.[ynn] very well done by [the] 1st as ill by [the] 2nd. Numbers pro 106 – cont – 253 – Contra Ld. Cornbury – Mr. Murray – (word scored out) almost all the Prince's family except P. & L., Srs. [E] Th.[omas] & Hume Campbell.

2d. With the Prince* – Discourse much the same as before – What could they ('2' crossed out by a and replaced with 'two') mean – The Tories left them yesterday – and they would be Dupes – Every one Gentle Waller & Dodington so, everyone but <?...> – Chester[field] so Carlisle so – /f. 27r/ Ld. Cobham had more sense than to divide the House of Lords – There was a Division yesterday about Mr Dodington's

Borough of Weymouth – 28 to 14 – and Lord Cobham not there – Dodington looked very ill upon him, & has lost his Borough – Ld. Hilsborough would be with the C[ou]rt. on the Troops –

17th Decr. With the Prince* – Talked with him about T. P. to keep him still longer in the Country if possible – if not, to tell him that 'twas impossible for him to serve him and vote against him – He was trusted with his Interest in the Country, and therefore upon a different foot from a Groom – Would talk himself to him – more moderate as to L. & P. The Opposition was now over – what could they have to find fault with next year – The H.[anoverian] Troops – would be no more brought on – He (viz the Prince*) still held the Balance – The Majority was /f. 28r/ but 53 – which he could have turned as he pleased – As to the Measure he did what he could to support it – The Estimate another thing – He entered not into Accounts – The levee money – The King* would never be popular – whoever would serve him must carry these points for him – He had not seen Ld. Cartt. since, never sent for him or any of the Ministers – they might come to him –

21st. With Ld. Cob. who was against T P. coming to Town – I had wrote to stop him – Qre. the effect of it – All the Affair of the Hanover Troops would come over again – Whether the Prince* would turn him out – The Prince* said there was a great difference betwixt one who was trusted with his Interest and one who put on his Shoes – 'Twas impossible that he could be misled whilst in Opposition –

Concerning Ld. Orford – That they (Qre. who) had threatened to bring him in again – That he, the Prince*, had said, that as soon as ever he came in, /f. 29r/ he, the Prince*, would go out –

25th. With the Prince* – Recd. Orders and Instructions from him for T. P. – Conversation – What if the Dutch should come in at last – Should agree to march 20,000 Men for the assistance of the Queen of Hungary – What if this should produce a Peace – That next year 2s in the L. Tax should be taken, part of the Forces disbanded – money should be reduced to 3 pr. Ct. a great sinking fund made for paying off the National Debt – Where then would all these Politicians be, who had been opposing the Ministry that brought about all this – Time would shew – Events only can determine – by this twelvemonth we shall see – The Prince* hoping rather for War.

27th. Sent by the Prince* to meet T. P. and to persuade him to get out of the Opposition – Found him as undetermined as his Brother was determined – The year ending in confusion – The Prince* given up /f. 30r/ to the Court – without much Consequence there – State of Affairs – Well thought of as I am told by the Ministry but where I might have expected – from his no consideration – least likely – The Reconciliation not half perfect – The Nation vastly poor, and discontented –

Jany. 9th. 1743 –

With the Prince – who settled a Pension on G.W.[86] of 100 per ann. – but much out of humour about it – bid me tell Lyttleton that there must be an end to these things – That he had already put M.[87] (*identified by a as 'Mallet': f. 29v*) upon him, and now another – He never designed it as a Pension, but only a gift of £100 – They called him stingy – He did not know what they might call him – bid me look into his Cash – but one Salisbury Bill of 20£ said he was poor – He paid £20,000 a year towards his debts – 10000 Interest and 10400 Pensions and Bounties – The list of Chaplains to be /f. 31r/ reduced no more to be added till they were brought to 36 –

25th. With the E. of Bath – Conversation – To ask me before Comp.[any] came in, if my Connection with *P.* & *L.* did not, or might, not hurt me – I hoped not – I was, ('and was' *crossed out*) permitted to be out of the quarrels – That Pol[itics] were above my understanding – the wisest, and best of Men differed about them – Fidelity, and Gratitude, were the only principles I went upon – and those were sure ones.

He said that he had advised the Prince* to proceed to no violences with P. and L. The Ministry might not thank him for it – but by no means – for they were Men of Parts. L. was moderate – P. too violent; especially upon the (*gap left in MS by original hand*) [Hanoverians]. What need he have called them odious?[88] – (L. of the same opinion). This may account for the temper with which the Prince* talked to me about them. He seems acceding to them – Had talked kindly to P. about his health – His conversation with me Yesterday the 24th was as if he wanted to bring /f. 32r/ them in, and make terms for them. P. will not let him make terms for <u>him</u> – Instructions from P. what to say to him; viz, that he will never be a young <u>Sands</u> – Not to come to particulars with the Prince* –

Jany. 26th With the Prince* – The Picture 30 – s15 1/2 – News that the P[eople] of Holland was come in – to try to stop what had been

---

[86] Gilbert West.

[87] David Mallet.

[88] Pitt used the expression in the debate of 10 December on the grant for payment of the 16,000 Hanoverian troops.

moved without concert by Ld S[89] – to be brought into the H. of Lds. next motion about the H. T.[roops].

Encore Jan. 25. Ld. B.[90] when asked why I did not get some one to answer the Pamphs.[91] said they could not be answered – the facts were true – it was not his business – let the Minister answer it – The Measure as managed not to be defended – but where was the good of trumpeting it about, only to do mischief to the family –

Feby. 1st. With the Prince* – The debate come on in the H. of Lds. apprehended that the Prince* would vote in it – /f. 33r/ Ld. Bath with him – He did not – thanks to Lady A. H. but was vastly incensed with P.

Feby. 19th – Returned to Town – with the Prince* in the Evening, who was in high Spirits with the news from Italy – The Country Politicians all mistaken – No violences ('heard of' *crossed out*) talked of, but Ld. Cob. could never hold it long – would no more be called to the Cab.[inet] Ld. Bath and he had the Balance in their hands – could make the King* [The King] hold the same language as usual about L. & P. –

22d. With the Prince* – About the Vice Ch. of Dublin the Primate Hoadly[92] would accept it – Kildare etc. asked me if I had not heard Mr. P. talk the latter end of last Summer of quitting him – No – About Maddox[93] would be [Archbishop] York if Sherlock refused it – was with the K. – Roxborough[94] the next Place –

March 22d. With the Prince* – Ordered by him to talk to Pitt* to tell him that he might be taken in on very good terms – that if /f. 34r/ he would not come in at least he might go Abroad – that he should travel at his Expence and no one know it – Offered these terms to Pitt* who absolutely refused to do any thing inconsistent with his Honor, or the Connexions he was in – for all the World – He knew he was not making his fortune – but would stand it out – not sanguine enough to expect that they should be the majority – but that still should make a formidable Minority – They were backed by the Nation –

---

[89] Lord Stair.
[90] Almost certainly the Earl of Bath (see below).
[91] The opposition whigs, spurred on by the Earl of Chesterfield, produced a series of pamphlets during the winter of 1742-3 attacking the employment of the Hanoverian troops. The most influential of these was *The Case of the Hanoverian Forces in the Pay of Great Britain*, which appeared on the eve of the parliamentary session.
[92] John Hoadly, archbishop of Armagh.
[93] Isaac Maddox. Maddox was translated from St. Asaph to Worcester later in the year.
[94] Robert, 2nd duke of Roxburghe.

26th. reported to the Prince* – frightened un peu – How could he then stay in his family? – £1000 – 200 per ann. joint lives – A.B. of York[95] dead – The Jealousy still subsisting – could do nothing for me – The King* [The K] would startle at my name – to be done by Sykes[96] – came very readily into it – As to foreign affairs – not in very high Spirits as to Germany – but /f. 35r/ what if a Peace should be made with Spain – & no search – The Embassadors from the 2 Sicilies had some such thing in agitation – The King* said when my name was mentioned to him – that he could not do it for Harris[97] – not considering (says the Prince*) the difference of the Men –

Il sensa sacramenta de Rosario 270000

1743 28th. With Ld. Bath – The Prince* had spoke to him before – would endeavour – Sherlock was not to be A.B. of Y., had refused it – A Meeting to be to Day – would open the whole Scheme if it was necessary – but the Jealousy still strongly subsisting – Proofs of it – The King* said, I know Pulteney has been 3 days following with P[itt] (*part of original word, possibly* 'Prince', *scored out by a*), which does not look well – When endeavored for an Act of Indemnity, the King* said – If I die the Rascal P[itt] (*part of original word, again possibly* 'Prince', *scored out by a*) (for he will call Names) I know will hang Ld. Orford – As to himself he was in a strange situation – He had lost all the little reputation with his own Party – and had /f. 36r/ got nothing for himself – Could not make a Tide Waiter – Had brought in some friends, and would have brought in some more if they would have let him – which might have made the majority – Wished that P. and L. had been more mod[erate] – L. was so as to foreign affairs – He could not tell what to make of them – That we seemed to have engaged in a War – without knowing how to conduct it, or having any fixed point in view. God only could deliver us out of it – That there must come a time when there must be a disconnection betwixt England and the Hanoverian Dominions

Saw Sr. L.[uke] Sch[aub][98] who had spoke to Lord Carteret.

29th. With the Prince – inter alia, that Ld. Gower would be turned out, and Ld. Chol. would succeed him. – That when Ld. Carteret desired it might not be so – the King* said if you will be kicked, I wont. – /f. 37r/

30th. With the Prince – Ld. Carteret had been with him – said there

---

[95] Lancelot Blackburne.
[96] Possibly Arthur Ashley Sykes.
[97] Not identified.
[98] Former British ambassador to Paris (1721–4) and a friend of the Prince.

was sense in my scheme – would cheat the King* into it if they <u>could</u> – Spoke very kindly of me – not much dependence on it – if it succeeds, good luck – Sykes comes very readily into it. Bsp. of Bangor[99] to go to York

Hutton to be Bp. –

Thomas of Peterborough[100] to be the next a. B[ishop].

April 17th. Hutton kissed hands on being made Bp. of Bangor –

Hays[101] made P. of West. – Do. Dr. Wilson[102] – 2 Prebends – neither of them could be obtained by the P. for a faithful Servant. –

Ld. Pembroke – given up –

Lord G. Beaucl.[ark] told me that Ld. B. was to be Lord Privy Seal – had been <u>shilly shally</u> about it – which had prevented Ld Cholys. being made – G. Wade to be made Commander in General of all the forces left in Brit. – had demurred – /f. 38r/ would talk to Ld. Cobm. – This said to me 3 months ago by the Prince* – The method I suppose of turning Ld. Cobm. out – Douglass said that Ld. Carteret would be at the head of the Treasury – and name the 2 Secretarys of State – The Prince* said that Ld. Cart. would not take the Treasury for him to make another Secretary of State at this time, before he had finished a Treaty, would be to put his Head in another Person's hands. –

Ap. 20th. Ld. Bath said he would let me know what turn that affair (viz. Sykes's) took.

21st. The House prorogued. –

Situation of Affairs – Perplexities Abroad, and Discontents at Home – What Events this Summer may produce, no one can foresee – On them will depend the ruin or continuance of this Min[istry] which seems to be divided – The Prince* has made himself <u>rien</u> – can neither get a Commission for his Page, nor Preferment for /f. 39r/ me – The Jealousy and Hatred full as high as ever – not of the Regency –

May 2d. K.[ing] landed in Holland –

4th. With Ld. Bath, who talked quite Patriotism – Asked how the Prince* had received Pitt – sent a Message by me to him, not to be too violent – it had been necessary for him to have been so – in order

---

[99] Thomas Herring.
[100] John Thomas, dean of Peterborough. Thomas was nominated to the bishopric of St. Asaph in December 1743, but was not consecrated. He was translated to Lincoln in the following year.
[101] Rev. and Hon. John Hay, son of the Earl of Kinnoul.
[102] Son of Thomas Wilson, bishop of Sodor and Man.

to raise him the height he was at – That he was now at the head of the Party – Lytt. not so violent –

The King* not only jealous of, but hated the Prince* – did not care whether he succeeded him or not – Would not be sorry if he was disappointed of the *(the original hand has here inscribed a symbol, a heavily drawn circle with a dot in the middle of it)* [Crown] – aversion so great that Lord Harringt. had half ruined himself – by playing at Cards with the Prince –

Ld. Carteret aiming at the sole Power – Affairs Abroad very bad – Had great fears for this Country, even with Success – We should be in great danger – /f. 40r/

May 15th. With Pitt* had been treated with great politeness during this *(gap left in MS)* by the Prince* – In a Conversation entered un peu into foreign affairs – differed, but civilly – the Prince* said to him, I say now before the D. of Queensb. that whenever things are in my hands, I hope I shall take such Measures as shall have your approbation and assistance.

21st. With the Prince* – Full of schemes for my Advancement. I desired him to let it alone – that as matters stood betwixt him and the King* – it would be impossible – He would tell me fairly that Ld. Cart wished me well and thought me a man of parts, but <u>dared</u> not serve me – As to his speaking to N.[ew]C.[astle] he was so connected with Bath & Cart he did not care to take an Obligation from N[ew]c[astle] – the temper the King* was in – so covetous that he would not contribute more than 10000 towards L[ouisas] Marriage,[103] tho' he was very desirous of it – so suspicious that /f. 41r/ he was very angry at the Duke of Cumberland* [The D of C] coming to take leave of the Prince* – He swore that they were all (even Drax). (who told this) debauched from him –

Great professions on both sides – The Prince* said that the King* had said that he was glad to see that *(word scored out)* Prince Edward* [P Edward] *(also identified by a:* f. 40v) had spirit, and hoped he would to be a Plague to them all –

23d. With the Prince* – Very sanguine as to the Successes in Bavaria – vastly elate as to them – but in the same letter – Malhereux pour les Anglais in the W. I.[104] – very little on that point – true we had been unhappy as to them – and it would never do there – Conversation as to Pitt* would make him Governor some years hence to Prince George*

---

[103] Princess Louisa was contracted to Frederick, Prince Royal of Denmark.
[104] West Indies.

(*identified by a:* f. 40v) – The Story of the Watches shocking – The [late] Q. to the D. of Rut.[land]

31st. With the Prince* – Had letter from Ld. Cart. – Things go well abroad – a passage in an intercepted letter from Secendorf[105] – viz – the /f. 42r/ Emperor must make a Peace coute que coute

June 25 With the Prince* – in great spirits on account of the Victory gained over the French – delivered to him a £1000 for which he granted me an annuity of £200 per ann. during our joint Lives – but redeemable – The money was advanced by Captain Tench[106] – 500£ on account of his wife – £500 I gave my Bond for –

Baltimore & Johnson –

The Battle of Brenan[107] – Qre. Whether the advantage so great as has been represented? What will they now say? – The emperor at Franckfort – will put himself under our protection –

June 26 With the Prince* – hoped much they would come in – they would always find his arms open to receive them –

Augst. 25th. – At Stowe with Ld. Cob. who then said that Pelh[am] would be at head of the Treasury –

30th. In Town – Pelh. was then appointed /f. 43r/ first Com. and is to be Chan. of the Exch. – Ld. B. would have accepted it – Qre. –

Sepr. 2d. – at Clifden with the Prince* – Long Conversation about Pitt* and Lyttleton* – Would they come in or not? They would bring him under great difficulties – They could not go on so. – Talked of bringing Thomas Pitt* (*identified by a as* 'Pitts Elder Brother': f. 42v) to act with the Min as Head of the family would have a great Effect – The Prince* said he would add 500 pr ann. – to be paid at the end of every Session. Would keep him his, and would not let him belong to the Minister – On conditions, viz, that he should vote as he would have him – should let him name 2 Members at O[ld] S[arum] for 1500 each – and the other Members at a settled price – I told him I could not come into any scheme to hurt Pitt at O. S[arum] – that his Election there was his Birth-Right – and that Thomas Pitt* could /f. 44r/ never stand the Clamours of the World, if he did not choose him – The Prince* still insisted upon the nomination, and would put by Pitt* as likewise Lyttleton* at Oke[hampton] –

Sepr. 4th. With the Prince* again – Had then altered as to the 500 pr.

---

[105] Count Freiderich Heinrich von Seckendorff, Imperial Field Marshall.
[106] Not identified.
[107] i.e. Dettingen.

ann. – Whatever I did for Thomas Pitt* with the Minister, he would know nothing of it – That I should take care for Pelh. was a slippery —— That the King* was out of Order, and had swelled legs – The Prince* still warm for Ld. Cart. – The same as ever with a view to a change – His Father was acting for him to make his Reign easy – Ld. B. and Sands would be satisfied – Ld. G. Sack. Sr. Ch. Wy.[108] Boo: one continued scene of low Idleness.

Mem. Sund. July 31st – the Prince* – on Femme – Lady Char. Edw[in] – Essing the dancing master – The Taylour /f. 45r/ of the Play House –

Augst. 1st. by 6 in the morning dans le jardin avec ces. –

Sepr. 17. Dr. Wil. told me that the Ministry designed to offer Pitt* the Office of Secret. of War – that Sr. W. Y[oung] was to have a share in the Pay Office – That he advised them to apply to him by me –

Sepr 20th. Advanced by Mr. Franks[109] to the Prince* the Sum of £5000 at the rate of 5 pr. ct. – to be repaid in 2 years time – Half at Michalmas 44 – the other at Michs. 45 – Promise at a future Cor. Witness Reynolds[110] moi meme –

25th. With the Prince* –

Octr. 17th. With the Prince* – Much Conversation about Pitt* and Lyttleton* – Offers had been made to Pitt* which he had refused – This the Prince* had heard from Furness – People very angry – What did Pelh. mean by acting as Minister and offering Places without knowing their /f. 46r/ will? The particular Place he did not know – There was nothing now to be done but bringing in Thomas Pitt* – would now give him 500 pr ann. more – it should pass through my hands – Desired that I (word scored out) would make the most of him –

Octr. 10th. With the Prince* – told him that I had talked with Maddox – who approved of my applying for the D.[eanery] of Linc[oln] but should write immediately to Ld. Cart. I wrote, and shewed the letter to the Prince* – The purport of the letter was to say that Thomas Pitt* was I believed well disposed to the present Admin – that I would endeavour to confirm him – That he had generally done me the honor to ask and follow my advice – That I would answer for him – The only mark of favor that he expected from His Maj. was my Preferment – Dean of Lincoln – The Prince* said he had talked to Marquis of

---

[108] Sir Charles Wyndham, M.P. for Appleby.
[109] Not identifed.
[110] William Reynolds, a page in the Prince's household.

Tweedale who approv'd /f. 47r/ of it. The Prince* made me enclose my letter to Mr. Wolst.[111] and He, the Prince, delivered it to Retzau to send on to Furness. Deus adjuvet – I had before shewn Thomas Pitt's* letter to William Pitt*. He advised the very method I followed, and said 'twas the very best thing that could be done for Thomas Pitt* – to receive from the Prince* £1500 – and 2000 post ob. The Prince* insisted upon leaving out of Pitt*, Lyttleton*, Lyd.[112], Banks[113] that he should not know what to do if Pitt* & Lyttleton* grew personal in their Opposition – How could he keep them in his Service – Spoke tenderly of Lyttleton* – Pitt's* damned tongue – Marq of Tweedale said that (gap left in MS) betrayed them at the last Election to humour D. of Arg[114] – Churchill had told the Prince* so before – and now it appeared from the D[utchess]s' will and disposition of his Affairs Q. Stone had told the Prince* – that their numbers would be 320 – Qre. – To go /f. 48r/ to meet Thomas Pitt* – Webster – Q.

D. of Bed[ford] not to come to Town this Winter unless Ld. G. was turned out – That Ld. G. had done – Q.

Sunday Octr. 23. With the Prince* – apparently in some fright about the Officers returned – Whether they should bear Evidence about the malconduct of the Army Abroad, and the partiality about the Hanover. Troops – Ld. Winch. had given him hopes – Had told him that the D. of Marl. said he would go into the Country to avoid answering Questions – Could such a one as he who had left in such a manner throw up? – D. of Rich. had published Matters – had said that the King* was so ill for 3 weeks after the Batt. of Det. that they could do nothing –

To set out to Morrow to meet Thomas Pitt* with Instructions – The Prince* would have £3000 added /f. 49r/ to them for both –

Octr. 27. Met Thomas Pitt* at Axmynster Shewed him the Proposals – which he agreed to in general – it would end a quarrel betwixt him and Pitt* – Wrote for me to Ld. Cart. –

31st. Returned to Town – with the Prince* – vastly satisfied with what I had done – thanked me, and would never forget it – Shewed him Thomas Pitt's* letter to Ld. Cart. – The Prince* told me that (word scored out) Miss Dives[115] was to marry a Broth. of Dr. Wilson – That P.

---

[111] Not identified.
[112] Probably Richard Liddel, M.P. for Bossiney. Liddel remained in opposition after 1742.
[113] William Banks, M.P. for Grampound. Like Richard Liddel, Banks remained in opposition after the fall of Walpole.
[114] Presumably a reference to the Earl of Ilay's reputed treachery at the last general election.
[115] A maid of honour in the Prince's household.

Louis was to ask for him the D. of Linc[oln]. The Prince* said that H[enry] Conway had talked much – The other Officers mod[erately] – had seen Capt. L.[116] – The Prince told me that Ld. Cart. had wrote to the Q. of H[ungary] to offer to assist her in the conq. of some Prov[inces] in France for her S.D. Whito.[117]

Novr. 1st. With the Prince* who told me that Drax had desired to succeed Lyttleton* in case he threw up – that if Ld. Arch. Hamilton had died Drax was to have succeeded as Surveyor – The office of cofferer to /f.50r/ have been sunk –

Novr. 5th. Recd. Ld. Cob. at R. Ch. – very much out of humour with the Times –

Novr. 6th. in Town with the Prince* who gave me 250 for Thomas Pitt* – With Lyttleton* – The discontents ran higher than ever – The Han.[overian] Tro.[ops] gave more universal disgust than either the Excise or Convention – Told Lyttleton* what had passed betwixt me and Thomas Pitt*, and as to the letter to Ld. Cart. Lyttleton* warned me strongly against any applic[ation] to Ld. Cart. – said he would not hold in 6 months – the Officers in the Army would declare – Qre. Duke of Marl had thrown up – Qre – They would shake the throne – The Prince* said, how was it possible to keep such men in his Service – The Prince* had lost all popul[arity] said un feu de paille – Lyttleton* said would push it with Decency but Strength. 'Ch. Hamilton'

Jones & Smith – Te Deu –[118] /f. 51r/

The Ministry would remonstrate to the King* – Report of his Illness – D. of Rich. palliating still – No particular offers had been made to Lyttleton* – not more particular than that what I had made from Dr. Wils[on]: They were reduced to a dilemma – They might choose the least Evil – perhaps make some good out of it –

Novr. 11th. With the Prince* – a long Conversation about the Han. Troops – They would carry them if they would by 30 – Pelh had told Vasner[119] that they should have difficulty, but that they could carry them – The Officers would be quiet in the House, all except Conway –

---

[116] Richard Lyttleton. Lyttleton had been aide de camp to the Earl of Stair at Dettingen.

[117] Possibly a reference to Maria Theresa's husband, the Grand Duke Francis of Tuscany, who was deprived of the duchy of Lorraine as part of the peace settlement which concluded the War of the Polish Succession (1733–35).

[118] Almost certainly a reference to the ballad *Old England's Te Deum* and the populist pamphlet *A True Dialogue between a Trooper and a Serjeant*. Both provoked the ministry to take action to prevent their circulation (see PRO TS/982).

[119] Ignaz von Wasner, Austrian minister in London.

Ross, and another[120] – Qre Whether Pelh – will support Cart., Bath and Sands would be quiet – On the other side the Prince* seemed very yielding – Other Troops, viz – Saxony Gotha &c might do as well – The King* in that case would /f. 52r/ not go Abroad – By this the Opposition would gain 2 great points – How would the King* (*identified by a as* 'King': f. 51v) bear it – He could not tell, and nothing certain till the King* came Home – Suppose the Duke of Cumberland* (*identified by a as* 'Duke of C': f. 51v) to Command in Chief – with the assistance of the D.[uke] of Aremberg – and another D.[uke] a German – whom the Q. of Hungary was very fond of – and who was an excellent General – Would not losing the Han. Troops ruin Ld. Cart. – no says the Prince* – why should it – It would shew that Cart. could carry what no one else could carry – But the Prince* added Cart. was tired of the King*, and would leave his Place of S.[ecretary] (and take another) if he could not go on with his plan – He would leave it very willingly – (Looks as if he could not hold it).

Ld. Tweedale came in.

Pelham jealous of Cart. – D. of New. would not suffer him to make a Treaty[121] – like all little minds, afraid of a superior – Would let Stone[122] or Schaub make a Treaty, but not Cart. and yet no one equal to him –

An union talked of betwixt Pelhs. and Pitt & Chest. – Yes says the Prince*, the King* would take them in if they would vote for the H. Troops and Civil List Debt – which they wont do – Another supposition to give the Q. of Hung. £400,000 & let her take care of Troops – His (the Prince's*) great Object was carrying on the War with France – He loved England – The King not well – knew nothing of the Flame here – would be in a Fit – P. G. (*identified by a as* 'Prince George': f. 52v) le petit verola – Deus opt. mox fabrum reddat.

The Prince* in good spirits, & seemingly under no apprehensions. – Pelh. had said that if the Prince* would stand by them, they could do it – The Prince* had said before that the Pelhs.' would betray Cart.

Novr 13th. Conversation with Pitt* – would /f. 54r/ never come into any scheme with Ld. Cart. – Knew and hated his ma[xims] (*part of the original word,* 'manners', *scored out by a*) – If he would offer the Oppos.

---

[120] Probably William Strickland, who joined Charles Ross in attacking the Hanoverian troops in the Commons on 6 December.

[121] A reference to Newcastle's opposition to the secret articles of the Treaty of Worms, signed by Britain, Sardinia, and Austria on 2 November.

[122] Andrew Stone, M.P. for Hastings, Newcastle's private secretary, and Under-Secretary of State.

their own terms, he would never come into them – Sir W. Ir.[123] would not vote for H. T.[roops] had talked with an Off. who said 'twas much worse than we knew, or thought – Sr. E. Thoms. said the D. of Mont.[ague] would resign not only his Reg. but Ld. of the BedCh. – Talk of granting Money – or the H. Troops again to Q. of Hung.

Oppos. will oppose every scheme that can preserve Ld. Cart. –

Pitt* warned me again against Ld. Cart. – K. expected to Morrow – Prins. to Night.

14 – The Princess of Wales brought to Bed of a Son.

15 – The K. came home.

Novr 17 – With Ld. Cart. taken in from the Levee – gave him Mr. P.'s letter – He read the letter – answered that this can't be done – /f. 55r/ Told him that my good friend the Bp. of Worcester had told me that the D. of New. was pushing for Dr. Barnard[124] – That I should be glad to succeed him as Dean of Rochester – only to shew that I was not proscribed – any mark of His Majesty's favor – He said I need not doubt of his good dispositions, could then talk explicitly with me – there were so many People waiting –

With the Prince* – had the Oppos. heard how the K. was rec. in the City? – Were they not knocked down with it? – No they were sanguine – The Prince* said that Pel. & Cart. would draw together – The King* did not speak to the Prince* at the first Meeting – The Prince* came too late – after the King* was got into the Drawing Room – by a mistake of the G. Usher –

18th Convers. with Pitt Twas hard to know the genuine sense of Mankind – What did people, moderate sensible People of Property say – Were they for taking things short – and recalling the Troops at once – throwing up the Continent? – /f. 56r/ Ld. Cobh. was violent – said we were in the same situation as last year – which Pitt* said was not so – Pitt* I think more moderate.

---

[123] Sir William Irby, M.P. for Launceston, Vice-Chamberlain to the Prince. Irby did in the event vote against continuing the Hanoverian troops in British pay on 18 January 1744.

[124] William Barnard. Barnard had been gazetted to the deanery of Rochester in April. He was appointed Bishop of Raphoe in May 1744.

LEICESTER HOUSE DIARY INDEX